BREAKING THE RULES

BY ALEXANDER CASELLA

GENEVA
ÉDITIONS DU TRICORNE
2011

Alexander (Sacha to his friends) Casella was born in Naples, Italy, in 1936. His mother came from a secular Jewish family from Prague and was successively a biologist, a classical pianist, a choreographer and a psychologist. His father, a publisher and bibliophile came from an old Neapoletan family. His parents met when his mother was called from Prague to organize a series of classical Greek choreographies to be performed in the newly-discovered Roman amphitheater in Pompei in the early 1930's.

In 1943, after the Germans invaded Italy, Alexander and his mother fled to Switzerland where they arrived as refugees. Over the following years Alexander acquired a degree in literature and philosophy from the Sorbonne in Paris as well as an MA and a PhD from the Geneva Graduate Institute for International Studies. From 1965 to 1975 he was a lecturer, consultant, and independent journalist covering essentially China and Vietnam. In 1975 he joined the Office of the UN High Commissioner for Refugees where, over the following 20 years he served in Vientiane, Hanoi, Geneva, Beirut and Bangkok. He retired from UNHCR in 1996 as Director for Asia.

Alexander Casella lives in Geneva with two cats and his American-born wife and currently writes for *Asia Times Online*.

ISBN 978-1463-6654-32
© 2011 Alexander Casella

Éditions du Tricorne
14 rue Lissignol
CH 1201 Genève
www.tricorne.org

INTRODUCTION

I

In February 1982, I was invited by the Aspen Institute to attend one of their seminars for senior corporate leaders. The title was 'Ethics and Values' and its purpose was to sensitize leaders of large corporations to the fact that, even in a market economy, profit was not the only benchmark of success.

By the end of the third day I had earned myself the nickname of 'the Swiss cynic'. If a cynic is someone who is distrustful of the motivations of others and in particular of those who claim to act for selfless or lofty motives, than I was indeed a cynic, and for good reason too.

After having spent some ten years as a journalist covering the Vietnam War, in 1975 I accepted an offer by the then United Nations High Commissioner for Refugees, Prince Sadruddin Aga Khan, to join his organization.

I had never viewed myself as a humanitarian and even less as a UN bureaucrat but I could not resist the challenge that I was presented with: coaxing the hard core communist regime in Hanoi to enter into a dialogue with UNHCR at a time when the Vietnamese communists, like their Soviet allies, viewed the UN with a hostility bordering on paranoia. On paper it was mission impossible and therein lay its appeal.

When I joined UNHCR I shared the generally perceived view that the humanitarian world was populated by the selfless, the kind and the giving whose sole concern was to alleviate the lot of the suffering. I was soon cured of this misperception. During the subsequent twenty years that I spent in the cutthroat world of humanitarian action, from Hanoi to Beirut to Bangkok to Hong Kong, the humanitarians I encountered included more than their share of the self-righteous, the unimaginative and the careerist. And as for the philanthropic organizations they served in, while these were certainly doing some good they were also spending an inordinate amount of time stabbing each other in the back as they vied for visibility and a larger slice of the public's money. To my mind the worst of the lot were to be found among the so-called 'advocates', those who had made it their mission to preach rather than to act. Vain, arrogant, self obsessed and with human right violations as their daily bread they would on occasion not hesitate to fabricate fodder in the race to appear more proactive than their competitors.

Granted, it could be argued that as a UNHCR staff member I was part of that throng. Indeed I was but with one caveat. I had no pretenses about being a humanitarian. Thus I embarked on this journey with no illusion or expectation about doing any good but at least with the confidence that I would be doing no harm.

In time, a combination of luck, guile and pragmatism along with the backing of a small team of like-minded cynics who shared some of my travails ensured that more good than I ever expected came of this agitation.

Thus, if there is a lesson to be learned from these twenty years of agitation on the front line of humanitarian action it is still one of hope albeit tinged by concern.

Hope because somewhere, somehow in the swamp of international bureaucracy where mediocrity reigns supreme and lack of accountability is the rule, there is still some good that can be done. Yet it is a counterintuitive fact that in times of crisis when humanitarian bureaucracies can no longer rely on a 'business as usual' approach there is no substitute for the pragmatic cynic, the humanitarian maverick who dares to break the rules because his overriding ethical principals command that he do the right thing rather than he do things the right way.

Concern because in the modern world, as bureaucracies balloon and rules become more pervasive, the voice of the principaled cynic who gets things done is being steadily silenced by the ever increasing bellowing of the legions of mediocrity.

DECEPTION IN DAMASCUS

'Sir, could I bring up the issue of the Afghans.'

S Essam Al Naeb, the Syrian vice foreign minister, cut me short. 'There are no Afghan refugees in Syria' he growled in a low measured tone which conveyed anger far more effectively than any raising of the voice.

Al Naeb knew perfectly well that what he was stating so emphatically was not true. There were Afghan refugees in Syria, several thousands of them. He also knew that I knew and that I knew that he knew, but that was not the issue. The issue was the date, December 11, 1984. The Cold War was in full swing; the Soviet Union had invaded Afghanistan and millions of Afghan refugees had fled to neighboring countries. Syria was the closest Soviet ally in the Middle East and with the regime in Damascus totally dependent on the Soviet Union for its weapons the Syrians could not afford antagonizing Moscow and had made it a point of closing their borders to the thousands of Afghan refugees who were floating around the Middle East. This was at least the official policy. In practice however, the Syrians had closed their eyes to the presence on their soil of a few thousand Afghan refugees. The Soviets were of course aware of this presence but as long as it was not made public had decided to ignore it. But the issue remained a delicate one that could blow up in the face of the Syrians anytime and it was therefore not surprising that all I had to do was mention the word Afghans to provoke the minister into a restrained rage. And yet I could not let the matter rest.

One week before, I had landed in Beirut with the somewhat daunting title of Regional Representative for the Middle East of the United Nations High Commissioner for Refugees. I had joined UNHCR some ten years earlier and this was my second field posting and not one to be taken lightly. I was now responsible for all refugees throughout the Middle East with the exception of the Palestinians who were covered by another UN agency. To compound the problem I was based in Lebanon and more precisely in the Moslem-controlled West Beirut. Lebanon at the time was mired in a brutal civil war and street fighting, kidnappings and car-bombings were a daily occurrence. So not only had I to take care of whatever refugees came my way; I also had to survive in West Beirut.

My function demanded that I visit every country in the region and after one week in Beirut I decided to start my rounds by first going to Syria, taking along my deputy Abdel Mawla El Solh. Born in one of the most prominent Lebanese families, Solh was the pillar of the UNHCR office in Beirut. He had served there for years, knew everyone there was to know throughout the Middle East and had achieved the miracle of being trusted and accepted by all, whatever their faith or political inclination.

In peacetime the journey by road from Beirut to Damascus normally took two hours but we were now lucky to have made it in five, and, after having gone through half a dozen checkpoints manned by armed factions of any color or creed, we had arrived in Damascus by mid morning and had headed straight for the Foreign Ministry.

While on the road Solh had briefed me on the Afghan refugees in Syria. There were several thousands of them and most had found jobs and were managing. Their problem was that schooling in Syria was not free of charge which meant that some 600 Afghan children were not getting any education because the parents could not afford the school fees. My job now was to get the children to school. 'Be very careful,' advised Solh, 'the Syrians are very edgy when it comes to the Afghans.' It was if anything an understatement and now I had a very angry Syrian minister glaring down at me.

There was a moment of silence and then keeping my voice as low and as even as possible I turned to the minister avoiding his stare. 'Sir, I don't think I ever said that there were Afghan refugees in Syria.' I could feel Al Naeb hesitate. 'So you agree,' he replied, 'that there are none.' 'Of course,' I replied, 'we completely agree on that, there are none. There are only a few foreigners of undefined nationality who cannot send their children to school because they cannot afford the fees. So perhaps through some voluntary agency or with the help of your Ministry of Social Affairs we could provide the school fees for the children.'

Al Naeb broke out laughing. 'As long as they are not Afghan refugees you can do what you like' he said. As we parted I felt that he had enjoyed the exchange.

That afternoon I sat down with Solh and went over our various aid projects in Syria. One, for which we had budgeted 130,000 US $ per year, was targeted to provide assistance for a small group of 132 Eritrean refugees currently in Syria. It was exactly the type of project I was looking for and we started fiddling. To the existing Eritrean refugees we added 600 more which we qualified as 'primary school children,' budgeted 300 US $ per child per year to cover school fees, some clothing, books and food for a total of 280,000 US $ and the trick was done. The revised project would not have survived an audit but the accounts were kept in Beirut and given the lack of security in Lebanon no UN auditor was liable to come near the place for the foreseeable future. I could of course have sent a lengthly memo to our Headquarters explaining why I had to artificially inflate the number of Eritreans refugees in order to help the Afghans and asking for clearence to do so but this would never have worked.

None of the beancounters at UNHCR would have taken the personal risk of approving what was a programming lie so my memo would have slowly worked its way up the hierarchical ladder. There would have been meetings and more meetings, discussions and delays with the strong probability that my memo would have been leaked, all this while the Afghans would be waiting for aid. So if I wanted to help refugees, fibbing was not an option. It was a duty.

As we finished drafting the project I could feel Solh's approval. Clearly I was no dreaded UN bureaucrat and for me doing the right thing came before doing things right. What Solh did not know was that I had been well schooled. Two years in Hanoi sparring with the UN bureaucracy on one side and the wily Vietnamese on the other had provided me with an education that I was not likely to ever forget. And in the process I had learned that working for the UN can be fun and that, on occasion, it can also do some good provided one is willing to fib, lie, obfuscate, cut corners and break all the rules.

It was an education that I had not planned for and that had come unexpectedly my way as I was sipping a cappuccino on a Geneva sidewalk café in September 1972, twelve years prior to my pulling into Damascus.

ONE STEP AT A TIME

S 'So, you cover the Vietnam war. From the American side I suppose?' The tone was condescending and the criticism implicit. Clearly I was just another one of those Western journalists who covered the Vietnam War from their own narrow ethnocentric perspective. Zia Rizvi was a tall, slender dark-skinned Pakistani with an elegant bearing, penetrating eyes and the somber good looks of a Rudolf Valentino. Unlike many of his kind he was sparing with his words and rather than deluge his interlocutors with idle prattle he exercised them sparingly but with the deft agility that a Florentine would have used in drawing a stiletto.

I hesitated to respond to his taunt but then decided that I would not let him get away with it so I answered with feigned detachment. 'Actually I have far more contacts with Hanoi and the Viet Cong, the South Vietnamese Liberation Front, than I have with the Americans.'

It was not the answer he had expected but he was far too vain to let it show so he just changed subjects and then shortly after announced that he had to go. 'I'll call you,' he said as he took his leave.

I would never have met Zia Rizvi had not one of my friends at Geneva University, an American, Jim Becket, arranged to have coffee with him on a lazy Sunday afternoon in early September 1972 and, for no particular reason, had decided to take me along. Jim actually barely knew Rizvi. 'He works for the UN Refugee Agency' he commented 'but this is all I know.' As for me I had no idea why he would want to call me and assumed he was just trying to be polite as he took his leave. Rarely was I ever to be more wrong.

I was born in Naples in 1936. My father was a well known Italian publisher and bibliophile. My mother came from a Jewish family from Prague and had made a name for herself in Vienna first as a classical pianist and later as a choreographer. From what they told me, they had met while my mother was on a visit to Pompei, and married in 1930. While my parents never divorced, over the years they had drifted apart with my father staying in Naples and my mother and I moving to Geneva in 1943. After I finished high school, my mother moved on to Paris and I stayed behind.

Alone in Geneva, a grey comfortable reassuring city, I had enrolled at the University and, after having obtained an MA in Political Science, for want of ambition or good advice had drifted into writing a doctoral thesis at the Graduate Institute of International Studies while my father kept me going with a small monthly allowance.

I had put Rizvi out of my mind when five months later, in early February 1973, the phone rang. It was Rizvi. 'I would like to see you,' he said, 'it is about Vietnam.' The next day I called at his office in the UN building in Geneva.

Rizvi's office was small, spartan and anonymous with a metal desk, a shelf, low table and two armchairs. As I was ushered in by a secretary, Rizvi pointed to one of the armchairs and settled into the other.

It did not take me long to discover that there were two Zia Rizvis. One I had met at a sidewalk cafe, wearing slacks, a dark blue polo shirt and a beige V-neck sweater, blissfully drawing on an oversize Cuban cigar as he sipped his cappuccino with concentrated rapture.

But the man I now had in front of me was a coiled cobra. He was wearing a dark grey suit with fine white stripes that emphasized his height, a white shirt and a wide polka dot tie. This, I thought to myself, is not your run of the mill UN bureaucrat or oily, rambling babu, more intent on listening to himself than to what others had to say. In another age I could have visualized him as a conqueror, leading an army on the windswept plains of Mesopotamia. I would have been less than candid had I not conceded to myself that this was one of the few people I had encountered whose presence I found somewhat unnerving.

For the next half hour, under the guise of an amiable, meandering conversation, I could see that he was trying to size me up. Why was I interested in Vietnam? How did I get my contacts with Hanoi and the Viet Cong? Did I believe that the Paris Peace Agreements on ending the Vietnam War which had been signed with great fanfare two weeks before on January 27, 1973 would hold? If it had been a test, I passed. 'Come,' he said, 'I will introduce you to the Prince.'

Sadruddin Aga Khan was the son that the old Aga Khan, the leader of the 30 million Shia Moslems who adhered to the Ismaeli branch of Islam, had by his second wife, the French-born Andrée Carron. His older half brother, Ali Khan, was a high profile figure who had married and divorced among others Rita Hayworth, served in the French Foreign Legion, represented Pakistan at the UN and managed to kill himself in May 1960 by driving his Lancia into a tree in the early hours of the morning in the Bois de Boulogne in Paris. Normally the title should have passed to Sadruddin, but the Aga Khan had decided to skip a generation and nominate as his successor Ali's son, Karim, Sadruddin's nephew.

There was never any evidence that the decision disappointed Sadruddin and he proved to be very much his own man. After having graduated from Harvard at the age of 21, he had chosen to dedicate himself to public service and, following various assignments for the UN, was elected in 1966 at the age of 33 to the post of United Nations High Commissioner for Refugees. Ironically, the only government that hesitated to endorse him was the United States. An impeccable record in public service, an American education and a wealth of contacts spanning the whole American political spectrum were not enough to endear him to the State Department bureaucracy. Actually his qualities played against him: he was too wealthy, too good-looking, too articulate, and too educated. But ultimately the State Department found preventing him from being elected too much of an effort and he got through.

The man to whom Rizvi introduced me proved to be as good as his image. He had the gift of putting people at ease as well as the ability of grasping the essentials and leaving the nuts and bolts to be worked out by those in his service. We chatted in French about Vietnam and he seemed satisfied with my observations. Strangely enough Rizvi, whose presence was generally overwhelming even when silent, had faded into the background, almost as if he had ceased to exist. Here, I thought, is the complex relation between the absolute Monarch and his Richelieu, both supremely intelligent and each playing his own role, the Master needing the Slave just as the Slave needed the Master to exercise the authority he has been empowered with.

The meeting must have gone well because, back in his office, Rizvi offered to hire me as a consultant with the title of Special Advisor for Asian affairs. I would receive 200 US $ per month, with travel expenses paid and my task would be to convince Hanoi and the Southern Liberation Front, the Viet Cong, to establish a dialogue with UNHCR with the ultimate purpose of setting up an aid program for the civilian population in the communist-controlled areas of Vietnam.

Officially UNHCR's mandate was to provide assistance to refugees, these being defined as people who were fleeing persecution and were outside their country of origin. On this basis, UNHCR had no grounds to intervene inside Vietnam where the only population movement was one of internal displacement. But in 1963 the UN General Assembly had passed the Good Offices resolution which stated that, if requested, UNHCR could also provide assistance to internally displaced persons. The resolution opened a whole new vista for UNHCR and provided the rationale for it to intervene in Vietnam but on one condition: it must be requested to do so by one or more of the Vietnamese parties. The Saigon government was savvy to how the international system operated and would have known how to seize this opportunity to get more aid but this was not what Sadruddin wanted. He wanted a request for assistance to come from all the contending Vietnamese parties and my job was to get the communists to do so.

On paper the assignment was impossible. Hanoi was not a member of the UN and the communists considered the organization as being nothing more than a tool of the US. On the plus side, UNHCR had been the only UN organization which, throughout the war years, had not been involved in channeling assistance to the Saigon government. Despite US enticements, Sadruddin had always insisted that what he aimed for was a permanent solution to population displacement in Vietnam and that as long as the war went on, any assistance from his Office would be wasted and so he had kept out of Vietnam altogether.

With the signing of the Paris peace agreements the situation had changed, at least on paper. Nominally, peace had returned to Vietnam and permanent solutions to population displacement could now be envisaged. In addition, the Paris agreements had endorsed the existence, in Southern Vietnam, of 'two South Vietnamese parties', namely the Saigon government and the Liberation Front. Thus, officially there were now three Vietnamese entities: Hanoi, Saigon and the Liberation Front.

This in turn had led UN Secretary General Kurt Waldheim, in an attempt to appear even handed, to request all UN agencies to provide assistance to the whole of Vietnam. The keyword here was 'whole' meaning the North, the areas controlled by the Saigon government and those controlled by the Southern Liberation Front, the Viet Cong.

As the head of a UN agency which was operating mostly in the third world, Sadruddin was particularly sensitive to the polarizing effect that the Vietnam war had had on the international community. He had managed to keep out of Vietnam during the war years but the war was now, at least on paper, over and he knew he would soon receive a request for aid from the Saigon government. With the war over, he could not turn down such a request but this would have trapped him into helping only one side. This he wished to avoid at all costs and not so much for reasons of substance but of form. The issue here was a matter of image. UNHCR had to appear even handed. To this end, UNHCR needed to be able to claim that it was assisting all sides that is to say not only the Saigon government but also Hanoi and the Viet Cong. The problem for Sadruddin was that UNHCR could not initiate an offer of assistance. It could only respond to a request. That the Saigon government would know how to present such a request, and that it would do so was obvious. That the communists would be too mistrustful, too apprehensive and too lacking in international sophistication to do likewise was also obvious. But Sadruddin wanted a request from all of the three warring parties. The Saigon government he could take care of. Hanoi and the Viet Cong he could not and this is where I came into the picture.

Paradoxically, while my encounter with Rizvi had been the pure product of chance, this was a mission for which, through no merit of mine, I was singularly well prepared for.

A TOUCH OF ASIA

I In 1956 I was in my second year at the University of Geneva. The summer holidays were around the corner and, at the unripe age of 20, I was at a loss about what to do with my time when I received a letter from my mother in Paris.

Her latest foible was the Rorschach test—the inkblot test—and she must have made a name for herself at it because some of her friends had brought her work to the attention of Kuo Mo-jo, the President of the Chinese Academy of Science. Kuo was known for having an inquisitive mind and in turn invited my mother to come to China for a fortnight to lecture at Beijing University on the Rorschach test and I was welcome to tag along.

There were few countries that I knew less about than China but I was vaguely aware that it was considered a rogue state, excluded from the UN and unrecognized by the overwhelming majority of the countries of the community of nations. But that was only part of the picture. Over the following days, as the word of my coming journey spread, I was able to gauge the conflicting emotions that it brought to light. While my fellow Swiss students reacted with indifference not so the handful of Americans that I had befriended. Most would no longer talk to me and those who still did tried studiously to avoid me as if I had become the bearer of some contagious disease. Why China would arouse such emotions among Americans was a mystery until I leafed through the likes of Time Magazine and the Readers' Digest. There, with no room for ambiguity, I found the explanation for their dread. China was not just another nasty country. It was the embodiment of evil summarized in the words of a Belgian missionary, Father Raymond de Jaegher, whose sentence stood beyond appeal: 'The Chinese communists are not Chinese; the Chinese communists are not human; the Chinese communists are living devils.'

It was thus fully forewarned of the perils that awaited us that after a 30 day sea journey from Marseilles and a brief transit through Hong Kong my mother and I landed in Beijing in the late afternoon of September 1, 1956 where a room had been booked for us at the *Hsin Chiao* hotel.

For the following fortnight, every morning after breakfast, my mother would be picked up at our hotel by a black Volga sedan with lace curtains that would take her to the university and she would only reappear for dinner.

Left to my own devices, armed with a rudimentary map of the town, I spent my days roaming the streets either on foot or by bus. Getting lost was not an option but a certitude, albeit one that carried no consequence for one good reason; I was a foreigner. All I had to do was to stop at a street corner and consult my map for a half a dozen children to congregate around me offering to help. Grown-ups were no less welcoming. I had with me the address of the hotel written in Chinese and all I had to do, as a last resort, was to show it to be guided by a relay of Chinese by bus or on foot until I had reached the vicinity of the hotel.

The political message conveyed by this behavior was unambiguous. Capitalist governments, so went the official propaganda line, were the enemies of China but foreign people were the friends of China. I was a foreigner permitted to come to China, hence a friend to be looked after. In its simplicity, and irrelevant to its accuracy, the message struck home, undoubtedly helped by the fact that foreigners were few and far between.

Apart from the foreign diplomatic corps made up mostly of fat Eastern Europeans, a small community of western expatriates did exist in Beijing and through the Peace Committee we were introduced to one of them. Rewy Alley was a ruddy down to earth New Zealander who had been active in the labor movement in China in the 1930's and had decided to stay on. He ran an open house and whenever we felt like it, in late afternoon we would drop in to see him and have a cup of tea, unannounced but always welcome. It was during these congenial gatherings that we came across some of the other expatriates who like Rewy had chosen to serve the Chinese cause. Israel Epstein, Sidney Shapiro and Sidney Rittenberg were all Americans and shared a burning commitment to the Chinese Revolution.

For me, an unripe 20 year old hovering in the background who had never encountered anyone possessed by such a burning commitment to any cause, they were a source of unfathomable mystery which I asked my mother to elucidate. 'Oh,' she replied with a touch of disdain, 'Jews looking for a cause.' It obviously did not occur to her that she could have been speaking about herself.

By mid September our stay in China had came to a close and as we reversed our steps to Hong Kong and from there to Geneva, this time by air, a journey which took three days in a lumbering Lockhead Constellation, it did occur to me that an extraordinary voyage had been essentially wasted on an unperceptive twenty year old youngster who failed to understand how lucky he had been. And yet not all had been lost on me.

I had been in Paris on an overcast day in March 1954 when the afternoon papers came out with headlines that took up one third of the front page: Dien Bien Phu has fallen. I knew of course that it was some sort of French position in a part of the world that went by the name of Vietnam but it was nothing I could relate to. Now, though I had only spent one week in Saigon when our ship had berthed there on her way to Hong Kong, Vietnam had become a reality. I had smelled the air, eaten the food and talked to some of the people. The same I could say about China. Before, it was a name without a face, distant and undefined, a threat ruled by a man named Mao. Now the name had a face and it belonged to people, real people, live people. And whatever the nature of the regime, it bore no relevance to the caricature that it had been made into.

Over the next successive years, as I obtained my MA and for want of a better alternative embarked on a PhD at the Geneva Graduate Institute for International Studies, I kept my contact with the Chinese consulate and when curiosity prompted me to apply for a tourist visa in the summer of 1965 to go back to China, it was promptly granted.

By then both my parents had passed away, my mother at the age of 63, my father at the age of 80 in Naples, and what he left me was enough to keep me going at a modest pace until I found a job.

The jet age had arrived and a journey to Hong Kong that took 30 days by sea in 1956 now took 22 hours. This time, not being a guest of the Chinese government, I had made my own travel arrangements through the China Travel Service in Hong Kong which organized my train journey to Canton and an onward booking by air for Beijing where a room had been reserved for me at the same *Hsin Chiao* hotel that I had stayed at on my previous visit.

The Beijing I had known in 1956 was a vast city with the atmosphere of a small town, an aggregate of neighborhoods surrounded by massive walls that dwarfed the city they were meant to safeguard.

By 1965 the old city walls had been leveled, Tien An Men Square had been enlarged ten fold and was now flanked by two massive government buildings but the rest of the city appeared untouched and I recognized many of the landmarks I had seen ten years before.

I had given myself ten days to explore Beijing after which I retraced my steps to Hong Kong and the comforts of a consumer society. One of my fellow classmates at Geneva University had joined the Shell Company after graduation and, after two years spent in Saigon, was now based in Hong Kong where he offered to put me up during my stay. He and his wife were wonderful hosts, his apartment luxurious, his friends numerous and the resulting temptation to linger in Hong Kong great. But after a week or so it was time to return to Geneva and to get back to working on my thesis, were it only to get it out of the way.

When I shared my plan with my friend he countered with an alternative. 'Why don't you stop for a couple of days in Saigon on the way back? I have a good friend, Charles Regnault, who works for Shell there and he will be happy put you up and take you around.' The suggestion was tempting. I had only a vague recollection of Saigon, from 9 years before, but with the Vietnam War going full swing and making the headlines daily I did not need much persuading.

Getting a Vietnamese tourist visa and rerouting my ticket proved no problem and on the morning of September 18, 1965 I boarded the daily Cathay Pacific flight to Saigon.

SAIGON 1965

South Vietnam might have been at war but this was visibly of no concern to the immigration and customs officers at Saigon airport who nonchalantly waved me through after having barely looked at my passport. There was a small crowd outside the terminal building waiting for the passengers and as I stood by my suitcase, somewhat at a loss about where to proceed, one of them looked at me. We made eye contact and he stepped towards me with outstretched hand and the touch of a quizzical smile on his face. 'Mister Casella, I presume.'

As we drove through the airport complex in his nondescript Peugeot 203, Charles explained that he would put me up in one of the guest rooms of the Shell complex where he had his apartment, but before that we would go downtown for lunch.

I had had coffee at *Brodard*, your typical French bistro with its zinc-covered bar, small brown tables and mirrored walls in 1956, and it was as I remembered it, unchanged. Most of the patrons were French and I could have been in Paris having a lunch of steak and French fries washed down with a pitcher of cheap red wine.

After lunch we drove to Charles's flat in the Shell compound on Truong Minh Giang street. Shell treated its expatriate staff well. All the apartments had spacious rooms, high ceilings and generous verandas and were allocated according to grade and family size. Charles was a bachelor and as such only rated a one-bedroom apartment, but on the ground floor there were guest rooms for visitors and I was given one of them.

The following morning I drove with Charles to the Shell building in downtown Saigon from where I made my way on foot past the cathedral and the post office to the crossroad between Dong Koi street and Le Loi boulevard, next to the old French theatre framed by the *Caravelle* hotel on one side and the *Continental* hotel on the other. This was the very heart of Saigon. Traffic was intense and chaotic, made up mostly of motorcycles, old French cars in various states of disrepair and military vehicles.

After having wandered about for a couple of hours, bought a street map and had coffee at the cafe *Givral*, I decided to go back to Charles's home for lunch by walking up the boulevard Pasteur till it intersected with Truong Minh Giang street.

As I proceeded up the boulevard I saw on the left side a sign on a four-storey building saying *Ambassade d'Italie*, Italian embassy. Without giving it much thought I entered the building's lobby. The embassy actually occupied only the two upper floors but it had a reception desk in the lobby behind which a middle-aged man with a handlebar moustache was reading the sports page of an Italian newspaper.

As I introduced myself he suddenly jumped to attention, his eyes focusing behind me. I turned around. A man had just entered the lobby. He must have been in his mid-fifties, with dark hair and a long and distinguished face, wearing an exquisitely tailored white linen suit with black shoes and a dark blue and white polka dot tie. The man nodded towards the receptionist and then turned to me with an inquiring look, as if to say, 'and you are?'

I had no idea who the man was but there was an air of elegant authority about him that required that I introduce myself, adding that I was just a tourist visiting Saigon for a few days. 'Casella?' he said in a questioning tone, 'are you by chance related to the publisher Casella?'

'Yes,' I answered, 'I am his son, but I live in Switzerland, and my Italian is not as good as it should be.' The observation elicited the semblance of a smile. 'If you are free will you join me for lunch?' he asked.

Giovanni D'Orlandi came from an old Italian family and did justice to his origins. In 1962 he had been posted as Italian ambassador in Saigon and he proved an instant success. His allure, intelligence, manners and discretion were instrumental in enabling him to establish a network of contacts, both among the diplomatic community and the Vietnamese elite, based on a degree of mutual trust that extended far beyond the reach of most ambassadors. Too sensitive to be a cynic but too level-headed to fall prey to mechanical anti-communism, he was said to have once commented that if all the American aid to Vietnam would have been distributed to every single Vietnamese in cash on a per capita basis, communism would never had stood a chance.

Over coffee D'Orlandi suggested that I prolong my stay in Vietnam and see some of the country. The idea was appealing but in a country at war where communications were hazardous and security unpredictable it was easier said than done.

'What is the main newspaper in Naples?' he asked. *The Mattino*, the Morning, I replied. 'Do you know someone there?' he asked.

'Not personally but my father was a friend of the editor and he knows of me,' I replied.

'Then it is all settled' said D'Orlandi. 'I will give you a letter requesting your accreditation as a correspondent for *Il Mattino* and you will write some articles for them on your return. You will get an American press card and with that you will be free to travel with the American forces.'

'But remember one thing,' he added, 'this is not only an American war. It is above all a Vietnamese war. Never forget that.'

When I left the embassy after lunch, instead of proceeding towards Charles's home, I turned right and returned downtown where I proceeded to the MACV (American Military Assistance Command Viet Nam) press office located in the *Rex* hotel. The US military press officers were both efficient and eager to please and I was soon the holder of a 'non-combatant certificate of identity' issued by the Department of Defense which, I was told, gave me a priority 3 on all military means of transportation after combat troops and liaison officers.

Armed with my new press card I took a pedicab back to Charles's home somewhat overwhelmed by the fact that my first day in Saigon, for reasons quite beyond my control, had been fruitful far beyond any expectation.

My American press card gave its bearer practically unlimited access to the American war effort in Vietnam, whether it was going on patrol with an American platoon, spending time on an aircraft carrier or having lunch in the officer's mess of one of the many bases the Americans had built all over the country and I shame-lessly profited from this bonanza. Overall it was a spectacular show in which only one constituent was missing: the enemy.

Hardly ever seen except by a minority of combat troops and even then often undistinguishable from the local farmer (in many cases he actually was the local farmer), he was an elusive intangi-ble that went by the name of Gook, Dink or Charlie. The one and only time I came across him was on the outskirts of the US base at Chu Lai. It was mid-afternoon and I was at the press center of the base when suddenly a major commotion erupted nearby. Some 100 yards from the base perimeter there was a Vietnamese cemetery in which a Viet Cong unit of some 50 men had positioned themselves, presumably to attack the base at night. They were discovered and a South Vietnamese unit was brought in to dislodge them. The firefight that followed was short but intense. Outgunned and out-numbered the Viet Cong did not stand a chance but they fought to the last man. I arrived on the scene a few minutes after the last shots had been fired in time to see a group of South Vietnamese instructed by the Americans to collect the bodies of the dead Viet Cong and pile them up next to the base perimeter while a bull-dozer proceeded to dig a trench to bury them in.

No sooner had the bodies been collected and piled in a heap that some sort of a tremor went through the Chu Lai base. Liter-ally from nowhere, American soldiers from inside the base started to converge towards the heap of bodies. What started, as a trickle became a rush, and then a stampede. More and more came. Kodak Instamatics clicked away; some of the soldiers posed in front of the bodies, alone or in groups; others bent down or twisted sideways to get a better angle for their pictures. They were all enlisted men, at most in their early twenties, and these were most certainly the first and last Viet Cong they were ever to see. Finally the throng, having taken its fill of pictures to send to the folks back home, slowly dis-persed and the bulldozer moved to maneuver the dead into their freshly dug grave. As its blade steered through the mass of mangled corpses of what had been 18-year-old Vietnamese farm boys dressed in black pajamas with the trousers rolled up to their knees, some of the bodies seemed to come back to life. Broken limbs, shattered torsos and severed heads, slowly rolled over as they were eased under the sod. Soon all that was left was a patch of recently moved soil as the bulldozer slowly made its way back into the base.

After three weeks, I felt that I had seen about all there was to see about the American military presence in Vietnam. Likewise, there were enough American correspondents and press services to cover the American war, and there was nothing I could have added to their reporting. And yet, I felt there was something I was missing as I remembered the words of Ambassador D'Orlandi. 'Try to look beyond the American war. There is a Vietnamese war far more complex, more convoluted and more multifaceted. That is the real war.'

The key to that war was not to be found in the briefing room of eager, confident, US army press officers in starched fatigues armed with statistics and colored charts. It was not even to be found going on patrol with an American unit and a non-combatant Certificate of Identity provided no access to it. For that, I had to look elsewhere.

There was still a small French community in South Vietnam and the more educated among them intermingled effortlessly with the upper crust Vietnamese, many of whom had graduated from prestigious French universities. Through Charles and his French friends I got to meet quite a few of them—doctors, lawyers, engineers, business men, officers and the like and the message they conveyed was unmistakable. None of them wanted to live under a communist regime. Many were Northerners who had fled South when the communists had taken over the North and they had seen the communists first hand. What they resented was not so much the lack of political freedom—there was no political freedom in the South either—but the regimentation not to say the restrictions placed on the every day life of the individual. For this group the war was not a conflict between two states, North and South Vietnam, but between two segments of Vietnamese society. Ultimately, it was a civil war with most of the communist leaders based in Hanoi actually not being Northerners and most of the anti communist leaders who ruled from Saigon not being Southerners. It was a war that the anti communist Vietnamese had already lost and it was only America's direct intervention in Vietnam in 1965 that saved them from the scourge of communist rule.

When the Americans landed in force in South Vietnam in early 1965 the South Vietnamese, that is those who were not on the communist side, awed by so much power, so much money and so much certitude watched and said nothing. They knew that their enemy was not encamped beyond an abstract 17th parallel. He was in their own back yard, which was also his backyard. But America had now taken over the war and America was too powerful to lose. Many among the better-educated South Vietnamese withdrew into their own shell. Others, the merchants, the petty bourgeois, the shopkeepers and most of the military, were too cynical, too cowardly or too indifferent to get themselves killed when the Americans were doing it for them. For these, making money became the name of the game. For the rest of the population, surviving was the most they could hope for.

Not so the communist leadership. Fired by a revolutionary zeal and a messianic belief in the justice of their cause, they soldiered on against incredible odds but never faltering in their will to win. And as for the rank and file, most of them could not tell the difference between a rice bowl and dialectical materialism but that was irrelevant. They were not fighting for communism, they were fighting foreigners so as to reunite their country under the benevolent eye of their uncle Ho and that for them was cause enough.

A JOURNALIST BY DEFAULT

F Founded sometime in the 19th century, the *Journal de Genève* was not so much a newspaper as a turn-of-the-century gazette dedicated to analysis, perspective, opinion pieces and financial reporting, a concern much in keeping with the newspapers' backers, the Geneva banking community. Whatever news it carried was at least two days old but this was of little concern to its editor, an austere Calvinist who used to say; 'If you want the news turn on the radio.'

I had received an introduction to the editor from one of the professors of the Graduate Institute and after having politely listen to my account of my visit to Asia he told me that he would be interested in three feature articles on my trip to China and six more on Vietnam. For each article I would receive the equivalent of 20 US $, a token payment, but then the *Journal de Genève* could not afford more.

Overwhelmed by an order of this magnitude, and lacking any journalistic experience, I set myself a number of empirical guidelines. Local color, the reader must somehow be made to feel that he is on the spot. Facts, not too many but contributing to the general picture. A human touch, a dash of political analysis and finally, to create an appearance of erudition, the ever essential 'perspective'.

I was now convinced that, whatever the effort and expenditure, the direct intervention of the United States in Vietnam was at best a stopgap. The US could prevent the communists from taking over the South but unless enough Southerners could be motivated into standing up to the communists with more than words the effort was doomed unless the Americans elected to stay in Vietnam for ever.

That was not what the readers of the *Journal de Genève* wanted to hear. They were good, hardworking conservative Swiss who believed in the virtues of freedom, democracy and free enterprise and loathed anything that smacked of dictatorship. Communism to them was anathema and they were acutely aware of the fact that only the US stood between them and a Soviet takeover of Western Europe. To see a country with which they shared fundamental values go awry in Vietnam and that at the hands of communists was not exactly good news to them. 'Don't upset them too much,' recommended the editor of the *Journal de Genève*. Writing proved laborious but the result must have pleased him for he published all nine of my pieces.

In the rarefied atmosphere of the small city of Geneva, my reputation was now made. Overnight I became an 'Asian expert' and a regular on local radio and TV talk shows.

One of the side-benefits of my newfound reputation was that I started to receive invitations from an odd assortment of groups and NGOs to make presentations on Vietnam and it was at one of these many gatherings, held in Geneva, that I met a Czech academic who ventured that he could get me introduced to the North Vietnamese embassy in Prague.

For me the offer was a major piece of good fortune. I had all the access I needed to the South Vietnamese and the Americans but the 'other side' remained an inscrutable mystery. Granted the North Vietnamese had an office in Paris and a small consular presence in London but getting to them, unless one was a recognized communist sympathizer, belonged to the realm of the impossible. Now, finally, luck had come my way.

In April 1967 I obtained a one-week tourist visa to Prague and the day after my arrival called at the North Vietnamese embassy where a meeting with the North Vietnamese acting ambassador Pham Duong had been set up.

Occasionally one encounters people to whom one takes an instant dislike. Pham Duong was one of them and I suspect that the feeling was mutual. His French was fluent, a sure sign that he came from an educated Vietnamese family but this in no way seemed to affect his demeanor; the French call it speaking with a wooden tongue, namely the mindless parroting of the official party line. Having systematically read the various policy pronouncements emanating from Hanoi, I already knew them by heart; The US had to unconditionally suspend the bombing of the North and withdraw from South Vietnam and if there was to be any negotiation it should be between Washington and the Southern Liberation Front, that is the Viet Cong. Of course it was not up to someone of the level of Pham Duong to deviate from the official line but it was delivered in such a dogmatic manner as to render it indigestible to any but the most thickheaded communist party members; and yet worse was to come.

After our formal interview I stayed on to chitchat and for no particular reason the conversation moved to Switzerland and from there to the Swiss army. I explained to Pham Duong that every Swiss male at the age of 18 was drafted in the army for four months of basic training followed by a refresher course every year until the age of 50. This being a militia army that could be mobilized in 48 hours, every soldier was required to keep his military kit including his rifle at home. 'What about the ammunition?' inquired Pham Duong.

'Also the ammunition,' I added.

Pham Duong looked startled. 'Impossible,' he said. 'Why?' I asked, somewhat surprised. 'Because,' he answered with no hesitation in his voice, 'the workers would revolt.'

It was my first encounter with a North Vietnamese official and after leaving the embassy it occurred to me that I must have come across the most obtuse of the lot because that if they had been all like that they would have lost the war years ago.

Back in Geneva I wrote a piece on the interview under the title 'Hanoi unyielding' and sent it to all the newspapers I was writing for. They all ran it and the responses I got were all positive. Those with American sympathies felt it portrayed the communists as uncompromising and those with Viet Cong sympathies felt it portrayed the Vietnamese as unwavering in their just struggle. For me, the reaction was a lesson. If you use the right expressions, you can please everyone because they will all have interpreted your words to suit their own opinion.

My journalistic career was now on solid grounds but I still operated under one major handicap, namely that I was Italian. Clichés have a life of their own and particularly so in the Anglo Saxon world where the word 'Italian' is more associated with good food, sunshine and Roman ruins than with hard work and serious, factual reporting.

So the time had come for me to become Swiss. The procedure lasted two years and required 12 years of residence and innumerable interviews in order to established that I behaved and thought like a Swiss but I passed the test and at the age of 31, I swore an oath as a new Swiss citizen. My credibility as a journalist made a quantum leap forward. Who could doubt the word of a 'Swiss correspondent'?

By now my network of newspapers had expanded beyond Italy and Switzerland and I was regularly contributing to German, English, Italian, American and French newspapers, as well as to the Far Eastern Economic Review.

I had also gone twice more to Prague to meet with the new North Vietnamese ambassador as well as the representative of the Liberation Front and while they had repeated the official party line which I could find in any of their many publications, getting a face to face interview had two advantages; it had a ring of authenticity and they were getting to know me personally. Thus, slowly, I was building my image with the 'other side'.

TET 1968

January is a dreary month in Geneva. By contrast it is the best time of the year to visit Saigon, where I arrived on January 26, 1968. The end of January heralded the coming of the Vietnamese New Year, the Tet, the most important festivity of the year. For close to one week the country would come to a stop as families got together to celebrate. Even the war would wind down as an informal ceasefire took place, albeit a noisy one as South Vietnamese soldiers and their Viet Cong counterparts would, contrary to orders, celebrate the New Year by discharging their weapons in the air.

Charles Regnault had left Shell but he had handed me over, so to speak, to his successor Jacques Morin and his wife, Françoise. They were planning to spend the Tet in Bangkok but before leaving had put me up in their guest room, gave me the key to their apartment and told me to make myself at home. My only responsibility was to feed their cat, a huge brute of uncertain lineage that took an instant liking to me.

On January 31, after sharing with the cat the diner that the maid had left for me in the fridge, I went off to bed at 10.30 pm and turned off the lights.

It must have been 6 o'clock in the morning and dawn was just breaking when I was awoken by what sounded like firecrackers going off nearby. I knew the Vietnamese liked to set off fireworks for Tet and initially did not think too much of it until I decided to get up and open the window. The din was infernal, but mirth was not what this ruckus was about. I could see tracer bullets slowly drifting up and down Truang Minh Giang street on a background of heavy explosions and the rhythmic ponging of 50 caliber machine guns. Several fires had started nearby and a heavy column of black smoke rose in the direction of Tan Son Nhut airport.

By 8 am the firing in the vicinity of the Shell compound had died down and I gingerly left the building to cast a cautious look down the street. It was totally deserted except for a lone pedicab driver who was nonchalantly cycling in the direction of downtown. I waved to him, handed him a 10 US $ bill pointed in the direction he was going, and got into the seat. After some 20 minutes without having seen a soul, we arrived near the cathedral. On the left, in the direction of the US Embassy, I could see some movement and signaled the driver in that direction. He complied and in another five minutes we were in front of the embassy and I waved him goodbye.

The embassy had visibly been attacked a few hours before. There were two dead Viet Cong sprawled on the embassy grounds, dressed in civilian clothes and wearing red armbands. One had taken a shot in the head that had partly blown off his face. The other suffered from multiple hits that had torn apart his ribcage and his stomach. A third body was being manhandled on a stretcher by four embassy guards wearing yellow rubber gloves. Rigor mortis had set in, meaning the Embassy had been attacked quite a few hours before and he kept on slipping off the stretcher. By that time the minibus that ferried some of the secretaries to the Embassy every morning had arrived, delivering its lot of clerical staff, blissfully unaware of what had been going on. It was obviously the first time they had come face to face with war. Horror, disgust, repulsion at the sight of the dead bodies were mirrored on their faces as they silently walked to the embassy door. Some started crying and dabbing their eyes with neatly embroidered handkerchiefs.

That the embassy had never been breached was obvious. The main door had taken one hit from a rocket-propelled grenade but had resisted. Whatever fighting there had been had occurred in the garden around the embassy, between the outer wall and the main building itself.

There was not much for me to do at the embassy so I set out on foot towards the US press center in the *Rex* hotel building some 20 minutes away. Except for an occasional car the streets were deserted and all shop windows closed. Firing could be heard in the distance punctuated by the occasional explosion. At the press center a handful of American correspondents were trying to piece together from two distraught press officers what had happened. Apparently the Viet Cong had launched a massive, coordinated attack throughout South Vietnam. Practically every city had been hit. In Saigon, Viet Cong sappers had attacked the radio, the US embassy and various army Headquarters. While none of these attacks had succeeded, large parts of the town had been infiltrated including the area near the Phu Tho racetrack where heavy fighting was ongoing. Tan Son Nhut airport was closed down and the road leading to it was not safe. All Americans were asked to keep to their quarters and stay tuned to the AFVN, the American Forces Viet Nam radio.

While it was impossible to judge the seriousness of the situation the fact that combat rations were made available at a nominal cost to correspondents at the press center was not a good sign. I bought two boxes of 12 rations each with no idea how I would get them back to the Shell compound when another lonely pedicab peddled by. I gave him a 10 US $ bill, got in the seat and pointed. We sailed through a deserted city as I kept on pointing and finally made it safely home.

For the next two days I stayed in the apartment. Firing throughout the city was intermittent but ongoing, moving from one part of town to the other. By night the sky over Tan Son Nhut airport was a red glow interspaced by brilliant flashes. With all shops and restaurants closed, my meals consisted of combat rations, which I shared with the cat. He clearly took a liking to them and we got along like a house on fire.

On the third day, the firing became more sporadic and after lunch I ventured forth from the Shell compound down the Boulevard Pasteur until I reached the Italian embassy. Ambassador D'Orlandi had left Vietnam, I did not know his successor and I expected the embassy to be closed anyway, but on a hunch I went in.

There were two men in the lobby, one tall and gaunt, the other small and stocky with a dark handlebar moustache, as well as a strikingly beautiful girl in her twenties wearing Gucci sneakers and a Hermes scarf tied to the strap of an elegant leather bag. I introduced myself as the correspondent for *Il Mattino*.

The small man was the Italian military attache, Colonello Boschi, who was in charge of the Embassy as the ambassador had gone to Bangkok for the Tet. Boschi belonged to a cavalry regiment and was a keen horseman who had made a name for himself at horse shows. The girl, Francesca, came from the best Turin society and was also keen on horses. They had met at a show somewhere in Italy, and the rest followed. She had told her family that she would be going to Australia for a horse show but instead had headed for Saigon to see il Colonello whose wife, most conveniently, had stayed in Italy. The Tet offensive did not seem to have perturbed their romance and they had spent the last two days, he with brilliant dash and she totally oblivious to the danger, driving all over Saigon in one of the embassy cars. They were now setting out on another foray and they invited both me and the other man, an Italian journalist who went by the name of Carlo Gregoretti to join them which we both did with no hesitation.

Downtown Saigon was still mostly deserted but quiet and for want of a better destination Boschi headed towards Cholon, the Chinese part of Saigon, staying on the main streets. We had a map in the car, but most of the street signs had faded for lack of upkeep and we were soon totally lost. The atmosphere was eerie, the streets totally deserted and every shop and window had their shutters drawn.

'There is nothing here,' said Boschi, 'let's go back.' He made a U-turn on a large avenue that would have led us back to Saigon when he spotted some movement at the end of a side street. We drove some 200 yards down the street that narrowed into a lane leading into a maze of alleys. It was too narrow for the car to drive on so Boschi made another U turn and was ready to head back to the main street when we saw a boy—he must have been about 15— sitting on a stool next to a half-open shop window. Boschi stopped the car next to the boy and I got out. I did not quite feel up to asking him if there were any Viet Cong around so I just said Phap, meaning French just as a way of indicating that I was not an American, hopefully in the right tone. The boy smiled, indicated that he did not understand and pointed to the inside of the shop. As

I entered, it suddenly occurred to me that the boy had an AK 47 under his stool. The boy was a Viet Cong.

Inside the shop I found two other somewhat bemused youngsters, both with AK 47s, as well as a 3-person French TV team headed by a well-known journalist, Brigitte Friang. She had a reputation for being fearless, audacious to the point of recklessness, and acerbic. Now she was restrained.

'Stay quiet,' she said in a low voice, 'they have sent for someone and they don't want us to leave the shop.' I waited in silence. Minutes passed and then Gregoretti stepped in. He saw the two youngsters, understood and said nothing. We waited. Then Francesca, with her Gucci sneakers and Hermes scarf, came in.

'Are you buying the whole shop?' she asked with an inquisitive smile.

'Stay quiet,' whispered Gregoretti, 'they are Viet Cong.'

'Really,' she answered, 'interesting.'

A minute later Colonello Boschi barged in. 'What are you doing?' he bellowed.

'Stay quiet,' said Gregoretti, 'they are Viet Cong.'

'I am going,' roared Boschi, moving towards the door.

From the corner of my eye I saw one of the youngsters slightly raise his AK 47 as Gregoretti took Boschi by the arm and growled in a low voice, 'stay quiet and don't move'.

We waited in silence. The tension was palpable; the two youngsters had faded into the background, their faces expressionless as if disconnected from reality. Outside we could hear an occasional shot. Suddenly a man walked into the shop. He was in his forties and held a Colt 45 pistol in his right hand, arm outstretched, pointing towards the floor. With his left hand he motioned us to follow him. As we set off with him in the lead, through a maze of alleys, two other Viet Cong with AK 47s followed behind.

As we moved from one alley to another we spotted more and more Viet Cong, crouching in doorways or in the shadows of walls. Most carried AK 47s, others rocket launchers. They hardly cast us a glance as we passed by. All were in civilian clothes with red armbands.

We finally reached a blind alley, some 20 meters long. The man with the pistol had disappeared as the two remaining Viet Congs motioned us to sit down on the ground. Both then chambered a round in their weapon and shouldered it, pointing at us. Not one word had been said and the only sound was coming from Colonello Boschi who had started to sob.

Suddenly another man appearing from nowhere cast an eye into the lane from a sidewall. He shouted something. The two Viet Cong lowered their weapons. The man who carried a Colt 45 pistol in a Sam Brownie holster motioned for us to follow him inside a nearby house. It was a typical Vietnamese home, built in stone on one floor with a main room that also served as kitchen and a bedroom in the back. The owner of the house and his wife, both well-past middle age, were seated at the far end of the room on a wooden bench. Both seemed unconcerned as we were made to sit on rickety plastic chairs. The man with the pistol then said something to the owner who turned to us and asked in impeccable French, 'who are you?'

'Do you mind if I speak for all of us,' I asked Brigitte in a low voice. She nodded silently. I then turned to the man with the pistol.

'We are not Americans; we are journalists from France, Italy and Switzerland.'

Slowly the old man translated. The man with the pistol barked back. 'You have entered the liberated areas without authorization from the Front. You are guilty.'

It was now or never for me to put to good use the jargon that I had had to put up with when dealing with the Vietnamese communists I had interviewed in the past as well as the set formulas that their propaganda was churning out with abandon. Using the wrong expression or phraseology I knew could be fatal and much, if not all, depended on how the old man would translate my words. Slowly I started.

'We recognize our guilt. We present our apologies to the Vietnamese people and to the National Liberation Front of South Vietnam, the only authentic representative of the South Vietnamese people. All we can say is that we have been deceived by the American imperialists and their Saigonese valets. They said that there were no Liberation forces in Saigon. They lied. It was not our intention to violate Vietnamese sovereignty and enter the liberated areas without the authorization of the Front. So our intentions were not bad. But we committed a mistake. We are guilty. Our fate is now in the hands of the Vietnamese people and their representative, the Liberation front. Whatever decision they will take in our regards, we know it will be a just decision. May I add that we are progressive journalists and that our readers all support unconditionally the just fight of the Vietnamese people for freedom and independence because as President Ho Chi Minh said, 'nothing is more important than freedom and independence.' As the old man translated, little by little I could see a change in the demeanor of the man with the pistol and when I finished speaking any overt sign of hostility had faded away and I could detect on his face a semblance of a smile. Visibly I had used all the right expressions. There was also a twinkle in the eye of the old man. He was no fool.

The man with the pistol now spoke. 'You are the guests of the Liberation Front.' He turned to the lady of the house and spoke a few words. She disappeared in the back and returned with a teapot and some small cups. The tea was the usual, bitter, foul Vietnamese brew but after we had emptied our cups I knew they would not shoot us, or at least not right away.

The man with the pistol got up. 'I will refer to the authorities,' he said. 'In the meantime you must stay here. I am leaving one of our fighters with you. You are not prisoners and he is here to protect you.'

For close to one hour we waited. Our guard, armed with an AK 47 was, from his weathered face and craggy hands, clearly a peasant. He wore plastic sandals, baggy khaki trousers and two shirts, one light blue and one white on top of each other. Two of his front teeth were capped in steel and he had an aluminum wedding band on the middle finger of his left hand. We made eye contact and his face broke into a wide smile as he nodded, reassuringly.

We waited in silence with Colonello Boschi occasionally blowing his nose. 'Do you think they will kill us,' he plaintively asked Brigitte.

'I dont know,' she snapped back, 'but if you don't like the idea change profession.'

As we sat silently on our chairs the household cat took upon himself to jump on my lap, cuddle into a ball and started to purr. I could see a lonely flea perched on the tip of his nose, and the predicament it represented suddenly overshadowed all my other preoccupations. Would the flea stay on the cat or would it change host?

At last we heard steps outside. The door opened and a man stepped in. There was an unmistakable air of authority about him as he spoke in Vietnamese with the owner of the house translating. 'The Front has examined your case,' he said. 'We accept your apologies and will escort you back to your cars. Until then we assume responsibility for your protection. After that, you are on your own.' We all got up and shook hands.

Our car was where we had left it and after having made a U-turn Colonello Boschi proceeded to drive back the way we came towards the main avenue. As we did so we passed a side street. Sitting on the ground there were about two dozen South Vietnamese soldiers in full battle gear. They had seen us drive towards the Viet Cong and had said nothing. Now they looked at us passing by the other way with the same indifference.

Once on the main avenue colonello Boschi stepped on the gas and 10 minutes later dropped Gregoretti and I in front of the Press Center in the *Rex* building where we arrived just in time for the daily 5 o'clock briefing. There, a US army colonel described how the Viet Cong had been pushed back throughout Vietnam with massive losses. Tet, he said, was an American victory and all it would take were a few more attacks like that for the Viet Cong to be wiped out. Militarily, he might not have been wrong.

It took another five days for the airport to reopen, bringing in a flood of correspondents who had been feverishly waiting in Bangkok as well as the Morins, slightly worried about the fate of their cat. They need not have been. The brute must have gained one pound during their absence and visibly preferred US combat rations to its usual fare. So, if nothing else, I left behind a contented cat as I boarded the flight for Bangkok and from there the onwards connection to Geneva.

In terms of enhancing my understanding of Vietnam my brief capture by the Viet Cong had been a non event which made for an amusing anecdote but not much else. It did however give a further boost to my journalistic career and also encouraged me to believe that I had reached a good level of proficiency in the use of the communist lingo. And it did make for a good conversation piece. Whenever I would mention the incident to the North Vietnamese or Viet Cong officials I would meet in Europe over the subsequent years the response, accompanied by a raucous burst of laughter would invariably be. 'So, you almost stayed in Vietnam for good.'

CONSULTING FOR UNHCR

By the time of the signing of the Paris peace agreements on Vietnam, in January 1973 I had a well established reputation as a Swiss scholar and journalist writing for the mainstream media untainted by any suspected left wing leanings and with contacts as good as any non communist westerner could have with the Vietnamese communists. Until now I had used these contacts to widen my perspective on the Vietnam war. Now, as a consultant I was expected to use them for a more tangible purpose: to get access for UNHCR to the regime in Hanoi.

The Paris agreements had endorsed the existence of two so-called South Vietnamese 'parties'. On one side there was the Saigon government which owed its survival to the American intervention and was now expected, with massive US assistance, to fight the war on its own. On the other side the Liberation Front which, in 1968, had given birth to the Provisional Revolutionary Government of South Vietnam, the PRG. That both the Liberation Front and the PRG were spawned by the Vietnamese communist party was a given. On paper the Liberation Front—or PRG—and the South Vietnamese Government were equal entities, each in control of a part of South Vietnam.

However, this was a contention furiously opposed by the Saigon government. Granted, it had signed the Paris agreement and therefore acknowledged the existence of 'two South Vietnamese parties' but what it had agreed to on paper was one thing and what it was willing to recognize in practice was another which meant that it continued to claim that it was the only legitimate representative of South Vietnam. To counter this claim the communist political strategy was now to build up the image of its latest incarnation, the Provisional Revolutionary Government of South Vietnam—the

PRG—in order to undercut Saigon's assertion of exclusive legitimacy in the South. In practice this meant that whenever an issue concerning the South was raised with Hanoi, the standard reply was: it is not our concern, go and talk to the PRG.

Now, while I was still a journalist, I was also a UNHCR consultant with the job of selling the refugee agency to the communist side and my problem consisted of finding the right angle of approach and the right bait for them to bite on. Offering only aid, I realized, would not get us very far as they were getting enough to cover their basic needs from the Chinese and the Soviets. Approaching Hanoi would have been not only useless but also counterproductive as the communist strategy was to promote the PRG and not the North, the Democratic Republic of Vietnam. This left me with only one card to play: to convince the PRG that entering into a dialogue with UNHCR would boost their international standing and so contribute to undermine Saigon's claim to exclusive sovereignty on the South. It was a long shot, but the only one available to me. Of course the approach would have to be coated with a humanitarian veneer: assistance, people in need, displaced persons would be part of the phraseology. In terms of substance however, it was pure politics.

In 1969 the PRG had opened an office in Paris and, in my journalistic capacity, I had met Pham Van Ba, its representative. Ba had a quick mind and while he must have been a communist party member of long standing, ideology had not gotten the better of his common sense so when I obliquely suggested that the Vietnamese revolution should also learn how to use the United Nations system his reaction was not negative on principal. During one of my visits, Ba introduced me to another Vietnamese, Nguyen Van Thu, 'he is the President of the Liberation Red Cross of South Vietnam' he explained. While the function sounded innocuous I knew there was more to it than it appeared. When governments who are not on speaking terms want to enter into some sort of negotiation without giving the appearance that they are doing so they often use their respective Red Cross organizations, given that on paper these are not government organizations. The ruse deceives no one but appearances are saved.

This approach was adopted in 1959 when Thailand and North Vietnam, through their respective Red Crosses, negotiated the repatriation of some 40,000 Vietnamese from Northern Vietnam who had sought refuge in Thailand during the first Indochina war and now wanted to return home. And the head of the Red Cross delegation from Hanoi at the time was none other than Nguyen Van Thu.

Born in Saigon but educated in Paris and slightly older than Ba, Thu had the manners of an upper class Frenchman with the slightly perplexed expression of a basset hound.

It was difficult not to get along well with either and whenever I would drop by in Paris to see them I would gently coax them into considering some sort of dialogue with UNHCR. The arguments I used were deceptively straightforward: the Vietnam war had now acquired an additional diplomatic dimension. This made it imperative to build up the international image of the PRG. What better way of doing this than to establish a dialogue with a UN organization and even more so one which was considered the best of the litter. There was no danger in trying and the political benefits could be substantive. And if nothing came out of it, it would at least do what the Vietnamese did best: further confuse the enemy. Obviously neither Ba nor Thu had the authority to decide on my proposals and all I could hope for was that they would transmit them further up the hierarchy. However, for them to do so required that they first be convinced that they had some merit and stood a chance of being accepted. On the downside, neither they nor their superiors knew how the UN operated and, like all communists, had an inbuilt aversion to dealing with multilateral organizations.

I did not expect progress to be fast and it was not. I also did not expect a call from the ICRC, the all Swiss International Committee of the Red Cross. But one morning, at home, my phone rang. A Mr Hocke, the new chief of operations of the ICRC, wanted to see me. Could I come over to their offices?

The man who received me visibly did not hail from the upper crust of Geneva's Calvinist bourgeoisie and cultivating appearances was not his forte. Six feet tall with light brown hair and a round, slightly chubby face, he wore off-the-peg clothes and an ill assorted tie. But what struck me the most was his gaze. He seemed incapable of looking you straight in the eye, or if he did so with only one eye, the other wandering off. Here was a man not to be trusted, I told myself.

Belying his appearance, he proved most congenial. Over the years the ICRC had built its world-wide credibility on being accepted as a neutral party by all sides in a conflict. Having failed to be recognized as such in Vietnam with the communists rejecting its presence altogether and the Americans turning it into a sham was a stain on the organization's record and Hocke wanted to set it straight but he did not know how to go about it. All his efforts to contact Hanoi or the PRG had met with a rebuff and so he turned to me. He had read my articles and had heard about me and wanted to take me on as a consultant. 'Get me to Hanoi' he said. How it was to be done, was left up to me. For my services I would receive the equivalent in Swiss francs of about 700 US $ a month and was to report to him and no one else.

Accepting Hocke's offer meant that I would be serving two master but none had requested exclusivity and serving one entailed no disadvantages for the other. So I accepted the offer and found no need to inform either Rizvi or Hocke that they were not my only clients.

There was one question that I found no need of asking myself at the time namely, why was I doing all this? But if I had, the answer would have been deceptively simple: for the fun of it. I enjoyed the company of Sadruddin, Ba, Rizvi,Thu and the like. And I also took a somewhat perverse Machiavellian pleasure in trying to goad the Vietnamese communists into dealing with a UN organization and finding the arguments to induce them to do so.

Promoting ICRC with Mr Ba and his cohorts was not quite the same as promoting UNHCR. They knew nothing about UNHCR whereas they had had over the years sporadic contacts with ICRC and had come to take exception to it. On the plus side the communists, like their Christian counterparts, also believed in redemption. Confess your sins and you might be forgiven.

In 1971 I had written an article on the issue of prisoners in Vietnam and had been critical of the ICRC's inability to understand that this was not a conventional conflict and that insurgency demanded a new approach to the POW issue. The article had not endeared me to the Swiss political establishment which viewed any criticism of the ICRC as tantamount to blasphemy but it did single me out as having a particular expertise on the prisoner issue in Vietnam.

I now felt the time had come to write a follow up story on the subject. The gist of the piece was that the ICRC had started to reform itself; there was a new President, a new chief of operations, all of whom understood why they had failed in Vietnam and wanted to make up for it. It was not quite true nor was it completely wrong. When I showed the piece to Hocke before publishing it he briefly leafed through it and just shrugged his shoulders: 'I don't care what you write,' he said, 'just get me to Hanoi.'

Ba had read my first article and he reacted positively to my second one. 'They are starting to understand' he commented.

'Maybe it is time to talk to them,' I said laughing.

'Maybe,' he answered.

After eight months I still had nothing to show for my efforts and was wondering if I had not taken on a hopeless task when in August 1973, Mr Ba came out with the first piece of concrete information I could work on. Apparently, the proposal for the PRG to establish links with UNHCR had been submitted to the higher echelons where it was still being dissected. Further probing elicited the information that this higher echelon was actually *Madame* Nguyen Thi Binh, the PRG Foreign Minister, and it would be useful if I could meet her. Ba's comments actually did not make sense. No foreign minister would ever decide on his own whether his government was to establish or not a dialogue with UNHCR. Such an option would be considered by a working group and then the various options submitted to the minister for a final decision. Given that Mrs. Binh's understanding of the UN system was probably non-existent my meeting with her could in no way result in a decision on her part on the matter. So why should I meet Mrs. Binh? Given that I would never know the answer I did not bother to ask the question but if it had to be Mrs Binh, so be it.

The other problem was where to meet her as she was constantly on the move. Mr Ba did not have her schedule but he knew that she would attend the non-aligned conference in Algiers in September. 'Why don't you try to meet here there?' he suggested.

When I passed the information to Rizvi I saw a spark in his eyes. colonel Boumedienne, Algeria's President, had invited Sadruddin as his personal guest to attend the conference. Sadruddin had other engagements and could not accept but why not send me as his representative? There, with some luck, I could try to approach *Madame* Binh.

Sadruddin liked the idea and the next thing I knew I was on an airplane to Algiers with another UNHCR staff member, Ghassan Arnaout. If UNHCR had been a court, Arnaout would have been the jester. Syrian, educated in Beirut and in Paris, quick, funny, articulate, a tremendous gossip with a sharp political mind and no practical sense whatsoever, he was the sort of person who could speak the truth or even insult those around him and get away with it because nobody took him seriously. Serving UNHCR was for him more of a pastime than a job, but one that he enjoyed as it gave him access to the diplomatic community and provided him with an open field where his gusto for intrigue could exert itself in full. Not that he was trying to achieve anything through it. Intrigue for the sake of intrigue was his nature, a trait that made him a real son of the Middle East.

Hosting the non-aligned summit was a great honor for Algeria and the government had pulled out all the stops to ensure the success of the get-together. The venue selected was a large hotel and country club complex outside Algiers and the whole area had been sealed off by a triple-cordon of elite troops supported by tanks and anti-aircraft guns.

When we landed at the airport in Algiers, our identities were repeatedly checked, and after having received special passes we were driven directly to the conference complex where rooms had been allocated to us. In terms of protocol the participants were divided into three groups: Chiefs of State, Prime Ministers and Ministers, each provided with a corresponding level of accommodation, restaurant facilities and restricted areas. Sadruddin had been invited as a Chief of State but as we were only his representatives we were downgraded to the level of Prime Ministers. Good as it might sound it was not what I had wished for. *Madame* Binh was corralled with the other attending ministers and, given the security constraints, moving from one area to the other was almost impossible. With the opportunity of approaching her either in a restaurant or the corridors now practically nil, my only opportunity of making contact with her was at the general meeting in between sessions.

My chance came after Colonel Khaddaffi, resplendent in a white uniform, had made a fiery speech that was followed by a torrent of applause. A half an hour recess was then announced and as the delegates dispersed I noticed that *Madame* Binh had not moved from her allotted seat. Slowly working my way down the aisle against a flow of exiting delegates I finally reached her seat, sat down on my heels to bring myself to her level and, as she turned her head to me, pronounced in a tone that I hoped was low but intelligible: '*Madame* Minister, I am a friend of Pham Van Ba and he asked me to talk to you, would you kindly give me a minute or two of your time?'

She smiled. 'Of course,' she said. It suddenly occurred to me that she was a very beautiful woman. Trying to be as concise as possible I explained that, unlike other UN agencies, UNHCR had never compromised itself with the Saigon regime, that following the Paris agreements we wanted to bring some assistance to the Vietnamese people and our priority was to help those who lived in the liberated areas. This aid should be seen as a gesture of solidarity and it was up to the Vietnamese people to determine what their needs were and how it should be distributed. So we are ready to enter into an agreement with you. There was a moment of silence and I could see her thinking.

'And how will you deal with us?' she asked.

'Exactly as you are,' I answered, 'as the Provisional Revolutionary Government of South Vietnam.'

'So you recognize us,' she said.

'Of course, *Madame* Minister,' I replied.

She smiled again. 'Then it is fine,' she answered, 'you can move ahead with Ba.'

The summit lasted for two more days and I could not decently leave before it ended, so I spent the remaining time by one of the pools. We were not yet home free but finally I could see some light at the end of the tunnel.

Back in Geneva I reported to Rizvi. He was the sort of person who excelled at showing dissatisfaction and only reluctantly displayed approval but this time he found it difficult to hide his satisfaction. He had been the one who had found me. He had introduced me to Sadruddin and any success I achieved would reflect well on his judgment. Two days later I was in Paris where a bouncy Ba informed me that he had heard the good news and that a letter from the PRG requesting assistance from UNHCR would arrive shortly in Geneva.

One week went by, then a second, then a third and still no letter. Rizvi was getting worried and so was I. Then I had a flash of inspiration. Did Pham Van Ba know how to draft a letter to a UN agency? Probably not. If he did not know, it was logical to assume that he would not write it. Would he admit not knowing? Unlikely.

I spent two hours with Rizvi in a Geneva cafe next to the UN drafting two letters. One was the type of letter that we would have liked to receive from Ba. The other was a draft of the letter that Sadruddin would write in response to the first one.

The next day I was back in Paris to see Ba. After half an hour of light banter over a cup of coffee, as I got up to leave I handed him a plain envelope. 'By the way,' I said, 'just for your information this is the sort of letter that we generally get from governments and this is how we answer.'

Three days later a letter from Paris arrived at UNHCR Headquarters in Geneva, written on PRG letterhead and bearing an official seal. It was an exact duplicate of the draft I had given to Ba. That same day a letter signed by Sadruddin was sent to Ba acknowledging his request, informing him that it had been accepted in principle and that further technical discussions would be held with him to determine the precise nature of the assistance to be given.

Rizvi, although he tried to hide it, was as pleased as punch. Sadruddin was satisfied. Ba could claim that he had achieved the first recognition of the PRG by a UN agency and I had enjoyed myself. But while things could not have gone better we were still not out of the woods and the challenge now was how to give some substance to an assistance request that was still undefined. So I returned to Paris, this time with Rizvi.

It was the first time Rizvi had met Ba, or any Vietnamese communist, but he instantly got the hang of the situation. While by nature he tended to think conceptually he also knew how to look at problems from a practical angle, a rare virtue for anyone, and even more so for a UN bureaucrat.

In theory, providing assistance to the civilian population in the PRG-controlled areas of South Vietnam was a noble endeavor and even more so as these had been the hardest hit areas of the country, but what was the assistance to be? It had to be useful, easy to deliver, cost effective, not impossible to monitor and, last but not least, bear a humanitarian trademark. This last point was essential for UNHCR. As the first assistance program to the 'liberated areas'—the expression used by the PRG and which Rizvi and I had adopted—by a UN agency it had to be cosmetically correct.

No one knew to play this game better than Rizvi. What he proposed to Ba was that UNHCR begin its assistance by providing 100,000 US $ worth of plain cotton material, half black and half dark blue for displaced persons who could then make clothes out of it. To emphasize his point he drew from his pocket two samples which Ba, having fingered enthusiastically, approved. To simplify matters, and to Ba's visible relief, he informed him that he would send him a letter confirming our agreement and specifying that UNHCR would undertake both procurement and payment and that the goods would be delivered to the PRG representation in Hanoi which would then be responsible for transporting them South. Subsequently the PRG would provide UNHCR with a report on the number of beneficiaries of the project. With Ba literally bouncing up and down with glee, Rizvi then suggested that someone from the PRG, or from its Red Cross, Rizvi was a quick thinker, come to Geneva to pay a call on UNHCR.

'Excellent idea,' said Ba, I will let you know next week.

The Vietnamese had their own idea of what the telephone was for. It was not made to convey information, only to make an appointment in which the information would be passed on face to face.

So one week later I was back again in Paris in Ba's office. Nguyen Van Thu was also there and it was he, I was told, who would be coming to Geneva to visit UNHCR. Perceiving a possible opening I suggested that he also take the opportunity of calling on the ICRC, adding 'it can do no harm and possibly some good will come out of it.' 'Yes,' he said, 'why not.'

Back in Geneva I conveyed the news to Rizvi, who feigned indifference and to Hocke who was ecstatic.

Ten days later Thu flew in from Paris for the day. We had decided that lunch with Sadruddin would be a more conducive first step to congenial relations than a formal meeting at the UNHCR office, so I picked him up at the airport and whisked him directly to Sadruddin's home, the Château de Bellerive on Geneva's lakeside.

After the customary introductions, with Thu looking approvingly at the subdued opulence of the surroundings, we sat down for lunch: Sadruddin, his wife Princess Catherine, Rizvi as ever the silent observer, Thu and myself.

It was the first time that Sadruddin had come close to a dyed-in-the-wool Vietnamese revolutionary and I could see that he was trying to find the most innocuous possible grounds on which to start a conversation.

'Your French is really impeccable. Did you study it France?'

'Yes, I attended high school in Paris; we used to live there.'

'I suppose you lived in the Latin Quarter?'

'Not really, we lived in rue de la Pompe.'

'Oh,' said Sadruddin, 'that is where my mother lived. Have you been to Switzerland before?'

'Not really. I was supposed to come to Switzerland to play in a tennis tournament against a Swiss school but then the war came and our trip was cancelled.'

'What school were you going to play against?'

'If I remember, something called "Le Rosey".'

'Oh,' said Sadruddin, with a sparkle in his eye, 'that is where I went to school.'

One was a Prince from one of the world's wealthiest families. The other was a dedicated revolutionary but actually they were birds of a feather and the conversation moved uninhibitedly to the better things in life, leaving the UN, Revolution and Liberation far behind. They parted as if they had been life-long friends, and I drove a jubilant Thu to his next meeting with Hocke at the ICRC building.

While they met, I made it a point of not joining them and waited for Thu in the lobby of the building. I had no doubt that Hocke would say all the right things but, for no specific reason, in the eyes of Thu I preferred to be seen as having a closer association with Sadruddin than with ICRC.

Half an hour later Thu reappeared, a large grin on his face. As I drove him back to the airport he confided that Hocke had given him a cheque for 25,000 US $, no mean sum at the time, as a first contribution from the ICRC to the Liberation Red Cross of South Vietnam.

Hocke was a quick learner. He was keen to establish a dialogue with the North Vietnamese but the condition for his doing so was to establish a prior relation with the PRG and by donating 25,000 US $ to Thu he had potentially bought his ticket to Hanoi.

So Thu came back from his one day in Geneva pleased as punch with 25,000 US $ in his pocket and the implicit recognition of the Liberation Red Cross by the ICRC. Hocke could claim that he had finally established the groundwork for a dialogue between Vietnam's communists and the ICRC and Sadruddin had had an entertaining lunch.

With my clients basking in contentment, I could nor repress and unworthy thought. Why? Why was UNHCR so keen to set up an aid program for Vietnam? Why was Hocke, now that the war was officially over and that there were no longer any Prisoners of War to monitor—the prime function of the ICRC—, so eager to establish a dialogue with Hanoi? If the Vietnamese communists were really in such a need for aid would they not have been capable of asking for it by themselves? And yet, here I was, hired by UNHCR to actually entice the Vietnamese communists into presenting a request for assistance. And why was ICRC involved in a similar quest?

Vietnam, at the time, was fashionable. It was the main show in town and everyone wanted to be part of it. Helping the Saigon government was fine but commonplace, not to say banal. Conversely, claiming that one was helping all sides carried with it a badge of impartiality to be worn with pride. So ultimately, did UNHCR actually need the Vietnamese communists more than the communists needed UNHCR? Was the donor chasing the beggar because without the beggar he could not aspire to the status of a donor?

While the answer to me was increasingly obvious—I was working for a solution in search of a problem—actually, I did not care. I was having fun.

Procuring 100,000 US $-worth of cotton material for the PRG would normally have been a straightforward procedure for UN-HCR. Rizvi however was looking to exploit the political potential of the operation by using it as a door opener towards China. For years Sadruddin had tried to establish a dialogue with China but all his attempts had been rebuffed on the grounds that UNHCR had provided aid to refugees from Tibet. All his direct approaches for a dialogue with Beijing having failed, maybe it was time to try something more subtle. Rizvi and I discussed the matter at length and we finally agreed that maybe, just maybe, procuring the cotton for the PRG in China could start a process that might slowly get the Chinese more involved with UNHCR.

Approaching the Chinese directly would have been counterproductive. They would simply not have responded. Rizvi's solution was simple. 'You know China,' he told me, 'well go there and buy the cotton.' When I told him I knew nothing about procuring cotton he would have none of it. 'Learn,' he said.

My next move was to go and see the Chinese consul in Geneva, Mr Hsu.

'I suppose you have come to ask for a visa,' he laughed.

I explained that yes, I did want a visa to go to China but not as a journalist. All I wanted was a visa for the Canton, now renamed Guangzhou, trade fair to buy cotton material for the liberated areas of South Vietnam. In a few words I gave him the background of what I was up to, making it clear that although UNHCR would pay for the cotton, the actual procurement would be done by me. China would not be entering into a sales contract with the UN, I assured him. One week later I received a call from Hsu. My visa was ready and the Foreign Ministry had made the necessary arrangement for me to meet the China National Textile Export Corporation at the trade fair.

Change of name apart, I found a city very similar to the one I had visited in 1965. The smell in particular was the same, the blend of kerosene, rotting vegetables and car exhausts. This time however I had two guides rather than the usual one, both of whom spoke English; one from the China Travel Service and one from the Foreign Ministry.

The morning after my arrival I was escorted into a large room in the grounds of the trade fair and introduced to three officials from the Textile Export Corporation.

'We hear that you want to buy some cotton,' said my guide, 'so please explain what you want.'

The question was obviously rhetorical. Mr Hsu must have sent a full report of our conversation to Beijing and my interlocutors could not have not read it. Assuming that they knew some of the background of my visit I decided to give a more ideological slant to my presentation.

UNHCR, I told them, had established a warm relation—they loved the word warm in describing relations, a step above good, —with the South Vietnamese people through the intermediary of the PRG. As a gesture of solidarity we wished to contribute some cotton to the displaced people in South Vietnam with which they could make clothes. We knew about the close relation between the Chinese people and the Vietnamese people and for this reason I had come to China to buy the cotton material. This was not a commercial transaction. We were not buying this cotton to sell it and make a profit. We were buying it for the heroic people of South Vietnam.

I took out my two samples. 'This is more or less the cotton we are looking for half in black and the other in dark blue.'

They fingered the samples. 'Yes,' they said, 'they could provide this quality of cotton.' There was a silence round the table. 'What was I thinking in terms of price,' they asked.

I had no clue about cotton prices and this was the time to play the only card I had.

'This,' I explained, 'is not a commercial transaction, we have 100,000 US $ available to purchase cotton and have it shipped to the office of the Provisional Revolutionary Government in Hanoi. We will give you this 100,000 US $ and it will be up to you to decide how much cotton you will give to your Vietnamese brothers. So if you agree you can perhaps prepare the contract and it will be signed.'

Silence settled around the table. By making the transaction an ideological issue I had cornered them and they could not possibly cheat me because by doing so they would have betrayed everything the regime stood for. Not that they would have been incapable of doing so, but not for a mere 100,000 US $. As we got up, having decided to meet after lunch, I did not have the feeling that I had been their favorite customer.

When we met again they produced a flurry of official-looking documents which were neatly lined up on our table and then the man who appeared to be the head of their delegation spoke.

'We have agreed on how much cotton we will provide, but there is a problem.' Silence fell around the table. 'We are a National export corporation and the recipient of the cotton material is a government. A corporation cannot sign a contract with a government because the two organizations are not on the same level. So what shall we do?'

'I agree with your position,' I replied, 'but there is no problem. I will sign the contract.'

'Yes, but in whose name?'

'In the name of the Provisional Revolutionary Government of South Vietnam.' I drew a paper from my briefcase and handed it to them. I had coaxed it out of Pham Van Ba before leaving for China, on official letterhead paper with a signature across a large seal: this is to confirm that Mr Alexander Casella is authorized to sign in the name of the Provisional Revolutionary Government of South Vietnam a contract for the purchase of cotton material for a value of up to 100,000 US $.

I was back in Hong Kong the next day from where I sent the contract to Rizvi by courier. As for the technicalities of the payment, this I left to the bean counters at UNHCR.

POLITICS ÜBER ALLES

B By late 1973, the first act of a comedy of mutual make believe had been played out. UNHCR as well as the ICRC had 'recognized' the PRG. What good it would do to the Southern revolution even in the ethereal world of political theatre would remain unknown. But it was the price an organization had to pay to have the privilege of talking with Hanoi, and that price had been paid.

In January 1974 I was again back in Paris, but this time to see the North Vietnamese. The head of the delegation, Mai Van Bo, was a gentleman of the old school who must have come from the best of families and attended the best French schools. Mercifully he did not offer me the habitual welcoming cup of Vietnamese green tea but a cup of coffee and had one brought in for himself. Building on this good omen I briefly explained to him the work of UNHCR, told him that I had been sent by Prince Sadruddin Aga Khan, the High Commissioner For Refugees, to convey to him the hope that his organization could establish good relations with the government in Hanoi. Mai Van Bo professed to have never heard of UNHCR but the name Aga Khan rang a bell. Had this anything to do with Rita Hayworth, he asked? I spent half an hour relating the little I knew about the Aga Khan and his various children, much to the interest of Bo, who visibly delighted in social gossip.

Finally we got back to UNHCR, at which point a deadpan Bo explained that the priority for any organization should be to help the South and the PRG. Feigning surprise I replied that we had done so a long time ago and our relations with them was excellent. However, we also believed that Vietnam was one and so too the sufferings of the Vietnamese people and we now wished therefore to extend to the whole of the country the assistance we were providing to the people in the Southern liberated areas. Mai Van Bo expressed surprise followed by satisfaction. He must have been a very good actor because I could scarcely believe that he was not aware of my dealings with Ba and Thu but appearances had to be preserved. Bo promised to convey my offer to Hanoi, 'I will refer,' he said as we parted on the best of terms.

That afternoon I went to see Ba and told him about my visit to Bo. Perhaps, I suggested, the PRG could intercede on our behalf with Hanoi. We would also like to pay a visit to the PRG in Vietnam—where in Vietnam I did not specify—and perhaps take the opportunity to call on the authorities in Hanoi. Which authority in Hanoi was irrelevant. Any authority would do or maybe even the Red Cross. It was pure Alice in Wonderland peering through the Vietnamese looking glass. Hanoi had created the PRG and here I was asking the PRG to intercede on our behalf with Hanoi.

In mid February 1974 I was back in Paris to see Ba. The cotton material we had procured for the liberated areas had apparently arrived at its destination, he told me, and we would soon receive a report on the location and number of beneficiaries. It was of course pure cock and bull. UNHCR in the first place had never seen the specific cotton material that had been purchased from China and even if we had had someone on the spot in the liberated areas monitoring its distribution, it could have been any cotton and not the one purchased. But this was immaterial. For the PRG the cotton was worth its weight in gold in terms of political recognition. For UNHCR it was a foot in the door to Vietnam. Given the benefits for all concerned, the price tag of 100,000 US $ was cut-rate.

But Ba had even better news for us. We, that is Rizvi and I, were invited to pay a call to the PRG liaison office in Hanoi. Our visa was ready at the North Vietnamese embassy in Vientiane, in Laos, to be picked up anytime we wished. We should then send a cable to the PRG liaison office in Hanoi, cable address DAZIMINA, giving the date of our arrival and they would make arrangements for us to be picked up at Hanoi airport.

For me the visa was the culmination of ten years of efforts to get to Hanoi. It was of course not as a journalist, but just getting there was more important than what label I did it under.

For Rizvi it was the confirmation, especially as regards Sadruddin, that the strategy he had advocated was now bearing fruit. I had also come to realize that within the upper echelons of UNHCR, Rizvi was not a liked man. His youth, intelligence, arrogance and closeness to Sadruddin had earned him many enemies, and while none had the courage to display openly their enmity, there were many who would have rejoiced in seeing him fail on Vietnam.

If getting to Hanoi was important for Rizvi's personal standing within UNHCR, it was also central to the overall credibility of the organization within and beyond the UN system. This was a dimension which I had not grasped when I had been first hired by Sadruddin but was now becoming increasingly apparent to me. Practically all UN organizations have overlapping mandates. UNHCR's responsibility towards refugees, be they men, women or children, included feeding them, addressing their health problems, providing them with a livelihood in case of repatriation, and more. To address all these needs the UN also had a World Food Program, a World Health program, a Development Organization and UNICEF, the children's fund, not counting outside the UN, the International Organization for Migration which was lurking in the background, ready to pounce on any piece of the pie that would come its way. In order to survive, all these bureaucracies needed to be seen as doing something, as this was the inescapable prerequisite for their being funded. Funds, in turn, were finite which meant that a pack of organizations were all scrambling for the same resources. Ultimately, they all got a slice of the cake, with the more visible, or aggressive ones getting the bigger slice. Market share was the name of the game.

UNHCR had a competitor in Vietnam, UNICEF, and in particular its Director for Vietnam, Jacques Beaumont. Beaumont, a fast-talking Frenchman, had made inroads with the communists and in fact had visited Hanoi some months before our visa had come through. Rizvi had dealt previously with Beaumont and while the two men professed to get along, Beaumont disliked Rizvi and Rizvi detested Beaumont in whom he saw a competitor. Thus, for Rizvi, carving a niche for UNHCR in Hanoi meant not only catching up with but also getting one better on Beaumont. There was therefore no time to be lost if we wished to win the second round of the race.

Rizvi had planned for us to arrive in Vientiane on a Monday morning, go to the North Vietnamese embassy that very afternoon to pick up our visas and proceed to Hanoi on the Tuesday. It was easier said than done.

We arrived in Vientiane early Monday afternoon as planned and after dropping our bags off at the only passable hotel in town, the crumbling *Lane Xang*, headed for the North Vietnamese embassy to pick up our visas in time to take the Tuesday flight for Hanoi. According to a current saying, the Vietnamese plant the rice, the Cambodians watch it grow and the Lao listen to it grow. This blissful state of mind must have rubbed off on the Vietnamese embassy. The sign on the door said it was only open from 7.30 to 11 am and Rizvi's repeated banging on the door proved of no avail. We then proceeded to the offices of Royal Air Laos, which provided the only air link to Hanoi, where a lonely clerk surveyed us with drowsy eyes. Yes, we could buy a ticket to Hanoi but the Tuesday flight had been cancelled and the Friday flight might also be cancelled but he was not sure. However, there might be a flight on Sunday. Could we buy a ticket? Yes. Now? Yes, come and pick it up tomorrow.

Vientiane was more of a village than a town. Cows wandered through the main streets and most buildings were no more than one storey high. Altogether it was a friendly, unhurried place, cheap, easygoing and well stocked with a wide choice of French provisions sold by small groceries along the main street.

The next morning we called again at the Vietnamese embassy where we were ushered into the Ambassador's office while our visas were being processed. A jovial fellow much advanced in years, the ambassador was something of a historical figure in Vietnam. Not only had he been one of the signatories of the declaration of independence in 1945 but, being something of an amateur composer, he had also written the music of the national anthem. This last accomplishment alone would have justified his posting to Vientiane, where he could end his days sheltered from the American bombing and the no less lethal Hanoi winters and sweltering summers.

'Come back anytime for a drink,' he said as he escorted us to the door, 'and don't forget to telegraph Hanoi your arrival day. No need to tell them the time,' he added laughingly, 'the planes are always late.'

With the next Royal Air Laos flight to Hanoi scheduled for Friday we now had three more days in Vientiane with nothing to do when luck proved again to be on our side. At the hotel desk we were told that the current rumor held it that the Friday Royal Air Lao flight to Hanoi would now be flying on Thursday. The rumor turned out to be true and after a hurried cable to DAZIMINA in Hanoi informing them of our arrival we boarded, on Thursday morning, a derelict DC 3 and two and a half hours later, landed at Hanoi's Gia Lam airport. Finally, I had made it to North Vietnam.

For some indefinable reason, I was expecting to find a smaller facsimile of China. I was totally off track. What I came across was an echo of France.

Gia Lam airport had been built by the French sometime in the 1930s and was very much in the state they had left it when they pulled out of North Vietnam in 1954. Passengers got off the aircraft on the tarmac and then walked some 200 meters to the terminal, a small building in art nouveau style. Luggage was brought in from the aircraft either by porters or by truck, depending on the availability of either, and unceremoniously dumped at one end of the terminal's only hall, leaving it to the passengers to find their own. That, at least for Rizvi and myself, was not a problem. Apart from ourselves there were only three other passengers on the flight.

As we stepped off the aircraft, a man and a woman who had been standing on the tarmac came up to us.

Monsieur Rizvi, *Monsieur* Casella, they said in French, welcome, we are from DAZIMINA.

We quickly learned that nobody in Hanoi referred to the Delegation of the PRG in any other way than by their cable address, DAZIMINA. They walked with us to the terminal and summoned two men in uniform who had been lolling in a far corner of the hall. Forms printed on rough paper in Vietnamese, Russian and French were handed to us, one for immigration and one for customs. Were we bringing in any bicycles, sewing machines, alarm clocks, wristwatches, gold jewelry or foreign currency? Formalities were perfunctory and with stamped passports and luggage we were led back to the tarmac where a battered Russian Volga sedan of uncertain vintage had been parked. We piled in, luggage stowed in the trunk, drove round to the front of the terminal and after having zigzagged past a number of sheds reached the main road to Hanoi, four kilometers away.

Driving into Hanoi was like moving back into a time warp. The French had built Hanoi in their own image, with elegant villas in late Empire style and large public buildings of elegant demeanor as if they were to stay in Vietnam forever, and though they had departed 20 years earlier the city stood as they had left it. Perversely, it was not so much the sight of a French town, so far away from the original model, that looked incongruous as the sight of the Vietnamese crowding the streets of a city built by foreigners for foreigners. But France's enduring presence was more than the optical illusion created by an empty stage.

The PRG had booked us into the hotel *Hoa Binh* in the city center. Originally built in 1932 under the name of hotel *Splendide*, it had been until 1954 one of the two best hotels in Hanoi, no mean feat in a town which had been the first in South East Asia to have electricity and until the onset of World War II, the premiere city in the region. At a time when Singapore was a swamp, Hong Kong a fishing village and Bangkok a sleepy native capital, Hanoi vied with Shanghai in boasting the best universities, the most modern hospitals and the most vibrant intellectual and literary social set in the region.

Like Hanoi, the hotel *Splendide* was only a shadow of its former self. The front desk was deserted but our two escorts finally located an attendant who condescended to hand over two room keys before disappearing back into the recess from which he had been unearthed.

It was now three in the afternoon and as Rizvi and I lugged our bags upstairs to our rooms on the second floor, our hosts informed us that they would be back within an hour to take us to our first meeting at the PRG delegation.

My room was vast and featured an immense four-poster bed encased in a mosquito net while the large electric fan hanging from the ceiling as well as the massive iron radiator by the window stood as silent reminders of Hanoi's peculiar weather that could be succinctly summed up as Glasgow winters and Bombay summers.

The heat combined with the humidity was overwhelming and as I unpacked I threw the switch on a large brass casing set in the wall which appeared to control the fan. At first nothing happened and then a delicate wisp of blue smoke emerged from the casing as the fan slowly came to life. After three revolutions the smoke turned black, a sound of frying came from the casing, followed by a large spark and the fan came to a dignified standstill.

The rest of the room was hardly in a better state. The windows did not close properly, the iron bathtub had lost most of its enamel and the water that emerged from the tap was a pale brown. On the plus side however the mosquito net that enclosed the bed was clean and two open glass bottles filled with water stood on the night table, drinking water I assumed, next to a candle and a box of matches.

A 4 o'clock sharp our hosts appeared in the hotel lobby. 'The PRG delegation is only five minutes away,' they said 'but it is still hot and we will drive there.' The PRG delegation in Hanoi was housed in a spacious French built villa that, we were told, had been the seat of the American consulate in 1945. Upon arrival we were ushered into a spacious room in which a large table covered in dark green felt cloth had been set up. There were half a dozen Vietnamese sitting at the table and as we were pointed to our seats one of them rose and, in impeccable French, identified himself as Mr Tam, the deputy head of the PRG delegation in Hanoi.

After the usual welcoming remarks by Mr Tam it was the turn of Rizvi to speak and the performance he gave must have been one of his best. Speaking in a low, even voice, he first acknowledged the obvious, namely that many, and for good reason, saw UNHCR as an instrument of the West in the Cold War. He was clever enough not to elaborate but simply to point out that in Vietnam, UNHCR had refused to get involved in the South as long as the war endured and only one side would benefit from its presence. After the Paris agreements, he added, UNHCR had made it a point to provide assistance first and foremost to the liberated areas of the South, the only UN agency to do so. UNHCR, he added, wished not only to increase this aid but also to extend it to all the people of Vietnam. He concluded by suggesting a technical meeting with the PRG regarding the nature of further assistance and expressed the hope that they would intercede on our behalf with the North Vietnamese authorities so that our assistance could be extended to all the Vietnamese people.

There was no reason to prolong the meeting beyond what Rizvi had to say so by five we were back at the hotel where it was suggested we should have dinner and were pointed towards the dining room. Having taken our seats at the only table that had been set up—it looked very much as if we were the only guests—we were presented a menu written by hand in a strange mixture of French and Vietnamese on a single sheet of paper torn from a notebook. There was sup which we assumed meant soup, gai, which I knew meant chicken, bifteck next to a mysterious *biftok* and an incongruous *kreme karamel*.

The waiter, who spoke some French, informed us that no, there was no gai, bifteck was a piece of buffalo, but no, there was none, *biftok* was also buffalo but minced, yes it was available and so was *kreme karamel*. To drink we could have either water or Ngoc Dua, meaning pineapple juice in a recycled bottle without a label. We finally settled for boiled rice, *biftok* and *krem karamel*. The meat was tough as leather but the creme caramel did not come any better. Visibly, French colonization had left something good behind.

After dinner, at seven sharp, Mr Tam appeared unannounced. He was all smiles, which led us to believe that we had passed our first test. As we set down on the well-worn, leather-covered armchairs that adorned one of the reception rooms next to the lobby he drew a piece of paper out of his pocket.

'This is the program we would like to suggest to you,' he said. 'Tomorrow at eight you will have a working meeting at the hotel with the PRG to discuss further aid to the liberated areas. At nine we would be taken on a tour of Hanoi. At twelve,' continued Mr Tam, 'you will have lunch at the hotel and at three you will have a meeting with the Red Cross of the Democratic Republic of

Vietnam, here at the hotel. Then at six thirty the PRG will host a dinner for you, and the day after you will leave Hanoi.'

I could guess what Rizvi was thinking. The breakthrough was the meeting with the North Vietnamese Red Cross. Until now, all our meetings had been with the PRG. Now, finally, we had graduated to talking with the Democratic Republic of Vietnam, or in other words Hanoi. In substance of course both were the upshots of the same master, the Vietnamese communist party but that was not the issue. The issue was form and the theatrics that went with it. Granted, we would still not be dealing directly with the government in Hanoi but only with its Red Cross but again that was just a matter of show. It was the first visit of UNHCR to North Vietnam, Hanoi was not a member of the UN and the Vietnamese were still not quite ready for an official relation with a UN body. A meeting with the Red Cross which officially was not a government organization could therefore be passed off as inconsequential if so required, even if in reality meeting with the North Vietnamese Red Cross was the same as meeting with the government, but that was to remain unsaid.

After thanking Mr Tam for his program, Rizvi indicated that he would like to venture one request to the PRG. It was common for UNHCR, while on mission, to contact some foreign embassies that were interested in our work. Would it be possible for the PRG to request for us a meeting with the Soviet and Swedish ambassadors? If Mr Tam found the request unexpected he did not show it and promised to do his best. He left us with these words as Rizvi and I retired to out respective rooms.

To say I spent a good night would have been stretching it. The excitement, the oppressive heat, compounded by the humidity and the sorry state of my mattress did not contribute to a good night's rest but this was of no consequence. As Rizvi and I sat down next morning for a breakfast of overcooked eggs, excellent coffee and a baguette like the best one finds in Paris both of us were fired up at the thought of what the coming day would bring.

Mr Tam and three of his colleagues appeared punctually at eight and directed us to one of the meeting rooms at the back of the hotel where a table had been set up for us. Green tea in minute cups was served as we took our seats and Mr Tam extracted a collection of Japanese catalogues from a plastic handbag. Apparently he was interested in bulldozers for clearing land for new housing and in motorized rice farming machinery. The conversation soon became quite technical with Rizvi wanting to make sure that, with its vast labor pool, agricultural mechanization was a priority for the liberated areas. Many of the details of the exchange escaped me, were it only for lack of interest, but it was finally agreed that UNHCR would provide two large Komatsu bulldozers and sixty pieces of motorized rice farming equipment. I could sense that Rizvi had his doubts as to whether the liberated areas did not have other and more urgent needs. But on the positive side, this new aid agreement which would require many months to implement guaranteed a continuity in our relationship with the PRG. Were it only for this reason, such an agreement, from a UNHCR perspective, was a plus.

Our meeting was coming to a close when Mr Tam was called to the telephone, our first indication that the telephone in Hanoi actually did work. When he returned he informed us that, as we had requested, the Soviet Ambassador would receive us at ten and the Swedish Ambassador at eleven. This took care of our planned tour of Hanoi. 'You will have to come back' said Mr Tam with a large grin.

At ten sharp we were in front of the Soviet embassy where a burly Russian opened the gate and motioned us inside. As he led us to the first floor another heavyset Russian sweating profusely followed us from behind. With one Russian leading and the other in tow we were led to a large reception room, furnished with dark, oversized leather armchairs where, for good measure, we were kept waiting for fifteen minutes before the ambassador, accompanied by an aide, briskly stepped in. Soviet ambassador Boris Chaplin was no demure career diplomat. A member of the Central committee of the communist Party of the Soviet Union, he was the man who, under politburo orders, had sent bulldozers some years before to level an outdoor exhibition of Russian dissident painters. In Hanoi, he represented both the Soviet state and the Soviet communist party and was a power to be reckoned with. As an added bonus he spoke perfect English and visibly had no patience for idle formalities.

'So,' he said, 'you wanted to see me. Why?'

Rizvi knew his was fighting an uphill battle. The Soviets had no sympathy for UNHCR which they considered an instrument of the cold war. While allies of Vietnam, and its major arms supplier, they were jealous allies, always suspecting that the wily Vietnamese would try to get the better of them. Any attempt by the Vietnamese to broaden their spectrum of relations beyond the Soviet Union, be it even with other Eastern European countries, was looked upon with misgivings, fearful as they were that it might erode the hold they had on Hanoi. When this new interloper turned out to be a UN organization, suspicion could easily become hostility. The last thing Rizvi wanted was having the Soviets pressuring the Vietnamese into no longer dealing with us. So, pacifying the Soviets was essential.

Speaking in a slow voice Rizvi explained the ins and outs of our visit to Hanoi. UNHCR was now, he further explained, planning to finalize an aid agreement with Hanoi to assist displaced persons to return to their home villages. Agricultural support would be essential to enable the returnees to become self-sufficient and this in turn would require tractors.

Vietnam is a socialist country, he added, they already have Soviet tractors and they know how to maintain them. So if UNHCR wants to give tractors to Vietnam, the logical thing to do would be to purchase them from the Soviet Union. Would the ambassador be so kind to let us know whom we could contact in the Soviet mission in Geneva to help us with the purchase?

It was probably the last thing the ambassador expected to hear from us. Of course he would help us. He was delighted that UN-HCR planned to purchase Soviet tractors for Vietnam and looked forward to seeing us in a more congenial setting next time we came to Hanoi.

As we proceeded to the Swedish embassy, I could see that Rizvi was eminently pleased with himself, and for good reasons too. Hopefully he had ensured that the Soviets would not put pressure on the Vietnamese to hold back on their relations with us.

The Swedish ambassador was away and his deputy did not have any particular advice or insight for us. But keeping in touch with the Swedes was important for UNHCR. Sweden had litterarily been having a love affair with Vietnam and they would be among the first to contribute funds to any assistance program we would be planning. Interestingly, he seemed to be particularly intrigued by which hotel we were staying in. According to his explanation, Vietnam was very much a Mandarin society where rules of order and hierarchy were strictly observed. Visitors held in high esteem were generally booked at the *Thong Nhut* hotel, the former *Metropole*. Visitors one-step below were put at the *Hoa Binh*. While both hotels were equally bad the issue was one of hierarchy, not comfort. That the dinner that the PRG would host for us that evening was to be given at the *Thong Nhut* was, he said, a good sign. Slowly we were moving up the totem pole.

For lunch we returned to the *Hoa Binh* hotel where at 3 o'clock sharp Mr Tam appeared in the lobby. 'The delegation from the North Vietnamese Red Cross is already here, they are waiting for you in the meeting room,' he said leading the way with Rizvi following and myself behind. As we entered the room I heard Mr Tam introduce to Rizvi someone he described as the head of the delegation. Then my turn came and as we shook hands I recognized Pham Duong, the diplomat from the North Vietnamese embassy in Prague I had met four years before who had stated with unshakable conviction that if all Swiss had weapons available, the workers would revolt. From his surprise at seeing me it was obvious that he had not checked our names before the meeting and I could perceive a slight embarrassment in his voice as he muttered that he was now working for the Red Cross. Of course, I replied, and in dealing with UN organizations they can profit from your international experience. My words were intended to put him at ease but I could tell that all they had achieved was to further his suspicion that I was being sarcastic. Anyhow, whatever the outcome of our meeting it was gratifying to see that for all practical purposes we were dealing with the North Vietnamese Foreign Ministry.

After the usual exchange of compliments kept thankfully short by the Vietnamese, Rizvi made his pitch. It was all about the fact that UNHCR had kept out of Vietnam during the war, our good relations with the PRG, and how the Vietnamese people were one and we wanted to help those in need wherever they were so they could return to their homes and become again self sufficient and so forth. For good measure he threw in the encouragement he had received from the Soviet ambassador in Hanoi. 'To conclude,' he said, 'we are ready to discuss the practical modalities of an assistance program for displaced persons in the Democratic Republic of Vietnam with the Red Cross as implementing partner.'

Speaking slowly, Pham Duong replied that the Red Cross welcomed such a move. What he proposed was that we sign first an agreement of principle, stating what the purpose of the assistance would be and later on a more technical agreement that would specify the type of assistance given.

'If we agree,' continued Pham Duong as he drew a paper from a plastic bag lying on the floor next to him, 'here is our proposal.' The text he gave us, one copy each, had been typed in a large old-fashioned font on thin paper using carbons to make multiple copies. It was very much a statement of principle, entailing no commitment for either side, an innocuous document except for the last paragraph which stated: the Red Cross of the Democratic Republic of Vietnam is gratified by the positive attitude taken by UNHCR as regards the Provisional Revolutionary Government of South Vietnam. That simply would not do.

Washington was already fretting over the assistance we were giving the PRG even though none came from American funds. Granted we were on safe ground legally as the Paris agreements had endorsed the existence of 'two South Vietnamese parties', but this was politics not legal niceties. That Sadruddin personally knew Kissinger helped in keeping Washington pacified but only as long as our dealings with the PRG did not become excessively conspicuous. Thus the last thing we needed was a written agreement with Hanoi, Red Cross or no Red Cross, which included a paragraph for all to see congratulating us on our relations with the PRG and which the communists would not fail to make public.

Rizvi had of course also immediately identified the trap and I was looking forward to observing how he would handle it when he turned to me. 'Mr Casella,' he said, 'is specifically responsible for relations with the PRG. So I think we should ask his opinion.'

It was Rizvi at his best. He knew we could not accept this paragraph. He knew somebody had to say no but he did not want to be the one. So he passed the problem on to me. By now I knew that there were many ways of saying no to a Vietnamese, with the exception of one: one does not say no. Alternatively, yes can mean many things. It can mean yes, it can mean maybe and it can mean no. So now I had to say yes while meaning no. Actually, given the context, it was not very difficult. For years, evidence to the contrary, Hanoi had maintained that the Southern liberation front and the PRG were independent entities which owed nothing to Northern support. Now the time had come to give the North Vietnamese a taste of their own propaganda.

'The PRG,' I said, speaking slowly and thoughtfully, 'as we all know, is a sovereign and independent government and it is in this capacity that we have been dealing with it. Of course we are extremely gratified that the Red Cross of the Democratic Republic of Vietnam wishes to compliment UNHCR for having taken a correct attitude'—they loved to use the expression—'as regards the PRG and we will certainly convey this to the High Commissioner. So on principle we thank you for this paragraph. The problem is that we deal with each government individually, as independent entities, which they are. So if in an agreement with the DRV Red Cross we make reference to another government, be it the PRG or any other, this could be interpreted by that government as an interference in its internal affairs. So while in spirit we take note of this paragraph and thank you for it, I think that as a gesture of respect for the sovereignty of the PRG it is better not to retain it.'

I had used all their own arguments regarding the sovereignty of the PRG against them and there was nothing they could do about it, but at least I had said no without making them lose face. 'Well done,' whispered Rizvi as we left the room.

It was now four in the afternoon and we told our hosts that we wished to wander a bit around town and would make our own way on foot to the *Thong Nhut* hotel, half a mile away for dinner at 6.

By late afternoon the streets were crowded as people headed home from work and the overall impression they conveyed was one of dignified poverty. The most common attire, both in men and women, were dark trousers and a white shirt, all impeccably clean from what we could see. Traffic consisted mostly of bicycles, thousands of them leisurely weaving their way up and down the avenues and completely indifferent to the efforts of a handful of police officers to regulate traffic at crossroads. No one seemed to ever stop but no one ran into each other either as if, by some unwritten rule, they all knew when to proceed and when to give way. Although we were the only visible foreigners no one seemed to pay any attention to us, as if we were a normal sight.

As we unhurriedly proceeded to the *Thong Nhut* hotel I could not help reflect as to why the North Vietnamese had made the effort of slipping us a banana peel and such an inconsequential one too. Whatever propaganda points they might have gained by publicizing their approval of our dealings with the PRG these were insignificant compared to the negative fallout that it might have generated for us. The Americans, UNHCR's major donor, were already not too happy about our relation with the PRG and had they become too cheesed off there is no doubt that Sadruddin, as a good politician would have taken a step backwards. Actually, we had bent backwards in accommodating the theatrics of deception that they had constructed around the PRG and rather than being appreciative of our efforts and making life easier for us they were pushing the envelope for more. This, as I was slowly to discover was a trait of character. Whether by game or some form of natural-born duplicity they just could not keep themselves from being too clever and would more often than not end up tripping themselves in the process.

While in the same state of disrepair as the *Hoa Binh*, the *Thong Nhut* hotel in its heyday must have been one notch above, considering the size of the lobby, the marble floor of the dining room and the adjacent salons where a table for six had been set up for us. Our host Mr Tam was in an excellent mood and his conversation with Rizvi soon developed into a heated debate as to when was the most appropriate time of day to smoke a cigar. We were halfway through the meal with neither willing to concede any ground when in the middle of a sentence Mr Tam paused and said: 'I have news for you.'

'Yes?' replied Rizvi.

'The Provisional Revolutionary Government, continued Mr Tam, invites you to visit the liberated areas.'

It was the sort of invitation that puts a humanitarian organization on the map and most would have given an arm and a leg to get one. For Rizvi it was a further vindication of the policy he had advocated for UNHCR; returning to Geneva with an agreement with the Hanoi Red Cross was already a major achievement. An additional visit to the liberated areas of South Vietnam to boot would have been a personal triumph.

'We planned for you to leave after tomorrow,' added Mr Tam, 'by road, and the journey will take about eight days.'

'I am very honored,' replied Rizvi, 'but unfortunately I cannot go. Silence suddenly settled around the table. There is an international conference in Bangkok next week where I am supposed to represent the High Commissioner for Refugees. All the arrangements have already been made and I just cannot cancel.'

Mr Tam looked stunned. It was the last thing he had expected. Rizvi went on. 'However I can come back in two weeks time, if you agree of course, and then I would be very happy to go.'

Mr Tam regained some of his composure. 'Of course, of course,' he said, 'but are you sure?' He did not continue but I could guess what he was thinking: this is a ruse to avoid going to the Liberated areas?

Rizvi turned to me, 'and you?'

'I have been invited to participate in a workshop on Vietnam during the spring term at the university in Geneva,' I replied 'and have already missed two weeks of classes, I cannot let my students down and have to be back in Geneva, so this time unfortunately I cannot make it, but perhaps later.'

By now I knew enough about Rizvi to guess that, deep down and much as he liked my company, he did not mind doing what was a first all by himself. So as the meal came to an end it was all settled. Rizvi would come back to Hanoi within two weeks and then go South and I would go back to Geneva to my students.

As we took leave of Mr Tam, with Rizvi out of ear reach, he whispered to me. '*Monsieur* Hocke is coming next week to see us.' Clever, I thought and another point in my favor.

Our return flight to Vientiane the next day proved uneventful and so was my onwards journey to Bangkok and Geneva. One week after my return I phoned Hocke. 'How did your trip to Hanoi go?' I asked.

He sounded surprised. 'How do you know?'

I explained to him that I had been in Hanoi the week before his arrival and that the subject of his visit had come up. He laughed. I did not want him to think that he had made it all by himself.

Three weeks later, Rizvi was back in Geneva and I asked him how he had enjoyed his visit to the South. 'It was not a bad trip,' he said, with an air of feigned detachment and then added 'we must do more things together.'

'Yes,' I told him, 'perhaps this is only the beginning.'

After Rizvi returned to Geneva, even those within UNHCR who least liked him conceded that he had achieved what, months earlier, had seemed near impossible: putting UNHCR on the map in Vietnam. On the subject of his journey to the liberated areas of the South, or more specifically Quang Tri province, which bordered North Vietnam, he was rather tight-lipped. Actually he had spent altogether six long days on the road and one short day in Quang Tri but this was irrelevant to the issue. Ultimately it was all theatrics. The visit was cosmetic, it gave the aura of credibility, the 'I was there imprint' to a funding appeal that UNHCR would shortly present to those donor governments who would be willing to finance an aid program for Hanoi and the PRG.

Every year in October for the meeting of its executive committee UNHCR would establish a list of its needs, country by country, with an estimate of costs that was then submitted to potential donor governments. Contributions were purely voluntary and could be either un-earmarked or earmarked to be used specifically for certain aid projects to the exclusion of others. This mechanism permitted donors, if they so wished, to provide funds only to those programs or countries that they wished to support to the exclusion of others. The advantage for them of using the UN system to channel their aid, rather than giving it directly was purely cosmetic. A hundred million dollars of US aid for refugees from Afghanistan given directly smacked of political support; but the same hundred million dollars given to UNHCR on behalf of Afghan refugees could be labeled as humanitarian aid under a multilateral veneer. Ultimately, I had come to realize, there was no such thing as 'UN aid'. There was only aid, provided by governments but laundered through the UN system from where it could then be distributed to the recipients under the label of humanitarian assistance. Finally, there were the special programs designed whenever the need arose and for which funding requests were submitted to specific donors who had indicated their willingness to contribute to them.

For obvious reasons, our current two programs in Vietnam, the one for the PRG and the one for Hanoi, came under the heading of special programs and we expected contributions to come from the likes of the Scandinavian countries or Holland.

While I was spending my time dealing with Hanoi and the PRG, Rizvi, were it only for the sake of maintaining the semblance of a political equilibrium, had also in the pipeline a program for assistance to displaced persons in the areas controlled by the Saigon government. Washington was of course ready to pour any amount of funds into that program but Rizvi had ensured that it be kept deliberately small so as to avoid an excessive imbalance between what would be available for the Saigon side on one hand and for the communist side on the other.

By the spring of 1974, UNHCR had a firm foothold in Vietnam. With aid programs for the North, the Liberated areas of the South and the Saigon government UNHCR had carved out a unique niche for itself within the humanitarian community as the only organization that could claim to be present in the whole of Vietnam.

A TWO-SIDED AFFAIR

Summer was now upon us and as the whole of Europe settled into a collective disconnect and with even Rizvi on leave it was a good opportunity for me to take stock of the situation.

It was clear to me that as a journalist I would not have received my visa to Hanoi and that it had been granted to me only because of my connection with UNHCR. On the other hand without my interventions UNHCR would not have had its entrée to Hanoi either. In turn, if I had gained over the past years access to the PRG it was because they believed that I was useful to them and that my writings contributed, albeit in a minute way, to their struggle for power. I had then moved one notch further up the scale by suggesting that it would be in their interest to enter into some relations with both UNHCR and the ICRC and when they did so they had not been disappointed.

In purely objective terms this made me a communist ally, but things were not that simple. By the same token an American journalist of whatever political persuasion writing, as many did, that Diem was a catastrophe, the Saigon regime with a few exceptions was essentially an aggregate of crooks, scoundrels and cowards and the American record in Vietnam in terms of the promotion of human rights abysmal could also be defined as a communist ally.

Ultimately it made for a perverse situation in which reporting the plain, unadulterated truth did indeed play into the hands of the communists. But if this was the price that had to be paid to ensure that a free press remain free so be it. Ultimately there was only one benchmark to go by; the truth, whatever side it happened to serve or be perceived as serving.

The problem for me was somewhat more complex. My use to both UNHCR and the ICRC derived from the fact that I could bring to them something they could not get by themselves. For me to continue to be of use to both organization required in turn that I preserve a minimum of good relations with Hanoi and the PRG. Too good relations with either, however, would have eroded my credibility with my readership which basically was center-right and by definition pro-American. This last point, the issue of 'anti-Americanism', was a sensitive one in Europe at the time and for me in particular. I was acutely aware that had the US not shouldered the main burden of World War II my mother would have gone up in smoke and I would be lucky to speak German. Had the US not shielded Western Europe from the Soviet Union I would presumably be learning Russian. This debt as well as a communality of values, however, did not provide an escape from the fact that the US was shooting itself in the foot in Vietnam and that it was legitimate for me to say so. So I had to tread a fine line between being perceived as 'friendly' albeit not a communist by one side and free of any pro-communist bias by the other while simultaneously being critical of the way the US had managed its venture into the Vietnamese quagmire. This exercise in tight rope walking was considerably facilitated by my being Swiss. Say Swiss and what springs to mind is neutrality, hard work and precision and I unashamedly rode the cliché as far as it would carry me. Being factual, reasonably honest and using adjectives sparingly made up the rest.

Back in Geneva I had made it a habit of dropping by the UNHCR office about three times a week and would call unannounced on Rizvi for a cup of coffee. Sadruddin's secretary Marie-Thérèse would generally let him know that I was around and, now and then, he would call Rizvi and I to his office for a chat and if it was near mealtime would invite us home for lunch.

Sadruddin lived in the château de Bellerive on the left bank of lake Geneva while the UN building was on the right bank. To go home he would park his Volkswagen beetle by a pier on the right bank where his launch, piloted by his butler, would pick him up for the short crossing of the lake. Sadruddin was one of those rare men whose wealth is not in excess of their taste and who did not need to pretend to be more than they were. When there were only the three of us we would often eat in the kitchen, albeit served by a butler in a white jacket. All his house staff were Sudanese Moslems, of Ismaeli rite, ensuring not only quality of service but also total devotion.

I also kept in touch with Hocke at the ICRC, were it only because I was still receiving a retainer from him. There was nothing more I could do for him as he now had his direct contacts with Hanoi and there was no reason for him to keep me on his payroll. However, when I suggested that maybe he no longer needed me he insisted that I stay on board. Why, I could not imagine but I supposed that having me around was reassuring for him. I acquiesced reluctantly. Being underpaid by UNHCR I could put up with but being overpaid by the ICRC made me feel uncomfortable.

In mid October Rizvi called me to his office. As his secretary brought in tea for him and coffee for me he put on the expression he favored when he had something important or unexpected to say, half closed eyes and a distant unfocussed gaze. He wanted, he told me, a permanent UNHCR presence on the ground in Indochina but the cosmetics had to be right. The South Vietnamese government would of course have loved to have a full time UNHCR Representative in Saigon, but without an equivalent office in Hanoi and one in the PRG controlled areas the cosmetics would have been wrong. With neither Hanoi nor the PRG quite ready for a permanent UNHCR presence on their territory he had decided to create a regional UNHCR office which would cover the whole of Vietnam as well as Laos and locate it in Vientiane. 'Would I,' he asked me, 'be interested in joining UNHCR and assuming the position of regional representative in Vientiane?'

Accepting Rizvi's offer would have meant that I assume a senior position within UNHCR without knowing anything of the interior workings of the organization which would put me at a disadvantage within the system. That I could have lived with but less so with the fact that the job did not sound particularly interesting. Granted I would be going regularly both to Hanoi, where I would be well received, and to Saigon, where I would presumably be less well received, but this would be mostly to work on programming, which consisted essentially of designing, managing and monitoring aid projects rather than scheming and conniving for whatever end was required. By now I had seen enough of UNHCR to understand that while Rizvi used programming as a creative exercise, the actual running of a program was the equivalent of managing a grocery store and I saw little attraction in it. I explained all this in detail to Rizvi who saw my point. By the same token I made it clear to him that I did not exclude, at one point or another, taking a full time job with UNHCR but I would have liked something more political. In the mean time I would be more useful to him in my present role as a consultant rather than as a full staff member. We agreed on this and pending a more intellectually demanding position, I decided to bide my time.

UNHCR opened its regional office in Vientiane in November 1974. To head the office Rizvi chose a Swiss, Jacques Cuenod. It was a well thought out choice. In his early fifties, Cuenod was one of the more experienced officers in the organization, with a solid, no-nonsense approach to programming and a dry sense of humor which served him well when required.

By the end of 1974, the situation in South Vietnam appeared superficially stabilized but it was only an appearance. In mid December the communists struck.

Phuc Long province, some 75 miles North East of Saigon was poor and sparsely populated and of no particular strategic importance but it was here that the Politburo chose to strike using the regulars of the North Vietnamese army against the outgunned local South Vietnamese forces. By early January 1975, the whole province including its capital was in communist hands. For the Saigon government it was not so much a military defeat as a political one. At Phuc Long the communists had been testing the waters. For the first time since the signing of the Paris peace agreements they had seized a provincial capital in South Vietnam and Washington had not reacted. The lesson was not lost on the communists. Washington, so they concluded, had for all practical purposes given up on South Vietnam.

THE LAST OFFENSIVE; MARCH 1975

O n March 10, 1975 the Politburo struck again but this time at Ban Me Thuot, in the central highlands of South Vietnam. Again they were testing the water but this time with far heavier means than those used against Phuc Long.

The South Vietnamese president, General Nguyen Van Thieu, had come to power in 1965 following a successful coup. While lacking any tested military ability, Thieu proved an adroit politician and, for the successive decade, out maneuvered all those who tried to overthrow him. This he did by surrounding himself with cronies, promoting his followers to key positions, sidetracking potential competitors and constantly reshuffling the officer corps. As long as the Americans were fighting the war for him, this was of little consequence, but after the American pullout he found himself with an army in which personal loyalty to him was the only criteria for promotion to senior rank.

Led by an incompetent general the defenders of Ban Me Thuot, facing elite divisions of the North Vietnamese army, stood no chance and the city fell the day of the attack. Thieu then took the most disastrous decision of his career; he ordered all his forces in the highlands to pullback towards the coast. Their commander, General Phu, started by evacuating himself and his family by heli-copter leaving behind some 200,000 men and in a matter of hours the retreat turned into a rout.

Their easy victory in the central highlands led the Politburo members to review their strategy. They had initially planned for an offensive spread over two years with the taking of Ban Me Thuot being the first phase. Now, they felt, the time might have come for a quick victory.

Five days after the capture of Ban Me Thuot the communists unleashed the North Vietnamese divisions that they had concentrated in Quang Tri province and headed for Hue. On March 25 Hue fell and the house of cards that had been South Vietnam started to collapse. At this point the Politburo pulled out all the stops and decided to go for Saigon.

By the end of March I sat down with Rizvi to review the situation. Events had taken an unexpected turn and waiting on the sidelines was not an option. If we wanted to keep UNHCR on the map we had to be on the spot and the only way to do so was to go to Hanoi. So it was agreed that Rizvi would cable the Red Cross in Hanoi indicating that we wished to come and see them to review the situation. In parallel, I called Ba in Paris asking him to support our visa request and also indicating that, with events developing as they did, we could soon envisage a much more substantial program for the South, or to put it in plain English, it looks like you are winning the war so let us sit down and discuss your needs after victory.

One week later, a cable from the DRV Red Cross arrived at UNHCR. Our visas had been granted and were available at their embassy in Vientiane.

Royal Air Lao had now gotten its act together and had four regular flights per week to Hanoi which actually left on time and we arrived there on April 8, somewhat haggard from the long flight from Geneva but exited by the feeling of being at the very spot where history was in the making.

While the car that the Vietnamese had sent to pick us up at the airport was the same battered Soviet Volga as the one used on our previous visit the hotel they had booked us into this time was the *Thong Nhut*, a clear sign that we had moved one notch up on the totem pole.

Likewise, they must have felt more at ease with us and this was reflected by our relations becoming less convoluted. On our previous visit we had come, officially, to visit with the PRG delegation. Now, after one perfunctory call at the PRG office all our subsequent negotiations were with the North Vietnamese Red Cross. Mercifully, the noxious Pham Duong had vanished from the scene and we now had an official counterpart in the person of *Monsieur* Bai who actually was really part of the Red Cross and the head of their external relations department. *Monsieur* Bai was no pushover but at least he was someone we could, over time, build a personal relationship with and that in itself was a major plus. What was becoming increasingly obvious to Rizvi and I was that, while from the outside the system appeared as a nameless bureaucracy where every move was meticulously planned and calibrated and all decisions were taken based on political calculations, it was also made up of individuals who more often than not had their own idea of how the party line was to be implemented. Clearly, the decision to deal with UNHCR had been taken at the political level. However, how they would deal with UNHCR would also very much depend on how they perceived Rizvi and I at a purely personal level. Ultimately, and even if it played in their favor, they had no respect for the gullible and I suspected that they had admired the way we had wiggled out of including a remark on the PRG in the agreement with the Hanoi Red Cross that they had proposed on our first visit. It was the sort of subtle sparring they enjoyed and in a way they found it reassuring to know that they were dealing with people who could, when called for, be as astute, not to say as devious, as they were.

Likewise they knew that the Soviets did not look positively on any step they would take aimed at enlarging their web of relations beyond the Socialist bloc and must have therefore appreciated the fact that we had approached the Soviet ambassador with an offer to purchase Soviet tractors. But did they want Soviet tractors? From our discussions it became apparent that they were great consumers of western technical publications and whenever we discussed tractors or bulldozers they would pull out a stack of recent catalogues from Komatsu, Caterpillar, John Deere and the like. Soviet bulldozers, solid but unexciting, were not what they dreamed of.

By mid April there was no more doubt that South Vietnam was crumbling. Hue and Danang had fallen to the communists and nothing could stop the North Vietnamese army as it headed for Saigon. As we headed back to Geneva, I could sense that Rizvi was already looking forward to carving out a major role for UNHCR in the post-war reconstruction of Vietnam. Ten days later, on April 30, 1975, Saigon fell and on May 1, without giving it much thought, I accepted an offer by Rizvi to join UNHCR as a fulltime staff member.

A UN BUREAUCRAT. MAY 1975

By 1975, the lucky streak that had carried me for ten years had come to an end. The Vietnam War was over and although Indochina continued to be a crisis area, it no longer commanded the interest that it had when the Americans were directly involved in the fighting. In China, the Cultural Revolution had run its course and Nixon's journey to Beijing had started an irreversible process. China was no longer the hostile enigma it was perceived to have been and was increasingly viewed as a normal country. Over the years I had build my reputation and derived my revenue from reporting on war, mayhem and confrontation. Peace, albeit imperfect, was now driving me out of business. So the offer to join UNHCR came just at the right time for me.

The fact that for the first time in my life I would now be operating within a structured system did not worry me too much, especially as I would still be reporting to Rizvi with continued access to Sadruddin. This and the fact that I would still be involved with Vietnam alleviated whatever qualms I might still have harbored about joining UNHCR.

The two questions that remained to be solved were my function and my grade. Grades for professional officers within the UN went from P1 to P5, followed by Director (D1) and senior Director (D2). At the time to finish one's career as P4 was honorable, as P5 was good, as D1 very good and as D2 outstanding, if not unheard of and to whit there were only two D2 slots within the whole of UNHCR.

Rizvi's grade was P5, which meant that I could only be a P4, which was fine with me. As for my function, Rizvi was convinced that UNHCR would soon be opening an office in Saigon and had identified me for that position with the title of Representative. However, until an agreement on the opening of such an office had been reached with the PRG I could hardly be given that title. So we sat down to try to devise an appropriate label for me pending my taking office in Saigon.

Officially the PRG had styled itself as the government of the 'Republic of South Vietnam' as opposed to the 'Republic of Vietnam' which had been the name of the Saigon regime which had now ceased to exist. So, in keeping with the world of make-believe in which we operated we decided that my title would be 'Special Envoy to the Republic of South Vietnam'. What this title actually meant was at best nebulous and so was this mythical 'Republic of South Vietnam' but pending UNHCR opening an office in Saigon it served its purpose by putting me on hold while implying that I was in the meantime responsible for relations between UNHCR and whoever ran South Vietnam.

While my employment contract was being finalized I informed Hocke that I was now assuming a full time job with UNHCR and could no longer work as a consultant for him. He expressed some regret but I assured him that I would stay in touch with him.

In early June Rizvi went to Hanoi from where he proceeded to Saigon. That he did not take me along was in keeping with his personality. Initially I had been indispensable to him but now I was no more than useful and he wanted to get the message across to me. Actually it served my purpose. The more he felt in control the easier he was to deal with.

On paper Rizvi's trip was an unqualified success. At a time when the rest of the UN system was desperately trying to get a foot in the door to Vietnam he had struck gold.

The agreement that he had signed with the PRG specified that UNHCR would open an office in Saigon, provide assistance for the rehabilitation of displaced persons, ensure the repatriation of Vietnamese who wished to return and assist in evacuating foreigners who could no longer leave South Vietnam due to the suspension of all air transportation.

But that was not the only document Rizvi brought back from Saigon. He did not tell me at the time but he carried a letter from the PRG to UN Secretary General Waldheim requesting that South Vietnam be accepted as a full member of the UN. Waldheim, under

US pressure, did nothing about it and soon the request was overtaken by events.

On the day he came back to Geneva, Rizvi called me in, showed me the agreement. 'I want to start an airlift to Saigon immediately,' he said, 'that's the priority.'

If there was one thing that most humanitarian organization dreamt of it was setting up an airlift. Airlifts were cool. They were highly visible and projected an image of urgency and efficiency. But airlifts to Vietnam had gotten off to a bad start.

Following the fall of Saigon, UN secretary General Kurt Waldheim had entrusted one of the UN heavyweights, the Australian Sir Robert Jackson, with the task of airlifting humanitarian aid to Vietnam. That the communists had not requested it was besides the point. The move was political and its main purpose was to enable Waldheim to say that he had responded to a crisis situation. Sir Robert was immediately provided by the Australian air force with a C130 military transport aircraft, which duly landed in Vientiane with a cargo of supplies intended to be flown onwards to Hanoi. It never got there. The Vietnamese had not forgotten that Australia had contributed troops to the US war effort in the South and there was no way an Australian military aircraft would be allowed to land in Hanoi. After three weeks on the tarmac in Vientiane, where it was a source of considerable mirth, the aircraft returned to Australia and Sir Robert tiptoed back to New York.

Conscious that we were operating in a highly politicized environment, Rizvi did not want UNHCR to suffer the same fate as Waldheim's aborted airlift. This meant that, unless we chartered an aircraft from a country that was acceptable to the communists, our airlift to Saigon would never get off the ground. Time was also an issue. Rizvi wanted us to start flying at the earliest and we did not have months to negotiate the like of air routes and landing authorizations. This did not leave us many options.

China was not one of them. Even if the Chinese had accepted to lease us an aircraft, I had the gut feeling that the Vietnamese, given their closeness to the Soviet Union would have been uncomfortable with the idea. They would not have said No but would have delayed giving us a landing permit and would have resented us for having created a potentially embarrassing situation for them. The other option would have been to charter an aircraft from the Soviet Union or from a country of the Soviet bloc but this, in turn might have irritated the Chinese and we did not want to do that either.

Fortunately, the solution lay on our door step. Royal Air Laos had not only three scheduled weekly flights to Hanoi but, until April 1975, had been flying regularly to Saigon, which meant that not only was the airline accepted by all parties in the region but its pilots knew the area. On the minus side its fleet had more in common with a museum of vintage aircraft than with a modern airline and its accident rate was astronomical.

But that was beside the point. Safety record apart, Royal Air Laos was exactly what we needed and Rizvi shot a long telex to the UNHCR office in Vientiane asking them to negotiate a charter agreement for an airlift to Saigon.

Jacques Cuenod, whom Rizvi had chosen to be the UNHCR representative in Vientiane, was a solid professional who could be counted upon to do a good job. However, while Rizvi recognized his competence the two had no great affinity for each other so the ever suspicious Rizvi decided that he wanted someone in his pay to keep an eye on Cuenod.

Darryl Han was a Burmese who before joining UNHCR had spent several years at Cornell from whence he had emerged with a law degree which he delighted in advertising and a green card about which he was somewhat more discreet.

Everything about Darryl was round. He was small, with a round head sporting round horn-rimmed glasses over a rotund body. The first time we met he went on and on about how he had read my articles and how honored he was to work with me. Of course I did not believe a word of what he was saying and told myself that here was a slimy, smooth-talking toady who was not to be trusted. Rizvi, however had taken a liking to Darryl and had him assigned to Vientiane. Cuenod who was no fool quickly realized what Rizvi was up to, so he assigned to Darryl the overall responsibility for running the UNHCR airlift to Saigon. Rizvi, who was also no fool, than suddenly realized that his protégé Darryl might have been given more than he could handle and that if something went wrong with the airlift Cuenod could wash his hands of the mishap arguing that he had entrusted responsibility to run it to Darryl, who in turn had been assigned to Vientiane by Rizvi.

To his credit Darryl did a good job and one week later UNHCR Vientiane informed us that all was on track. A charter contract with Royal Air Laos had been signed, the North Vietnamese embassy in Vientiane had been informed and so had the PRG office in Hanoi and all we were waiting for was the green light to commence flying. But it was not coming and Rizvi was becoming uneasy.

In the meantime UNHCR had submitted my name to the PRG for accreditation as Representative in Saigon and was waiting for approval, upon which I could then proceed to my post. All this, even in the best of cases, took weeks. In the meantime Rizvi was getting increasingly nervous about our airlift to Saigon. Cuenod, he realized, was doing his job but no more as the airlift was not at the top of his priorities. And as for Darryl, Rizvi had also now realized that whatever the high opinion he had of himself he did not quite have his feet on the ground when dealing with practical matters was required. Ultimately the airlift was Rizvi's baby and if something went wrong he would be the one to be blamed.

So Rizvi did the obvious. 'Rather than wait in Geneva for your accreditation to go to Saigon,' he told me, 'I want you to go out there and keep an eye on things. You can then go to Saigon later when your accreditation comes through.'

On Saturday June 28, I arrived in Vientiane where Darryl informed me that clearance for the UNHCR airlift to Saigon had finally arrived and that the first flight had flown the day before carrying in two tons of canned meat and 45 passengers out. These were all foreign passport holders, mostly French and a few Hong Kong Chinese who had then proceeded to Bangkok by their own means. The second flight was due on the coming Monday and Darryl would be on it. To this effect, he had received a visa for Saigon from the North Vietnamese embassy in Vientiane, which he proudly showed me. It was in fact a regular visa to North Vietnam in which the port of entry, Hanoi, had been crossed out by hand and replaced by Saigon. Apparently he had asked for a similar visa to be delivered to me but the green light from Hanoi had not arrived yet and I should wait for it before going on a flight.

The flight left as planned on Monday with Darryl on board and I went to the airport late afternoon when it was due back.

The terminal building in Vientiane was small and friendly, built in the modern colonial style favored by the French before the age of air conditioning and in keeping with the number of passengers using the airport which rarely exceeded 50 at one time. I had been provided by the UNHCR office with an access badge to the airport which I pinned to my shirt, but no one checked it as I wandered back and forth through immigration, on to the tarmac and up to the control tower under the indifferent gaze of a handful of Lao airport staff sprawling on whatever benches or chairs were available.

The flight landed after sunset. It was a four-engine DC4 which had first come on the market in 1938 and the first person to emerge was a visibly shaken Darryl. 'We got back on three engines,' were his first stuttering words.

'You mean on the first flight you got back on all four. That is unheard of,' I replied. With Darryl, there was another UNHCR staff member, a young Swiss, Pierre von Gunthen, also hired by Rizvi. Contrary to Darryl he was unflappable and appeared totally indifferent as to the number of engines the aircraft would come back on, provided it came back.

The next day Darryl informed me that the next flight to Saigon was scheduled for the coming Wednesday but there was no longer any need for him to accompany it as Pierre von Gunten would be on board. Of course I could also go, he added, provided my visa had arrived. Suddenly Darryl had lost all taste for flying.

On Wednesday morning at six, just in time for sunrise, Pierre von Gunten and I arrived at the airport. Hardly anyone was around as there were no flights due until mid-morning and we made our way to the tarmac where the DC4 was parked. Two mechanics were fiddling with one of the engines while the tanks were being topped up from an old fuel truck. As we waited, Pierre explained to me the flight procedure which had apparently been agreed upon by Darryl and the Vietnamese.

At six in the morning the Vientiane control tower would radio Hanoi airport requesting authorization to land in Saigon. By seven, if everything went well, Hanoi would radio back with the OK. Vientiane would then radio back with the Estimate Arrival Time in Saigon (ETA) and the aircraft would then take off.

With Cambodia under the Khmer Rouge a no-fly zone, the aircraft first would head towards Bangkok then turn out to sea following the coast until it reached the tip of South Vietnam, and from there take a left over the Southern delta before landing in Saigon, a journey which at an average speed of 200 miles per hour would take about four and a half hours. Once on the ground there was more waiting in store. For some unknown reason passengers in Saigon were not permitted to go to the airport by themselves and had to report to the downtown city air terminal. From there a bus would transport them to the airport but it would depart the city terminal only after the aircraft had landed. Bringing the passengers to the airport, checking their documents and inspecting their luggage was a four-hour affair during which the aircraft had to wait. Adding the flight time to Saigon and back this made for a thirteen-hour day not counting the time spent in Vientiane preparing the aircraft and waiting for clearance from Hanoi. Compounding the problem, Vientiane airport would close down after the day's last scheduled flight, which was at four in the afternoon. Having a flight come in at eight in the evening required that at least some of the staff be back at the airport were it only to man the radio in the control tower and turn on the runway lights. This was easier said than done. Most of the staff did not have a home telephone so someone had to be sent on a bicycle to make the rounds and persuade them to come back to the airport. 8 o'clock was the limit. Raising them from their repose any time later was not even to be contemplated. The end result was that if our aircraft was not airborne by eight thirty in the morning at the latest the flight had to be cancelled.

By now it was seven thirty in the morning and there was still no news from Hanoi. Just to make sure the message had gone out I went to the control tower where the lone Lao radio operator assured me that it had been sent and acknowledged. Would he send it again? Of course, no problem, he said as he started fiddling with his dials. Finally, the answer came shortly after eight. It was short and to the point: flight not cleared.

The following morning at six thirty, Pierre and I were again at the airport as the mechanics prepared the DC4 for its flight to Saigon. Request for clearance had duly been radioed to Hanoi and we were waiting for a reply. At eight thirty it came in: flight not cleared.

As Pierre and I drove back to Vientiane it was now obvious that somehow, somewhere along the line something had gone wrong with our airlift but what? Fortunately, the next day there was a flight to Hanoi and by early afternoon I was back at the *Thong Nhut* hotel and its battered mattresses. On paper we were still supposed to deal with the PRG on matters involving South Vietnam but as I was driven to the PRG office the morning after my arrival I decided not to raise the issue of the airlift as my first priority but start by trying to find out what sort of UNHCR program they envisaged for the South and, last but not least, when did they expect the approval for my accreditation to Saigon to come through. The discussion that followed proved surreal. I had three counterparts, none of whom I had ever met before and none of whom had the least idea of what we were talking about. One of them even suggested that as the cities in the South were dirty they could use some garbage trucks. While I knew that Rizvi would not hesitate to stretch UNHCR's mandate to the limit this was more than the traffic would carry and I gently told them so. When we finally came to the subject of the airlift, I drew a total blank. 'Yes,' they said, 'they were aware of some problems, but I should discuss these in Saigon.' I thanked them for their advice but pointed out that until I had access to Saigon, I could not communicate with the authorities there, to which they silently nodded. Finally, almost as an afterthought, they added that the military were also involved but they had no idea where they could be contacted. As for the issue of my accreditation, this they said, was being processed. How long the processing would take they did not know. The meeting ended with an exchange of smiles and enthusiastic handshakes but nothing else.

At a loss about what to do I then went to see *Monsieur* Bai. I knew, I told him, that he was not responsible for the South and I had come to see him in a purely personal capacity as a younger person asking the advice of an older, more experienced one.

After explaining to him in detail the problems we had with the airlift to Saigon I cautiously added that I would be grateful for his guidance. He smiled and after a short pause said two words: 'Be patient.'

Be patient. Like the Oracle of Delphi *Monsieur* Bai spoke in riddles except that there was no one to interpret them for me. Be patient. The more I thought of it the more it was clear that the advice he had given to me was to wait and do nothing implying that there was nothing I could do about the situation.

In other words something unforeseen over which we had absolutely no control was taking place. What these events were, he left to my imagination and short of a crystal ball my only option was to wait, but to wait for what? By now I was slowly starting to realize that I was faced with a puzzle where most of the pieces were missing and there was nothing to assemble into a coherent picture. And when, much later, the pieces started falling into place the picture that emerged was far remote from the one Rizvi, and to a lesser extent myself, had imagined for Vietnam.

Ho Chi Minh had once written that his goal was to see a free, independent, unified and socialist Vietnam. The first three of these wishes were now met; all that was left was to make Vietnam 'socialist' albeit communist on the Leninist model. But building communism required communists and these, in the South, were in short supply. But this was not the only predicament the Politburo was confronted with. There were two others; China and Cambodia.

The first requirement of building 'socialism' in the South was that the security situation be brought under control. By May 1975 the communists had succeeded in rounding up some 200,000 former Saigon officers and civil servants and consigned them to reeducation camps, thus alleviating their more immediate security concerns. The second requirement was the setting up of a state controlled economy but achieving this goal required that the regime first break the back of the Southern mercantile establishment which was in the hands of the Chinese and concentrated in Cholon, Saigon's Chinatown.

From a French communist journalist whom I had met in the dining room of the *Thong Nhut* hotel I learned that on May 1, the day after the fall of Saigon, practically every home in Cholon had hoisted the flag of the People's Republic of China. It was not the sort of display that anybody in Vietnam would undertake spontaneously so someone must have given the instruction to the Chinese to show the flag and it was obviously not the Vietnamese. This raising of the flag actually harked back to 1956, the year Diem, the then dictator of South Vietnam, imposed Vietnamese nationality on the country's Chinese minority. The move at the time had been denounced by both Beijing and Hanoi as invalid, meaning that China could now claim as its own the ethnic Chinese community of South Vietnam. So the instruction to raise the flag could only have come from Beijing. Clearly however, the Chinese leadership would not have raised the issue of the Chinese residents of South Vietnam had it not had other and more serious bones of contention with Hanoi. While on occasion these did surface during the war they were kept out of the limelight in the name of 'socialist solidarity' and the imperative necessity of the leadership in Hanoi to preserve its supply of weapons from China. But now the war was over and the priority was 'building socialism' rather than keeping up the semblance of good relations with China. This now demanded that the Vietnamese communists decapitate the massive Chinese commercial establishment of Cholon, a tall order indeed and even more so if in the process they had to take on the People's Republic of China.

The Politburo's predicament was further compounded by the problem of Cambodia. Starting in June 1975 there were a series of major border incidents between the Vietnamese forces and the Khmer Rouge as the two communist brethrens took to settling their score through gunfire.

By July 1975 the Politburo came to the conclusion that the challenges it faced in the South were of such magnitude that they could not be addressed by the meager forces of what was left of the local communist infrastructure, even supported by an influx of Northern cadres and the likes of the North Vietnamese army. So the decision was taken to opt for immediate reunification. There would be no semi-independent South and no foreign or UN diplomatic presence in Saigon.

Rizvi had gone to Saigon in June. At the time the communist leadership still envisaged a semi-autonomous South Vietnam and an international role for the PRG and the agreement he had signed was in line with this policy. By July however, the Politburo had opted for immediate reunification and the agreement he had brought back was dead. But who was there to know? We were getting no indications from the Vietnamese that they had moved the goal posts and with no hard evidence to go by, Rizvi was not ready to accept that the agreement he had signed in Saigon was no longer worth the paper it had been written on. As for me I was getting uneasy. I knew that if the Vietnamese communists really wanted something to work, it did. Conversely, if it did not work this could either mean that it was not a priority and could be left floundering or that they actually did not want it to work. But which was which? It would have been out of character or them to let us know.

One week after my visit to Hanoi I was in Bangkok having dinner with Rizvi who had flown in from Geneva that morning and as we reviewed the situation I could see he was getting impatient. Why was I not yet in Saigon? Why was the airlift not operating? Rizvi did not like delays and when obstacles arose he believed it was only so that they could be overcome. Make it happen, was one of his favorite answers when told something did not work. Are you sure you are doing enough, you should be out there in Hanoi putting pressure on them. Putting pressure on the Vietnamese? I held myself back from commenting that if ten years of American bombing had not done the trick one pathetic UN civil servant was not going to do any better. All I could suggest was that he come to Hanoi.

It was his fourth visit to Hanoi and *Monsieur* Bai was now starting to feel at ease with him. He was also keen to get things moving in terms of an aid program for the North and he and Rizvi came rapidly to an agreement. UNHCR would set up a buffalo breeding farm and a chicken breeding facility both of which would be part of a rehabilitation plan for the countryside to facilitate the return of displaced people to their villages of origin. It was the sort of grass-roots, down to earth program that Rizvi was best at and the Vietnamese were delighted.

Overall it was a successful mission and even *Monsieur* Bai, the incarnation of restraint, had started to warm up. Then Rizvi, almost as an afterthought and with feigned innocence, made his move. Could he have a very junior UNHCR staff member come to Hanoi for a few weeks to give a hand with coordination? Mr Bai nodded. And could the Red Cross provide some secretarial support, of course paid by UNHCR. Again *Monsieur* Bai nodded.

Only then did Rizvi make a reference, albeit obliquely, to our airlift to Saigon. He had pretended that he did not quite believe me when I explained to him the problems I was encountering but actually he had understood perfectly well that he could not force the issue. We have a humanitarian airlift to Saigon, he said but there are still some technical problems to be ironed out. We are patient, he added, everything will come in due time. *Monsieur* Bai nodded or at least gave the impression he did.

Rizvi was pleased and flew back to Geneva while I returned to Vientiane. Keep at it, he said before leaving. How, he did not say.

While getting flight clearance for our airlift was still my main concern the decision was entirely in the hands of the Vietnamese and there was nothing I could do about it. So, while I waited for a hypothetical authorization I turned to the more mundane question of getting the logistics right.

Royal Air Laos had only two aircraft that could fly to Saigon; a DC4 and a twin jet Caravelle. While the Caravelle was flying under Lao colors it was for all practical purposes an Air France aircraft with a French crew leased to Royal Air Laos for the symbolic fee of one Franc per year. For some unknown reason Darryl had chosen the DC4 but it was a bad deal. The aircraft could take 50 passengers, and cost us 680 US $ the hour. Conversely, the Caravelle could take 100 passengers and cost 2,000 US $ the hour. It took no genius to calculate that the Caravelle which flew the same distance in half the time would cost us 80 US $ per passenger as opposed to 110 US $ for the DC4. So I redrafted the contract negotiated by Darryl and the Caravelle was now ours to fly.

When Saigon fell, the only foreign airline company whose representative stayed behind was Air France. The French had long believed that they had some sort of privileged relationship with Vietnam and hoped to resume flights within weeks of the fall of Saigon since the airport was undamaged but the Vietnamese would not hear of it. What followed was a lengthy negotiation during which the communists were as contrary as they could be (which was saying a lot). Landing fees, traffic rights, radio frequencies, and the price of tickets became the objects of lengthy and often acrimonious exchanges. For UNHCR the issue was not peripheral. It was clear that if Air France had resumed its flights to Saigon there would have been no reason for our airlift. But we were also aware that the Vietnamese were quite able to claim that they did not need Air France because they could rely on us to fly, and use this argument to raise the ante with the French.

I was aware that Sadruddin had always enjoyed excellent relations with the French government and the last thing we wanted was the Vietnamese using our flights as an argument against Air France, a point that I made clear to the French ambassador in Vientiane, visibly to his great relief.

Another issue I had to deal with was the so-called humanitarian assistance I was supposed to bring to Saigon. When Rizvi had gone to Saigon in June the Vietnamese were adamant. We were welcome to fly in assistance but there would be no 'evacuation' flights from Saigon. Unless the word 'evacuation' carried some sinister meaning in Vietnamese that we were unaware of, the assertion did not make sense. There were thousands of foreigners stranded in Saigon which the new authorities had no interest in keeping so why not let them leave? Finally, it all proved a matter of semantics. Evacuation was a no go but 'family reunion' was fine and the deal was made. We would be flying in assistance and as the aircraft would by flying out empty the Vietnamese would be free to put on board foreigners who wished to join relatives abroad. Given that every foreigner stranded in Saigon had potentially one relative abroad appearances were preserved, but on one condition: we had to fly in with something. In the summer of 1975 there was hardly a single item or piece of goods that was not available in Saigon but it took more to put Rizvi off. He had gotten hold of an undetermined amount of canned beef and had arranged at great expense for it to be flown to Bangkok from where it was transferred in install-ments to Vientiane for onward transport to Saigon. The Caravelle could easily carry two tons of cargo in addition to its passengers but that was not the problem. The problem for us was to have enough canned beef available in Vientiane to ensure that, in case our airlift did indeed take off, there would be enough of it to load on each flight so as to substantiate the fiction that the purpose of the airlift was to bring in aid. That the Vietnamese had no use for the beef was irrelevant to the issue.

On July 22 I was in Bangkok to check our stock of beef when a telex came in from our office in Vientiane. They had received a phone call from the North Vietnamese embassy saying that a flight to Saigon had been cleared for July 24 and that they had received approval for my being on board.

The flight was uneventful and as we came in to land I recog-nized a familiar landscape. Hundreds upon hundreds of bomb craters had transformed the countryside around the airport into a lunar landscape. Our pilot, captain Simard, had landed before in Saigon and, knowing his way, brought us straight to the terminal where he cut the engines.

I had known Tan Son Nhut airport as one of the world's busiest but as I got off the rear ramp of the aircraft I had the impression of stepping into a ghost city. The silence was deafening and except for one other aircraft on the tarmac, a Soviet-made IL 18 with North Vietnamese army markings, we were alone.

Two men in civilian clothes and one in uniform with the insig-nia of senior captain were waiting for us and motioned us to follow them to a waiting room some 50 meters away. As we were invited to sit down in an assorted set of shabby plastic-covered armchairs I surveyed our surroundings. Several of the windows had been smashed by what appeared to be shell fragments that had embed-ded themselves in the wall, but there were no traces of bullet holes.

After tea had been brought in by a young woman wearing North Vietnamese army fatigues one of the civilians turned to us and in perfect French announced that while the crew would stay at the airport, I would attend a meeting and lunch in town before returning to the airport for take off.

As we drove towards downtown the changes were unmistakable. Traffic had diminished by at least half and consisted now mostly of motorcycles. One shop out of two was closed and the hustle and bustle that was the city's trademark had become a thing of the past. The driver headed for the hotel *Majestic*, by the riverside at the far end of Tu Do Street, where we got off. The lobby was deserted except for a lonely receptionist and two burly men in civilian clothes with a visible bulge under the right side of their shirts overhanging their trousers who eyed us with suspicion as we headed straight for the restaurant on the top floor.

As we sat down the *maître d'hôtel* came hesitantly towards us, a menu in hand. He was an old frail man who must have been with the *Majestic* hotel forever and whom I vaguely recognized from a past visit. Conversely, the three waiters who converged on us looked so out of place in their badly cut slacks that I could not help wondering what they were doing here when it suddenly all became clear. These were North Vietnamese. With an occasional foreign visitor staying at the hotel the authorities did not want to take any chances with security, and apart from the old maitre d', they had cleared out all the old hotel staff and replaced them with hastily assembled replacements from the North. Security had no doubt taken a quantum leap forward but quality of service an equal leap backwards.

My host, who introduced himself as Mr Tam, was a French-educated long-standing revolutionary from Saigon who had moved North in 1954 and had now returned to the South. He made no secret of the fact that there was no such thing as a PRG running the South. Saigon, he explained, was under the control of a Military Managing Committee and the rest of the country was for all practical purposes under direct North Vietnamese army rule. And as for our airlift, he was equally forthright; it was controlled from Hanoi.

According to his explanation, the Saigon Military Management Committee had a master list of foreigners who were authorized to leave Saigon. Whenever Hanoi informed Saigon that one of our aircraft was due to arrive, a list of passengers who were authorized to board the coming aircraft would hurriedly be posted at the downtown office of Air Vietnam at around nine in the morning. 'The procedure,' said Mr Tam, 'could not be changed because flight clearance was given by Hanoi only on a day-to-day basis and there could be no advance planning. People,' he explained, 'had been going to the Air Vietnam office with their luggage day after day, every morning to see if there was a flight and if so, if their name was on the list. People on the list would, once our aircraft had landed, be transported by bus to the airport to go through check in, including a thorough inspection of their luggage, with the whole procedure taking three to four hours upon which the aircraft and passengers could depart. As for those passengers who were on the list but had not checked it that morning, well they would not be leaving.'

By one thirty I was back at the airport where some of the passengers had starting boarding the aircraft and by two we were airborne. As the coast of Vietnam faded in the distance I went through the cabin. The passengers were a mixed lot. French teachers with their families, Hong Kong businessmen, an occasional Indian, and some Italians. All had tickets issued in Saigon for which they had been required to pay 125 US $. By any standard this was theft. We had made our aircraft available free of charge to the Vietnamese authorities to repatriate foreigners stranded in Saigon and now they were making them pay for the fare. But after giving the matter some thought, I decided to do nothing about it. We had enough problems as it was without raising ethical issues. After all, this was politics.

At three thirty we landed in Vientiane and I was looking forward to a shower but it was not to be. A note was waiting for me at the hotel lobby. Rizvi would be in Bangkok the next day and wanted to see me urgently. I barely had time to pack my toilet kit and some underwear and rushed back to the airport. The Caravelle was due to leave for Bangkok any minute and immigration had already closed down, so I ran through the terminal and just made it to the aircraft as they crew was closing the door. That I had neither a ticket nor boarding card was beside the point. I finally did get to take my shower, but it was in Bangkok.

While I had been struggling with our airlift Rizvi had been busy. After the Vietnamese had half-heartedly agreed to having a UNHCR staff member in Hanoi to act as a liaison he had hired a young Swiss for the job who had already arrived in Hanoi where the Vietnamese had allocated him one room in the *Thong Nhut* hotel as an office as well as a support staff of two. We now also had a cable address in Hanoi, HICOMREF Hanoi, and a box at the central post office.

Rizvi also informed me that in order to strengthen our relations with the Vietnamese authorities he had recruited in Geneva a young Vietnamese, Nguyen Tang Canh, whom he had decided to send to Hanoi on a mission. Canh, he told me, was expected to arrive in Vientiane any day to pick up his visa at the North Vietnamese embassy and would then proceed to Hanoi.

The move was pure Rizvi. He was constantly fearful of being the subject of some sort of plot or of being denied information and just as he had sent Darryl to keep an eye on Cuenod he now had hired Canh to report on me. He also enjoyed destabilizing those around him and by hiring Canh he was making it clear that he now had his own contacts with Hanoi and could therefore, if he so wished, dispense with my services. Ultimately it was pathetic, especially in someone as brilliant as he was, but it was in his nature and I left it at that.

I had met Canh at the Graduate Institute where he had been a student and I had not been impressed. His surname Nguyen Tang indicated that he was related to the former imperial family and he derived great pride from it. He also claimed to have all sorts of contacts in the government in Hanoi and had obviously impressed Rizvi.

When Rizvi broke the news to me I had my doubts but kept them to myself. The communists, I knew, had little empathy for those Vietnamese who had spent the war years comfortably ensconced in Paris or Geneva, only to claim their allegiance to the revolution once the war was over. I therefore did not see what Canh could do for UNHCR but had I said so to Rizvi he would have become even more suspicious of me so I left it at that.

One week later Canh arrived in Vientiane. Normally he liked to feign modesty but this time he was downright cocky. His visa was being processed, he announced, and meetings were being prepared for him in Hanoi. High-level meetings, he emphasized. He would report on them directly to Rizvi who would inform me as he saw fit.

Three days later, as I dropped by the UNHCR office I ran into Canh whom I thought was now in Hanoi. 'What are you still doing here,' I asked.

'No problem,' he answered, 'there is a small delay with my visa but they said it was only technical.' Technical. I had heard the expression before in Hanoi. On paper it meant that something had been approved but that a small glitch had delayed implementation. That was the official explanation but like most things in Vietnam it had to be read backwards. Technical actually meant no, but poor Canh had not got the message.

A few days later I ran again into Canh. 'Well,' I said. 'What about your visa. Any news?'

'It's technical,' he replied, but the certainty had gone out of his voice. Two weeks later I again came across him in the UNHCR office as he was readying his ticket to go back to Geneva. As I passed by him I could not help myself. 'It's technical,' I whispered. As for Rizvi, he kept Canh on the staff but never mentioned him again to me and I did likewise. Rubbing in the point would have been of no use. He had tried to be just a bit too clever, he had made a fool of himself, he knew it and he knew that I knew it.

The following six weeks were a nightmare come true. We had planned for three flights a week from Vientiane, on Mondays, Wednesdays and Fridays, leaving in the morning and coming back by mid-afternoon which would enable the Caravelle to then proceed on its daily and only flight to Bangkok. On the days we had planned to fly I would arrive at the airport at five in the morning and by six the fuelling of the aircraft would start. At seven we would radio Hanoi for clearance and then wait. With some luck by eight we would get an answer and in two cases out of three it was an unambiguous 'flight not cleared'. I would then return to my hotel with nothing to do all day until the next try. Whenever I would try to get some explanation from Hanoi and send a cable to the Swiss fellow that Rizvi had posted there I would get the same answer: 'Authorities inform be patient.' After half a dozen cancellations I had reached the conclusion that we should close our airlift altogether but Rizvi would hear nothing of it. Visibly he felt that the credibility of UNHCR was at stake and as news of the repeated cancellations had not spread either within the UN system or in the media he could still claim that we had an ongoing airlift to Saigon. Perversely, each time I felt I had come close to convincing him to throw in the towel one of our flights would get clearance. 'You see,' he would say, 'You must keep on trying.' But I could feel that even he was starting to have his doubts and the issue now was how to close down the airlift without losing face. The solution came in mid-August from where I least expected it.

One afternoon as I was peacefully reading in the UNHCR office in Vientiane the incredible happened. Rizvi was on the phone. He had called from Geneva and the call had actually gone through, the first and last time this would ever happen. Apparently, he explained to me, an American Quaker group had heard of our airlift. They had several tons of children's medical supplies in Hong Kong and had received a license from the US government who had an embargo on Vietnam to have them shipped to Saigon. Could we provide transportation from Hong Kong to Saigon they asked? Rizvi had immediately answered in the affirmative. This was the stuff he dreamt of. High visibility, worldwide recognition, medicines for children, as an operation it did not come any better.

This, we agreed, would also be our last flight. Air France had now resumed flights to Saigon albeit irregularily and our airlift was no longer needed.Not that there ever really had been an airlift but that was another matter.

Flying our airlift from Vientiane to Saigon I had told Rizvi was one thing; flying from Hong Kong to Saigon was quite another ball game. So I told Rizvi to be prepared for the worst. 'Not to worry,' he said, 'but make sure that things have been cleared at both ends,' he added.

Given that the direct air corridor between Vientiane and Hong Kong had now been closed the idea was to plan a flight which would proceed from Vientiane to Saigon with its usual load of canned beef, proceed from there to Hong Kong, where it would spend the night, return to Saigon the following day with the medicines, and fly back to Vientiane with some passengers. It was an easy route, entailing no particular problems, political or technical, or so we thought.

I now had to do my rounds to get clearances for the flight and my first stop was Hong Kong.

Royal Air Laos already had landing rights in Hong Kong and the Caravelle met all the technical requirements to do so, so this was not an issue. The problem was that the Hong Kong control tower needed confirmation from the Hanoi control tower that the aircraft had been cleared to take off from Saigon. The two control towers had not communicated since 1954, when the communists took over North Vietnam and re-establishing the radio link proved a major headache in more ways than one. The Lao had informed me that the call sign of the control tower in Hanoi was 7 HN 2 HAN and the radio frequency was 8854 but this was just the beginning.

Firstly, Hanoi still communicated in Morse code. By and large, the world had given up Morse in the early 1950s and there was no one at Hong Kong airport who knew Morse code or even had a Morse key. Fortunately, one of the technicians working in the control tower remembered having met a retired Chinese radio operator who still knew Morse and collected vintage radio equipment. Contacted by phone, he promised to come to the airport with his gear and felt certain that something could be put together.

Secondly, Hanoi had been out of the loop of civil aviation for so long that what might have been its radio frequency in 1954 had been allocated somewhere else by the International Civil Aviation Organization. This meant that the use of frequency 8854 by Hong Kong would be illegal, but fortunately for us the flight controllers were so exited by the idea that they would be contacting Hanoi control tower that they chose to overlook this minor detail.

By now the news that an aircraft from Vietnam, the first since the fall of Saigon would soon be landing in Hong Kong had hit the local media and strange calls started coming in.

One came from a man who identified himself as Joseph Lee, the South Korean consul in Hong Kong. Apparently the South Koreans had not succeeded in evacuating their diplomats from Saigon before the fall and were afraid that the Vietnamese would hand them over to the North Koreans. 'Could we do something about it and eventually bring them out,' he asked. 'No we could not,' I told him; it was up to the Vietnamese to decide. 'You should work out something with them directly,' I told him. 'You mean the communists,' he said. 'Yes,' I told him, 'the communists, who else.'

I then had a call from the hotel reception informing me that someone was waiting for me in the lobby. I was expecting no one but decided to give it a look.

In the hotel lobby I found a Chinese man who claimed that he was some sort of Member of Parliament, or whatever they had as a representative in Hong Kong. He appeared most agitated and wanted to know what we were doing about 'our refugees', in Saigon. Actually he was referring to Hong Kong residents stranded in Saigon who wanted to go home.

First, I told him, they are not 'refugees'. A refugee is someone who had to flee his country of origin to escape persecution. These are people who just got stuck in Saigon and can't get out. Air France now flies to Saigon and it is up to the Vietnamese to release them and you should get in contact with them.

'You mean the communists,' he replied with a horrified look.

Suddenly I lost patience with him. 'Of course,' I answered, 'you could try General Thieu in Taiwan, but yes, the communists, who else.' He stepped out of the hotel the very image of despair.

Having hopefully cleared things in Hong Kong I then proceeded to Hanoi ready to face the battered mattresses of the *Thong Nhut* hotel. The rainy season had set in and in addition to the oppressive heat, the humidity was overwhelming, but there was nothing to be done about it: air conditioning was not even on the horizon. While these were not shortcomings that one could blame on the Vietnamese who were still shouldering the burden of thirty years of war, lack of comfort in my eyes carried no redeeming value, so this time I had packed an extra suitcase with an electric water kettle, instant coffee, sugar, condensed milk, two rolls of toilet paper, a dozen tins of canned beans, some mosquito spray and two pairs of bed sheets.

The young Swiss that Rizvi had temporarily assigned to Hanoi to act as our liaison officer was now in place and at first glance looked as the most unlikely candidate for the post; an emaciated, slightly stooped, creepy-looking character with a goatee and a suspicious gaze. He rarely spoke and spent most of his days poring over figures. This, and the shortage of candidates for a post as uncomfortable as Hanoi, is probably what motivated Rizvi's choice, who obviously wanted a man with few material needs who found his fulfillment in program management.

The Vietnamese had allotted him two rooms in the *Thong Nhut* hotel: one as an office and one for his own use, but he would have been unable to function without some local assistance and an arrangement had been made by Rizvi with the Foreign Ministry to provide us with some Vietnamese staff.

Rizvi had never mentioned to me the Vietnamese who had been assigned to us and the first I became aware of his presence was when I stepped into the office room that had been allocated to us at the *Thong Nhut* hotel. There I found a middle-aged gentleman who greeted me in French with well-mannered caution.

Mr Khoang was in his 50's and coming from one of the wealthier families of Hanoi had enjoyed both a comfortable and studious youth.

In December 1946, Khoang was 20 and his future as an educated youngster from a well-to-do family was assured. But he was to choose a different path. After months of negotiation, the uncertain truce between the French colonial forces and the communist-oriented Viet Minh nationalists had broken down. Fighting had spread and the first Vietnam War had begun. Literally overnight Khoang gave up the life of a privileged urban Vietnamese and joined the resistance. For eight long years he lived and fought in the jungle; there he met a young girl who like him came from a privileged milieu and they planned to marry once the war was over.

One day, he told me, she happened to be based with a guerrilla group in a village next to his position and he got a pass to visit her. On his way back to his camp there was a major attack, which lasted several days. The village where she had been based was hit by French artillery and he never saw her again. 'She was the love of my life,' he told me, 'and after I lost her nothing was the same. Several years later I married but afterwards I realized that she was the only woman I would ever love.'

Khoang did well in the resistance and became the editor of the newspaper of one of the Viet Minh's crack divisions. In a society which valued scholarship and the gift of literature it was a prestigious position, and when he came back to Hanoi in 1954 with the victorious communist forces he was a respected figure in his own right. Such was the esteem in which he was held that he was invited to join the communist party and offered a government position. He turned both down.

'I told them,' he explained to me, 'that I was ready to give my life for my country but that the party had just too many meetings and I would get bored. I also was not interested in government service. I was interested in literature.'

So Khoang followed his own course and chose to devote his time translating the classics of French literature into Vietnamese. The pay was miserable and the print runs small (about 1000, which was a lot given the scarcity of newsprint in war-torn North Vietnam), but he had chosen his own way. I asked him once how much he earned and he told me he was paid 120 Dongs for every book he translated, which was the equivalent of three months pay for a factory worker.

'It is the standard pay for a translation,' he said.

'But,' I asked him, 'let us imagine that one translator does a good job and his book sells well while another translator is not so good and his book does not sell, do they both get the same pay?'

'Yes,' he answered.

'But do you think it is right,' I asked.

He paused for a second and then answered with a slight smile: 'It is socialism.'

Most of his classmates had by now reached prominent positions in the party or the government, and their doors were always open to him; though of little means and with no official position he was looked upon with considerable respect.

Khoang took a visible liking to me and when I explained to him that I had come to Hanoi to obtain clearance for a last UNHCR flight from Hong Kong to Saigon, he got the message and by the end of the day he had three appointments set up for me for the next morning.

My first meeting was a first in more ways than one. Until now, UNHCR had officially been dealing only with the North Vietnamese Red Cross and not with the government. This time, however, my meeting was at the Foreign Ministry, a clear indication that our relations had been upgraded to government level. But even better news was in store for me. I had expected to be received by a mid-ranking official. The man who received me was none other than Vice Foreign Minister Nguyen Co Thach. The name was of course familiar and I had seen numerous pictures of him at the Paris peace talks where he was the right hand man of the North Vietnamese negotiator Le Duc Tho.

A protégé of Tho, Thach had a forceful personality with no patience for idle talk and gave straight answers to straight questions. By Vietnamese standards he was heavily built, not fat but muscled, and he carried himself with assurance and authority.

I thought it pointless to go into the details of the past problems we had encountered with our airlift and decided to focus exclusively on Hong Kong. We had, I told him, a consignment of medicines donated by the Quakers and would like to obtain authorization for one flight, and one flight only from Hong Kong to deliver them to Saigon. Only one, I reiterated, possibly on August 26. As I spoke I could see that the idea did not appeal to him and that some convincing would be required.

Most of the Vietnamese ruling elite in Hanoi had gone to French schools and, in the process had acquired a solid dose of Gallic Anglophobia. 'Les Anglais', the English as they would say, were not to be trusted and perfidious Albion was more than just an abstract. During the war years Britain had been a steadfast ally of the US in addition to providing expertise in counter-insurgency. In practical terms this had been inconsequential but it reinforced the inbred Vietnamese mistrust of all things English. And while they neither liked nor respected the Americans they were still in awe of their power and money. By comparison, the British were third-rate Americans with neither the money nor the power.

Instinctively then, Thach was liable to say no to anything involving Hong Kong which at the time was a British colony.

Finally, however, after I underlined the fact that this was really a matter involving UNHCR and the Quakers and that there was nothing the British in Hong Kong would stand to gain from it, he relented. All right, he said, one flight, and one flight only. This time I had no doubt that there would be no impediments to the flight, and that it would also be the closing chapter of our airlift.

My last meeting, at the PRG office was a matter of form and even more so as it had not escaped me that it was the North Vietnamese Vice Foreign Minister in person, and no one else, who had given me clearance for a flight from Saigon to Hong Kong with the PRG nowhere in the picture. By the same token it was now obvious to me that, while South Vietnam was, in relation to Hanoi, supposedly run by a separate government, even the communists were paying less and less lip service to this fiction and that UNHCR would never open an office in Saigon independent from Hanoi.

SHOWDOWN IN HONG KONG

O
On August 26 at 5 pm, after a brief stopover in Saigon where I unloaded our last shipment of canned beef, the Royal Air Laos Caravelle landed in Hong Kong. I was expecting the flight to pass unnoticed but the Hong Kong government had decided otherwise.
As I got off the aircraft a police officer was waiting for me and escorted me to a police car which, I was told, would bring me to the government secretariat. While I welcomed the hospitality extended to me, I was finding the procedure somewhat strange but refrained from asking any questions to the portly English policeman dozing next to me on the back seat. On arrival I was escorted by a guard to a third floor suite of offices. There, settled around a round table, were two Hong Kong immigration officers, the aircraft pilot capitaine Simard, the local head of Air France and Ivor Jackson the UNHCR representative in Hong Kong. Presiding the meeting was Hong Kong's Political advisor, Charles Drace-Francis.

While Hong Kong had its own civil service, consisting mostly of expatriate Englishmen, some of the key positions were filled by officials detached from London and Charles Drace-Frances was one of them. He was strictly Foreign Office and his post was equivalent to Foreign Minister of Hong Kong.

There was a dead silence around the table as he started to speak. The tone was haughty, the demeanor arrogant and the English impeccable. Visibly he had been to all the right schools, possibly Eton and certainly either Oxford or Cambridge. The message he conveyed was unambiguous and not open to discussion. 'There were,' he told us, '49 Vietnamese stranded in Hong Kong who had overstayed their visas. All wished to go back to Vietnam and the government had decided to expel them. Here is a court order,' he said, as he handed a paper to Simard. 'Tomorrow at 9 am the Vietnamese will be put on board of the Caravelle and will be flown back to Vietnam together with the shipment of medicines, end of story. So, it is agreed,' he concluded.

There was silence around the table. No one looked at each other as I decided it was my turn to speak.

'We would be very happy to fly these people back to Vietnam,' I said, provided of course that they wish to go home and that the Vietnamese authorities agree to their return. We will be happy to bring their files to Saigon for clearance but unfortunately we cannot fly them back until their return has been approved by Vietnam.

Drace-Frances drew himself up. 'Did I make myself clear,' he barked, 'I am not asking you, I am telling you. Tomorrow at 9 am the Vietnamese will be on board the aircraft.'

I could feel Ivor Jackson fretting next to me. This was his territory, he was senior to me and it would have been inappropriate not to let him intervene so I turned to him. As he started to speak I recognized the type. A lawyer and a creature of Headquarters, well versed in the arcane ways of refugee law and totally devoid of any practical sense. His assignment to Hong Kong was a temporary one and he longed to go back to his law manuals.

Next to me, Jackson was wringing his hand with a look of despair on his face. 'Charles, Charles, how can you do this to us.'

Drace-Francis snapped back with undisguised glee, 'Well, I obviously can.'

'But Charles,' I could see Jackson desperately seeking for the right word which would convey the greatest possible degree of indignation, finally he found it, 'it is unfair.'

'I know it is unfair,' Drace-Francis barked back, with a joyful sneer. 'So what?'

Suddenly Jackson seemed to collapse on himself. He had put up as good a fight as he was able to and now he was a spent man. 'Do you want me to proceed,' I whispered to him.

'Yes, do, please,' he answered in a broken voice.

I said nothing. Again there was silence around the table. Drace-Francis hesitated. So it is all settled he said.

'What is settled,' I asked in as innocuous a tone as I could conjure.

'That at 9 am tomorrow the Vietnamese will be on board.'

'Fine,' I said. 'If this is what you wish, I can't stop you.'

'Very well,' he answered; 'these are the court orders,' he turned to Capitaine Simard and handed them to him. Simard took them and said nothing.

'Excellent,' he said, they will be on board. Capitaine Simard seemed to nod. There was silence around the table. No one moved. I thought I detected a brief look of concern on Drace-Francis's face quickly replaced by a smile.

'So,' Drace-Francis turned to us, 'it is done, the Vietnamese will be on board,' there was a moment of hesitation, 'is there a problem?'

'Ze problem,' Simard spoke slowly in a heavily accented English, 'is zat I vill not turn ze engines on.'

'What,' exploded Drace-Francis, 'I order you to.'

'I only take ze order from Mister Casella,' he replied.

'Then you will go to jail,' he barked back.

'If Mister Casella tells me to go to ze jail I will go to jail.'

'Of course,' he added, 'I can turn ze engines on and zen put ze power and put on ze brakes. You vill have ze airplane with zi blown tires in ze middle of ze runway.'

By now Drace-Francis was screaming. 'I will have your aircraft impounded.'

'I don't care,' answered Simard in a calm, even voice. 'Zis is not my aircraf.'

At this point I felt it was time for me to intervene.

'Let us look at the problem under another angle,' I said. 'The aircraft belongs to Air France, which is owned by the French government, flies under the colors of Laos and is chartered by the United Nations to bring medicines to the children of Saigon. If you want to impound it, I can't stop you and frankly I don't care. Of course the French will go berserk. You might also end up with a riot in front of the British embassy in Vientiane, the UN will start bellowing about the evils of colonialism and every bleeding heart in the world will accuse you of denying medicine to the sick children of Vietnam. If this is what you want, so be it. Personally I think it is a bit of a high price to pay to get rid of 49 Vietnamese, especially as you will not have repatriated any of them anyhow, but it is really up to you.'

Again silence settled round the table. The two immigration officers, old Hong Kong hands, had their eyes on the ceiling, a blank expression on their faces, but I suspected that they did not mind seeing a young whippersnapper imported from London put back in his place. Capitaine Simard had his eyes half closed, as if he had drifted away but I knew he was enjoying it all. The Air France man was doing his best not to grin and poor Jackson lay slumped on his chair.

By now Drace-Francis had regained some of his composure. 'Well, I see, we might have to look at this again,' he said. It was now 10 pm and everything had been said.

'Are we actually detained,' I asked Drace-Francis, 'or can we go back to our hotel?' 'Detained, of course not,' suddenly he was his most charming self, 'you must have had a long day; I'll call you in the morning.'

For me there was one last thing to do and this was to get Jackson to call Geneva, brief them and ask them to call London. Half an hour later the phone rang in my hotel room. He had got through to Headquarters and spoken to the deputy High Commissioner who in turn had called the Foreign Office in London. They were horrified and said they would take care of the matter. The next morning at 8 am Drace-Francis called. He seemed in the best of moods. 'Don't worry,' he said, 'London called and I have been overruled.' He seemed to think it was all a huge joke.

'Why did you do it?,' I asked.

'Why not,' he answered, 'it can't hurt to try and it might have worked.'

The return flight was uneventful and by mid-afternoon I was back in Vientiane, exhausted but content. Altogether, we had flown to Saigon some 15 tons of canned beef which nobody needed and flown out 528 people who would have gotten out anyhow, albeit a few weeks later but that was besides the point. What was not was the fact that we had gracefully exited the scene with our last flight from Hong Kong.

But it was not the end of our airlift, or at least not quite. In October I was twiddling my thumbs in Vientiane when a telex arrived from Rizvi who was in Geneva. I was to charter a DC 3 from Royal Air Laos and be in Hanoi on the morning of October 30 to fly out some foreigners. More details he did not provide me with and I knew better than to ask but by 10 am at the requested date I landed in Hanoi in a dilapidated DC 3.

The airport was deserted except for a lone Vietnamese official who pointed me towards a small side building. There I found a small group of Westerners who eyed me uneasily as two other Vietnamese officials came up to me. 'These are foreigners,' said one in French, 'who have expressed the wish to be repatriated. The PRG,' he added, 'has decided to agree to their request and they have been brought to Hanoi to be handed over to UNHCR. Here is a list of them. Please sign.'

As I took out my pen I glanced through the list. There were 9 names on it; a Canadian woman missionary, two Canadian missionaries, an American missionary couple, the Johnsons with their five year old daughter Luanne, a scholar from Cornell, Jay Scarborough and two other Americans, Paul Struarik, a State Department official based in Ban Me Thuot and James Lewis later identified as a CIA officer.

From what they told me on the flight back to Vientiane from where, after a short stop we proceeded to Bangkok, they had all been captured in the South Vietnamese highlands by the advancing North Vietnamese army, had been brought to Hanoi by road through the Ho Chi Minh Trail and had nothing to complain about their treatment. Their only concern was how long they would be held and they were only told they were being released upon arriving at Hanoi airport.

The whole foreign press corps was at Bangkok airport when we landed and, except for Lewis and Struarik who were whisked away in a black limousine the moment the aircraft door open the rest of the passengers showed no reluctance in submitting themselves to a media frenzy.

For UNHCR as an institution, the release was a major plus. We had demonstrated that were present on the ground in Vietnam, that we were efficient and that we were a credible interlocutor and the governments which supported us could not have asked for more.

A MIRAGE TOO MANY

By the time Saigon fell, on April 30, 1975, some 130,000 Vietnamese had stampeded out of the country, about half evacuated by the Americans and the rest having found the means to leave on their own.

By June some 2,500 among the evacuees, some of whom were already in the US and others scattered among the countries of South East Asia, were clamoring to return home arguing that they had never intended to leave Vietnam in the first place.

The question of their return had been raised by the PRG with Rizvi when he visited Saigon in June 1975 and he had been informed that the evacuees were welcome to come back to Vietnam and UNHCR should assist with the return process.

By early August 1975, UNHCR had registered some 2,500 candidates for return and their applications had been given to the Red Cross in Saigon with an additional copy to the PRG office in Hanoi. All we needed now to start the repatriation were the first clearances.

Weeks went by and then more weeks and no clearances came our way and whenever we would ask the Vietnamese when the repatriation could start it was always the same answer: the matter is been taken care of, the first clearances will come soon, everything is on track, just be patient.

Had circumstances been different UNHCR could have hoped that our planned role in a repatriation process that was becoming increasingly dubious could have just faded away with none the wiser but it was not to be.

Rizvi had gone out of his way to advertise the fact that we had been asked by the PRG to assist with repatriation and expectations had been raised. Now, with no clearances for return forthcoming, we were taking part of the blame for the delay in returns. Again, this would have not been more than a passing nuisance had the blame not originated from our major donor, namely the United States.

Of the 2,500 Vietnamese who had expressed a wish to return to Vietnam some 1,500 were actually in the US and were becoming increasingly rowdy. At a loss about what to do with the group the Americans, by August, had moved them all to a camp on Guam pending their repatriation by UNHCR. With no repatriation date in sight the group had become restless. There were demonstrations, barracks were burned and some Vietnamese even threatened to cut off their fingers and send them to President Ford if they could not return home. The situation was not helped by the broadcast of Radio Hanoi claiming that the group was being held hostage by the Americans who were preventing their return. This led the Americans to increase their pressure on UNHCR which found itself caught between Washington's insistence on a speedy repatriation and Vietnam's procrastination regarding clearances.

Had the Vietnamese told us that repatriation was on hold we could have disengaged but just like they never told us to close down our airlift and only made things difficult for us until we got the message they left us in the dark as regards the beginning of the repatriation and would only repeat that they were doing all possible efforts, that time was needed and that we should ba patient. By now of course I had my doubts but these were still a matter of hypothesis. All that I knew for sure, as Rizvi announced to me, was that Sadruddin would be coming to Hanoi in mid September on an official visit and that his mission had better be a success.

I had never gone on a mission with Sadruddin and I owed it to him to get things right, and even more so as he would be traveling with his wife, princess Catherine. Rizvi did not particularly like Catherine whom he considered spoiled and since I could hardly count on his advice on how to deal with her, I decided to phone Sadruddin's trusted secretary, Marie-Thérèse. So I took the first flight available from Vientiane to Bangkok and got on the line as soon as I landed.

Sadruddin, she told me, was not fussy and when on field trips ate what was offered and slept where available. Princess Catherine was not particularly fussy either but she had two quirks. She was allergic to pepper and was particular about the water she drank, Évian being her favorite. Almost as an afterthought, but probably remembering that I was new to the organization, she added that when he traveled on official business Sadruddin had the UN flag flying from his car.

This last piece of information, I felt, needed immediate attention. Where could I find a UN flag? Marie Thérèse connected me to what she called Registry, a unit which I had no idea existed in the dark recesses of UNHCR. There I got a Frenchman on the line to whom I explained my predicament. Yes, he could get me a UN flag. And maybe also a flagpole that could be fixed to a car? How about a second flag in case something went wrong with the first one? What could go wrong with a UN flag? Well, this was Vietnam where everything could go wrong. The weather was awful, it rained a lot, the flag could get torn, he did not want the High Commission traveling in a car flying a torn UN flag, did he? He got my point and I was in luck. The UN had a weekly pouch which would be leaving the next day for Bangkok and the flag would be in it, addressed specifically to me. I spent the next three days by the pool of the hotel *Erawan*, waiting for the flag. Finally, with flagpole, flag and a spare secure in my carry-on bag, I returned to Vientiane.

Most of the small grocery stores owned by Vietnamese who stocked imported goods for the benefit of the foreign community had now closed down, but the one next to the French cultural center was still in business and miraculously still had two twelve-bottle crates of Évian water which I purchased on the spot.

Armed with the two indispensable ingredients to a successful visit, a UN flag and two crates of Évian water, I landed in Hanoi two days before Sadruddin's arrival. Khoan had come to pick me up and as we started on the fifteen-minute ride to the *Thong Nhut* hotel he turned to me and asked with a tone of expectation, 'is he coming with Rita Hayworth?' It must have been 30 years since Khoang had seen an American movie and at the time he must have been up to date with Hollywood lore. Alas I had to disappoint him. Rita Hayworth had been married to Sadruddin's half brother, Ali Khan, some 20 years his senior. His current wife was charming, but Rita Hayworth she was not.

The next morning at nine Khoang had arranged a meeting for me at the Foreign Ministry with the protocol department which was responsible for organizing Sadruddin's visit. It was the first time they were to receive the head of a UN agency and they wanted to get everything right. The program they showed me seemed fine for a stay that was a little on the long side. Sadruddin would be arriving on a Friday afternoon, on Saturday there would be a visit to Ho Chi Minh's memorial, on Sunday he would drive to Vinh, returning on the Tuesday, leaving three days for meetings in Hanoi before departing for Vientiane on Saturday and from there on to Geneva. No mention was made as to whom he would meet in the Government; they probably had not decided yet and would play it by ear, depending on what he said, his attitude and whether they liked him. 'Did I have any question,' they asked? 'Yes,' I replied, 'there is just one small detail left, the flag.' 'The flag, what flag?' 'The UN flag.' I explained that wherever the High Commissioner traveled, he flew the UN flag from his car. 'Yes, but Vietnam is not a member of the UN,' they said. 'That does not matter,' I replied, 'he flies the flag even when he visits countries which are not UN members.' Fortunately they did not ask which ones, as I would have been hard put to answer.

Here was a hurdle, and a major one for them, which they had not expected and therefore not planned for. There was a long exchange in Vietnamese, which Khoang did not translate, and then one of them turned to me with a look of relief. 'We do not have a UN flag,' he said. 'That's not a problem,' I answered, 'I have a flag.' Consternation hit them. There was more chatter in Vietnamese; obviously they could not agree. Finally, as if to break the deadlock, one of them turned to me and asked, 'Can we see the flag?'

I was ready for the move and drew from my attaché case my UN flag, the model, made to fly from a car. The response was unanimous. 'It is too big.'

'Would it help if it were smaller?' Hesitantly, they said yes. I pulled out my Swiss Army knife, the one with scissors and under their horrified gaze proceeded to desecrate the emblem of the UN by cutting off a few inch lengthwise and in height. 'Here it is,' I said, as I handed over to them flag and flagpole.

While Rizvi would be staying at the *Thong Nhut* hotel I was told, Sadruddin would be accommodated in a government guest-house, where I proceeded to with Khoang. It was a small French villa, impeccably clean with whitewashed walls and French furniture that must have dated from the 1930s. Sadruddin would be taking most of his meals here and I was introduced to the cook who spoke some French. I explained to him that Princess Catherine was allergic to pepper and we would also be bringing in a crate of Évian water. There should always be one bottle on the High Commissioner and his wife's night table and one in the dining room. Empty bottles he was welcome to keep, a suggestion that elicited a large smile. 'You have made him a great present,' Khoang whispered to me. 'He can sell them for a lot of money.'

Sadruddin and his party arrived on schedule on Friday on the Royal Air Lao DC3 and we drove up next to the aircraft in three cars; one car for him and his wife, one for Rizvi and myself and one for the officials who were receiving him. As Sadruddin stepped off the aircraft and was pointed towards his car I saw his eyes focus on the fender and then turn to me. 'The flag,' he whispered. There it was, a miserable, truncated UN flag limply hanging from its mast. 'I know,' I replied, 'I will explain.'

As we drove into town I explained the flag episode to Rizvi who shook his head in disbelief. Our first stop was Sadruddin's residence where all the staff and a few more officials had lined up to receive him. His luggage was carried to his bedroom and when Princess Catherine saw the Évian bottles on the bedside tables, she turned to me.

'Sacha, I know it is you, thank you, thank you so much.' Behind me I could feel Rizvi glowering. He would be thinking I was currying favor, but why not? If Catherine was happy, Sadruddin was happy, and it was all for the good.

We left the next day at seven in the morning for Vinh in a three-car convoy. It was my second visit and I could have done without it but it was part of the job. So was the bottle of Évian water that princess Catherine found on her night table in the very simple bungalow where we had been put up and where she seemed perfectly at ease. 'Sacha, it is again you, thank you,' she exclaimed, while I could feel Rizvi grumbling in my back as he muttered: 'How many bottles did you bring.'

By the time we were back in Hanoi two days later it was clear that Sadruddin had enjoyed every minute of the visit and even Rizvi conceded that it had been a success. As for me, after an early dinner at the *Thong Nhut* hotel of the usual *biftok* and *Krem Caramel*, I was looking forward to a quiet evening when Khoang suddenly appeared in the dining room and came up to me.

'Two people from the Foreign Ministry are here and want to see you right now,' he said, 'could you please come. They are outside.'

As I stepped out of the hotel I saw two men next to Sadruddin's car. 'Look,' they said. The source of their concern was clear for everyone to see. My cutting the UN flag down to size might have solved one problem but it had created another one. The flag had not been hemmed and after some sixteen hours on the road it had started to come apart and it now looked like an old mop with threads unraveling in all directions.

'We can't go on like this,' said one of the officials, to which I noddingly acquiesced. 'What shall we do,' he hesitated, 'you would not happen by chance to have a second...' the words were held in suspense.

'Actually, yes, I have a second flag,' I said, 'but... this time,' I did not have to specify, they nodded. I went up to my room, got the second flag and handed it over to them to their visible relief. The next day, for the first time ever, an un-truncated UN flag flew in the skies of North Vietnam.

Attitude is something the Vietnamese pay close attention to and from that perspective Sadruddin's visit to Vinh had been an unqualified success. He had visited farms, village communities as well as Ho Chi Minh's birthplace, had said the right things, listened carefully when called upon to do so and had asked the relevant questions. When he had first flown in to Hanoi he had been received with guarded courtesy. Upon his return from Vinh the atmosphere had changed and the Vietnamese had actually developed a liking for him.

The next two days were spent on meetings and soon an air of familiarity set in. Nguyen Co Thach, the vice foreign minister and one of the rising stars of the new generation of communist leaders, dropped by Sadruddin's residence for tea and stayed for two hours. Both knew Kissinger, Sadruddin on a personal basis and Thach as an adversary and Rizvi and I who happened to be present reveled in hearing the two exchange jokes on his many foibles. It was only towards the end of the meeting that Sadruddin raised what I knew was to him a subject of concern; repatriation to the South. The Americans, he reminded Thach, had assembled in a camp in Guam some 1,500 South Vietnamese who wanted to return to Vietnam. UNHCR had been asked by the PRG to assist with their repatriation and we had forwarded to Saigon the files of the returnees but the PRG had yet to respond. The Americans were now getting impatient and were blaming UNHCR for the delay. They had also readied a ship, the *Truong Tin*, which they intended to give to the returnees to sail home on their own with or without clearance.

'You will get the returnees whether you want them or not,' Sadruddin told Thach. Thach, who was well informed about the issue, did not agree.

'They will not dare,' he said.

'We'll see,' said Sadruddin with a big smile.

As I accompanied Thach to the door I mentioned to him that our assistance programs in Vietnam were expanding and that we needed some sort of formal presence in Hanoi. Could I submit to him a draft text of an agreement. He paused for a second and then said: 'Send me a proposal by tomorrow morning.'

Rizvi had followed the exchange and suddenly went into high gear. 'Well done,' he commented, 'let's get moving on a text.' A quarter of an hour later we were back at the *Thong Nhut* hotel battling with a manual typewriter. Rizvi could not type and I typed slowly, but one page was enough. It was agreed that UNHCR would open an office in Hanoi with the task of assisting the authorities in the rehabilitation of displaced persons and other humanitarian matters, a definition kept purposefully vague. Either party could terminate the agreement any time... it was important to reassure the Vietnamese that they would not be stuck with us forever. But there was one last point which could not be avoided. What would the status of the office be? Would it have diplomatic status? Was the staff subject to Vietnamese law? Could we import our office equipment duty free?

The issue could take months to clarify, especially as there was no precedent for a UN office in Hanoi, which was not even a UN member. But Rizvi knew his job and I dutifully typed, 'the privilege and immunities of the UNHCR delegation will be subject to a further exchange of letters'. The potential deadlock was circumvented and needless to say the further exchange never took place. First thing the next morning, with the draft in hand, Khoang was dispatched at full speed to the Foreign Ministry. He returned two hours later with a big grin. It is OK, he said, tomorrow morning at nine, Thach and Rizvi will sign the agreement.

The signing was if anything an anticlimax and, as Sadruddin and I looked on, took barely a few minutes but it was the first agreement between Hanoi and a UN agency. Following the signing Sadruddin paid a courtesy call to the PRG office in Hanoi. The head of the delegation was all smiles but was visibly out of the loop and a gracious Sadruddin diplomatically refrained from raising any substantive issues. Clearly the days of the PRG, even as a sham, were over but form still had to be respected.

That afternoon at five the authorities gave a farewell reception for Sadruddin. It was decided that we would all go together with Sadruddin in one car, and as Rizvi and I went to pick him up at his residence we passed a large sign in Vietnamese. Look, I told Rizvi, this is Ho Chi Minh's favorite slogan: there is nothing more precious than freedom and independence. Driving back along the same route with Sadruddin, as we passed the sign Rizvi pointed to it and said: 'Prince, this is Ho Chi Minh's favorite slogan: there is nothing more precious that freedom and independence.'

At the reception, apart from Thach and *Monsieur* Khoang we knew none of the two dozen present but they included a good number of high ranking army officers, impressive with their weather-beaten faces and sober uniforms. Thach's speech was short, straight and to the point. UNHCR had shown itself to be an effective organization and Vietnam looked forward to a strengthening of relations in the future. Sadruddin's speech was equally short and could have almost be passed off as perfunctory had he not ended it by adding, 'and over the years you have gained the respect of the world because you have never wavered from your conviction that there is nothing more precious than freedom and independence'. The applause that followed his words was genuine. As for me, I considered it a privilege to be associated with someone like Rizvi to whom you could throw an idea, confident that he would pick it up and bounce it on to Sadruddin who would know how to put it to good use.

The end of the mission coincided with my last bottle of Évian and we were fortunate enough the next day to catch the connection from Vientiane to Bangkok, and from there onwards to Geneva.

Being back in Geneva was a welcome break after a chaotic summer but it left unresolved what I was supposed to do within UNHCR. On paper I was still Special Envoy to the Republic of South Vietnam. In practical terms this made me special envoy to a fading mirage.

This consideration notwithstanding, Rizvi still liked to believe that UNHCR would open an office in Saigon and that I should be kept available for that position which meant that, pending my future hypothetical assignment, I was in limbo, albeit a comfortable one. But having spent the previous three months on a fourteen hour a day schedule seven days a week I did not have the feeling that I was short-changing the organization. So I decided to bide my time, show up at the office for one hour a day at the best and just wait.

On October 17 I was called in by Rizvi to go with him to see Sadruddin and we found him chuckling. The day before, the Americans had announced that 1,546 Vietnamese had left Guam on the *SS Thuong Tin* headed for Vietnam. None had been cleared for return but the US having provided them with a ship to sail home they had decided to take things into their own hands. It was exactly what Sadruddin had predicted to Thach and what the Vice Foreign Minister had claimed the Americans would never dare to do. Eight days later the ship arrived at Cam Ranh Bay and both Hanoi and the PRG went ballistic: violation of Vietnamese sovereignty, unilateral act, provocation were the mildest terms used. But words notwithstanding, faced with a '*fait accompli*', the communists had no option but to permit the returnees to land thus turning a potential propaganda victory had they cleared the returnees—refugees returning to a communist country was a rare event—into a major loss of face with one caveat. Maybe Vietnam's communist leaders, having won the war, no longer needed propaganda victories. As for the returnees, they all ended up in detention under the suspicion of having been sent back by the CIA to create problems for the new regime. For once the winners were the Americans who had gotten rid of the troublemakers and, in passing, Sadruddin who had proven correct in his assessment. Even Rizvi, who was at heart anti-American, felt the Vietnamese authorities had gotten what they deserved. Ultimately, the real losers turned out to be the returnees and many years later several were identified among the boat people who were fleeing Vietnam in droves.

The *Thuong Tin* interlude notwithstanding I still had nothing to do when one morning as I was having a late breakfast at home I suddenly got a call from Rizvi; he wanted me to go back to Hanoi at the earliest. Sadruddin would be returning to Vietnam but this time more specifically to Saigon and I was to be there to receive him and make sure that everything was under control.

Sadruddin's previous visit to Hanoi had basically been a courtesy call and no substantive issues had actually been discussed. It was not that there was a shortage of such issues but they mostly concerned the South and with the fiction still in force that Hanoi was not responsible for the South and that the Provisional Revolutionary Government was an independent and sovereign entity, Sadruddin now had to go through the motions of going to Saigon to discuss what could have been more profitably raised in Hanoi where decisions where actually made.

For Sadruddin these were not just technical problems. By accepting the request of the PRG both to assist with repatriation and to help with the evacuation of foreigners stuck in Saigon, Sadruddin had put the credibility of UNHCR on the line. We had wiggled out of our comatose airlift and he had succeeded in washing his hands of the *Thuong Tin* affair but there were still, in Thailand, Malaysia and Indonesia small groups of Vietnamese who were clamoring to return home. With repatriation ostensibly the responsibility of UNHCR, the organization was expected to deliver and it was now the Asian governments, who wanted to get rid of their Vietnamese at the earliest, who were holding us responsable for the delay in returns.

For the Vietnamese communists Sadruddin's visit to Saigon was not without its ambiguities. On one hand they had requested UNHCR to open an office in Saigon, assist with the evacuation of foreigners stranded in the city and promote the repatriation of Vietnamese from abroad who wanted to return home. But on the other hand, having visibly opted for a rapid reunification, they did not want to consolidate the international image of the PRG which meant that UNHCR would never be allowed to open an office in Saigon. Likewise, repatriation appeared now to be indefinitely on hold and as for the evacuation of foreigners stranded in the city this was being achieved through the resumption of the Air France flights and, of all people, by the International Red Cross.

During the French colonial era, in addition to the French, various other groups had drifted towards Vietnam and after Saigon fell the new authorities were suddenly confronted by a total of some 6,000 Indians, Pakistani and Yemenis whom they perceived as a leftover of colonial imposition and decided to get rid of them.

The Vietnamese communists could have justified their expulsion on ideological grounds claiming that there would be no room for these people in a socialist regime that made no allowance for private enterprise. But they did not bother. This was ethnic cleansing, albeit without the violence, and they had to go simply because they were not Vietnamese. The only problem was how to organize their departure.

In the weeks prior to the fall of Saigon, Hocke had decided that the ICRC delegation in the city would stay put. It was a gamble and initially it did not pay off. The communists made it quite clear to the ICRC representative in Saigon that they had no use for him and it was only a question of time before he would be sent packing. But they did not count on Hocke's sharp wits. Not one to miss an opportunity, or to create one if none was at hand, Hocke prevailed on the Indian and Pakistani governments to officially request the ICRC to repatriate their citizens from Saigon. The communists resented the ICRC but they were not the sort of people to miss a good opportunity. Here they had on the spot an organization whose presence carried no diplomatic implications and which could turn out to be useful. So, overnight the ICRC found itself a new role: repatriating not only the Indians and Pakistanis from Saigon but also the Yemenis.

Rizvi was not unaware of these developments especially as in November the government of Yemen has sent a request to UNHCR asking the organization to repatriate some 500 of its citizens from Saigon. With now two cooks on the scene, one of whom was actually in the kitchen and the other not, Rizvi wisely decided to forward the Yemeni request to the PRG office in Hanoi and leave it at that.

With repatriation to Vietnam stalled and evacuation in the hands of the ICRC, Sadruddin's coming mission to Saigon, notwithstanding the personal esteem in which he was held, was not a guaranteed success. That it not turn into a failure was, at least in part, up to me to ensure.

I arrived in Hanoi on Saturday, December 6, and proceeded to Saigon on the following Monday. Sadruddin and Rizvi were expected on Wednesday, which gave me one free day for whatever would need to be done in preparation for the visit. Mineral water for Princess Catherine was this time not a must; there was plenty of it left in Saigon.

On Tuesday morning I was picked up at my hotel by a Vietnamese official who, in impeccable French, explained to me as we drove to the offices of the Red Cross that there were a few issues that the authorities wished to discuss with me. 'It will be a short and informal meeting,' he added. By now I knew enough about the Vietnamese to understand the real meaning of the term informal: it actually meant that this was going to be a serious, substantive meeting and I'd better be on my guard. The two gentlemen who received me, who also both spoke French, went straight to the point. There were in Saigon, they said, some 2,000 Taiwanese and 700 Yemenis whom they wanted to get rid of. When could UNHCR start with their repatriation?

Suddenly I was in a major fix. In the absence of Rizvi I was certainly not going to commit UNHCR to anything but I also had to give them a credible answer. So it was a question of finessing it while making it clear to them that we were not fools either.

'We are among friends,' I told them, 'and we will study your request carefully.' (Study in Vietnamese jargon meant that we would look at a proposal, maybe say yes, or maybe never answer.) 'But I understand that the ICRC is currently repatriating the Indians and Pakistanis so the logical thing would be to give them also the Yemenis and the Taiwanese. In addition,' I added, 'we are a serious organization and when we undertake a mission we want to do it well but to do this job one must be present in Saigon and they are and we are not.'

Translated in plain English, I had told them that since they had decided not to let us open an office in Saigon they could not expect us to do the job, and if they had chosen to deal with ICRC that was fine but they should stick with it. I could see that they were not expecting the answer I had given them but a line had to be drawn somewhere. I then continued, 'I will refer the question of Yemenis to my Headquarters'—which in plain English meant no, we will not deal with them—'but concerning the Taiwanese, as you are aware, this is a very complex issue, there are many implications which you are well aware of and I think that a private organization like the ICRC is best equipped to handle such a problem.'

With the UN having recognized the government in Beijing as the only legal representative of China, there was no way UNHCR, as a UN organization could have even come close to touching the Taiwanese, and on that issue I had given the Vietnamese a straight No. As for our repatriating the Yemenites, I had given them an indirect no and was confident that this is what Rizvi would have wanted me to do.

After lunch I had a free afternoon and wandered around downtown Saigon. The sleepy, gracious city I had known in 1956 had become, years later, a frenzied urban sprawl, fuelled by easy money and shady deals. Now, it was the dying capital of a dead regime. Most shops were closed and when open everything was on sale. Hundreds of food stalls had been set up on the sidewalks, mostly consisting of a few chairs and tables where groups of youngsters with long hair, bell bottomed trousers and tapered shirts would congregate sipping lemonade or drinking weak Saigon beer. Occasionally a group of North Vietnamese soldiers would walk by, generally unarmed, in their baggy green uniforms and rubber sandals. They were all of the same age but their eyes never made contact as if they belonged to two different worlds, on one side the winners, on the other the losers.

The change of regime meant another change of names for Saigon's streets. There was now a Dien Bien Phu street and an April 30 street. To Do street, meaning 'freedom', had become Dong Khoi, 'General Uprising' street, dear to communist mythology. That Saigon had never known either freedom or a general uprising was beside the point. The two French doctors who had done so much for Vietnam, Yersin and Calmette, retained their original streets but, for some unknown reason, Pasteur lost his. Actually, he was to regain it some years later again for reasons no one could fathom. Alexandre de Rhodes, the Jesuit missionary who in the fifteenth century created a new Vietnamese writing system still in use today based on the Latin alphabet and who was instrumental in enabling Vietnam to break away from the fetters of Chinese ideograms, proved a difficult case. As a foreigner, a missionary and a Roman Catholic he was anathema to Vietnam's Marxist ideologues. Conversely, there were few men who had done as much to consolidate Vietnamese culture and render its writing accessible to the masses. The debate within the Party hierarchy must have been intense and short of a consensus a compromise was reached. The plate was not removed from the street that carried his name but on the city's official maps the street appeared as carrying no name.

Sadruddin, with Princess Catherine and Rizvi, arrived on schedule on Wednesday at eleven and I went to the airport to meet them. There were two black Oldsmobiles waiting on the tarmac, one for him and his wife and one for Rizvi and me and without even stopping at the terminal building, we headed straight for downtown. This time there was no UN flag flying from the fender of Sadruddin's car. I had gotten fed up with the theatrics and Rizvi had concurred.

After a superb lunch served in the large dining room of the opulent villa where we were all lodged—the former residence of the British ambassador as we were later to discover—we started to do the rounds that had been planned for us.

Our first meeting with Hoang Bich Son, the Vice Foreign Minister of the PRG, was formal and consisted of a stilted exchange of platitudes. Son belonged to the new Soviet-trained generation of communist leaders: he spoke no western languages, his comportment was wanting and he lacked the culture and easy-going manners of his French-educated predecessors. Ultimately of course, in terms of substance, it made no difference. They followed the same policy line, were all equally sly, devious and conniving except that some did it with more *'savoir vivre'* than others.

Saturday proved intellectually more rewarding. At nine in the morning a meeting had been arranged in one of the many reception rooms of the residence. We had expected two or three Vietnamese officials to come but a dozen showed up, all French-speakers and for two hours they gave us a presentation on how they planned to solve the key problem of the South: population displacement. According to their plans some eight million people would have to return to the countryside to what they termed 'New Economic Zones'. These were either areas that had never been cultivated or former farmland abandoned during the war. To accommodate the newcomers the areas would first be identified and then demined. Then roads would be built, wells dug and basic shelter erected. The first settlers would be provided with food rations, farm tools, fertilizer and seed. Each farmer would receive a private plot of some 2,000 square feet while the rest of the land would be collectively owned and cultivated. In parallel, schools and health facilities would be set up as well as permanent housing. Little by little new villages would emerge which would become self-sufficient at best in six months' time and, step-by-step, re-establish a normal population balance between cities and the countryside. The whole project should be completed in some three to five years upon which the countryside would produce an excess of rice that would enable Vietnam to achieve self-sufficiency in food.

As the description of the project unfolded we realized that this was the regime's master plan for South Vietnam. On paper it made sense. Whether the regime had the administrative and material means to implement it properly was a question that we could not answer, but given the clarity of its formulation a cautious optimism was not unreasonable.

Sadruddin seemed attracted by the idea as the rehabilitation of displaced persons was a problem he was sensitive to and he reacted with a practical proposal. UNHCR, he said, would be willing to be the focal point of a 100 million US $ UN rehabilitation program for South Vietnam. Such a program, based on one comprehensive appeal to donors, would involve all the various agencies of the UN system in a co-coordinated fashion and enable the Vietnamese to deal with one UN focal point rather than with a large number of individual agencies. While Sadruddin was making his point I could see his interlocutors nodding but that was the last we heard of his proposal.

The Vietnamese communists had just emerged from a 30 year-long war which they had won to a large extent by fuelling confusion among their enemies. Secrecy, duplicity and mistrust had been their daily fare and though they were now at peace old ways endured. Confusion was the environment they were the most comfortable with and promoting confusion was still an instinctive reflex.

It was therefore in their psychological make-up to believe that they would get a better deal by playing the various UN agencies one against the other rather than dealing with one focal point. That the UN agencies compared their programs and that donor governments knew exactly how much they were contributing to each UN agency and for what projects never occurred to them and using the international system to their advantage was something they had not yet learned to do. Sadruddin had been ahead of his time and he never received a reply to his offer.

After the meeting Sadruddin went back to his rooms and as the other participants took their leave, two men from the Red Cross indicated almost conspiratorially that they would like to have a word with Rizvi and me. We moved to a smaller room and after settling down in comfortable sofas they voiced the subject of their concern: the joint communique.

It was a common practice, particularly in communist countries, that after a high level state visit the two parties would issue a joint communique. Granted this was an issue that the Vietnamse had not raised when Sadruddin had gone to Hanoi but then it had never been quite clear if his visit had been as High Commissioner for Refugees, as Sadruddin Aga Khan or both. A joint communiqué was mostly a matter of protocol with both parties expounding on their good relations, real or imagined but when substantive issues were at stake it would also give an indication of what results, if any, had been achieved. The Vietnamese seemed to be keen on having such a joint communique and suggested that we start working on an informal draft. Rizvi must have discussed the matter with Sadruddin beforehand and went straight to the point. The High Commissioner, he said, was under considerable pressure from many governments to implement some voluntary repatriation to Vietnam and could not afford to come back empty handed. 'That is no problem,' they replied, 'we will say that the Vietnamese side is totally committed to the principal of voluntary repatriation and is undertaking all efforts to ensure its implementation at the earliest.' 'No,' said Rizvi, 'the earliest is not good enough. We need a date; a firm date by which even one Vietnamese, only one, it can be a woman or an old man, will be approved for return.' Silence followed. 'We could say as soon as possible,' they suggested. 'No,' said Rizvi, 'we need a date, a firm date.' More silence. 'This,' said one of our interlocutors in a slow voice, 'we cannot do.' 'Fine,' said Rizvi, 'we are friends, we remain friends but you will have to understand that, under the circumstances it is best that we agree that there will be no joint communique.'

It was an elegant way out. The system had decided that there would be no UNHCR office in Saigon and no repatriation and that was that. But if this was really the case why did the PRG request Rizvi, in June 1975, to open a UNHCR office in Saigon and to assist with repatriation? The answer was ultimately deceptively simple. Because at the time the Politburo was still operating on the principle, as espoused throughout the war, that reunification would be gradual and that the semblance of a PRG would be kept alive in the South. By July, however the situation had changed and faced with an unmanageable South the Politbureau had opted for accelerated reunification. Had Rizvi asked to go to Saigon three weeks later than he did, after the Politburo had opted for accelerated reunification, not only would he not have received a request for assistance by the PRG but he most probably would not even have received a visa. Ultimately, his bad luck was to have moved too fast. Granted, the communists could subsequently have given us some indication to the effect that our airlift was no longer required, that repatriation was a non-starter and that we would never open an office in Saigon and they actually did, but in their own way by procrastinating. Our only problem was that it took so long for Rizvi to see the light. Later in the day Sadruddin met with PRG President Huynh Tan Phat and his message, in impeccable French was unambiguous: with security concerns still the number one priority, the practical implementation of voluntary repatriation was simply not in the cards.

The dinner that evening, hosted by the Vietnamese in one of the private rooms of the former Caravelle hotel, was a congenial gathering. Thu, the President of the PRG Red Cross and now a member of the Military Committee which managed Saigon and whom Sadrudding had received at his home in Geneva, was there in the best of moods and so was Sadruddin. At the end of the meal a Vietnamese lady seated next to me, who had introduced herself as from the Red Cross,—I marveled at how many Vietnamese were working for the Red Cross—turned to me and said in French in a low voice: 'The High Commission has been firm and we respect this.' Short of a commitment to repatriation it was the best compliment Sadruddin could have received.

Hanoi, where we landed the next day, Sunday, was cold and overcast and a light rain was falling. Sadruddin was due to leave the next day for Vientiane and further on to Bangkok when word came that the Royal Air Laos Monday flight had been cancelled and no one knew when the next flight was scheduled. The prospect of getting stuck in Hanoi had no appeal for Sadruddin and even less for Princess Catherine.

'Sacha,' she said, 'get us out of here.' It was not an easy proposition. With most of Royal Air Laos' DC3s grounded as pilot after pilot fled to Thailand our only hope was the Caravelle but the problem was Gia Lam airport. It had been built before the age of the jet and the runway was perpendicular to one of the Red River dykes which required that incoming aircraft come in at a steep angle before leveling over the runway, a maneuver easier done by a propeller driven aircraft than by a jet. A flurry of cables with our office in Vientiane followed until Captain Simard finally agreed to try to come in, although he could not promise to actually land. Rizvi, I could see, was not pleased. 'The aircraft will never make it,' he said, 'and anyhow it is good for Sadruddin to wait and suffer a bit. You are just trying to curry favor,' he looked at me reproachfully.

The next morning on Tuesday at ten we were all at the airport when the Caravelle broke through the cloud cover, circled the airport and then came in. The moment it touched the runway there was a loud crack as Simard deployed his braking parachute and the aircraft taxied to the terminal.

'Sacha, you have saved us,' exclaimed Princess Catherine. The Vietnamese officials with us were just as impressed. It was the first time ever that the Caravelle had landed at Gia Lam, and the first time they had seen the deployment of a breaking parachute.

I had expected to leave with Sadruddin but Rizvi told me that the two of us had to stay behind. Rizvi was generally tight lipped about Sadruddin's private affairs but as we drove back to Hanoi and the ubiquitous *Thong Nhut* hotel I asked him who would pay for the charter of the Caravelle. 'Oh,' he answered with feigned indifference, 'Sadruddin pays from his own pocket and he also donates his salary to UNHCR.' He then proceeded to explain to me why we had to stay in Hanoi. A few weeks before, Sadruddin had been contacted by the Vietnamese. They had invited representative Sonny Montgomery, a longstanding member of the US House of Representatives Armed Forces Committee to come to Hanoi to receive the bodies of three American MIAs, and they wanted UNHCR to be the go-between. 'He will be coming from the US to Bangkok,' explained Rizvi, 'go there immediately and arrange a flight to Hanoi.'

One week later a car provided by the local UNHCR office drove me to the far end of the Bangkok airport terminal where the Royal Air Laos Caravelle, was parked. The rear ramp had been lowered and a number of Americans in uniform were cautiously easing three military coffins into the aircraft cabin. The coffins were huge, some seven feet long and almost three feet wide made of polished wood with brass carrying handles and had to be placed on their side to fit in the aisle between the two rows of seats. Montgomery then arrived with three aides in a car provided by the US embassy and we were off. Our first stop in Vientiane was perfunctory. The aircraft had not requested clearance for a direct flight from Bangkok to Hanoi and we had barely touched ground in Vientiane when we were off again for Hanoi. Simard was at the controls and ventured that he was glad he had already landed once in Hanoi as he was now sure he could bring the aircraft safely down.

The sky had cleared before we touched ground in Gia Lam and this time Simard did not have to use his breaking parachute. As the aircraft came to a stop next to the terminal Montgomery and one aide stepped down while the other two remained in the aircraft out of sight. There were about a dozen Vietnamese officials as well as Rizvi waiting for us as we were led to a larger room at the far end of the terminal building where a long table with a green velvet tablecloth had been set up. On the table were three brown, wooden boxes some three feet long and about 18 inches high and wide, the sizes of the standard French military coffins used to transport the remains of soldiers who had been buried and the bones subsequently recovered. A Vietnamese official took his seat at one end of the table, motioned to Rizvi to take his place at his right and to Montgomery at his left. Papers were produced and signed. Hands were shaken. Montgomery, Rizvi and their escorts then left the room and headed for the main entry of the terminal where cars were waiting to take them to Hanoi while I returned to the Caravelle followed by three Vietnamese airport staff, each of whom nonchalantly carried under his arm one of the boxes which he delivered to the aircraft's door.

Soon we were heading for Bangkok. Throughout the flight there was considerable rummaging in the back of the aircraft where the Americans, who had stayed out of sight during our stopover in Hanoi had, obviously found something to do for themselves. I did not care to find out what and made myself comfortable in one of the seats next to the front of the aircraft.

As we approached Bangkok Simard had one of the crew call me to the cockpit. 'We have a problem with the control tower,' he was smiling, 'I told them we are coming from Hanoi and they will not let us land. I suppose it has taken them by surprise,' he added. It must have indeed. For the past 21 years no aircraft had flown from Hanoi to Bangkok direct.

Finally after 20 minutes we got permission to land and were then instructed to taxi to the military Terminal of Bangkok's Don Muong airport. As he cut the engines, Simard turned to me from the pilot seat. We have one small problem, he said, I can't open the rear ramp, it's probably jammed but it doesn't matter, we will exit from the front door. But it did matter.

As I stepped off the aircraft I found myself in the middle of an American military pageant. There was a band, a guard of honor in full uniform, officers were standing at attention, and flags were flying. As the band started playing, six soldiers in full uniform wearing white gloves stepped up the gangway and disappeared into the aircraft. Minutes passed, there was a slight shuffling near the front door of the aircraft and I suddenly realized what had happened. During the flight the Americans on board had opened the ceremonial coffins and put the small wooden boxes holding the remains of the MIAs inside. The guard of honor was now expected to carry the coffins down the rear ramp of the aircraft but the ramp had jammed. The only way to get the coffins out of the aircraft was now through the front door but to do so the coffins had to be stood up on end and rotated through the galley. As they did, the first coffin got stuck between the door and the galley and had to be manhandled back into the aircraft to be pried loose. The spectacle was too much for me. Fortunately there was a small shack some 100 feet away and in its shadow I broke out in to the most uncontrolled fit of laughter that has ever overcome me as the band played on in the distance.

The next day I was back in Geneva, just in time for Christmas and as I looked back on the past months it occurred to me that it had been an interesting year. Granted, in the process I had not come across a single refugee, but who was there to care?

REPRESENTATIVE IN HANOI

B By January 1976 Rizvi finally acknowledged reluctantly that even he now had some doubts as to whether UNHCR would ever open an office in Saigon. Intellectually he could accept that circumstances had changed but he still had a problem reconciling his gargantuan ego with the fact that, just once, something he had set his mind on had not materialized as expected.

Personally I never had any problem dealing with his ego and I actually welcomed it. It was a flaw in his armor, and, like all flaws, if properly massaged it made him vulnerable to manipulation. The only problem I had with him was his attitude towards the UN. He actually perceived the organization as some sort of mythical organism entrusted with a hallowed mission of peace by an indefinable entity called the community of nations. It was a quasi-religious approach and however much he despised the priests who officiated in this cult, namely your average UN bureaucrat, his faith in this God remained unchanged. And though he was well attuned to the realities of politics he still believed that the sum total of the governments that made up the UN represented some sort of an ideal, albeit one that I believed he would have had problems defining. But an ideal it was and I knew better than to challenge him on the issue. As for me, I found my satisfaction in my personal relation with Rizvi and Sadruddin and the fact that, through UNHCR, I had had the opportunity of getting involved in a set of events which otherwise would have been quite beyond my reach. In this confused but entertaining hodgepodge I had set out, more by nature than design, to do my best in all circumstances while possibly retaining a basic sense of humor, without falling prey to vanity or losing my perspective.

Though still reluctant to concede that our office in Saigon had been a mirage Rizvi made me a new proposal. If by May we had not opened an office in Saigon, would I accept the job of representative in Hanoi? It would be a far less comfortable post than Saigon, still awash in the leftovers of a consumer society, but at least it would enable me to observe first hand how Vietnam's communists operated and it was an opportunity not to be missed; I accepted on the spot, to his visible relief.

Rizvi wanted the Hanoi UNHCR office to be a success and I alone could certainly not do the job. 'Don't worry,' he said, 'I will get you some good people.'

There was no substitute for a good administrative secretary, someone who could manage the office, supervise the accounts, find her way through the labyrinth of UN administrative rules and, above all, keep her cool in all circumstances, and Joan Edwards was that type of woman. In her mid-thirties, with light blonde hair, blue eyes and a severe, uncompromising expression which would give way to a cheery smile when she so chose, she was the stuff the British Empire had been built on; unflappable and uncompromising whatever the heat, the humidity or the circumstances.

As my deputy, Rizvi chose Joan's opposite. Pierre Jambor was Italian, looked the part and acted it to the hilt. He was bright, handsome, quick, witty, articulate, moody, hard-working, and unpredictable and could deal with anything that came his way in addition to being, above and beyond the call of duty, an inveterate flirt.

To assist Pierre with programming, Rizvi had chosen a young aristocrat whose French Huguenot ancestors had sought refuge in Prussia in the seventeenth century, He was a tall, quiet, pleasant young man of impeccable manners and considerable culture and it took a discerning eye to perceive that he was gay. It bothered no one except Pierre who was a monument to every single macho Italian prejudice but this was more than made up for by Joan, who took him under her wing.

By April, the team was ready to move in, a motley assembly of an atypical Swiss, a sex-crazed Italian, a young English woman of Victorian deportment and a well mannered gay German aristocrat.

I had originally been hired by UNHCR as Geneva-based and my moving to Hanoi had major salary implications. Base salaries throughout the UN system were uniform, according to grade, but they were only part of the remuneration package. The other part was the so-called post adjustment, an additional monthly sum calculated on the basis of the cost of living in the place of assignment. Post adjustment took into account rent, food costs, entertainment, utilities and the like. In high-cost locations such as Geneva, Tokyo, London or Paris it was considerable and could almost double the base salary. Conversely, in most third world locations, it was almost non-existent, and for good reason. Rents were minimal, food in the market was cheap and utilities, when they existed were cut-rate. That the water was not drinkable, the housing sub-standard and entertainment non-existent was not factored in. For the UN a steak was a steak, whether from corn-feed cattle on sale in a New York supermarket or from a mangy buffalo gently rotting on a Vientiane food stall. The only consolation for being assigned to what was warily classified as a hardship post was that home leave was granted every year instead of every two years, a small relief for a massive cut in salary.

Living expenses in Vietnam had not yet been the object of a UN assessment and consequently Hanoi did not have a post adjustment. So for want of a better solution UN staff members assigned to Hanoi were given a fictitious posting in Bangkok from where they would be on so-called mission status to Hanoi and for which they would receive a daily subsistence allowance (DSA) of 40 US $. The solution might have been good for the UN but for the staff it was a kick in the teeth. Bangkok had one of the world's lowest post adjustments and this meant a major pay cut barely supplemented by Hanoi's 40 US $ per day. While on paper at the official exchange rate, this was adequate to pay for our meals and hotel room it made no allowance for any necessities one wished or rather had to import.

The personnel service at UNHCR was well aware that these rules were made for a Headquarters-bound bureaucracy comfortably ensconced in its New York offices and not for a field oriented organization but there was nothing they could do about it. The end result was that the combination of a low post adjustment in Bangkok and an unrealistic DSA in Hanoi made an assignment to Vietnam something most UNHCR staff members would have sought to avoid at all costs.

I left Geneva on May 26, 1976, impoverished but excited about what lay ahead for me.

After an overnight stop in Bangkok I arrived in Vientiane from where I was to proceed to Hanoi.

Laos was now no longer a kingdom but a republic under communist rule and not only the regime had changed. For one, Royal Air Laos no longer existed. It had been replaced by a new company called Lao Aviation except that there was no Aviation. All the pilots of the defunct Royal Air Laos had fled to Thailand in the hope of being resettled in France or in the US and as for the Caravelle, it had gone the way of Franco-Lao relations. Since 1954 the French had a military mission in Vientiane. It served no practical purpose but in keeping with French tradition it had a well-stocked commissionary replete with fine wines, the best cognacs and the likes of goose liver pate.

For unknown reasons one of the first moves by the communists when they took over Vientiane was to impound the French commissionary. Confronted with this gastronomical tragedy and wary of things to come, the French took urgent action. The following morning the Caravelle took off for its daily flight to Bangkok but this time with its full crew and three of the prettiest Lao flight attendants. No sooner had the aircraft landed that a swarm of painters descended on the jet. The Royal Air Laos logo was painted over and replaced by Air France and a new French matriculation code was stenciled on the fuselage. It was the last the Lao saw of the Caravelle.

This meant that the Bangkok to Vientiane route was now exclusively served by Thai Airways and it was up to the Vietnamese to ensure some air service from Vientiane to Hanoi. While they were short of civilian aircraft they succeeded in scavenging an old Soviet twin engine, high-wing 50-seat Antonov 24 that flew the route twice a week. The Antonov was a slow, relatively safe aircraft with one quirk. When the engines were turned on and what stood for the air conditioning was engaged the cabin would suddenly be engulfed in a swirl of water vapor which often was so thick that one could barely see the passenger next to whom one was seated. It was therefore literarily in a cloud that, at the age of 40, I arrived in Hanoi on Saturday May 29, 1976 to take over my new duties.

The major change to the UNHCR office since my last visit was that we now had two cars, a Toyota sedan and a Volkswagen Westphalia camping bus. The Toyota was the standard UNHCR office car but the Volkswagen was pure Rizvi. In his mind we would be regularly going on field trips to our project sites and would need a vehicle in which we could sleep and cook, so he had chosen a model which included a wash basin, gas stove and fridge, plus a large folding bed. It did not occur to Rizvi that in North Vietnam practically every village had some sort of facilities, often only a simple bamboo hut but a hut nonetheless, for visiting party officials and none of us ever needed to sleep in the van. As for the gas stove and refrigerator, these were powered by liquid gas, a commodity unknown in North Vietnam. The one piece of equipment that would have been of use was air conditioning, but Rizvi did not believe in air conditioning and we made up for it by driving the van with the sliding side door open.

With our cars came a driver provided by the Foreign Ministry. In his mid thirties he had served for some ten years in the North Vietnamese army as a sergeant. He was probably the biggest wheeler-dealer in town and knew all the tricks: where to find contraband goods and how to change dollars on the black market. Shortly after the fall of Saigon, through army friends of his, he had managed to import a small generator from the South and was making a fortune renting it out by the hour to people in Hanoi who were giving parties and did not want to have their good time interrupted by the constant power cuts. In no time Pierre and he were as thick as thieves and they would disappear at lunchtime into the back alleys of Hanoi where they would savor a bowl of homemade noodle soup in some unregistered family run eatery that endured in spite of all the dictums of a collectivized economy.

I had taken over the room which had originally been allocated to UNHCR on the third floor of the *Thong Nhut* hotel, and it was as good as they came except for needing a new coat of paint. So I called Khoang and the hotel painters were summoned. There were five of them and after having looked at the room with concerned expressions they ventured that painting the walls off-white would cost the equivalent of 10 US $ and take four days. 'That is perfect,' I told them, as Khoang translated. 'But you are all outstanding revolutionary workers and I am sure you can do the job faster and also impeccably well. So as a contribution to your efforts I will give each one of you 10 US $ if you can do the job in one day.' At seven sharp next morning they were in my room and by five in the afternoon the job was finished to perfection. 'Your method is not very socialist,' commented Khoang, 'but I can't say it is not effective.'

Office space was my next concern. As more and more governments recognized Vietnam, Hanoi saw an influx of western diplomats, all of whom were housed in the *Thong Nhut* while they looked for residences. The Germans, Swiss, Belgians, Finns, Australians and Pakistanis were among the new guests and while rooms were still available they were no longer in unlimited supply. Compounding the problem was the fact that the *Thong Nhut* was government property although no one seemed to know which government service was actually the owner. As state employees the hotel staff were on a fixed salary which they received whatever the number of guests; as a result of which their main occupation was to ensure that the hotel stay as empty as possible. Thus any improbable foreigner—Vietnamese were not allowed in the hotel—who stepped up to the front desk asking for a room would get the inevitable answer: do you have a reservation and if he did not the answer would be no room even if plenty were available. But who could make a reservation? The answer was unclear. According to one rumor the State Tourist Office had been allocated a number of rooms but as there were no tourists the rooms stayed empty. The Foreign Ministry, we knew, had also been allocated a number of rooms but these were now in short supply and all their efforts to have some of the empty rooms held by the Tourist Office reallocated to them had come to naught. With the Foreign Ministry and the Tourist office now locked in mortal combat I was caught in the middle. For an office we had been given one room but fitting in the four of us plus two Vietnamese assistants was physically impossible and I had to find a better solution. Our office did have a communicating door with the room next door which was empty but our pleading with the hotel's director to give us an additional room had been met with a stony silence. At my request Khoang contacted *Monsieur* Bai from the Red Cross but he said there was nothing he could do and the Foreign Ministry gave us a similar answer.

I felt we had exhausted every avenue when Khoang had an idea. A new Vice Foreign Minister had just been nominated, a Mr Phan Hien who he knew well and who could perhaps help. I found Phan Hien a delightful man who spoke perfect French and gave the impression that he did not quite know why he had been made Vice Foreign Minister. But he listened with sympathy to my sad tale and promised to look into it. Two days later Khoang triumphantly produced a paper on Foreign Ministry heading. By order of the Vice Foreign Minister the hotel director was instructed to provide us with one more room. 'He is furious but he can't refuse' laughed Khoang.

My next job was to get the office actually functioning. In terms of communications with our Headquarters there was nothing we could do to improve the system. There was no telex connection, the fax had not yet been invented, so we had to rely on telegrams at the exorbitant price of 0.40 US $ a word. On paper the telephone did work but took about two days to get a connection via Moscow to Geneva and when it did get through the line was so bad as to make conversation almost inaudible. This kept communications to a minimum, which was actually a blessing.

Once a week we were supposed to receive the pouch from Geneva, a large sealed heavy canvas bag marked UN and containing all documents, memos etc that were too long to be sent by telegram or were of a less urgent nature. The pouch left Geneva by airfreight for Bangkok where it was supposed to be put on the flight to Vientiane and from there transferred to the flight to Hanoi. On paper the journey took three days. In practice it took at least ten days with the pouch regularily missing the connecting flight either in Bangkok or in Vientiane or, more often, in both. There was no delivery service at Hanoi airport and whenever the pouch was due one of us would drive to the airport, wait for the flight from Vientiane to land, walk up to the aircraft and grab the pouch provided it was there as it was unloaded from the hold with the rest of the luggage. Currently we had received no pouch for three weeks and I promised myself to look into the matter. More urgently however, I needed to furnish our office.

Before I left Geneva, Rizvi had reluctant conceded that I could not run a UNHCR office without a minimum of equipment. Normally this would have been far below his level of concern but he had taken a proprietary interest in the Hanoi office and wanted to know exactly what I was planning to purchase. For some unfathomable reason he was opposed to air conditioning but finally relented when I explained to him that in the prevailing humidity paper clips rusted in six weeks and our electrical equipment would follow the same route. But my crowning achievement was to persuade him that a photocopier was not a luxury.

Having squeezed out of Rizvi the approval for the office equipment I then went to personnel service for instructions on how I should actually proceed with the procurement. While they did not have the ideological hang-ups of Rizvi they had other obstructions to contend with, namely UN rules which made no allowance for any support for staff in the sticks. But they were understanding and agreed to provide each staff member in Hanoi very exceptionally, they insisted, with the use of one refrigerator and an air conditioner, provided it came under the heading of office equipment. To that end I was now authorized to go to Hong Kong for four days to procure the basics to run our office in Hanoi. One thing is essential, I was told as I was handed a thick manual, you must follow UN procurement rules.

One look at the manual convinced me that to get things done, the one thing I should definitely not follow were UN procurement rules. This was confirmed to me by one of the gnomes in the UNHCR administration who, very much off the record, suggested that the only rule I should follow was to get three quotes for every item I was planning to buy and provide some explanation however zany if I were to choose anything other than the cheapest item. 'Just claim it was cost effective,' he added, 'and you will get away with a lot.'

Armed with this vital piece of knowledge I proceeded to Hong Kong.

In the early 1930's Air France had a weekly flight from Hanoi to Hong Kong with a total travel time of five hours. Thirty years later technology had improved but politics had not. In 1976, the only connections out of Hanoi for Hong Kong consisted of the bi-weekly Chinese flight to Nanning with a connection to Canton for an overnight stay followed by a four-hour train ride to Hong Kong: a total travel time of 26 hours if all went well.

Ho Chi Minh's testament had included an injunction to the Vietnamese people to the effect that 'there is nothing more precious than freedom and independence'. According to a joke making the rounds in Vietnam, the first part of Ho Chi Minh's last will had been implemented: 'There is nothing.'

My shopping list was a fair reflection of this reality, or more prosaically, of what it cost Vietnam to win the war. For the office, my list included four desks, seven air conditioners, four refrigerators, fifteen electrical equalizers, two dehumidifiers, one electric typewriter and a manual one, one photocopying machine, two electric heaters, a complete tool kit, a large assortment of electric light bulbs, wire, nails, hooks, screws, tape, glue, string and extra Freon gas and all the stationary I could think of. For myself it included a hot plate, pots and pans, 40 pounds of spaghetti, canned tomatoes, olive oil, a bed with a foam mattress, blankets and pillows, instant coffee, powdered condensed milk, salt, sugar, ten pounds of lentils, canned beef, detergent, toilet paper, tooth paste, soap, a sewing kit, a small washing machine, some bookshelves, a large piece of carpeting, a water filter, a Hi Fi set in addition to two crates of Coke and two of beer.

There was at the time in Hong Kong a company called Andrews that specialized in supplying diplomatic missions in Beijing. They had a vast catalogue, their prices were competitive and all I would have needed to do was go to their office and pick out my order and it would be delivered, fully packed, at the railway station to the China Travel Service freight department. But my problem was the three bids required by UN rules. Getting them would take days. When I explained to them my predicament, they understood: for all major items Andrews provided me with two other quotations at a slightly higher price on different letterhead and the trick was done.

I left Hong Kong followed by 22 large wooden crates, destination Guangzhou. My original idea was to send them on by train to Hanoi but in Guangzhou I discovered to my surprise that while the cost of shipping freight by express rail to Hanoi was 4 US $ the kilo, by air it was only 50 cents the kilo for overweight, and 30 cents by air freight. China must have been the only country in the world where airfreight was eight times cheaper than freight by rail and there was no hesitation; I would ship everything by air. However, the clerk at the Freight department of the China Travel Service was not convinced. 'The airline will not take it,' he said. When I asked him why he said it was 'too much' and the airline did not like crates. I did not ask him how much was too much but took his word for it. Was there a cheaper freight rate by train? 'Yes,' he said, 'you could send it by slow train but it could take a month or perhaps two or three, no one knew, but by express it will take one week.' I decided to take his word for it and ship the crates by express train with the exception of four crates containing my new bed, one air conditioner and food, which I was going to try and take by air as overweight. The clerk looked uneasy. 'Are you sure?' he said.

'No,' I replied, 'I am not sure but I will try.'

I almost did not get away with it. The dour attendant at the airline check-in counter next morning who spoke a surprisingly unaccented English was adamant. 'You can only take two crates' he snapped at me. It was clear from his tone that asking him why would only have aggravated him further so I tried another tack. 'I will pay, whatever the rate.' That was not a good idea. He looked straight and me and barked back: 'We do not work for money.' It was my tough luck to have fallen on a true believer. So I had to try another tack.

'You are quite right,' I said, 'you follow the teachings of Chairman Mao, you don't work for money, you serve the people.' It was the last thing he was expecting to hear and it completely threw him. 'OK,' he said, after a pause, 'this time you can take four crates, but only this time.' In case he had any lingering doubts I assured him that it would indeed be the last time, and I meant it too.

At noon that day I was back in Hanoi with my four crates and Khoang set out to ensure that the hotel electrician and mason would be in my room the next morning. They worked fast, with no need for any further incentive, and by the afternoon the air conditioner was installed and my bed was assembled. That night I had my first good sleep in Hanoi.

One week later, Khoang suggested we go to the railway station. 'But we have received no notification that the goods have arrived,' I told him. His only answer was a slight smile and I got the point.

Hanoi's railway station was an elegant building built by the French at the turn of the century in what could pass as an architectural style reminiscent of Louis XIV. One wing had been bombed by the Americans but overall the building was unscathed as we wandered from office to office, our shipping documents in hand. No one had heard of our shipment and we were on the point of giving up when a clerk seemed to remember that, yes, he had heard that some crates had arrived from China. He led us to a huge store room piled up to the ceiling with boxes, crates and bundles of all sizes and suggested we look around. By pure luck I identified one of our crates and two hours later all eighteen of them were lined up on the sidewalk in front of the station. The problem now was how to get them to our office. Two fitted in the Volkswagen, but what about the rest? There were a few pedicab drivers lolling around and Khoang motioned to them to come closer. Half an hour later, with the Toyota leading the way and the Volkswagen taking up the rear, a convoy of 16 pedi cabs, each with a large crate on the seat, set off for the *Thong Nhut* hotel as the astounded citizenry of Hanoi crowded the sidewalk to watch us drive by. Word of our arrival had preceded us and the whole staff of the *Thong Nhut* hotel and his brother were waiting for us, ready to help us unpack. When I asked Khoang the cause for this enthusiasm, he said it was the wood and the nails. 'They will unpack for us but they would like the wood of the crates and the nails. They can sell them for a lot of money.'

My next preoccupation was the pouch. The logical route from Geneva through Bangkok and Vientiane was erratic so I started looking for other options. Every Thursday Swissair had a flight from Geneva to East Berlin, which connected to the East German airline, Interflug, that departed Berlin that very evening and arrived in Hanoi the next day. The schedule was ideal and we gave it a try. It never worked. Each time the pouch missed the connection and got stuck in East Berlin for a week. Was a heavy canvas bag with United Nations stamped on it, secured by a lead seal too much for the East German security to resist opening? I never found out but we gave up.

My last resort was Beijing. Every Friday, a Swissair flight landed in Beijing at noon just in time for the pouch to catch the Chinese flight departing for Hanoi. It was a tight schedule but we tried it and it never failed us. So one month after having taken my assignment in Hanoi I had my team in place and the semblance of an office. Now all that was left was to get down to the job with one rider: work, play, meals, week ends, programming, entertainment, health concerns, and the like, were all part of an unending daily struggle, mildly frustrating but always entertaining that came under the general heading of 'life in Hanoi'.

TAMING THE MINOR DRAGON

U UNHCR was exclusively dependent for its funding on the generosity of donor governments and all its programs carried the caveat 'subject to availability of funds'. Thus as a representative of the organization my job included not only keeping track of our programs—a task which I happily delegated to Pierre—but also staying in good terms with the embassies of governments that traditionally supported us.

By 1976, as more and more countries established diplomatic relations with Hanoi, the *Thong Nhut* hotel had acquired a sizeable number of permanent residents in the form of foreign diplomats waiting for a building to be identified and refurbished where they could set up their embassy and residence.

All the communist embassies which had been present in Hanoi for years had sumptuous residences with large gardens and ample living quarters.

Among the westerners, the French, who had always kept a foot in Hanoi, had a large compound in the center of town with their own generator, doctor and an ample supply of goods flown in once a month from France.

The British were also part of the long-timers but were not much the better for it. They had initially opened a consulate in Hanoi in 1945, which occupied a large French-built villa in the center of town and was accredited to the city's municipal authorities. In 1954, when the communists came to power in the North, the British thought they were being clever by keeping their consulate in Hanoi while simultaneously extending diplomatic recognition to South Vietnam and opening an embassy in Saigon. The communists were furious and initially wanted to close the consulate and throw the British out. On second thought however, it dawned on them that if they did so the British would retaliate by closing the

North Vietnamese consulate in London. Ultimately the communists had more use for a presence in London as an observation post than the British had for a consulate in Hanoi so they put up with the indignity but decided instead to make life difficult for the hapless British consul and his skeleton staff.

While the Vietnamese could easily have cut the water or the electricity to the British consulate in Hanoi this would have been too blatant a gesture so they chose a more subtle approach; refusing to allow the consulate to hire any local staff with the result that the English had to do their own cooking, laundry and house cleaning. Not that they lacked time to do so. With visa requests by North Vietnamese citizens wanting to travel to Britain being few and far between, ultimately the consulate had nothing to do. While the consulate had a car, the refusal of the Foreign Ministry to let them hire a driver meant that the British, lacking a Vietnamese driving license, could only move throughout the city on foot or by bicycle. This went on for years until a particularly enterprising young consul decided to do something about it and set out to obtain a local driving license. After repeated attempts during which he systematically passed the driving test but failed the written exam he decided to raise the ante and learned all the answers by heart. Again he failed the test. When he objected pointing out that he had answered all the questions word by word as they appeared in the driving manual his Vietnamese examiner did not disagree.

'Yes,' he said, 'we noticed that your answers matched the manual word by word. This means that you learned the answers by heart, which shows that you did not really understand them and this is why you failed the test.' So the consulate's car never left its allotted parking place, but it did occasionally serve a purpose. Whenever there was a power cut the consul had the option of getting into the car, switching on the engine and turning on the air-conditioner, thus enjoying a few moments of relief from Hanoi's stifling heat.

All this pestering came to an end when Britain established diplomatic relations with North Vietnam in 1973 and sent a full ambassador to Hanoi and from then onwards it was business as usual.

The Swedes had recognized North Vietnam only in 1969, but throughout the war years had been vocal supporters of Hanoi and, in reward, had been given in 1973 a piece of land on the outskirts of the city where they had built a compound which included an embassy building and several residences. Enter and you were in Sweden, from the smell of freshly cut pinewood to the sauna to the Scandinavian furnishing.

The foreign diplomats stranded at the *Thong Nhut* hotel in 1976 while waiting for an embassy building to be made available were the last of the lot among these countries that had recognized Hanoi and included the Japanese, the Italians, the Germans and the Swiss. The Japanese had moved into a set of rooms at the far end of the first floor, past the reception desk and kept to themselves. Occasionally some would emerge from their lair, never less than in groups of three, saunter apprehensively across the lobby and disappear into a waiting car. They never set foot in the dining room and it was said that they received all their food and drinking water by air from Japan through Beijing from where it was transported on the bi-weekly flight to Hanoi. Next to the Japanese the West Germans had three rooms, one each for the ambassador, his assistant and one as an office. They mostly spent their time in Bangkok and seemed hopelessly disoriented in Hanoi's peculiar environment.

The second floor was home to the Italians. The ambassador, Giuliano Bertuccioli, was one of the last of a dying breed, the scholar-diplomat. At heart he was a linguist and spoke fluent French, English, Chinese, German and Japanese but the love of his life was China. He had studied the language in Italy when the Foreign Ministry, short of translators, offered him a job with the Italian embassy in Nanking in 1946. One of his favorite anecdotes about this period, he would recount, happened shortly after his arrival. A local Italian businessman had allegedly committed some major misdeed and the Chinese authorities had sentenced him to death. The Italian ambassador had written to the government asking that his life be spared and Bertuccioli was given the task of translating the reply that the embassy had received. The request for clemency had apparently been turned down but the Chinese had conveyed the message in such a convoluted way that Bertuccioli misread the text and made a note to the ambassador saying that the Chinese had agreed to spare the man's life. Upon receiving the news the ambassador had rushed to the Chinese to thank them for their pardon. This put the Chinese in a major quandary. They were convinced the Italian deserved to be beheaded but if they did so the Italian ambassador would lose face. Finally, to spare embarrassing the ambassador they pardoned the businessman.

While in Nanking, Bertuccioli had met the daughter of a senior Kuomintang General whom he married. She was a tall, beautiful woman of impeccable manners and was in a class of her own. At one of the few diplomatic receptions in Hanoi she had met the wife of the Chinese ambassador and, politics notwithstanding, the two had become the best of friends. She would spend most of her time in the large compound of the Chinese embassy while Bertuccioli, who had brought with him an impressive amount of books, would devote his time to scholarship. As for his diplomatic duties, they were few and far between and he delegated them to his deputy Elio Menzione, a studious young man who had the foresight of bringing with him a guidebook of Hanoi. It was a French Madrolle published in 1936 and, except for the street names, it was still up to date. Altogether, the Italians cooked their own spaghetti, put up with the heat, never complained and seemed to look on all things Vietnamese with bemused empathy.

On the same floor, above the lobby, the Belgians had their realm. The ambassador had the absurd name of Vilain XIV which in English translated into Ugly Fourteen. The rumor went that one of his ancestors had acquired his name when some unknown king who was off hunting with his nobles decided to stop for lunch at a local inn. When the table was set however, they discovered that they were thirteen in all, a number which was known to bring bad luck, whereupon the king grabbed a passing peasant, a villain so the story went, seated him at the table and proclaimed him 'Vilain fourteen'.

Vilain XIV was an urban, educated man. Hanoi was his first ambassadorial post and he had decided to make it a success, ignoring the fact that there was nothing for him to do all day. A keen photographer, he was lamenting the fact that Hanoi was covered with signs saying no photographs and had cautiously expressed his disappointment to the Vice Foreign Minister Phan Hien.

'In what language are the signs?' Phan Hien had asked.

'In Vietnamese,' replied Vilain XIV.

'Do you read Vietnamese?'

'No.'

'So where is the problem?'

Television had just come to Hanoi in the form of one channel broadcasting in black-and-white, one hour a day from eight to nine in the evening. TV sets were a luxury that no Vietnamese could afford but 2,000 had been imported from Russia for viewing in public places and one had been allocated to the lobby of the *Thong Nhut* hotel. With Vietnam's TV production in its infancy, the authorities had to import material to fill their daily one-hour broadcast, but it could not be just any material. For ideological reasons it had to conform to their Marxist outlook and their options were limited to the Soviet Union and its Eastern European satellites but what they had to offer did not seem to have any appeal to a Vietnamese audience. Then the Yugoslavs stepped in.

Producing war movies pitting heroic communist guerillas against evil Germans fascists was a specialty of the TV studios in Belgrade and this was exactly what the Vietnamese relished. Henceforth, night after night, Hanoi's TV sets gushed forth with the sound of gunfire in the Balkans. At the *Thong Nhut* hotel, an enterprising electrician had hooked two additional loudspeakers to the lobby TV and the sound, set at full volume, was deafening. The Belgian embassy's room was located just above the lobby and with the TV going full blast it sounded like being on the front line of the battle of the Bulge. The ambassador had repeatedly pleaded with the hotel staff to lower the volume but all his efforts had proved to be in vain. Finally one evening, in desperation, his secretary descended to the lobby with a pair of scissors in hand and proceeded to cut the wires to the loudspeakers. A stunned silence followed as the assembled hotel staff, congregated around the TV set, stood petrified while confronted with such daring.

She could have saved herself the effort. A few days later, to the great disappointment of the citizenry of Hanoi, all the Yugoslav war films were pulled from Vietnam TV. I found it a strange decision and it was only after some prodding that Khoang provided me with an explanation. Apparently, the repeated showing of heroic partisans battling evil Nazis had created among the Hanoi citizenry an increasing aversion to the Germans. That those featured in the films had nothing to do with current Germany, East or West, was a point of detail that escaped most Vietnamese. The Germans were Nazis and the Nazis were evil and that was that. Things had come to a head when two East German diplomats had been insulted in the streets of Hanoi. The East German ambassador had sent a protest note to the Vietnamese authorities who, reluctantly, had decided to suspend the airing on TV of Yugoslav war films.

Every Monday the pouch came from Geneva and included, in addition to official communications, one week of the International Herald Tribune newspaper as well as two weekly magazines to which I had subscribed and which a friendly clerk in the registry would hide in an official envelope. These were *Paris Match*, a French version of *Life*, and *Jours de France*, a somewhat trashy French People magazine that kept us entertained for want of a better choice. With all foreign publications banned in Vietnam these stood as a bit of a reminder of what the rest of the world was all about, trivia included.

One morning, as I entered my room, I found the four hotel maids assigned to my floor seated on my bed avidly going through *Paris Match*. When they saw me they jumped up from the bed as if they had been caught doing some atrocious misdeed. As they stood in silent embarrassment I called in Khoang and asked him to translate. First I thanked them for cleaning my room so well, a statement that we all knew was preposterous. Then I told them that they were welcome to read my magazines. When I was finished with them I would carefully put them on top of my wastepaper basket and they could take them home. From that day onwards I had the cleanest room in the hotel. They would do it up between eight-thirty and nine when I was at breakfast, learned to use my vacuum cleaner and provided me with double the number of allotted bottles of drinking water.

'You did them a great favor,' commented Khoang, 'and they will become very rich.'

'Why,' I asked, 'are they going to sell the magazines?'

He smiled, 'Oh no, they are too clever for that. They will rent them out by the hour.'

Whatever work we had was enough to keep us occupied during the day. How to fill our evenings and weekends was another matter.

Unless on official business, foreigners were restricted to Hanoi and any request to travel outside the city had to be made two weeks in advance. Even if it was granted, the authorization was only valid for three sites: Tam Dao, Do Son and Sam Son. Tam Dao, at an altitude of 3,000 feet, was a mountain resort built by the French at the turn of the century three hours by road from Hanoi. Most of the French villas had been blown up during the first Vietnam War and the only hotel was in ruins. Do Son and Sam Son were seaside resorts, three hours and five hours respectively from Hanoi. While the beaches were untouched, they were also unkempt and the lodging facilities made the *Thong Nhut* seem like a luxury establishment in comparison. Having tried each one once, we decided that spending the weekend in Hanoi was the lesser of evils and we would while away the time reading or playing backgammon, shivering or sweltering depending on the time of year.

The only issue that caused us some concern was the medical services. The Vietnamese had some good doctors and one of them, Ton That Tung, was known as one of the world's best liver surgeon. But war and isolation had taken their toll and most doctors and their equipment were of the standards of the 1930s. With modern medicine or drugs at best two days away, either in Bangkok or Hong Kong, the concern was not just theoretical, especially when Pierre came down with constant stomach pains.

After one week of groaning, Khoang brought Pierre to the hospital where a French-speaking doctor had him ingest a foul mixture prior to taking an X-ray of his stomach. When Pierre returned to the hospital the next day for the result of the examination he found a somewhat perplexed doctor. 'Look at this spot,' he said as he raised the X-ray picture to a naked light bulb. 'It is either a moisture stain on the film or an ulcer but which of the two it is I can't tell.' By now Pierre had worked himself up into a state of panic and just to play it safe, I sent him to Bangkok. He came back one week later with a generous assortment of medicines. It was an ulcer.

Pierre's predicament among the western diplomatic corps was not an exception but rather the rule and the combination of the weather, the poor food and the lack of facilities engendered in many an obsession with health. Antibiotics were wolfed down at the least sign of discomfort and rumors abounded.

Shortly after my arrival the buzz spread among the foreign community that an epidemic of encephalitis had hit Hanoi. The first to react were the French and in a matter of days they flew in from Paris a lot of vaccines for their staff in an insulated container, packed in bags of ice packs to keep it cool. Upon arrival, the container was brought to the city's main hospital where, after examination, the vaccine was pronounced fit for use. A first group of French went to the hospital in the morning to get vaccinated. They all came back to their embassy clutching their shoulder in dire pain but glad nevertheless to have been spared from contracting the dreaded disease.

A second group went to the hospital in the afternoon and the first of them happened to be the son of a doctor. He had witnessed many vaccinations and was somewhat surprised to see that the liquid in the syringe with which the doctor was going to vaccinate him was blue. 'Can I see the vial from which you took the vaccine?' he asked.

'Of course,' replied the doctor as he motioned to an assistant who produced a bag of the ice-pack. If anything, the incident provided the scientific proof that ice pack, when injected, was not lethal to the human body.

When Pierre had come down with his ulcer and had to go to Bangkok to see a doctor, he had to pay for his own ticket. Of course I could have asked Geneva that he go on medical leave but this would have entailed obtaining a medical certificate based on an X-ray plate which left unanswered the question as to whether the spot it featured was due to either moisture or an ulcer and the reply would probably have taken weeks. Such were UN rules and by then I knew that to challenge them was a losing proposition. So, rather than a frontal assault on the system, we decided that the only way to deal with it was to circumvent it and even Joan, the guardian of the temple, concurred.

After having truncated our Geneva-based salaries by assigning us to Bangkok, the UN had allocated us 40 US $ a day to cover our daily expenses in Hanoi. How much that sum translated into the local Vietnamese currency was almost a metaphysical question. There were at least half a dozen official exchange rates depending whether the person changing the money came from a 'friendly' country, a socialist country or a capitalist country in additional to various commercial rates. We of course, coming from capitalist countries, had the least favorable exchange rate of 2.4 Vietnamese Dongs to the dollar. Given that our room and food cost us no more than some 20 Dongs a day, 40 US $, a day equivalent to 94 Dongs at the official rate, was generous. However, if one factored in the cost of an occasional trip to Bangkok or Hong Kong to have a bath, buy some books and replenish our stock of provisions it was grossly insufficient. After some initial qualms, we decided to use the services of Pierre to change our dollars to Dongs on the black market. He would pass the dollars on to our driver, *Monsieur* Hien, who knew all the ropes and provided us in exchange with wads of local currency at an exchange rate of 12 Dongs to the dollar. As we paid our hotel rooms in Dongs the end result was that out of our 1.200 US $ dollars a month as daily allowance we would spend 200 US $ at most in local currency, leaving us enough for an occasional trip to Bangkok.

On the first of every month Joan and Pierre would proceed to the State Bank of Vietnam where we had opened two accounts in the name of UNHCR, one in Dongs to pay local expenses and staff and one in dollars from which she would provide us with one month's worth of daily allowances. All transactions were in cash, provided of course that there were enough funds in the accounts. These were replenished at regular intervals by UNHCR from Geneva though the intermediary of a Soviet bank in Paris. It was only after our accounts had gone dry that we discovered that the average time for a transfer was six to eight weeks. When we asked the bank why it took so long they replied, as a matter of course, that this was the time it took for the cash to be physically transferred to Hanoi. This was the only way they knew how to make transfers.

This, like most other hurdles we encountered in Hanoi, proved inconsequential. It was mostly a matter of adapting or of finding a way around the obstacle, or both.

What we could not find our way around was the weather. Hanoi had possibly the worst climate in Asia. The summers, from March to October, were stifling with the humidity hovering at around 95%, then winter would hit with the temperature hovering just above freezing point, and it was not a dry cold either. The French called it the *crachin*, the spittle. Somewhere between a light rain and a heavy fog, it lasted for weeks on end and permeated every nook and cranny. Humidity dribbled from the walls and there was not a single dry spot in Hanoi. The Vietnamese were miserable and would pile on sweater upon sweater, with a layer of old newspapers in between for added insulation.

The central heating at the *Thong Nhut* hotel had been turned off in 1954 when the last Frenchman had left the city and had never been turned on since and we had to make do with a few electric heaters bought in Hong Kong. These, when combined with dehumidifiers, helped to bring the temperature up a few degrees and the humidity down to a tolerable level, when the hotel electric fuses did not blow that is. Fortunately, Pierre had identified the fuse box on our floor. The fuses were actually lead wires which he had the good idea of replacing with tin foil and from then onwards, our electrical supply was practically uninterrupted albeit at the risk of burning down the hotel but that was a chance we were willing to take. Apart from these inconveniences, what counted was that we were a good team, the job was challenging, dealing with the Vietnamese perversely enjoyable and, comfort or discomfort, none of us would have wanted to be anywhere else.

While on the personal level our relations with the authorities were cordial—which did not mean that they would not try to bamboozle us if the occasion arose—the fact that we existed as an organization must have been to them a source of enduring incomprehension further compounded by the fact that we had no identifiable agenda.

For the Vietnamese everything had a purpose, visible or covert, and they must have repeatedly asked themselves why we were helping them. That a number of Western governments, and capitalist ones at that, were providing funds to UNHCR to help the Vietnamese people get over the consequences of the war and this at no advantage to themselves was beyond their understanding. The end result of this search for a purpose which they could force-fit into their ideological bias meant that the best of intentions could take on, from their perspective, the dimensions of a sinister and convoluted plot.

Sweden's current Prime Minister, Olof Palme, had been a vocal supporter of Vietnam during the war years, to the point of alienating the US and one would imagine he would be considered a friend by Hanoi. Not so. Palme was a socialist, or more precisely a social democrat, and if there was one thing that the Soviets and their communist party allies outside the Soviet Union feared and hated the most, it was the socialists. Except for rejecting totalitarianism, the socialists shared with the communists the goal of creating a state-owned economy and an aversion to private property and entrepreneurship. With their respective electorates overlapping, the socialists represented the only political force in Western Europe liable to attract voters away from the communists. So just like in Vietnam where the conservative nationalists were perceived by the communist as their greatest challenge, in Europe it was the socialists rather than the Right that the communists considered as their main electoral threat. I had once discussed Olof Palme with *Monsieur* Bai, observing that he was a great friend of Vietnam. 'No,' said Bai, 'it is not the case; the Swedish people forced him to support us.' *Monsieur* Bai was an intelligent man but circumscribed as he was by his ideology, he had reached the limits of what he was capable of comprehending. Thus, what he saw in Olof Palme was the social democrat who preached a non-totalitarian left wing alternative to communism rather than a friend of Vietnam.

Rizvi, in his discussions with the Vietnamese, had kept on repeating that we were humanitarians but they could not possibly have accepted this as a full explanation. When I had first contacted them on behalf of UNHCR my argument had been that they would gain some political mileage by dealing with us and this was an argument they could relate to. But now the war was over and they no longer needed any political mileage but they were also practical people and if we could provide some assistance, why not?

Ultimately of course, they were right: UNHCR had an agenda and it was called survival. To justify its existence as a bureaucracy UNHCR had to be visible throughout the world wherever there was a crisis and what better visibility was there than to be present in Hanoi? So our agenda was therefore simply to be present in Vietnam; but to expect the Vietnamese to understand this would have been to assume that they had a knowledge of the UN system that they could not have possibly have had. And so was the fact that, for the sake of our image, we needed the Vietnamese more than they needed us.

But while this was an unquestionable reality, it was not the full picture. I had sold UNHCR to the PRG using the argument that dealing with us would contribute to their international legitimacy. I never discounted the possibility that I was decieving them, but if this was so it was only because they were decieving themselves. Whatever legitimacy we could give them was an illusion. It had no substance. It had no impact on reality and did not change one iota on the outcome of the war. Conversely our aid was not a mirage. It was real and while its impact was marginal as regards the whole of the country, for a few hundred thousand farmers—the bombed, the shelled, the defoliated, the displaced—those who had been at the recieving end of the war, it did make a difference. So, whatever the initial motivations of either UNHCR or the communists, the end result of this convoluted relationship was nothing anybody could be ashamed of.

Unlike foreign Western diplomatic missions, we had a daily working relation with the Vietnamese and as time went by we established the semblance of a personal relationship with some of our many counterparts. Belying the cliche that communist systems by necessity were represented by a faceless bureaucracy there were times when it looked as if we were dealing not with a government bureaucracy but rather with an aggregate of quick, funny, head-strong, crafty, perseverant, devious, articulate, manipulative, witty, quarrelsome and messy individuals barely kept in rein by a regime without which they would all have drifted into anarchy. And while singleness of purpose was perhaps their only common denominator, how to get there was quite another matter, and it sometimes felt as if we were operating not so much within one system as with a swarm of individuals each of whom had his own idea as to how the system should work.

As the war spread throughout the Vietnamese countryside the number of farmers whose homes were destroyed and who had to flee their villages numbered in the millions. With the return of peace getting them home became a priority and this is where UNHCR stepped in.

In 1975, before the official unification of the country, we had set up two programs, one for the North and one for the South. By the middle of 1976 these were merged into one comprehensive program totaling twelve million dollars that covered the whole of the country. Getting the farmers back to their home villages was not the problem. The problem was ensuring that they would be self sufficient upon return which in turn required a considerable degree of rehabilitation of the countryside. Rizvi, who had conceived most of the programs, was acutely aware that in a rural society the most effective projects and the easiest to monitor were generally the smaller ones, locally implemented and targeted to solving local needs. Our twelve million dollars ended up financing some 30 projects extending all the way from the suburbs of Hanoi to the Southern delta and included the likes of twelve rural hospitals, irrigation pumps, hand carts, clothing materials, fertilizer, small tractors, two large bulldozers, emergency food supplies and fishing nets for fishing communities. This was not exactly what the Vietnamese leadership, who had visions of building an advanced collectivized agricultural system, wanted so to sweeten the deal Rizvi threw in a set of incubators for chicken, a buffalo breeding farm and a technical training school in Vinh.

Vietnamese buffalos were hardy but gave no milk while Indian buffaloes were less burly but produced milk so a cross breed of the two which would have the qualities of both made sense. So we set up a special allocation to build a farm and import 200 buffaloes from India. Likewise Vietnam's chicken could stand some improvement of the breed and importing incubators made sense.

Visiting each site in order to monitor project implementation meant long days on the road, an ordeal that I had no hesitation in delegating most of the time to Pierre. But occasionally I also had to go myself and the first time I did *Monsieur* Bai uncharacteristically decided to follow suit.

After two long days on the road, during which we visited several sites, as we were sharing a bowl of noodles at a roadside inn *Monsieur* Bai looked unusually relaxed and I dared to address the question that had been constantly on my mind.

'*Monsieur* Bai, I hear you are an old revolutionary, may we dare ask what you did during the first resistance war against the French.'

Monsieur Bai seemed unconcerned by my question and answered matter-of-factly. 'I was President of a Revolutionary Tribunal.'

I could feel Pierre looking at me and as our eyes crossed we shared the same grisly thought. A Revolutionary Tribunal, tens if not hundreds of innocent souls sentenced to a gruesome fate by a latter-day Robespierre in the form of a merciless *Monsieur* Bay. We shuddered but the die was cast and I had to proceed with my inquiring. '*Monsieur* Bai, what were the cases that you most commonly had to deal with?'

Monsieur Bai looked unconcerned. 'Divorces.'

It was not the answer I had expected but at least I felt on safer grounds. '*Monsieur* Bai, could you tell us one of your cases.'

'Of course.' Suddenly *Monsieur* Bai came to life, a different man, animated and almost boisterous. 'Yes, I will tell you, it was so complicated, you can't imagine the headaches it gave me. There was a big battle and French troops came into a village, they were blacks—a look of horror passed across *Monsieur* Bai's face—there were caves nearby and all the inhabitants fled to them but one of the blacks found a cave, there was a woman there, and he raped her. The cave had several levels and on one of the upper levels the husband had hidden and he looked down and saw everything. After the French soldiers had left the inhabitants returned to the village and the husband wanted to divorce his wife. He said that while she was being raped she had raised her legs in the air, which meant she had enjoyed it and he did not want her any more. The wife said it was not true, she had not enjoyed it and as they could not agree I had to handle the case.

You can't imagine how much trouble it gave me. First I had to organize a meeting of all the women in the village to discuss the matter. Then a delegation of women went to see the husband to explain to him that when a woman raised her legs it was not necessarily a sign of enjoyment. But the husband did not quite believe them so we also had to organize a group of men to give their opinion. Finally, after unending discussions the husband was convinced and agreed to take his wife back. It was a good ending but you can't believe how much time and effort it took.'

Suddenly, I saw another man behind the dour bureaucrat that *Monsieur* Bai purported to be. Not only he had a heart but he also had a conscience and he had gone out of his way to save a marriage. But that was only half of the picture. I could visualize the same story happening in South Vietnam with this time the rape being committed by an American soldier. How many South Vietnamese officials would have made the same efforts as *Monsieur* Bai to mend a marriage between two simple farmers. None was the realistic assumption. They did not care. But the communists did care. They could be ruthless with their enemies, real or perceived, but they also cared for their own and that, ultimately, was why they won the war.

Keeping track of all the equipment that was coming in for our program was a major headache as it arrived in many distinct lots. Generally we would get a cable from Geneva informing us that this or that lot of equipment was due either at the port of Haiphong or by train from China and I would put Pierre on the task of keeping track of the goods. He was doing a good job but could not quite make sense of the fact that so many of the shipments arrived damaged. Two to three times a week we would have a meeting with *Monsieur* Bai and he would ceremoniously announce in a low, solemn tone; ten tons of cement: 32% damage; 40 bulldozers: 12% damage; 6,000 feet of fish netting: 18% damage. We would then have to get a written statement from the Red Cross, which we sent to our office in Geneva which would approach the insurance company, which would often ask us for more details. It was a time-consuming process, not to mention that I was not quite convinced that the alleged damage was what it was said to be, but with no proof there was nothing I could do. Of course we could have gone ourselves to inspect the alleged damage but it would have been a too visible show of lack of trust in the Red Cross; not that we trusted them but we had to find a way of showing our suspicion without making them lose face. As we groped for a way of addressing the problem without openly confronting the Red Cross, Pierre, by talking with Khoang discovered that Vietnam had a National Insurance Company called Bao Viet and arranged an appointment for us. The officials who received us in a dingy office did not speak one word of French and were visibly not used to dealing with foreigners and their reaction was initially guarded. As Khoang translated I explained to them that we loved Vietnam and rather than deal with foreign insurance companies we would much rather work with a Vietnamese one, provided they offered us a better insurance rate. If they were interested in the offer they should establish by telegram a direct contact with our Headquarters in Geneva and work the details out with them. By now the reaction of the Bao Viet people was enthusiastic and they promised to act on our approach immediately. Back in our office we sent a cable to Geneva and waited.

Six weeks later after a new shipment had come in we had our customary meeting with *Monsieur* Bai and the scenario started off as usual. 'There is a problem,' said *Monsieur* Bai, 'a lot of damage.'

Before he could continue, I smiled and said, 'it is all solved.'

'What is solved?' he asked suspiciously.

'The damage, you don't have to come to us any more. As you know we always give priority to our Vietnamese friends and instead of insuring the shipments with foreign companies everything from now onwards is insured with Bao Viet. They are just around the corner and if there is any damage you can deal with them directly.' It was the last time we were ever to hear about damage to a shipment.

Every month we would send a memo to Geneva by pouch with a progress report on each project. Likewise, as required by UN rules, the Red Cross was supposed to provide us with regular reports on how they were implementing projects. Thus when a project required some construction, their report was supposed to indicate when the cement had been delivered, to which port, when it had been unloaded, transported to its destination and put to use. It was not a complicated matter but the Red Cross had never done it before and the first reports they sent us were full of useless generalities and contained no hard facts which we could forward to Geneva so we would send them back to the Red Cross with requests for clarification, which never came. I could not really tell *Monsieur* Bai that his reports were useless, as this would have entailed a major loss of face for him so, in desperation, Pierre and I sat down with Khoang and asked him to come up with a way out for all of us.

The first proposal that he came back with was that the Red Cross would send us a draft report; we would correct it, send it back to them and then receive the final text officially. I told him that it was not a bad idea but that it would be time-consuming and we could do better. So he came back with a second solution. The Red Cross would give us a batch of blank paper with their letterhead on it, we would write the report and send it to them to be signed and stamped and they would return it to us to be sent to Geneva. The system worked flawlessly and soon I could report to *Monsieur* Bai that our Headquarters had asked me to convey their appreciation to the Red Cross for the quality of their reporting.

Rizvi had assumed that in Vietnam everything worked. We in Hanoi, after a few months on the ground, would have been justified in thinking that nothing worked. But it was not quite that simple. For 30 years the country had been geared up for war. It was a total commitment, material, psychological and organizational. The best brains had gone into the army and everything had been subservient to war. War was a state of mind, war meant also secrecy, and secrecy became a way of life. Orders and directives came exclusively from the top as the country was compartmentalized into parallel, hermetically closed components, each operating independently in an environment where lack of communication was a condition for survival. Priority was another issue. When the Vietnamese wanted something to work it did. But when it was not their number one priority it was left to drift by the wayside.

In 1975 the war was over, but the mindset that it had generated endured.

How many times did the Red Cross inform us that a shipment of cement and machinery had been unloaded at Haiphong for the technical training school we were setting up in Vinh and had left it at that. That they could have informed the local authorities at Vinh who were actually in charge of implementing the project never occurred to them. The end result was that we would have to spend two days on the road to go to Vinh, inform the local authorities that the goods had arrived in Haiphong for them and give them a few Dong so they could afford to send a couple of officials to Haiphong to identify the shipment and ensure its transportation to Vinh. Once in Vinh, however the problem was solved. Throughout the country the grassroots level administration functioned admirably. The same applied to the ministries we were dealing with in Hanoi, be it health, fisheries or agriculture. They knew their job. What did not function was communication from one ministry to another. And if ever one of our projects involved two ministries it was up to us to establish the link between the two.

Rizvi had once commented that Vietnamese chicken were much like the country. Small, hardy, resilient, skinny and tough. What he wanted to see in their place were big, fat hens. So he came up with a sensible idea. Why not set up a chicken breeding facility to improve the breed and distribute the super chicken to farmers where they would multiply for the good of all concerned. The authorities loved the idea and after some snooping we found a Japanese firm which wished to get a foothold in Vietnam and was willing to sell us, for the reduced price of 500,000 US $, a complete chicken breeding facility including a dozen, modern incubators which could produce half a million chicken a year. The facility would be located at Chem, in the suburbs of Hanoi, and the Vietnamese would ensure that a proper building be constructed to house the facility and the incubators. We offered to provide a Japanese technician to help assemble the equipment but the Vietnamese were adamant that they could do it themselves.

In June 1976 *Monsieur* Bai informed us that all the equipment had arrived and everything was proceeding according to plan. The facility, he told us, would be formally inaugurated by the end of December and production would start in early January with an initial lot of 15,000 eggs. All this was good news and I immediately sent a telegram to Geneva informing them that the project was on track.

By end November I asked *Monsieur* Bai if a date had been set for the inauguration of the facility but his response was so evasive that I suspected something had gone wrong and I asked Khoang to organize a visit to Chem. Generally the Red Cross would send someone to accompany us but this time they did not as Pierre, Khoang and I proceed to Chem on a rainy morning. It was only ten minutes away from downtown Hanoi but it could have been at the other end of Vietnam. There, in the open, on a large waste ground, two shivering Vietnamese were waiting for us next to a gigantic pile of wooden crates which seemed to have been dumped off at random. 'We could not set up the installation,' one of them explained, 'because many parts are missing.' 'Which parts,' I asked. 'There,' he said, pointing to a half-opened crate some 30 feet long, 'all the water pipes are missing.' With the help of Pierre I managed to pry open a side of the crate. It was full of carefully packed plastic pipes. 'What about this,' I asked him. 'Oh, this,' he said, 'it is plastic.' I did not have the heart to tell him that iron pipes had gone out of use some 20 years earlier and that all water pipes were now made of plastic.

It was the last we ever heard of Chem. By then I had also discovered that UNHCR had a short memory and it was not unusual for a project to drift into bureaucratic oblivion, so I sent a memo to Headquarters saying that the Chem project was on track and left it at that. Actually my fibbing was what the situation demanded. For UNHCR it would have been a major embarrassment to have to explain to donors that half a million dollars had gone down the drain. There would have been an investigation. Questions would have been put to the Vietnamese, face would have been lost all around and resentment generated towards UNHCR. But while we closed the book on Chem the memory lingered and twenty years later, three months before leaving UNHCR, I went back to the site. There I found a crumbling barrack that looked abandoned and I was on the point of leaving when an old man appeared. Yes, he explained in hesitant French, this was the chicken breeding facility at Chem and he was in charge. Vietnam was no longer the country I had known many years earlier and the old man, who had been there since day one, showed no reluctance to speak once I told him who I was.

'After the fall of Saigon,' he told me, 'the Ministry of Agriculture sent a team to the South to survey agricultural installations. They were all far more modern than what we had in the North but when we unpacked the equipment that arrived in Chem we realized that it was even more up to date then anything in the South. It was so advanced that we did not know how to set it up but no one wanted to admit it.'

What followed was predictable. The Ministry of Agriculture did not give up the project but simply pushed it aside, neither closing it down nor actively pursuing it but just left it ambling along. With time some of the technicians managed to set up three incubators but it was just the beginning of their woes. The site did not have any water so they had to connect it to the mains, which took further time. Then came the problem of the power supply and when Chem was finally connected to the grid, the inevitable happened. Two of the incubators were fried by a massive power surge and as for the remaining one, constant power cuts ensured that the temperature required to incubate the eggs could not be maintained. But this was not the end of the project. As a state owned enterprise in a socialist country, Chem could not be closed down so the staff was retained, year after year, as one after the other they slowly drifted into retirement. The technician I met was the last of the lot, serenely waiting for his retirement upon which Chem would be finally shut down and with it the last chapter of Rizvi's dream to provide every Vietnamese with a big, fat hen.

As I headed back into town I recalled Khoang's words, 20 years ago. We had just come back to the *Thong Nhut* hotel from surveying the stack of unopened crates that lay at Chem under the rain when he turned to me 'You know,' he said pensively, almost as if talking to himself, 'I still can't understand how we won this war.'

I could have provided him with at least part of the answer. Singleness of purpose, unwavering perseverance and the readiness to accept any sacrifice had won the war for them. And Khoang was no stranger to that endeavor.

Khoang lived on the outskirts of Hanoi and, during the December 1972 bombings peering through his kitchen window, he had seen a shot-down American pilot parachute near his home. His immediate reaction was to grab an old kitchen knife and go after him. The pilot was not far away but others captured him first, he told me, so he went back to his kitchen. I could imagine the scene, on one side a pitiful little Vietnamese long past his prime whose dream in life was to translate poetry, holding an old kitchen knife and on the other a well-fed six-feet-tall young buck for whom Vietnam was merely a set of coordinates on a map. 'What would you have done if you had been the first to reach him?' I asked?

'I would have told him to surrender. And if he had refused? I would have killed him.'

'But American pilots all carried handguns and you had only a knife. He could have killed you.'

'So what?' he responded.

On July 2, 1976, Vietnam was reunified and the Democratic Republic of Vietnam was merged with the non existant Republic of South Vietnam to create a new state, the Socialist Republic of Vietnam.

What's in a name? Everything. Calling Vietnam a Socialist Republic was not only an act of faith. It was also an act of supreme arrogance. Within the hierarchy of communist countries, only two states had had the audacity to qualify themselves as 'socialists'. The Union of Soviet Socialist Republics and Czechoslovak Socialist Republic. All the other communist countries had chosen to qualify themselves as Democratic Republics or the People's Republics, acknowledging that they were still a long way from achieving the status of a socialist nirvana. By following the Soviet model and choosing for itself the name of Socialist Republic, Vietnam was not only reaffirming an ideological choice. It was signally the other People's and Democratic Republics that it was one up on them. Actually, the choice of name was absurd, not to say pathetic. Socialist translated into the supremacy of the proletariat, the working class. But Vietnam had no industrial base and hence no working class of any significance. Granted, the party had tried to inflate the size of its proletariat by including in its numbers plantation workers and the like but it was a poor subterfuge. Basically Vietnam, the ideological delirium of its leaders nonetheless, was and remained a technologically backwards agrarian society.

The choice of names also ushered in a new phase of the revolution. Ho Chi Minh had advocated a Vietnam that would be Free, Independent, Unified and Socialist and out of these four aspirations the first three had been met. Now the time had come to embark on the fourth struggle, the struggle for socialism. From the perspective of the *Thong Nhut* hotel, there were few clues to the effect that Vietnam had for all practical purposes set out on a new war not so much this time against the French or the Americans, but against itself and collaterally, against China. But even the available clues would have been undecipherable had not one of my neighbors at the *Thong Nhut* hotel taken it on himself to guide me through this ideological labyrinth. Officially Michel Strulovici—we called him Strulo—was the correspondent in Hanoi of the daily newspaper of the French communist party, *L'Humanité*. In practice he was the representative in Hanoi of the French communist party and as such privy to the regime's inner workings. While Stroulo left the communist party after the collapse of the Soviet Union he was at the time a committed Marxist but no fool either and he was not blind to the foibles of the regime. Over time we had become friends and he proved invaluable in teaching me the art of Hanoiology.

On September 9, 1976, Mao Tsetung died and as the lone UN representative in Hanoi it was my duty to go to the Chinese embassy and sign the condolence book. Appropriately, it was like going to a funeral. The book had been set on a low table, surrounded by wreaths, next to which two Chinese officials in black suits stood to attention with frozen expressions. It would have been sufficient for me to write in the book 'with condolences' and sign my name and function but I decided to raise the ante and wrote 'deep condolences' followed by 'his memory will live for ever'. That afternoon I found Khoang chuckling in the office.

'The Chinese embassy called,' he said, 'they are very impressed with you. They wanted to know who you were. What did you write in the condolences book?' he asked cautiously. When I told him he paused for a moment and then asked, 'what do you mean by his memory will live for ever?'

'Whatever you want it to,' I answered. There was a second of silence and then he broke out in peals of laughter.

The Vietnamese had never really looked upon Mao as a Marxist. They were Leninists who considered the communist party as the supreme institution that overrode personal inclinations and had viewed with dismay Mao's wrecking of the Chinese communist party during the Cultural Revolution in order to secure his personal position. But ideology aside, Hanoi's relationship with China had always been ambiguous. On the one hand there was a past history of ten centuries of Chinese occupation and countless wars and on the other hand the vital assistance they had received during their wars against the French and the Americans. Ultimately of course, China's assistance to Hanoi was part of an overall geopolitical equation based on self-interest rather than romantic motivation. Mao had also been less than enthusiastic about Hanoi invading the South, preferring a divided Vietnam to a unified one. So upon his death, reservations against Mao as a person and against China in general were bound to surface, at least for those who knew how to read between the lines.

The mourning in China lasted six days and it was not until the fifth day that a Vietnamese delegation went to the Chinese Embassy to deposit a wreath on which was written: to the memory of Chairman Mao Tsetung, great leader of the Chinese people, great friend of the Vietnamese people.

'Things are really going bad between Vietnam and China,' commented Strulovici as I went to see him that day, 'look,' he pointed to the text of the communique lying on his desk, 'it is not what they say that is important, it is what they do not say. Did you notice, there is not one word about his being a Marxist or the chairman of the Chinese communist party? He is referred to as the leader of the Chinese people and nothing more. From their point of view, he could just as well have been a Chinese emperor.'

It was bad but it got worse. On September 2, on Vietnam's national day, the Soviet Union got into the picture. That day Moscow sent to Hanoi a note of congratulation which stated that 'loyal to the principles of proletarian internationalism the communist party of the Soviet Union and the Soviet people will continue their assistance to Vietnam in all fields, to consolidate the unity of the socialist countries on the unchangeable basis of Marxism'. 'Read carefully,' commented Strulovici, 'the message is unequivocal.' It indicates that Soviet support to Vietnam would continue in 'all fields' on the unchangeable basis of Marxism. In contrast the message from China was glacial: The people of China and Vietnam are brothers and our people have always supported and assisted each other and the Chinese people will do 'their share' to consolidate this friendship. There was no reference to the communist parties or to the governments of either countries and only the 'people' were mentioned. As for 'support' it was in the past tense.

I was by now aware that Hanoi was slowly drifting towards a closer relationship with the Soviet Union and hence a more difficult relation with China but signs of the ideological drift of the regime towards a more doctrinaire form of communism only came my way peripherally. But when it did come it was unmistakable.

I had learned from Rizvi to keep an eye open for anything which might contribute to our work in Vietnam and this led me to notice, on the road to the airport in Bangkok, a display of water pumps powered by windmills of the type used in the American West. During my many missions to Vinh the local authorities had often complained to me about the lack of water to irrigate the rice paddies. Apparently there was water but it was some fifteen feet below ground and they had no pumps to retrieve it. The area was one of the windiest in Vietnam and ideal, I thought, for wind-powered water pumps. They only pumped about 200 liters per hour but a few hundred of them would make a difference. So I picked up some documentation and sent a proposal to the Red Cross. We could bring in one test pump from Thailand together with two technicians to set it up and watch the results I told *Monsieur* Bai. My assumption was that it was an approach the Vietnamese should like; cheap, effective, easy to maintain and requiring neither electricity nor fuel. Three months later, with no answer in sight, I sent Khoang to investigate. When he returned I could see that he was both puzzled and amused. 'It has not been accepted,' he said.

When I asked him if he knew why, he replied with a smile, 'for ideological reasons'. I could not make heads or tail of his answer so he gave me the full explanation. Lenin had once defined socialism as 'the Soviet state plus electricity'. Vietnam was now building socialism. Had I offered electric pumps, even if there had been no electricity, they would have accepted. But windpower was not part of the Leninist picture. You could not build socialism with windmills so my proposal had been turned down.

During my second year in Hanoi I had started to think what I would do after the end of my assignment. Granted, UNHCR would have been happy to prolong my posting but I had decided I wanted out. It was not so much that the living conditions were getting to me but the challenge as I had known it was no longer there. Politically, with Vietnam now a member of the UN and the rest of the UN system slowly moving in, I was now treading a beaten path. So all that was left for me to do was managing the aid program or, as Rizvi would say manning the groceries store and while keeping track of cement loads or sparring with the Vietnamese on minor matters of arcane bureaucracy had been initially entertaining it was becoming repetitive and the charm was gone.

So out it was but to where? As far as journalism was concerned I felt I had done my time and having been an actor—albeit a very minor one—reporting news rather than contributing to making it had lost its appeal. So would I stay with UNHCR? It was an option I seriously considered, but after two years in Hanoi I felt I needed a break of some sort. Strangely, the longer I stayed in Hanoi, the more I was tempted to spend some time in the US. I had never lived in the US and when through friends I was informed that the Carnegie Endowment would be happy to have me for one year in New York as Senior Associate, I jumped at the opportunity. My job would be to write, give lectures and generally make myself available as the rare bird that had just spent two years in Hanoi.

I left Hanoi on October 7, 1977, and on my way back stopped for three weeks in Geneva to put my affairs in order. There my current contract with UNHCR was extended by two years with the understanding that in 1978 I would be on leave without pay before returning to UNHCR in 1979. What I would do next was unclear but given my privileged relationship with Sadruddin and Rizvi, I could expect to be given a reasonably challenging job. But as chance would have it, two days after I renewed my contract Sadruddin unexpectedly resigned from his post as High Commissioner for Refugees. Suddenly, the power structure of UNHCR as I had known it dissolved and the knives were out. Rizvi, I was sure would be the first to fall from his pedestal. Not that he would be fired, this did not exist in the UN system, but he would be moved to an unimportant post, away from Headquarters. It would be exile, but a comfortable one. After all, he was a senior director and assigning him to an excessively uncomfortable post would have set a precedent and no one one knew when the wheel would turn.

As for myself, while I had been closely associated with Sadruddin and Rizvi, I had never been part of any clique or aggravated any one. Likewise, Hanoi had not been a sought-after post and by accepting it I had not deprived anyone of a plum job. Nonetheless it was a good year to be away from UNHCR and let a new structure fall in place.

LIVING IN THE USA

I arrived in New York at the end of November 1977 with the expectation of having a good time. I was not disappointed.

The Carnegie Endowment was located in a side street off the UN building and made for a good 25-minute walk from my apartment. There I was given an office, a telephone line and, when needed, the support of a secretary. My functions were undefined on the understanding that I would contribute visibility to the Carnegie, be available for lecture tours, briefings and presentations as the rare Swiss who had just emerged from two years in Hanoi. Except for these obligation I was free with my time, could take long lunches if I wished and was not tied to a timetable or schedule as long as I did what was expected of me.

My start with the Carnegie was auspicious. ABC had recently purchased from Swiss TV a documentary on Vietnam which they edited into four segments that ran on Good Morning America with me appearing live doing the commentary under the label of the Carnegie Endowment. That alone put me on the map and by the same token it was visibility for the Carnegie. This, however, proved not entirely for the best. Shortly after the show I received a call from the UNHCR Representative in New York, Viru Dayal, requesting that I come and see him.

On first impression Dayal could pass off as an unctuous Indian but behind the façade he stood for the best of the Indian civil service. Bright, articulate, well mannered he was a diplomat at its best. The subject of his concern, he explained to me, was me.

Although on leave from UNHCR, he reminded me, I was still a UN civil servant and should therefore steer clear of political controversy. Apparently, after my TV program had been aired the head of the Vietnamese delegation at the UN had come to see him and had complained that I had 'earned money' by appearing on TV. The intervention, in diplomatic terms, was so unusual not to say incongruous that Dayal was wondering if the Vietnamese delegate had gone round the bend or if I had said something outrageous on the air. I could not make head or tail of it either and, by chance, asked him the name of the Vietnamese representative. Pham Duong, he answered. This was the man, I told Dayal, who a few years back in Prague had emphatically stated that the Swiss workers could not possibly have their military weapon at home because if they did they would revolt. Dayal found the story hilarious and told me to forget about what had happened while cautioning me to just be a bit careful. By now nothing about the Vietnamese was liable to surprise me but I could not help thinking that if this was the man that the system in Hanoi had chosen to represent Vietnam at the UN and report back to the Politbureau, then Vietnam was indeed in big trouble.

The combination of the Carnegie name, the fact that I had spent two years in Hanoi and that I was a Swiss with a PhD gave me an entree in academia, the foreign policy establishment as well as the leftovers of the anti-Vietnam war movement and the spectacle it provided me was mesmerizing.

Observing America, this strange, exotic, foreign and at times outlandish society, both alien and familiar, proved a fascinating exercise, the exploration of another facet of our Western world, as unfamiliar to me as the dark side of the moon. The door to this new world, New York, was some sort of oversized Ellis Island, no longer Europe but not quite America. Actually it was the best of both worlds, an intelligent, vibrant creative city freed from the social fetters of the old world and not yet strapped down by the bigoted insularity of the new. But what increasingly struck me was the dichotomy between the nation's wealth and the nation's government.

It was an incredibly rich country, which derived its wealth from a combination of size, population, natural resources, a rigorous work ethic, flexibility, innovation, creativity, good management and the intellectual freedom to take risks. This wealth not only supported a state apparatus which enjoyed almost unlimited resources but also a unique collection of academic institutions, foundations, intelligence agencies and research facilities, with a database of facts that was unequalled.

Already in Vietnam, but even more so now in the US, I could not shake off one nagging question. To what extent did the power elite tap into the nation's intellectual reservoir before coming to a policy decision?

There is little doubt that practically every assessment made in Washington regarding the Vietnam war and its wider context had proven wrong. There is equally little doubt that the whole thrust of America's policy towards China had been off track for three decades and even more so after Beijing had broken with the Soviet Union in 1960.

These, I had now come to believe, were not incidental malfunctions but rather an example of the ingrained predisposition of the American power structure to systematically overlook any objective fact that did not conform to its world vision. The ultimate result was the triumph of a Manichean vision that perceived the world as a struggle between absolute good and total evil, where the only choice was between right and wrong, real or imagined.

Politics thus became an exercise in religious fervor in which the whole compendium of power, Congress, government, foundations, NGOs, lobbies, military and intelligence complexes operating as an entity, functioned in gear with its own beliefs rather than with a geopolitical reality. Thus Taiwan became 'free China', never mind that in the 60s and 70s the regime was a nasty dictatorship which tolerated no political dissent and where the only freedom was at best economic. Likewise Diem, the radical Roman Catholic president of South Vietnam, became the 'Churchill of Asia' at the time when he was stifling all opposition to his personal rule.

This propensity to sugar-coat every ally, proxy or accessory with the attribute of free and hence of good, as opposed to evil probably was a direct by-product of a perception of foreign relations that studiously ignored geopolitical realities. The fact that any government seated in Beijing—whatever its ideology—would seek to surround itself with buffer states, would object to an enemy gaining a strong hold on its Korean and Vietnamese borders and would be far more comfortable with a divided Korea and Vietnam than with a unified one was never considered.

Within this context the immense reservoir of knowledge that America possessed was never put to full use because it rarely conformed to the world vision that had cast its hold on the power establishment. This, ultimatly, was a nation of believers and if knowledge and understanding contradicted belief, it would be overlooked. Understanding would have cast doubt on Washington's untenable contention that Taiwan rather than Beijing represented China, on the effectiveness of the bombing of North Vietnam or on the capacity of the Saigon regime to hold its own just like it would have cast doubt on Saddam Hussein's alleged involvement in 9 / 11 or possession of weapons of mass destruction. But doubt was not American. Certitude was. This I felt was the great American divide between on one hand a parochial, ideologically oriented decision-making process and on the other a reservoir of knowledge that remained ignored or untapped, if it proved to be at variance with a world view grounded in the moral absolutes of an imagined struggle between absolute good and absolute evil.

The problem, if anything, was compounded by naivety. The power elite, apart from a few exceptions, was not sensitive to plots, conspiracies, manipulations and labyrinths of ulterior motives or hidden agendas. They were straight, honest and believing and hence easy to manipulate; from Chang Kai-check to Nguyen van Thieu to Chalaby to Karzai they would repeatedly fall prey to the sirens who knew how to sing to them.

The one who finally found the solution to the Vietnamese component of this foreign policy aberration was Henry Kissinger. But Kissinger was not American. He was a bright Jewish kid from Erfurt who was lucky enough to have left his home town early rather than later through the chimney and obtained an American passport in the process. But below this American veneer he remained a quintessential central European in whose geopolitical perception of the world balance of power Vietnam stood out as a pawn rather than a crusade. And once the pawn had lost its relevance—real or imagined—discarding it not only carried no stigma; it was a duty.

Ultimately however, ignorance, naivety, cultural insensitivity, misuse of intellectual resources and blindness to any realities which did not fit a pre-conceived vision of the world were irrelevant to a single truth which was the defining component of political America. It was too big to fail. Where does a 500-pound gorilla sit? The answer is: anywhere he wishes. The country was so powerful, the depth of its wealth and resources so great, that it could do whatever it wished and overlook the consequences of its eccentricities. These, in proportion to its might, were insignificant: 150 billion dollars wasted, 58,000 dead, the loss of South Vietnam were ultimately of little consequence to the United States and the nation soldiered on none the worse for it having in the process learned nothing and forgotten everything.

Exploring America brought me in contact with what was left of the peace movement. It had been instrumental in forcing the power establishment to disengage from Vietnam and with the end of the war it imploded for lack of a cause. All that was now left of it was a small handful of individuals who had been opposed to the war from its inception for ideological reasons and, having ridden the wave of the anti-war movement, had gone back to being an insignificant sideline in American society. With no war to oppose they clung to their last straw, advocating US reconstruction aid for Hanoi. They were a lonely set who refused to see Vietnam for what it was, namely a Stalinist dictatorship committed to an absurd ideology. I remembered coming across one of their leading lights, Cora Weiss, a bright wealthy New Yorker at Bloomingdales. When I commented that Cambodia had just broken diplomatic relations with Vietnam, she replied forcefully: 'Not broken, suspended,' as if it mattered.

Representatives of these fringe groups regularly visited Vietnam where they kept telling the Vietnamese what they wished to hear, namely that American reconstruction aid was just round the corner. How off-target they were was reflected in the writings of one of their members, Candace Falk, who commented that by maintaining their trade embargo on Vietnam the US was 'losing out on lucrative opportunities for trade and investment'. Lucrative opportunities? Vietnam had no banking system, no rule of law, its exchange rates were purely artificial, it was broke, had nothing to sell and its 1977 foreign investment code was surreal. 'Lucrative opportunities' apart, the lesson, if there was any, was that the full range of the American political spectrum shared the uncanny ability of seeing in Vietnam what they wanted to see rather than what there was to see.

From the comfort of the Carnegie Endowment I watched the last chapter of a process that I had only marginally grasped while in Hanoi; the inexorable march of the Vietnamese communists on the road to their total alignment with the Soviet Union. In June 1978 Vietnam joined the COMECON, in November it signed a 25-year-long treaty of friendship with the Soviet Union and on December 4 it invaded Cambodia. By now the leaders in Hanoi had recreated the environment they were the most comfortable with; war, and Vietnamese children could chant to their hearts content 'khun tot Kampuchea, Hoa, My ... no good Cambodia, China and the US.' It was a tall order but not one to worry the leadership. Over the years they had defeated all their enemies and manipulated all their allies and had emerged victorious. They were invincible and no challenge was too great for them. The only situation they could not manage was peace but that was no longer in the cards.

By November 1978, as my time with the Carnegie was coming to an end, I had received a call from the Head of Personnel of UNHCR. They were ready to take me back as of January 1, 1979 and had found a position for me in the Asia section but there was a small problem. The current head was due to retire and they felt that an Asian should fill the job and they were thinking of Darryl Han. Of course he was junior to me but would I mind working under him? The call did not excessively surprise me. Darryl was a master at boot-licking his way up the UN bureaucratic ladder and, building on the fact that he was an Asian and hence the ultimate Asian expert, he was gunning for the job of head of the Asia section. Superficially I got along well with Darryl, but I was well aware that given my Asian experience he would perceive me as a potential competitor and the first thing he would to do would be to ease me out of the Asia section. By now however I had started to understand the inner workings of the UN; never say no, never confront, never express a difference of opinion and if there was any stabbing to be done make sure it was in the back. So I enthusiastically agreed. 'Darryl is a friend and superbly qualified,' I replied, 'of course I will not mind working under him.' Fate then took care of the rest. A few days later I received another call from Geneva. Darryl had found a house in a small community just outside Geneva and was peacefully driving home one evening when a speeding Turk coming from the opposite direction in an overloaded, dilapidated car jumped the lane and hit him head on. Another driver might have swerved in time but Darryl was not particularly skilled at the wheel and, severely wounded, died at the hospital the next day. I immediately shot a cable to Geneva conveying my heartfelt condolences and breathed a sigh of relief.

BACK AT UNHCR

A After two years in Hanoi and one in New York, at the age of 42 I was back in Geneva which I found exactly as I had left it. All my Swiss friends had the same jobs, holidayed in the same places, talked about the same subjects, held the same opinions and, more importantly, had made sure that they would not meet anyone they did not already know. It was reassuring that such a place as Geneva existed, a place to which one could come back as if one had never left. But it was not exactly a fount of great excitement and the price to pay for living in this Eden of comfort could be summed up in one word: boredom.

The new head of the Asia section to which I had been assigned was a genial Dutchman who was given the job that had been set aside for Darryl Han. He was overweight, dressed shabbily and his fingers were brown from the nicotine of the three packs of cigarettes he smoked every day and I could not have hoped for a better boss. He had a good word for everybody and as long as things were more or less on course had a natural proclivity for not interfering with anything or anybody. The fact that he was one year away from retirement if anything encouraged a natural bonhomie and he merrily told me that he had nothing for me to do but that this should not stop me from whatever I thought I might want to look into.

The departure of Sadruddin had brought a profound change to UNHCR. Under his rule, the organization had been a monarchy in which the subjects paid homage to their Prince whose judgment was unquestioned and whose wishes were commands. His successor Poul Hartling was if anything his opposite. A Dane who had started his professional career as a school master with strong links to the Lutheran church he had gone underground when the Germans occupied Denmark and became one of the leaders of the resistance. By 1945 he was a national hero and naturally gravitated towards politics where he became a pillar of the conservative estab-lishment. Over the years he became successively Foreign Minister and then Prime Minister before leaving Danish politics and being elected High Commissioner for Refugees in 1978. There, schooled in the ways of a Scandinavian democracy, he set up the semblance of a cabinet and rather than ruling by decree would seek out the opinion of his directors before taking any major decision.

On a visit to New York Hartling had come across Viru Dayal who was the UNHCR representative at the United Nations and had been impressed by his sharp mind, his administrative savvy and the wide range of contacts he had built up. Being new to the job and with no prior UN experience, he realized he needed someone with entries into the UN system and had brought him to Geneva as his Chief of Cabinet to replace Rizvi who had been sent packing to represent UNHCR in Rome. I had met Dayal several times in New York and while he was not personally hostile to me, I could feel that he was somewhat wary of what he considered to be a slightly adventurous style of work. Given that he was now Hartling's right hand man and a power to count with, some damage control on my side was needed and I was mulling on how to go about it when, on February 17, 1979, China attacked Vietnam.

It was obvious that after Hanoi had openly sided with the Soviet Union and had invaded Cambodia, Beijing could not just stand passively by and do nothing so they responded in kind, sort of. What followed was probably the strangest of all wars. Both coun-tries kept their diplomatic relations, neither used their respective air force and at the very onset of the conflict the Chinese went public as regards their strategy, namely that they would penetrate Vietnamese territory for a depth of some 20 to 30 miles, stay put and then withdraw.

As I kept up with the incursion mostly by reading American newspapers, which kept on underlining the problems the Chinese army had in dealing with the Vietnamese, a German expression kept on coming to my mind: Schadenfreude. Loosely translated it meant taking pleasure in someone else's woes as if after having been thoroughly trounced by the Vietnamese, the US were now rejoicing in the Chinese taking a similar or worse drubbing. That the Chinese found the going hard was unquestionable. The last time they had fought a war was some 25 years before in Korea and they lacked the battle-hardened veterans that Vietnam had in abundance. They had also spent the last ten years caught up in the domestic wrangling unleashed by the Cultural Revolution and their army had lost its focus as a defense force. So when the incursion started the Chinese proved hopelessly inept at co-coordinating the use of armor, infantry and artillery, with each operating independently of each other at no small cost to themselves. But this was irrelevant to the issue at stake.

The incursion was a show; it did not threaten the Vietnamese regime and left unanswered the question as to whether the Soviet Union would actually risk a war with China and a major confrontation with the US in order to come to the assistance of its Vietnamese ally. But it was a show that carried a message. It could be repeated anytime and this created for the leadership in Hanoi the single situation which they felt the most uncomfortable with; uncertainty.

The Vietnamese had also always fought an enemy, be it French or American, which had a shortage of ground troops. This was no longer the case. The Chinese threw 500,000 men in the incursion and could double the number any time.

The French and the Americans had also been casualty shy. The Chinese had no such compunction and fifty or a hundred thousand casualties more or less were of no concern to them. Last but not least, if the Vietnamese had broken the will to fight both of the French and of the Americans it was because these were democracies with dedicated parliaments and a vocal press where dissent was free to express itself. In China they found an enemy in their own image. With no free press, a controlled parliament and an unlimited supply of manpower to throw into the fray there was no anti-war movement to fuel and Hanoi's well oiled, propaganda machinery had nothing to work on. Finally while both the French and the Americans operated with expeditionary forces 12 000 miles from their home countries the Chinese were on the border of Vietnam literally breathing down their necks. The end result was that the Vietnamese communists had now to unlearn everything that two previous wars had taught them. Conversely, China now demonstrated that it was the only power who was currently not only ready to use force against Vietnam but could repeat the operation at its convenience.

As the incursion came to an end and China announced on March 5 that all its forces had pulled back from Vietnam another crisis unfolded; the boat people exodus. The first mass departure had actually started in 1978 when some 260,000 Chinese residents of Northern Vietnam were pushed over the border into China. By 1979 the exodus had spread to the whole of Vietnam, sweeping away both Chinese and ethnic Vietnamese and as tens of thousands of boat people started to arrive in neighboring South East Asia and Hong Kong old alliances crumbled and new ones gelled. Before it had been the US fighting the specter of China in Vietnam. Now it was China, ASEAN and the US confronting the Soviet Union and its local mad dog, Vietnam.

Boat people notwithstanding, I still had to find something to do. Hartling had kept Marie-Thérèse as a secretary and personal assistant so I went to her for advice 'I think he is interested in China,' she commented, 'perhaps you should try that'. It made sense. In 1974 Hartling had been the first prime minister from a NATO country to visit China and could not have been unaware that Beijing considered UNHCR as a hostile organization and had refused every attempt Sadruddin had made to establish even the semblance of a dialogue. If Hartling could overcome this hostility he would have opened a new chapter in the history of the organization.

Hartling came from a well-structured government where one went through channels and it would have been inappropriate for an officer of my grade to ask for an appointment or send him a note. So I decided to go and see Dayal. If I could sell him the idea that I could help on China, he might get Hartling interested. However if Dayal did not buy it, that was the end of it. It was a chance I had to take and so I asked for an appointment.

Dayal received me oozing with civility as he expanded on how pleased he was to see me again. Careful, I told myself, the man is no fool, you have to play it well and, without pretending, give him the feeling that you could be useful. Hyperbole did not work with

Dayal so I prudently kept to the facts without embellishing them. I had had a long relation with the Chinese, they had been helpful when I procured aid to Vietnam. In case Hartling was looking to improve relations between them and UNHCR I could approach them informally and see their reaction. At worse nothing would come out of it but if the approach was successful it could develop into something very important for UNHCR.

Dayal was an Indian. His country had been at war with China and the Chinese loathed the Indians. But he was also as loyal a UN civil servant as they came. If he, an Indian, could contribute to mending relations between UNHCR and China he would have, if anything, enhanced the concept that a UN civil servant is above whatever confrontation his country of origin is involved in. Dayal listened, made no comments and said he would get back to me. Keep this to yourself, was his only recommendation.

Two days later he called me into his office. This time he was all business and dispensed with the usual niceties. 'You can go ahead,' he said, 'and keep me informed. Be careful,' he added with a smile as I left his office. That I should report only to him was unsaid but understood.

Hsu Ching-mei, my genial contact at the Chinese consulate in Geneva, had been called back to Beijing and I was received by his successor, Mr Li. His English was fairly good and after the usual cup of green tea and some idle chitchat I came to the purpose of my visit.

As he knew, I explained, UNHCR had a new High Commissioner who, when he was Prime Minister of Denmark, had been the first Prime Minister of a NATO country to visit China. This, I emphasized, took some courage and demonstrated that in principle Mr Hartling was well disposed towards China. Currently UNHCR was very involved in assisting refugees who had fled Vietnam because they were persecuted. Many of these refugees were of Chinese origin and developments in Indochina were of course also of concern to China. So having the opinion of China was very important for Mr Hartling. Unfortunately this was not possible because there were no good relations between UNHCR and China. So Mr Hartling wished to improve these relations. I had come to convey this message in a personal capacity and as a friend of China. Personally, I added, I would not have passed on this message if I did not think Mr Hartling was sincere. I also thought that with the ongoing crisis in Indochina some sort of relationship between UNHCR and China would be a good thing. This relation could start informally (the Chinese liked this expression), step by step (they also liked that) and it could also be with Mr Hartling in his capacity as the former Prime Minister of Denmark and not necessarily as High Commissioner for Refugees. Mr Hartling was open to any suggestion in a spirit of good will.

Mr Li could only report my words to Beijing and I hoped not to have overdone the salesmanship. But it was clear that to get the Chinese to move I had to convince them that it was in their interest to do so, which in this case it was. With the whole world now ganging up on Vietnam and the exodus of boat people getting worldwide coverage, the Chinese had nothing to loose by appearing to be among those who supported a UN agency which was assisting refugees from Vietnam. Without going into details I reported my meeting to Dayal and went back to the splendid isolation of my office from where I could observe undisturbed the deterioration of the refugee situation in Asia.

The exodus of boat people from Vietnam had now reached crisis proportions with Hong Kong, Malaysia and Thailand at the receiving end of the outflow. The Vietnamese invasion of Cambodia had also provoked a massive exodus of Khmers to Thailand in a flow that included both ordinary people and former Khmer Rouge. At the point of departure, Vietnam, there was clearly a policy: class war combined with ethnic cleansing. At the various points of arrival there seemed to be no co-coordinated policy. Basically it was a mess.

Three weeks later, which was fast by Chinese standards, I received a call from Mr Li. Would I please come to see him. After the usual cup of green tea, he came straight to the point. Mr Hartling was welcome to visit China in his capacity as former Prime Minister of Denmark. Mr Li also wanted to know with whom Mr Hartling generally traveled with. This was a delicate issue. For questions of protocol he could not come alone but then there would have been no operational justification for his bringing along a team from UNHCR. So I replied that he generally traveled with his wife and one personal assistant who was generally his Chief of Cabinet. Would I be coming along too? I would let him know.

When I broke the news to Dayal he was visibly elated. Granted it was not a total breakthrough. Hartling would be coming to China as former Prime Minister and not as High Commissioner for Refugees but it was a first step and if things went well much could be built on it. Dayal was a shrewd diplomat and saw the opening it represented. Hartling was presumably less attuned to the circuitous ways of the East but this was something for Dayal to handle. Another question was my role. Dayal was too sharp to be finessed so I played it straight. The devil was in the details, I told him. The hotel Hartling would be staying in, who he would be seeing, where he would be going, how informal messages would be passed back and forth, all these were important matters and if he felt I could be useful in organizing the visit I would be happy to help.

Two days later Dayal called me in to meet Hartling. He came across as a quiet, sturdy man with a strict headmasters eye for discipline and after having asked me a few questions on my background he dismissed me with the semblance of a nod. A solid man, I thought, demanding but fair and probably far shrewder than he looked. I think you passed the test, commented Dayal with a smile as we stepped back into the corridor. And off course, he added, I hope you will be coming with us.

Hartling, accompanied by his wife and Dayal arrived in Beijing on Monday March 13, 1979, on the early evening flight from Geneva. I had preceded him by two days and went to the airport to meet him. There was no time lost on his arrival and after a perfunctory five minutes in the VIP lounge, he and his wife were whisked away in a Red Flag limousine while Dayal and I followed in a lesser car. It was 8.30 pm when we arrived at the Beijing hotel after what had been for them a very long flight and as they went to their rooms we agreed to meet next morning for breakfast at eight.

Hartling's visit to China was a showcase of understated diplomacy. Nothing the Chinese did was by accident and every detail had its meaning. But if this meaning was clear to the Chinese more often than not it was lost on foreigners. Dissecting every single Chinese signpost to ascertain it's meaning was an exercise too alien for Hartling to enjoy but Dayal found it highly entertaining.

As a former Prime Minister Hartling had been invited to China by the People's Institute for Foreign Affairs. While state-financed, officially it was neither a government organization nor a communist party organ and its uncertain status enabled it to operate in a political haze when the authorities saw fit to keep issues and relations undefined. The outcome in the present case was that, in the middle of a major outflow of refugees from Vietnam which was destabilizing the whole of South East Asia, a High Commissioner for Refugees could come to China under the inconsequential label of 'former Prime Minister of Denmark'.

The morning after Hartling's arrival we proceeded to the Foreign Ministry where we were received by our official host, Ling Qing, director of the International Organizations Department. Ling was the embodiment of Chinese diplomacy at its finest and radiated intelligence, sophistication and a natural elegance. The fact that he was a direct descendent of Lin Tse-tzu, the Mandarin who had burned the Opium that the British had forced the Chinese to import in the 1850s saved him from the worst excesses of the Cultural Revolution which he spent in limbo. Now he was again in his natural element and China was certainly the better for it. With Ling there was no longer any pretence that Hartling was in China only as former Prime Minister and the discussion centered exclusively on UNHCR.

According to Ling there were at present some 230,000 refugees from Vietnam in China, of whom about 20,000 were ethnic Vietnamese and the rest of ethnic Chinese origin. All had been temporarily allocated to state farms at a considerable cost. Hartling responded by suggesting that UNHCR could provide some assistance to facilitate the local settlement of the refugees. 'We will inform the authorities of your suggestions' said Ling with a smile as he rose to indicate the meeting was over.

Until now all of China's foreign relations had been exclusively bilateral on a state to state basis. Accepting Hartling's offer would have meant that the Chinese were now ready to go multilateral and, in parallel to their state-to-state relation, also operate through the UN system. Vietnam had chosen that route but initially it was only to promote the PRG and they had come to it almost circuitously. This was not the way the Chinese operated. Unlike the Vietnamese and their experimental approach, the Chinese were more structured and systematic and for them the choice to go multilateral would have been the result of a policy decision rather than an opportunistic approach. Hartling's visit notwithstanding, there was nothing to indicate that such a decision had been taken or was even considered.

After meeting with Ling we moved one step up the hierarchy and were received by Chang Wenjin who held the rank of Vice-Foreign Minister. Chang, a bouncy man who spoke good English, chose to embark on a long monologue on Vietnam. 'Vietnam,' he explained, 'has decided to impose its hegemony on the whole of Indochina. As a matter of principle this is unacceptable to China. Why has Vietnam chosen this route? For two reasons. First, having won the war against the Americans they have become arrogant and think they are unstoppable. Second, they are supported by the Soviet Union.

The Soviets have global ambitions and as they cannot further them in Western Europe they use Cuba to intervene in Africa and Vietnam to intervene in Asia. This is unacceptable to China and it is for this reason that we had to teach the Vietnamese a lesson with a military strike on the border. Of course we were not so naive to believe that this would make Vietnam change its ways. But we had to show that Vietnam was vulnerable. As for the future, we have kept the option open to again resort to a military operation if needed and if necessary we will teach them a second lesson. The crux of the matter is that we want stability in the region, which means that Vietnam must pull its troops out of Cambodia and Laos and stop threatening Thailand. But at present Vietnam has no desire to negotiate.'

That evening the Danish ambassador hosted a dinner for Hartling and as we were having coffee handed him a press release from the New China News Agency. It said, 'Chinese Vice Foreign Minister Chang Wenjin met former Danish Prime Minister Poul

Hartling. Mr Hartling visited China in 1974 and cherished friendship with the Chinese people.' The text was significant both for what it said and what it did not say. It said that Hartling cherished friendship... the past tense indicating that this referred to his former visit to China as Danish premier and not to his current visit and it also made no reference to his present position as High Commissioner for Refugees. To Dayal and me the implications were clear. Hartling was still officially only a former Prime Minister and relations between China and UNHCR were still on hold. So more work remained to be done.

While in Geneva planning Hartling's visit I had suggested to the Chinese that he might wish to see Shanghai and also perhaps Kunming. It was just a hunch but Kunming was where many of the refugees from Vietnam had arrived and it would bring Hartling closer to the action. I mentioned this to Dayal but all he said was: 'Do as you wish.'

The following day we left for Kunming and for the next 24 hours we went sightseeing which provided me with an opportunity to get to know Hartling. Anyone, I felt, who had fought the Germans must have had some merit but there was more to Hartling than just having been a former resistance fighter. He had his feet on the ground and if the schoolmaster in him made for a disciplinarian, it was with a human touch and despite his simple demeanor, not to be underestimated.

On the evening before our departure one of the officials who accompanied us told us there would be a change of program. You will fly to Shanghai tomorrow in the afternoon as planned but in the morning you will meet some refugees.

We were off by eight the next morning, Hartling and his wife in a Red Flag heavy limo and Dayal and I, together with half a dozen Chinese officials, leading the way in a minibus. The sky was overcast and occasionally we would pass convoys of military trucks. They were heavy machines of Soviet design, packed with troops who surveyed us with indifference as we drove past them. Attached by ropes to the back of each truck was a large cauldron with the outside blackened by what must have been smoke. I could visualize the troops getting off their truck, gathering firewood and cooking their rice in the cauldron; cheap, effective and so very archaic.

After about one hour on the main road we branched off to an unpaved track and after a couple of miles came to a stop next to a cluster of small brick buildings with corrugated iron roofs. We stepped from our cars onto the muddy ground and were pointed towards one of the larger buildings.

The building was actually a meeting hall with the floor made of packed earth and light provided by a few naked light bulbs hanging from the ceiling. At one end of the room there was a large wooden table covered by a plastic tablecloth. Facing the table about 50 people had gathered, sitting on a motley assortment of rickety chairs. They looked at us silently as we took our seats on the side of the table facing them. Most seemed in their forties and about a third were women. 'They are refugees from Vietnam,' said one of our interpreters to Hartling. 'They heard you were here and they wanted to meet you.' The explanation was absurd. How could the refugees possibly know that Hartling was nearby. But this was in keeping with the prevailing theatrics. The former Prime Minister of Denmark had no business meeting refugees in China but if refugees requested a meeting with the High Commissioner for Refugees, the Chinese authorities would generously abide by their wishes. But this said, the people were for real and so was their predicament.

There was silence in the room and then a woman in her fifties got up. As she started to speak in a slow, measured voice the interpreter next to Hartling translated. This was clearly no sedate housewife but a woman of authority who spoke her mind. As she spoke, her voice slowly started to rise in pitch. She was from Haiphong, she said, and had joined the resistance against the French in the early 50s as an underground trade unionist. After the creation of the Democratic Republic of Vietnam, she had made her way up the ranks of the local trade union and had joined the communist party. Then things started to go wrong between China and Vietnam and in the Spring of 1979 she, her husband and three children crossed the border into China. I could see Hartling listening attentively and at one point he interrupted her and asked: 'Did the

Vietnamese forcefully expel you.' There was a moment of silence. 'No,' she answered, 'they only took away our jobs, our ID cards and our rations and made outcasts of us. So what other choice did we have?'

Others spoke. One was a veteran of Dien Bien Phu who had spent fifteen years in the army. Another was a high school geography teacher. Hartling asked him if he had heard about Denmark. 'Yes,' he answered, 'the capital is Copenhagen.' There was also a crane operator from Haiphong and a miner from Honghai. As the meeting proceeded the tone changed, the atmosphere became electrified and the tension palpable. These were not actors reciting a script. These were people, real people, hard working people who felt they had been wronged and the sense of injustice they conveyed was genuine. All told the same story; their only sin was to have been born Chinese.

It was probably not often that Hartling had spent so much time listening to refugees and articulate ones too and as we headed back for Kunming to catch the flight to Shanghai I could feel that he had been touched.

It was a five-hour long flight from Kunming to Shanghai in an aging Soviet propeller-driven Iliushin 14 and after two hours in the air I could see that Hartling was getting increasingly bored. This I thought was the moment to catch his attention as I handed a one-page hand written note to Dayal. On it I had written that there was a distinct possibility that Hartling's visit might be a turning point in the relations between China and UNHCR. This would require that UNHCR have an assistance program to help the Vietnamese refugees in China which would lead to UNHCR having a presence in Beijing. Such a program would not only have to be well managed but would also require a keen understanding of China and of the political sensitivities at stake. This would require that UNHCR adapt its existing structure to address a new situation. On this basis, one of the solutions would be to devide the current Asia Regional Section in two and to create a new East Asia Regional Section responsible for China, Hong Kong and Japan. Such a section should be small and include a head, a program officer, one administrative assistant and a secretary.

Dayal looked at the paper and then passed it on to Hartling who read it, read it again and then passed it back to Dayal with a nod.

That the note was self-serving was obvious and for all practical purposes I had written a job description for myself. But I was also telling Hartling that there was something I could do for him. He could not say yes because we still had no official relations with China, but if this were to happen I was now confident that I had carved out a role for myself.

Our stay in Shanghai was uneventful and we proceeded to Beijing from where Hartling left for Geneva the evening of the following day. I had planned to leave China the day after through Hong Kong and went to see him off at the airport.

The day before Hartling's departure, I had sat down with Dayal at an old typewriter borrowed from the hotel and, on a blank sheet of paper, had drafted a one-page note entitled The Three Proposals: The title might have looked strange to a foreigner, but the Chinese had a habit of putting numbers to whatever they had to deal with; there were the three happiness's, the four pests, and the five evils so we thought it would be appropriate to make ours the three proposals. The first proposal was that UNHCR would contribute to China's efforts to settle the refugees that had arrived from Vietnam. The second was that China would offer 20,000 resettlement slots for Indochinese refugees currently in South East Asia and Hong Kong with all expenses paid by UNHCR. The third was that, given the crowded situation in the Hong Kong refugee camps, some of the refugees could be temporarily housed in a holding center on the Chinese mainland just across the border with the clear understanding that this was temporary and that not one refugee would stay on in China. As Hartling was about to leave I handed the paper to Mr Wang, the Foreign Ministry official who had accompanied us throughout our visit, saying off-hand that this might be of interest.

As my turn came to say goodbye, Hartling looked me straight in the eyes and said with a touch of a smile 'thank you'. It was a nice gesture.

I came back from China by way of Hong Kong where I spent two days and it was not time lost.

Hong Kong was at the receiving end of a double exodus from Vietnam, one from South Vietnam and one from the North. While both groups were nominally Vietnamese, they were quite distinct. The Southerners, who included a large number of Sino-Vietnamese, were either the victims of the policy of collectivisation, of ethnic cleansing or of both. The Northerners conversely included a relatively small number of Chinese the majority having already fled overland to China and a large percentage of ethnic Vietnamese, most of whom had no quarrel with the regime but could not make ends meet. This last group was particularly problematic as few Western countries were inclined to accept them.

As a British colony Hong Kong was constrained in having to apply western standards in an Asian environment. Unlike Singapore, which had simply decided not to let a single Vietnamese boat land, or Thailand and Malaysia who regularly pushed boats back to sea, any such measure taken by Hong Kong would never have been tolerated by London. Hong Kong therefore had no option but to let all Vietnamese boat people land. This, in turn, created a problem with the local Hong Kong Chinese population. Since 1980 it was the policy of Hong Kong to forcefully return to China any Chinese who came over illegally. Forceful return was not a matter of choice. There was no other option if the colony was not to be swamped by a wave of illegal immigration from the Chinese mainland. Overall, the Hong Kong Chinese accepted this policy as a matter of necessity even if this entailed forcefully returning relatives who lived on the other side of the border.

With Chinese expelled daily to China, it was politically not feasible for the British authorities to be anything but adamant about the fact that the Vietnamese permitted to land could only do so in transit to a resettlement country and that none would ever be allowed to stay. The problem was that many Western countries, including the US, were dragging their feet about resettling North Vietnamese from Hong Kong, arguing that their priority were the boat people from the South housed in camps in Thailand and Malaysia. Another distinguishing factor regarding the refugee camps in Hong Kong as opposed to all the others in the region was that they were 'open' meaning not only that the refugees were free to move in and out but also that they were allowed to work. With Hong Kong chronically short of unskilled labor, this was not only a boon to the economy but also meant that the refugees were self-sufficient and their upkeep did not burden either UNHCR or the Hong Kong authorities. On the downside however, this also meant that any out-of-work Vietnamese from the North, even if he stood no chance of being resettled, could come to Hong Kong and get a job which further fuelled the influx to the colony.

From Hong Kong I proceeded to Bangkok and from there to the Vietnamese refugee camp in Songkhla in Southern Thailand. My visits to China and Hong Kong had given me a pretty good idea of what had brought about the exodus from Northern Vietnam. South Vietnam, I knew, was an altogether different story. I knew the context but the human dimension of the exodus was something I had yet to come to grips with and to do so I had to come face to face with those concerned.

Dr Hung had attended medical school in Saigon and, in 1970, at the age of 30, was drafted into the army as a doctor with the rank of Captain. In mid June 1975 six weeks after the fall of Saigon a notice appeared in the local newspapers stating that all the captains in the former South Vietnamese army were to report to the Phu Tho technical school with food for ten days. 'We all thought,' he explained, 'that this meant that we would be detained for no more than ten days, so we all went.' Hung and all the other captains spent three days in the school building and were then moved by truck to the former army base at Long Thanh, outside Saigon, where he was held for one year. It was a camp for officers with the rank of captain but no distinction was made between those who worked in offices, those who were assigned to elite fighting units or those who were in the medical services. Living conditions were not easy but they were bearable.

In May 1976 all the captains, who until then had received equal treatment, underwent a classification process and were divided into three categories: A, B, and C.

Category A included detainees who were not only considered innocuous but had also high ranking communist relatives who could vouch for their future good behavior and sponsor their liberation. All those in this category were released.

Category B included officers from non-combat units such as doctors, technicians, communication specialist and the like who were considered 'well reeducated'. But, contrary to the detainees in category A did not have influential communist relatives to sponsor their release.

As for the C group, this included officers from elite units such as the rangers, marines or paratroopers as well as intelligence officers and all chaplains be they Roman Catholics, Protestants or Buddhists.

Following the classification exercise the camps were reorganized this time not by rank but by category, with one exception. Generals. Under its communist veneer Vietnam was still a Confucian society where deference to rank, even the rank of the enemy, was ingrained. 'Generals,' commented Dr Hung, 'enjoyed better living conditions than lieutenants and captains.'

Dr Hung had been classified as B and had been moved with other officers in that category to a camp in Tay Ninh, West of Saigon. While living conditions were tolerable what the detainees found most stressful was not being told how long they would be kept in the camp nor what the criteria for being successfully reeducated were. After one year spent in the camp Dr Hung was called in by the camp authorities. 'They told me that technicians should assist in the reconstruction,' he explained, 'and that I was free so I returned to Saigon.'

Following his release, Dr Hung's first move should have been to apply for a job with the Saigon health authorities but he did not. 'I was afraid to get in touch with the authorities,' he explained 'and also the pay was so bad that that I would have been unable to live on it.' With one wife and three children to care for he spent the following year taking odd jobs like pedicab driver, mechanic or electrician. By then Saigon had been organized into 20 family groups with an overseer assigned by the Party. 'He was almost illiterate,' said Dr Hung, 'and could only sign his name so when he asked me if I had registered with the health authorities I said yes and I showed him any piece of paper and he fell for it.'

While Dr Hung was not personally harassed, he felt insecure. When he had been released from detention he had been given a re-education certificate but it was only valid for six months before having to be renewed by the police and he felt it could be withdrawn at any time with no explanation given. So he decided to leave. 'I was Roman Catholic, I was a former officer and I was an intellectual and I felt that neither me nor my children had any future in Vietnam,' he commented. Fortunately he had a sister in the US who had some money. He claims he never understood how she did it but from the US, through intermediaries, money was paid to organize his escape. 'For the Chinese,' he said, 'there was no problem. Any Chinese with some money could go to the authorities and they would organize his way out. For us Vietnamese it was more difficult. But it still could be done.'

Le Dinh Nam faced a somewhat different predicament. Born in Danang in 1945 in a wealthy Buddhist family he was given the opportunity to study abroad and between 1964 and 1970 first attended Laval University in Quebec and then McMaster University in Ontario from where he graduated with a degree in chemical engineering. Upon his return to Vietnam in 1971, he was drafted in the army as a private. After having spent nine months in the military, his family, through some well placed bribes, succeeded in having him released and he found a job in the Ministry of Economy where he worked in the technical department dealing with chemical fertilizers.

After the fall of Saigon, his former rank as a private and his low position in the Ministry ensured that he was exempted from re-education and after three days of political lectures, of which he understood nothing, he was allowed to go home. Nor was he out of a job for long either. While the Ministry was being reorganized by cadres brought in from the North, the chemical fertilizer department to which he belonged continued to operate and he was soon back at work with a monthly salary of 80 Dongs. 'In the beginning,' he explained, 'things were not too bad but then the situation began to deteriorate. In 1975, the rice allocation for Ministry staff was thirteen kilos a month but by 1978 it had dropped to three kilos and with inflation I could no longer live on my salary.'

Another problem was dealing with his supervisors. 'The new director of our unit and all the leading officials,' he explained, 'were from the North and had all studied in the Soviet Union. Not only did they resent me because I had studied in a capitalist country but we had different ways of working and they started to make life difficult for me. So little by little I realized there was no future for me in Vietnam.'

Over the years Nam had saved 2,000 US $ and with this sum he managed to find a place on a boat for himself, his wife, two sisters and one nephew. The boat carried 293 passengers who, except for Nam and his family, were all Chinese. 'We passed ourselves off as Chinese,' he explained, 'and this made it much easier to leave.'

Nam and Dr Hung had sat out the war on the sidelines but in the eyes of the ideologues of the new regime this did not make them any less culpable except that their guilt lay not in what they had done but in who they were; class enemies. As foreign educated bourgeois they were on the wrong side of the new system, at best tolerated on the fringes of a 'socialist' society that had no room for them. And as for their professional talents, these were of little use in a society where the premium was on ideological loyalty rather than on expert qualifications. Ultimately for them, the choice was either to wither in their own country as ideological outcasts, or to leave.

Lieutenant Colonel Nguyen Minh Chau was in another league altogether. Born near Saigon in 1933, Chau joined the South Vietnamese army in 1954 where he stayed for the next 20 years reaching the rank of Lieutenant Colonel and district chief at the time of the fall of Saigon in April 1975. 'I was ready to fight to the end,' he told me, 'but all my superiors had fled and all my soldiers had deserted, so I just went home to my family and waited.'

In June 1975 a notice appeared in the local press saying that all lieutenant colonels were to report to the Don Bosco school in Saigon bringing with them rice for 30 days. 'I thought our detention would last for 30 days,' he said, 'and then I would be reunited with my family, so I went.' He smiled. 'I guess I was naive.' After two days at the school the odd 1,700 lieutenants colonels who had reported in were moved to a camp near Ba Ria were they were kept for five months. 'Life was not too hard,' he said, 'we would work eight hours a day in the fields and do some political study. For food we had 600 grams of rice per day with some vegetables and fish sauce so that was all right.'

In June 1976, all the detainees were shipped to North Vietnam where they were distributed in various camps with Chau and some 500 other officers ending up in the Yen Bay camp some 30 kilometers West of Hanoi.

'Here life was far more difficult than in the South and we had to work 10 hours per day clearing forests and planting rice. If the purpose was to punish us,' commented Chau, 'they did a good job of it but in terms trying to convert us to communism, it was a waste of time.'

In May 1977, for some unknown reason Chau and 91 other officers, including two generals from a nearby camp, were moved back to Saigon, and the following month were set free. 'I was quite weak,' he said, 'and suffered from an old war wound, so perhaps this is why they let me go.'

Back in Saigon Chau received a re-education certificate and thought his troubles were over. He was wrong. Three months after his release the police came to his home to arrest him. Apparently going through the records of the South Vietnamese army, the communists had discovered that Chau, in addition to his military functions and responsibility as district chief, had also been his district's coordinator for the Phoenix program.

The Phoenix program had been set up by the CIA in 1967 in an effort to neutralize the Viet Cong administrative infrastructure as opposed to the Viet Cong guerrillas. Neutralize was a euphemism. In practice it meant assassination. While the actual killing was done by Vietnamese mercenaries the program was totally American financed and directed and its operators were recruited from the ranks of the State Department, the Army or the CIA. Phoenix was probably the greatest single American human rights aberration of the Vietnam War. Arrests were arbitrary, torture was the rule and due process non-existent. Not that the communists did not have their own version of the Phoenix program or ever hesitated in wiping out members of the Saigon administrative infrastructure.

BREAKING THE RULES

At best, being closer to the grassroots, they were probably more selective about who they were killing but the principle was the same with one difference. They did not claim to represent freedom, democracy and Western civilization

Participating in an assassination scheme did not seem to bother the hundreds of Americans who worked for Phoenix with a few notable exceptions. One was Jacques Klein, an Air Force officer, who later became a General. Jewish and of French origin, Klein withdrew from the Program because, in his words, he would not endorse 'means and methods used by the Nazis in World War II'.

It is clear that if Chau had indeed been a district coordinator of the Phoenix program he would get no more mercy from the communists than he had shown them and he knew it. As the police kept banging at his door, he swallowed 40 tablets of Optalidon, a common French painkiller and collapsed. Giving him up for dead, the police left and it was only by a miracle that his wife got him to a hospital where the doctors managed to save him. Since then he had lived in hiding until he found a boat in April 1979 leaving behind his wife and six children.

Were Chau, Dr Hung and Nam refugees? The 1951 Convention defines a refugee as someone who is seeking asylum from persecution for political, ethnic or religious reasons, on the understanding that the persecution must be substantive and not just a matter of discomfort or lack of economic opportunities. So a point could have been made that, if one were to strictly apply the Conventions, neither Dr Hunh nor Nam would qualify as 'refugees'.

As for Lieutenant Colonel Chau, through his participation in the Phoenix program, he had been an accessory to assassination and the conventions had a clause that excluded all those who had committed crimes against humanity from the benefit of refugee status.

So how relevant was a convention, drafted in 1951 in a European context, to the final chapter of the Vietnam War? The simple, basic direct answer was that it was not, but again this was irrelevant to the issue. The Conventions were only as good as the nations which implemented them but this again had to be qualified. During the Cold War the Western European democracies would not have dreamt of sending back a Pole, Czech or Hungarian who would had succeeded in crossing the Iron curtain, and this irrespective of whether his status corresponded or not to the fine print of the Convention. So, ultimately, recognizing Chau, Hung and Nam as 'refugees' was the equivalent of applying a European solution to an Asian problem; all those who left were automatically refugees. But then the same could have been claimed regarding the Chinese who were fleeing to Hong Kong, many of whom were no less victims than the Vietnamese of the aberrations of their regime. And yet, they were all sent back to the mainland and no Western country and in particular not the US had ever even considered granting Hong Kong a resettlement quota for refugees from China. So the real issue was not asylum; it was that in a miserable country called Vietnam a confused superpower had lost a war and was looking for some sort of redemption to a pathetic outcome. Indeed, never in the history of human undertaking had so many with so much failed so miserably against so few with so little. To seek deliverance from this humiliation, America's response was to open the floodgates to an increasing exodus from their one time client state. That many of those who left, were actually part of a new class of outcasts was accidental. Suddenly America had a cause which no one could cast doubt on. Saving the boat people. America being what it is, it was not a cynical, thought-out political ploy but rather a mish-mash of bad conscience, posturing and self-righteousness amplified by the irrepressible urge to agitate.

Personally, I had no qualms about this policy. Life was by defini-tion unjust and if the likes of Dr Hung or Nam were lucky enough to find a developed country which would take them, so much the better for them. But what I found a bit more difficult to put up with was the posturing of so many of the so called refugee advo-cates for whom the Vietnamese were simply a means to purchase a good conscience on the cheap.

It was with these thoughts in mind, and possibly a better un-derstanding of what was going on in Vietnam, that I returned to Geneva.

Prior to my return the rumor had spread that Hartling's visit to China had been a success, and while I was still in a bureaucratic limbo with no precise function, I could feel that I was no longer looked upon as being entirely marginal. With no one feeling threatened by me and Darryl Han out of the way I could therefore look forward, at some point or another, to a post which would provide some interest and possibly a challenge but I had no clue when and if this would happen. So in the meantime, from the cover of my warren, and with nothing else to do, I observed.

All the counties of South East Asia are ethnic mosaics within which Malay, Chinese, Indians, Thai, Christians, Moslems, Khmer and the like keep to themselves and are wary of any development which might alter the delicate balance between communities. This was what they feared the boat people exodus might do. Thus all the countries in the region were dead set on one issue. Not a single Vietnamese would be permitted to settle on their territory. And if ever there was to be even a suspicion that the Vietnamese boat people who had landed on their shore would be in the country on more than a transit basis, they would have no hesitation in pushing all newcomers back into the sea. While occasional pushbacks would provoke the Americans into a frenzy of protest, the response of countries in the region was unequivocal; don't blame us, blame the Vietnamese for exporting part of their population.

By early 1979, the massive boat people exodus from Vietnam combined with the occupation of Cambodia had created throughout the region such a level of resentment against Vietnam that the leadership in Hanoi felt it had to make some sort of gesture. To do so they chose the issue that carried the highest level of visibility, the boat people.

On January 19, 1979, Hanoi sent a message to UNHCR indicating that it was ready to grant exit visas to a number of people who wished to leave Vietnam legally and by this measure contribute to a reduction of the boat people exodus.

It was the first indication ever that Hanoi might provide an avenue for legal departure for some of its citizens and the idea was pounced on by the deputy High Commissioner, Dale De Haan.

Dale, a former senate aid to senator Ted Kennedy was a dapper young man with an engaging personality who wore natty clothes and low, well-polished, trendy boots. His Dutch background must have included a touch of Indonesian and this no doubt accounted for his black hair and dark complexion strikingly set off by the light blue eyes of a Husky. The effect was dramatic and further emphasized by a winning smile. In Geneva his door was always open to anyone who wished to see him and I could well imagine that as a senate aide he was a roaring success. Unfortunately he was also an imbecile.

In February 1979, de Haan, convinced that he was going to make history by devising a system of legal departure from Vietnam which would bring to a close the boat people exodus, proceeded to Hanoi taking with him a team of four other UNHCR staff members. Not one of them had any experience in dealing with the Vietnamese and when I suggested that he also take my former deputy Pierre Jambor who was now stationed in Bangkok Dale's answer was an unqualified no. 'I want to turn a new leaf,' he told me. I did not try to find out what he meant but De Haan by then had made it known that he planned to achieved a major breakthrough in Hanoi and could see himself as the first US ambassador to Vietnam. That for once Vietnam needed UNHCR more than UNHCR needed Vietnam was of course totally beyond his grasp as he proceeded to Hanoi with the blissful obliviousness of a lamb being led to the slaughter.

The outcome of his visit was the so called Orderly Departure Program (ODP) that Dale signed with the Vietnamese on May 30 and which was to become one of the defining arrangements of the boat people saga.

According to the ODP agreement three lists would be set up. List A would include people that the US or other Western governments were willing to accept. List B included people to whom the Vietnamese authorities had given exit permits or, to put it in other words, wanted to get rid of. As for list C, it included those who were both on list A and B and were cleared for departure.

It is a prerogative of every sovereign nation to decide who it will accept for immigration. So list A made sense. What did not was list B. The fact that Vietnam could establish a list of its citizens that it wished to expel and impose on foreign countries was outrageous. As Dale explained triumphantly he had based his agreement on a similar arrangement reached between the US and Havana which provided for an avenue for legal emigration from Cuba to the US. What he had overlooked was the fact that Cuba did not have one million Chinese that it wished to export. Vietnam had. This peculiarity did not take long to come to the fore and the ink was barely dry on the ODP agreement when the Vietnamese presented UNHCR with a list of some 10,000 people who had been granted exit visas. On closer examination they all proved to be Chinese and amounted, in the words of a US official, to the equivalent of the Cholon phone directory. What followed and lasted over the years was a game of blackmail. If the Americans, wished to accept a Vietnamese to whom they felt some obligation the price to pay was to also accept someone on the Vietnamese B list whom Hanoi wished to get rid of.

For Hanoi, the ODP agreement was a gift from heaven. On July 20, UN secretary General Kurt Waldheim had convened in Geneva an international conference on refugees from Indochina where Vietnam would have stood out as an international pariah. Now, however, courtesy of Dale de Haan, the Vietnamese did not have to come to the conference empty handed and could claim that through the ODP agreement that they had done their share in trying to stem the boat people outflow by creating an alternative avenue through legal departure.

The first ODP flight from Saigon to Bangkok took place at the end of June, as a token gesture prior to the July 20 refugee conference. By the end of the year total ODP departures stood at exactly 1,979, and hardly made a dent on illegal departures. But the Vietnamese had what they wanted. A fig leaf for the Geneva conference. Not that the ODP did not ultimately work. Ten years later it did, but for that the Soviet Union had first to collapse.

The conference, which was attended by 65 governments including the Chinese, did not concern me but I found it interesting to hang around on its periphery. While lasting only two days it had been preceded by weeks of informal contacts and the decisions adopted were a foregone conclusion even before the conference started. First, there would be no embarrassing procedure to determine if every single boat person was or was not a refugee; prostitutes, politicians, prison guards, dissident intellectuels, former military, simple farmers, ethic Chinese, shopkeeper or the plain man in the street all now came under the same umbrella and would be automatically granted the status of refugee. Second, all the boat people would be permitted to land in the countries of South East Asia but third, on one, non negotiable condition; they would all be resettled in Western counties.

To say that the conference was a roaring success is an understatement. Practically all the participants got everything they wanted.

For Hanoi, it was an implicit endorsement of its policy of socio-ethnic cleansing. They could now expel, pressure to leave or close their eyes to the departure of any number of their citizens secure in the knowledge that it would not further aggravate their relations with the countries of South East Asia from where they would be subsequently resettled in developed economies. This ensured not only a continued outflow but a steady income. As more and more boat people were being resettled in the West they were increasingly sending remittances to their relatives in Vietnam and the exodus had now become Hanoi's major source of foreign exchange.

For Washington the exodus had become an after-the-fact moral justification for having intervened in Vietnam. Occurring in a Cold War context it was one more illustration of the evils of communism and every resettled Vietnamese was balm on America's conscience not to say bruised ego. But it was more than just balm. For the countless American NGOs and advocacy groups involved in processing the boat people the crisis was a bonanza, generating a prospering refugee industry where funds were plentiful and the opportunities to posture profuse.

For UNHCR the conference was manna from heaven. Almost unlimited funds and a major international role was more than the organization could hope for.

The last of the winners, but not the least, was China. The Vietnamese invasion of Cambodia combined with its alliance with the Soviet Union and the exodus of the boat people had sent tremors throughout South East Asia and while US economic might was still undiminished, Washington had demonstrated that it was not a credible player in a land war in Asia. Now the only power which appeared in a position to counter Hanoi was China. The Thais in particular lost no time in making overtures to the Chinese and the rest of the region was now following suit. The irony was that a war that had started as an American crusade against China had resulted in both Washington and Beijing now sharing the same interest in keeping Hanoi under control.

Last but not least, the boat people could not have hoped for a better outcome. All those who survived the sea journey were now guaranteed resettlement, that is emigration to a developed country, no mean opportunity for the citizens of a country that ranked among the world's poorest 5%. Granted not all survived the journey but coming from a country which had been for 30 years at war, danger was their daily lot and losses at sea could not have exceeded those resulting from mines, shelling and America's constant and indiscriminate bombings of the Vietnamese countryside.

On the morning of Saturday July 21, the second and last day of the conference, I came across Mr Wang from China's Foreign Ministry to whom I had handed 'The three proposals' strolling in the corridors of the UN building. He was attending the conference as part of the Chinese delegation. We exchanged some idle chitchat and as he prepared to move back to the conference room he commented almost as an afterthought, 'oh, by the way China has accepted your proposals one and two. Why don't we meet this afternoon to discuss things?' I will not deny that it was with some excitement that I cornered Dayal when the conference broke for lunch and gave him the news.

'Excellent,' he said, 'actually the Vice Foreign Minister is coming to see Hartling Sunday morning at ten. Please do join us.'

That afternoon I met Mr Wang in the UN coffee shop and I was impressed. These people were professionals, they had done their homework and Wang had come to Geneva fully prepared. According to his figures 251,855 refugees from Vietnam had arrived in China by June 30, 1979. Of this number 208,885 had been placed in 150 state-owned farms and 41,970 were still in holding centers. But the most intriguing was the breakdown by nationality. According to Wang, only 6,989 were Chinese nationals while 222,713 were

Vietnamese citizens of Chinese ethnic origin and 20,322 were ethnic Vietnamese of Vietnamese citizenship. The breakdown represented a 180-degree turn by China on the nationality issue. Beijing had always claimed that the ethnic Chinese in Vietnam were Chinese citizens. Now they were claiming that the overwhelming majority were actually Vietnamese citizens, and politically it made sense. Not only would the newcomers be legally entitled to refugee status (no one could be recognized as a refugee while in his own country) but it also raised in regards to Hanoi the specter of their repatriation in an undefined future.

If the Chinese had made a U-turn on the issue, so had the Vietnamese. Initially they claimed that all Chinese in Vietnam were Vietnamese citizens. Now, once they had been made to leave they were presented as Chinese citizens, thus implying that they would never have any claim to return to Vietnam.

To draw the attention of Mr Wang to these discrepancies would have been a provocation so I chose to overlook these minor points of detail and to concentrate on what UNHCR could contribute to China in terms of assistance to the refugees.

An influx of a quarter of a million refugees in a country of more than one billion inhabitants was, on paper, a negligible occurrence at the national level. But at the level of the grassroots it was not. With the People's communes owned collectively by the farmers who lived on them unable or unwilling to accept the newcomers, the only option the authorities had was to resettle them on state farms. These were owned by the government and generally operated at a loss that was made up for by the authorities. Most numbered from 2,000 to 5,000 farmers and were situated on land of indifferent qualities. It was obvious that the sudden arrival of a thousand or more refugees on an individual state farm meant that its whole economic base, which was already pretty weak, was suddenly put out of whack. Overnight there would be a sudden shortage of housing, schooling, food, jobs, and medical facilities not to say land and this in an establishment which was, at best, operating on the brink of a deficit. If the exercise was repeated in over 150 state farms the cost to the government would be significant and a contribution from UNHCR could play some role in alleviating the burden on the authorities.

Dayal had passed on the good news to Hartling and as I reported to his office on the Sunday he was as ecstatic as his Lutheran background permitted. Three months before he had gone to China as former Prime Minister of Denmark and now he was the head of a UN agency which in the past 24 hours China had acknowledged as an organization it could work with. For Hartling this was a major breakthrough and he made no bones about how pleased he was.

'This is a historic event,' he told Vice Minister Zhang, 'and I would like to thank you for working with us.'

'Don't thank us,' replied Zhang laughing, 'thank the Vietnamese; they forced us to work with you.' Zhang had clearly reached a level in the Chinese political hierarchy which dispensed him from having to submit to the usual clichés, and obviously considered Hartling an equal. The two men, both astute politicians, were clearly on the same wavelength and when Hartling, if only for the sake of politeness, mentioned how he had been impressed by the reception centre for Vietnamese refugees he had seen in China, Zhang interrupted him, 'they gave you the show window,' he said, 'you know the trick, if you send Mr Casella to China,' he turned to me, 'we will show him the real situation.'

'Yes,' replied Hartling laughing, 'I know it was a show window, it is always like this, but I will send Mr Casella to China and he can negotiate an agreement with your authorities to provide some assistance, and I promise you we will move fast.'

That Zhang had made it difficult for Hartling to send anybody but me to China was not an issue. There was no one else within UNHCR that Hartling would have wanted to send anyhow but it was gratifying to hear it from both sides. All there remained for me now was to negotiate with the Chinese a solid and technically credible assistance program.

Negotiating an assistance program was a task generally undertaken at UNHCR by a team of technocrats, something that I felt the Chinese were not quite ready to put up with. On the other hand undertaking the job alone was clearly beyond my ability. Fortunately Jacques Cuenod, who had been the UNHCR representative in Vientiane and who was now in charge of assistance planning in Geneva, stepped in; there was someone that he wished to recommend to me to take along and I leapt at the idea.

At first sight the most striking feature about Jacques Mouchet was his size: at best five feet. Born in the French Savoie of peasant stock he had been orphaned at a young age and had been reared by an aunt. After, I suspect, considering the priesthood he had studied law, found a teaching job in Vientiane, married a Thai from the Northeast and had drifted into joining UNHCR. He was amazingly cultured, quiet, analytical, and hard working with a strong sense of ethics. His only fault if any was that, whatever the circumstances, he moved at his own speed. He could not be accelerated but nothing would slow him down either. Ultimately I could not have hoped for a better assistant.

I arrived in Beijing with Jacques on August 14, 1979, not quite on edge but not totally at ease either. Over the years I had dealt with the Chinese as a journalist and subsequently as a UN civil servant but that had been in organizing Hartling's visit which was essentially a political undertaking. Now I would be dealing with the nuts and bolts of a program and I was not sure that my Vietnamese experience would be of any great relevance.

AN OPENING IN CHINA

I In Vietnam UNHCR had been the spearhead of the UN system and perversely we were now playing the same role in China and for this reason alone Jacques and I felt a personal commitment to its success. The responsibility went far beyond our job levels and grade, but circumstances had thrown us into this role and we intended to pull it off if only for the aesthetics, 'le beau geste' as the French would have called it.

None of our Chinese interlocutors had ever worked with UNHCR or knew much about the organization so I decided that from the start it was necessary to set the record straight. This meant impressing on them three things: first there would never be a UNHCR program in China but rather a Chinese program which would benefit from some UNHCR support. So it was up to China to identify both needs and determine how they would be addressed. Second, our role was to represent the international community and in this capacity provide some support to the efforts of China. Third, we were not operational. We did not physically implement programs but provided support to those who did, in the present case, the Ministry of Civil Affairs.

The day after our arrival in Beijing we left for Nanning, capital of Guangxi province, which bordered Vietnam. From there for eight long days, from dawn to dusk, we were on the road, going from one state farm to another. It was a miserable journey. Guangsi was one of the poorest provinces in China and it showed; a wide expanse of wastelands with hardly a tree on them and an occasional village built in stone and mud huddled under a few anemic trees surrounded by parched fields. The sky, day after day, was grey, the weather hot and muggy and the roads one long sequence of potholes.

At every state farm that we visited it was the same dismal tale. The sudden arrival of several hundred not to say thousands of refugees, whose only possessions were the clothes on their back, had driven the already stretched resources of the farm beyond breaking point. There was no housing and the refugees were temporarily quartered in schools or communal buildings. The authorities had provided the farms with emergency food assistance and milk for the children but only as a stopgap measure. Not only were there no jobs for the newcomers as all the available land was already under cultivation but reclaiming new land would require irrigation equipment and fertilizer, all of which were lacking. Altogether the picture was a depressing one of good people trying to cope with the odds stacked against them.

After one week on the road we arrived in the port city of Beihai, some 100 miles by sea from the Vietnamese border. It was a delightful little town, built in stone in typical Southern Chinese style with the sidewalks covered by arcades. In 1876 it had been declared an open city and half a dozen Western countries had set up trading houses with adjoining churches and schools, all of which had been carefully preserved. The local guesthouse was airy and comfortable, cooled by a gentle sea breeze and we had our first good night's sleep in a week.

The morning after our arrival we went down to the port. It was completely clogged up by hundreds of small boats. There were, we were told, altogether some 11,000 refugees on 916 boats which had sailed in from Northern Vietnam. Actually, most of the fishermen had lived on land while working on large boats but they also owned their own small boat which they used when fishing for themselves and it was on these that they had been made to leave. The journey had lasted from one to two weeks according to the sea and the winds and they had all put in to Beihai for want of a better destination where they were now living on their boats pending an alternative.

With none in sight the authorities were considering moving them inland to state farms, an option that the refugees viewed with apprehension.

'We are not farmers, we are fisherman, we only know how to fish,' explained one of them, 'to put a fisherman on a farm is like putting a salt water fish in a sweet water pond,' he added. When Jacques and I asked the authorities why they did not try to integrate the newcomers in the fishing industry, they said it was impossible. The boats they had come in with were not adequate for fishing and larger ones would have to be built but then the port of Beihai would not have been deep enough to accommodate them. Finally there was the question of fishing equipment and also where to store the fish.

It was now time for lunch and as we were on the point of breaking I indicated that I would like the meeting to resume early afternoon. Our hosts looked somewhat surprised as they felt all had been said and done, but they acquiesced and at three we were all back in the meeting room. Over lunch Jacques and I had hastily worked on a plan and it was now time to spring it on them.

First I concurred with their decisions to resettle the refugees on land for which, I emphasized, there was no alternative given the situation. However, if the situation was to change we could then look at other solutions.

'The refugees,' I said, 'were fishermen and they would serve China and themselves best by fishing and so rapidly achieving self-sufficiency. Now we have to look at the problem from the practical side. What is needed? Fishing boats. We know there is a shortage of wood in Beihai but we can import wood from Malaysia so larger boats can be built locally. We can also buy fishing nets and import marine engines from Japan. If the port is too small we can find concrete to build a new jetty and we can also rent a dredge to make the port deeper. For fish storage we could install a refrigeration facility. So in a reasonable period of time not only will the fisherman become self sufficient but they will contribute to China's economy.'

My arguments hit their mark. Rather than telling them that it did not make much sense to resettle fishermen on farms, which they knew perfectly well, I had offered them the option of implementing a better alternative, if they so wanted.

The next morning, before the long hot dusty ride back to Nanning, we had a last work meeting. The Chinese must have spent part of the night going over our ideas. They had picked up every single one of our proposals and developed them into a comprehensive program to which they would contribute part of the funding and UNHCR the rest.

It was my first experience of working with the Chinese and the natural reflex was to compare them to the Vietnamese. 'The Vietnamese,' the French ambassador in Hanoi had once commented to me, 'are Chinese, only smaller and more messy,' and he could not have been more right. Both shared a sense of form and protocol and the obligation to abide by set rituals but the similarities stopped there. The Vietnamese were constantly either on the attack or imagining plots where there were none. Their planning was erratic and improvisation often was an end in itself. Altogether it made dealing with them highly entertaining but in the long term it was for them a self defeating exercise and they ended up more often than not tripping themselves rather than their imagined foe.

The Chinese conversely were solid, professional, systematic and shunned hyperbole. When they had taken a position they would stick with it unless one could prove to them that there were better alternatives upon which they would be ready to reconsider their original stand.

Three days later, Jacques and I and a notebook full of figures were back in Geneva where Jacques, who was much better at it than I was, proceeded to translate all our notes into one comprehensive assistance program which I handed over to Dayal. 'Finally some good news,' he commented. It was only a few days later that I understood what he had meant.

When I left Hanoi Rizvi had chosen as my successor a 30-year-old Swede, Anders Johnsson. New both to Asia and to UNHCR, Johnsson arrived in Hanoi with all the romantic preconception that Sweden harbored about Vietnam. While he was far from stupid he was smug and his belief, encouraged by the Vietnamese, that as a Swede he had a privileged relation with them, got the better of him and they squeezed him for all he was worth.

When we had set up our buffalo breeding farm the Vietnamese had asked us for some automated milking equipment which I flatly refused to give them: with an excess of manpower they did not need it. One week after his arrival they asked Johnsson and he said yes, a decision that marked him out as a 'useful idiot' for the rest of his stay.

In the weeks following their invasion of Cambodia the Vietnamese had given Johnsson a letter from the new Vietnamese-installed Cambodian government asking for UNHCR assistance. 'This is highly confidential,' said the Vietnamese to Johnsson, 'and it is given exclusively to you as our special friend.' The letter never surfaced at UNHCR Headquarters which only could have meant two things. Either Johnsson sent it but without ensuring that it get the proper follow up and it got lost or, more likely, he just sat on it assuming he had the time to mull about its contents. What the Vietnamese had not told him was that they had given exactly the same letter, with the same admonition that it was confidential and should not be shared with anyone, to both the representatives of the ICRC and UNICEF in Hanoi.

Contrary to Johnsson, who considered himself a notch above the other internationals in Hanoi and did not deign to consort with them, the representatives of UNICEF and the ICRC compared notes regularly and soon realized that they had both received the same appeal. So, jointly, they went to the Vietnamese and informed them that an assistance program for Cambodia could be envisaged but only on the condition that ICRC and UNICEF be permitted to undertake a joint mission to Phnom Penh. After some hesitation the Vietnamese conceded and what followed was a public announcement to the effect that ICRC and UNICEF would soon undertake a joint aid assessment mission to Cambodia. The news hit UNHCR in the solar plexus. The main problems in Cambodia were displaced persons and the possible return of refugees and this was UNHCR's territory and no one else's. Confronted with this flagrant encroachment on his bailiwick, Hartling instructed Dayal to use all his influence to ensure that UNHCR be included in the mission but it was all in vain. In the cut throat world of humanitarian action, neither ICRC nor UNICEF would miss the opportunity to have UNHCR excluded from such a high profile operation and the mission proceeded without us. Both Dayal and Hartling were furious but there was nothing they could do about it. But if they had lost out on Cambodia they had China to fall back on.

In October a Chinese delegation came to Geneva and while meeting with Hartling came straight to the point. The Chinese authorities, they said would provide for most of the expenses to resettle the 260,000 refugees from Vietnam but would like UNHCR to contribute 50 million US $ towards the cost. Hartling had many qualities but I would not have said that being quick was one of them. I was wrong. Without batting an eyelid, and though the sum requested was far larger than he expected, he replied, 'Yes, over a five year period.' It was a minor stroke of genius. He had not demeaned himself by haggling with the Chinese and had accepted their request but had spread it over five years, which made it a credible proposal as regards UNHCR finances. As for the Chinese they were happy. They had asked for 50 million and had received 50 million and the fact that it was spread over time was only a technicality.

Hartling's next move was to announce that he had decided to split the current Asia Section in two and create an East Asia Section which would be responsible for China, Hong Kong, Japan and Korea. While the fact that I would get the job was a foregone conclusion, the organization still had to go through the standard theatrics and I was asked to draft a job description for the position. True to form I wrote that the incumbent was expected to have at least an MA if not a PhD in Asian studies, substantial experience with China and at least one posting as representative in an Asian country. By a strange coincidence I was the only UNHCR staff member who corresponded to this description and it was with the semblance of a smile that the Head of personnel informed me that the appointment board had selected me for the job. Then came the problem of my staff. All I really needed was a good administrative secretary, of which there were many within UNHCR and a program officer who spoke Chinese of which there was only one. Li Yuyen who had held the Vietnam desk while I was in Hanoi was the perfect—and only—candidate for the post and in no time

I not only had three comfortable office rooms but also a functioning unit. All I needed now was a finalized program and someone in Beijing to represent us.

By early November I was back in Beijing with Jacques. Since our last visit the Chinese had been busy and had redesigned their assistance program to integrate our contribution spread over a five-year period. It was good, solid work and unlike the Vietnamese where each ministry did its own thing the Chinese coordinated.

Likewise, working out of Beijing was a breeze compared to Hanoi. The Chinese allocated us two rooms in a new, nondescript building that they told us had been set aside for the UN. We bought furniture locally and it took us the best part of one day to open two bank accounts, get a telephone connection and a cable address. But we were doing things backwards; officially we did not have a UNHCR office in China.

It was an issue that had not escaped me and I had previously indicated to Mr Wang, our counterpart at the Foreign Ministry as if the matter was incidental that wherever UNHCR had a program we had also a presence. Mr Wang had nodded non-committedly and I had decided not to raise the issue again until one morning he dropped by my hotel while I was having breakfast and indicated that he wanted to have an informal meeting with me. Suddenly I remembered Vietnam and recognized the pattern. Substantive issues are discussed at 'informal' meetings.

UNHCR had originally been conceived as an organization which would promote the legal protection of people recognized as 'refugees' which meant ensuring that none would be sent back to a country where he was liable to be persecuted for political, ethnic or religious reasons. Over the years, by default, UNHCR had drifted into becoming a major assistance-providing agency but this was only in addition to its core function – the so called mandate – which remained the authority that governments had delegated to it to recognize a person as a refugee. If, with time, this protection role had shrunk in favor of the provision of assistance it was still the one single feature that made UNHCR distinct from any other UN organization as all of them in one way or another provided assistance. Now the very mandate that had been at the inception of UNHCR had become an obstacle to its work.

However, much as the government in Beijing valued the material assistance provided by UNHCR and the implicit political support it represented, they were not ready to see a gaggle of UNHCR lawyers gallivanting all over China recognizing refugees at will. Had the same situation arisen ten years later, they would have known that governments were adept at evading their obligations under the Refugee Conventions whenever they thought it necessary and that UNHCR was less than sanguine when it had to confront a major government on any asylum issue. However, having just emerged from the isolation of the Cultural Revolution, they were not aware that below the veneer of the Refugee Conventions reason of state always prevailed, and so were reluctant to accept an official UNHCR presence in Beijing. Granted they had not adhered to the Refugee Conventions and were not tied by them but they knew what mission creep was and once UNHCR had a foot in the door there was no telling where it would lead to.

In practice this meant that a formal UNHCR presence in China was not in the cards. And yet we could hardly have a program without some presence. This was a substantive issue that I had no authority to negotiate but a solution had to be found and possibly sooner than later so I took things in my hands.

'For UNHCR,' I told Mr Wang, 'formally opening an office in Beijing and signing an agreement with the authorities is not an issue. All we need is a technical presence in Beijing with Jacques Mouchet in charge and as long as the work gets done no one will be the worse for it.' Mr Wang nodded. Visibly I had offered him a solution that he had the authority to approve so we agreed on the spot that Hartling would write a letter to the Chinese Foreign Minister informing him that he would like to have a presence in Beijing to assist in the implementation of an assistance program for refugees from Indochina and assign the job to Mouchet. The Foreign Minister would not answer the letter but shortly after Jacques Mouchet would receive a visa for China.

Having worked out a solution with the Chinese my job was now to sell it to UNHCR and it was only when I had returned to Geneva that I realized how far I had put myself out on a limb.

There had recently been a reshuffle at Headquarters among the four directors and a new one had taken over Administration.

Homann-Herrimberg was a diminutive Austrian with a American wife and a minor title of recent vintage. His manners were impeccable, at least when he wished them to be so, but he had also the mind of a reptile. Wherever he turned he saw intrigue and subterfuge, especially if there was none. Calling him contorted would have done insult to a cork screw and seeing him operate provided a good insight as to the reason for the fall of the Austro-Hungarian empire. As soon as he had heard that we might have a presence in Beijing he had started to conceive a bureaucratic nightmare. There would be one senior officer as representative, one deputy, one program officer, one legal officer, one administrative assistant and one secretary, six people in all. It was enough to scare the Chinese away for good from us having a presence in Beijing and in desperation I went to Hartling.

'We are still walking on eggs,' I told him as I suggested Jacques Mouchet to represent UNHCR in Beijing, 'the Chinese know him, they feel comfortable working with him and we must proceed cautiously.'

'What is the grade of the post,' he asked.

'P5,' I told him.

'And the grade of Mouchet?'

'He has just been promoted to P3.'

He looked at me. 'Do you feel comfortable with him?'

'Sir,' I replied, 'I think you will feel comfortable with him.'

There was a short pause and he smiled. 'Fine,' he said.

It was probably the first time in the UN system that a staff member with a P3 grade took over a P5 post and it could not have worked better. To assist him Jacques was given a French secretary and the two of them proved more than adequate in fulfilling the tasks that the UN bureaucracy felt required six staff members. With time even Homan-Herrimberg began to appreciate Jacques and he even pretended to forgive me for having gone to Hartling behind his back.

Being chief of a regional section was my first line job as opposed to my previous undetermined status at Headquarters and I was now part of the system. But what was 'the system'? As I surveyed my surroundings one word came to my mind; a zoo. UNHCR had been set up in 1951 with a European staffing and Western funding to deal with the left over refugee population created by WWII. By 1979, all its funding was still exclusively contributed by industrialized democracies but the staffing however, had slowly mutated. Little by little the UN notion of 'regional representation' had taken hold and staff had been increasingly hired so as to reflect the spectrum of nations represented in the UN. Thus, while most of the senior staff was still made up of Westerners, the newcomers came increasingly from the likes of Africa, Asia or the Middle East. Now, to be hired or subsequently promoted, competence was not enough. Increasingly one had to come from the right country and have the right color of skin.

This tribalization of the organization had only just started but had already resulted in the emergence of regional mafias. There was the African mafia which had a stranglehold on practically all senior positions regarding Africa; an Indian mafia composed of Indians, Pakistanis, Sri Lankans and Bangladeshi who had set out to pretend that they represented Asia; an Arab mafia which claimed for itself all senior positions in the Middle East and North Africa, and the like. The end result was that the system of promotions became increasingly warped and groups would maneuver to place their own in plum positions with little regards for whether they were putting a round peg in a square hole. The same happened regarding assignments and the need to ensure 'regional representation' resulted in an Indian here, a Japanese there, an African here an American over there, balanced by a German and a Latin American, with the question as to whether the incumbent had the profile for the job either coming a poor second or totally ignored. Compounding the problem, each staff member brought with him his cultural background and it was a rare Japanese who in a crisis situation would take a decision on his own initiative or an Indian from a privileged milieu who was ready to sleep on a camp bed in a bug infested tent in Southern Sudan.

With most of the staff throughout the organization claiming to be overworked I had viewed my new posting with some concern until I realized that much of what was termed work was actually mindless agitation and that as far as substance was concerned the pace was pretty leisurely. But in this respect I must confess that I had a privileged position. While my staff was small, they were outstanding which meant that all the nuts and bolts of programming, the groceries, were taken care of. The same applied to a large extent to the countries I was responsible for.

China was under control, the Chinese were rigorous as regards program implementation and reporting and whenever a question arose Jacques Mouchet would solve it on the spot.

Japan proved a different proposition but not one I could really do anything about.

The Japanese had adhered to the Refugee Conventions simply because it was the done thing. In practical terms they had no intention of ever opening their door to any form of foreign immigration and the only refugees in the country were a few hundred Vietnamese boat people who had been rescued at sea by Japanese ships. These had been mostly parked in a camp in Okinawa, as far away as possible from the Japanese heartland, and all the Japanese hoped was that they would go away and be accepted by some other country, a wish fully shared by the Vietnamese, none of whom, given the choice would have wanted to stay in Japan. Fortunately, convincing the Japanese to integrate the Vietnamese was not my job. Since the advent of the boat people exodus Japan had become one of the major contributors to UNHCR and as such had become the privileged domain of our director in charge of fundraising. He was a Dane, close to Hartling, and his one concern was to keep the Japanese happy and I was not going to interfere with that.

As for Hong Kong, it was a mess but one best left to the Hong Kong authorities to manage and the fact that UNHCR had had a string of totally ineffective representatives in the colony proved irrelevant to whatever there was, or could be done.

The end result was that my work consisted mostly of delegating, keeping one eye open for any political problems that might arise and staying up to date with communications either received or originating from my section. In terms of hours my workload was minimal and my main concern was how to conceal this extravagance from the rest of the organization.

I was fully aware that once you had a reputation within the organization it was almost impossible to shake and acquiring a good one was a priority. This was not too difficult an achievement provided one followed a few simple rules: don't appear too bright, don't be a threat to anyone, lie low, and, above all don't create problems. Sucking up to the Directors was also a must but it had to be done discerningly. Volfing, the rigorous Dane who was in charge of fund raising, went for hard facts and possibly good ideas presented in as few words as possible. Conversely, Moussalli the Lebanese in charge of legal protection would gobble down any compliment that came his way. Jaeger the Belgian was a sophisticated man who enjoyed an intellectual approach. And as for the Austrian Homan-Herrimberg, he stuck to his coterie. All in all the formula for bureaucratic success was summarized by a gnome in personnel; rule number one, hide. Rule number two, if they find you, lie. While the formula had its merits it skirted one basic requirement. The need to appear hardworking which translated not so much in obtaining results as to being seen to put in long working hours.

I was driving a Fiat 500, a diminutive bright red car with a two-cylinder air cooled engine that sounded like a sewing machine and like all section chiefs I had my reserved parking in front of our office building which entailed that my presence, or absence from the building was for all to see. That was the chink in my armor. To circumvent this major handicap, at least once a week I would come to the office in my red Fiat, leave it overnight and go home by bus. With everyone keeping an eye on who was parked where and when, staff leaving late in the evening would marvel at seeing that I was still in the office while those arriving early in morning would do likewise assuming I had arrived even before they had. With all the directors in the habit of arriving at the office late in the morning and staying late in the evening there were also points to be gained by being seen rushing around the corridors clutching a file at eight in the evening.

After a while all these ruses paid off in the sense that with my reputation well established I was left in peace to do my job more or less the way I intended to.

When Dayal commented as regards China that finally there was some good news, he was not wrong in more ways than one. 1979 had been a bad year for UNHCR in Asia. Not only had UNICEF and the ICRC successfully conspired to exclude UNHCR from Cambodia but the organization, through its own bureaucratic bumbling, had also been on the brink of losing its foothold in Thailand and being excluded altogether from the Vietnamese refugee exodus, the largest refugee crisis since the beginning of the cold war.

Why UNHCR came so close to bureaucratic obliteration was, I came to believe, a matter of configuration. Large international institutions like UNICEF, ICRC or UNHCR are built around a core bureaucratic establishment that is essentially dedicated to self-preservation. That the function of the bureaucrats comes under the heading of humanitarian is purely incidental. Theirs is a job like any other, except that being the equivalent of a government civil service they are not subject to market forces and are essentially a tenured bureaucracy. So by their very nature they are resentful of change, innovation or anything that can disturb an established and foreseeable routine. While the bureaucracies were dependent for their continued existence on a succession of humanitarian crises, these in most cases were a matter of routine and were approached as such.

Ultimately none of the entrenched bureaucracies were intellectually equipped to confront at short notice the unfamiliar compounded by the unexpected. In these exceptional circumstances, when push came to shove and a crisis for which there is no previously set pattern looms on the horizon, the establishment takes a back seat to the individual, if one is available or on the scene. In Vietnam, our initial involvement was not so much that of UNHCR as an organization but rather of Rizvi as an individual boosted by Sadruddin and advised by me. It was only once the groundwork was done that the organization was made to follow suit.

The same happened with ICRC and UNICEF in Cambodia. It was not so much the two organizations that outmaneuvered UNHCR and grabbed for themselves the credibility that went with being the only official aid purveyors to Cambodia; the move was the outcome of the direct intervention of two individuals, Jacques Beaumont for UNICEF and Jean-Pierre Hocke for ICRC. Within UNICEF Beaumont was known as a maverick who operated on the margins of the system and had been the motive force in drawing the organization into the Indochinese landscape. As for Hocke, at the ICRC he was a law unto himself and had a tendency to act first and only inform the Committee later as an afterthought. If leadership is the ability to lead an organization where it would not go by itself, both were leaders, not to say brilliant mavericks which no organization seeking to preserve its market share could, in an emergency, do without. These were the people that in 1979 UNHCR was sorely in need of.

The Indochina crisis which confronted UNHCR after the fall of Saigon and the subsequent Vietnamese invasion of Cambodia was a complex emergency involving Vietnam, Cambodia, Laos, most of the countries of South East Asia, Hong Kong with its British connection, China and last but not least the US. Dealing with the resulting imbroglio was not a matter of routine and required more and different talents than those displayed by your average UN bureaucrat. This did not make the average bureaucrat any less indispensable to the system but rather demanded that the system retain the flexibility and intelligence needed to replace him at short notice with someone of a different profile when the situation required it.

In the fall of 1975, following the first outflow of Vietnamese boat people into Thailand, Sadruddin had already eased out of his post the then UNHCR representative in Bangkok, a lazy, ill tempered and pompous Iraqi named Usman Kadri. Kadri was fine as long as no demands were put on him but the moment there was a job to be done he had outlived whatever use he might have had. His successor, Leslie Goodyear, a genial Englishman, had one great passion in life: golf. Thailand for him was the ideal posting but he was hardly what UNHCR needed at the time.

BREAKING THE RULES

Nearing retirement age, his main concern was not to rock the boat and he had chosen to close his eyes to the looming humanitarian crisis on the Cambodian border as the Thais started to push back an increasing number of Cambodian refugees who had sought asylum in Thailand. The push backs were being viewed with increasing alarm by Washington but whenever the US ambassador in Bangkok, Morton Abramowitz, would go to the Thais to protest they would reply with a smile; 'It can't be as bad as you say because if it had been, UNHCR would have protested.' With the US embassy getting more and more incensed about the push backs and Goodyear giving no indications that he could be jolted even into the appearance of some action, my former deputy in Hanoi, Pierre Jambor, who had now been assigned to Bangkok as Goodyear's deputy, decided to move. In June 1979 following the push back of some 8,000 Cambodians not a few of whom lost their lives in mine fields, Pierre went behind Goodyear's back and sent a letter directly to Hartling warning him that if UNHCR continued to vacillate and refused to take a stand and confront the Thais more expulsions would occur. Dayal, who filtered all the correspondence to Hartling, was a man of integrity and while the bureaucrat in him disapproved of Pierre not going through channels he did raise the issue with Hartling albeit suggesting that the message was the doing of a young Turk which he qualified as bright but inexperienced.

Not surprisingly, within a month the Thais pushed back a second group of 23,000 Cambodian refugees. The latest expulsion was one too many for Washington and discreetly but firmly the US let it be known that if UNHCR did not take a stand on what was a major refugee issue, perhaps the organization should have no future role, at least in Asia. Hartling got the message and had Pierre called to Geneva where he asked him what he felt should be done. Remove Goodyear and send Rizvi to Thailand was the reply. By then the directors, who had been instrumental in having Rizvi unseated, had seen the writing on the wall and were close to a state of panic. So none of them objected when Rizvi was called back to Geneva from his Roman exile and offered the post of representative in Thailand. Cleverly he made his acceptance conditional. Either he would get an immediate promotion to senior director or he would return to Rome. Three weeks later he was in Bangkok with a new team and his promotion in his pocket.

After seeing Rizvi come back in I then witnessed Dale de Haan's inglorious exit. The man was a vain, friendly, well-meaning non-entity but that, if anything, in a UN bureaucracy was an asset. His undoing came from the fact that he started to agitate, running from one foreign mission to another, which in turn started worrying the directors least he acquire too much visibility. That would not have sufficed to ensure his undoing had he not also increasingly irritated Hartling. Granted there was a flippancy about him that tested the patience of the Danish headmaster but it was a minor peccadillo that proved to be the straw that broke the camel's back. According to UN rules at the time, staff members of the grade held by Dale were entitled to travel first class, but only on flights exceeding nine hours. Dale would regularly go to New York but instead of taking the daily direct Swissair flight that left Geneva at noon and arrived in New York around two, an approximately eight-hour long flight, he would take the early morning flight to Zurich and from there the connecting Swissair flight to New York which arrived around noon for a total travel time of some ten hours which entitled him to fly first class The explanation he provided was that by arriving in New York a couple of hours earlier he could plan some appointments in the afternoon. No one, least of all Hartling, was fooled. The man just wanted to fly first class. Had he done so occasionally he could have gotten away with it but it soon became a habit to the increased irritation of Hartling who saw it as petty cheating.

Except for Dale himself, who happened to be away that day, no one was thus very surprised when a memo suddenly was distributed to the UNHCR staff informing them that after two years of outstanding service and to Hartling's great regret, the Deputy High Commissioner Dale de Haan would be leaving his post.

The position of Deputy High Commissioner was reserved for an American and upon Dale's departure the State Department presented Hartling with a list of candidates.

Among those Hartling chose William Smyser. Of German Jewish origin, Smyser was a first class mind who after various postings with the State Department had been one of the main assistants of Henry Kissinger. After having reportedly been passed over for the job of ambassador to Germany, the State Department, not knowing what to do with him, had offered him to Hartling and America's loss was the organization's gain. In retrospect, he was the best deputy High Commissioner UNHCR ever had. Both by intellectual volition and by choice he did not pretend to be a bean counter and, rather than getting involved in the groceries, focused on what a credible deputy should do i.e. concentrate on policy and establish a productive intellectual interchange with the High Commissioner. Whenever I went to see him I would return from our meeting marveling at his political acumen and overall grasp of international relations.

But what UNHCR gained on one hand it was to lose on the other. 1981 saw the retirement of Gilber Jaeger, the Belgian Director for Assistance, and the other directors started looking for a replacement. Until now 'regional representation' had spared the upper reaches of UNHCR but the rot had set in and the directors decided they needed more diversity and the post would go to an African. With none available within UNHCR they extended their search to the rest of the UN system and one morning the rumor spread that someone had been found.

Our new Director for Assistance carried the improbable name of Maxime Zollner and hailed from the former German colony of Dahomey, now renamed Benin, of which he had been the ambassador at the UN. What qualified him for a senior post at UNHCR was to remain a mystery. He had never been involved in refugees, had no experience with aid programs or held a senior post with the UN, but if the prerequisite of the post was to be black and bland he was an outstanding contender.

Shortly after he took up the post I went to introduce myself. The first thing that struck me as I entered his office was a large, framed photograph hanging on the wall. It was a photo of himself. Next to it was a framed certificate in an elaborate script attesting that Maxime Zollner had been included in the Who's Who of intellectuals. As for the man himself he was not so much fat as massive, a huge, amorphous hulk with two small porcine eyes that surveyed me with suspicion. He showed no interest in my brief which I brought to a rapid end before proceeding to back out of his office with what I hoped was a sufficiently submissive bow. My next encounter with him occurred when, prior to a mission, I had sent my travel request for approval to him. In response his secretary called informing me that he wished to see me. The message he had for me was unambiguous. In the future, before sending him a travel request, he expected me to come and see him and explain to him why I had to go on the mission. The request made sense but this was clearly not the purpose of the exercise. What was required was that I come, knowtow to the chief and then only could I send in my travel request. I complied prior to my next mission but as he was away from Geneva at the time the request went to his deputy who promptly sent it back with his approval. From then on this was the procedure I adopted and, except for occasionally coming across him in the corridors this was the last I saw of Maxime Zollner, Director for Assistance, or as he put on his CV 'Worldwide Director for Assistance'.

Ultimately, the benign clutter that prevailed throughout the organization was manageable and played in my favor and short of a major crisis within my area of operation I could envisage the coming years at Headquarters, if not with serenity, then at least with the reasonable hope of being left alone to do my thing while being ready for the unexpected. That it would one day come I knew but even in my wildest dreams I never expected that the wake up call would come from Poland.

On December 13, 1981 the Polish government of General Jaruzelski proclaimed martial law, outlawed the Solidarity trade Union movement and arrested many of its leaders. Three days later I had a call from Mouchet in Beijing. Six Solidarity activists who were at the time touring China had come to his office requesting asylum. They were due to fly back to Poland shortly and were in no doubt that they would be arrested upon landing. The case put us in a major quandary. Technically, the six were unquestionably refugees that is fleeing from persecution but this was a label and not a solution. China had no sympathy for Solidarity which they correctly viewed as a dissident movement which had set out to bring down a fellow communist regime and would not hesitate to deport the group. As for the Polish embassy in Beijing it would also have been duty bound to require that the group be deported. The end result was that, in practical terms, an official intervention on our side would only have precipitated matters and there was no way we could have convinced the Chinese to show some leniency towards a group of opponents to a communist regime.

The first thing that Jacques and I agreed on was that we would not inform Headquarters. Had we done so the risk would have been considerable that the legalists within the Protection division would have made an official request to the Chinese demanding that the six be given asylum. Such a move would not only have precipitated the expulsion of the group but also branded UNHCR as a nuisance, with all the negative consequences this could have had for our continued presence in China. This we knew was of no concern to the legalists. Their job was not to save refugees but to take a stand and having done so they felt they had done their duty, whatever the result. The next priority was to gain time. So Jacques went to the authorities informing them that six foreigners—he deliberately did not mention their nationality—had come to the office and would like their visas prolonged for ten days to do some more sightseeing. The request in itself was innocuous and was met with no objection. Not that the Chinese were duped; they were fully aware of what the whole matter was about but obviously they had decided not to press the issue, at least for the time being. Jacques then went to the Australian Embassy and explained to them what the matter was about. Three days later the six Poles, all holding visas for Australia and air tickets provided by UNHCR, were escorted by Jacques to Beijing airport where they boarded a flight to Sydney, thus bringing the matter to a close. For all concerned it was a win-win situation. The Chinese did not have to turn down an asylum request that, on principle, they could not have granted. The Polish embassy in Beijing did not have to deal with a complicated deportation and the Polish Solidarity activists were safe. With the six Poles out of harm's way in Australia I went to Dayal with the full story. Well done, was his only comment.

With China under control, Japan best left to its own devices, the only territory in my region that required a more involved approach was Hong Kong. Like Japan, Hong Kong had an advanced economy with an effective government, but the resemblance stoped there.

Contrary to boat people arrivals in other transit countries most of the those that landed in Hong Kong came from Northern Vietnam and therefore could not claim that their departure was due to the takeover of the South by the communists. However, given that the 1979 conference had decree that all Vietnamese boat people with no exception would be granted refugee status this made them as much 'refugees' as the Southerners and likewise entitled to resettlement in a Western country. On paper it made for an easy solution for Hong Kong but reality proved otherwise. Coming from the North, the boat people were of no interest to the Americans to resettle and, in addition, Hong Kong being a British colony, there was a general feeling that it was up to Britain to take most of them. So resettlement from Hong Kong proved a far more difficult proposition than from the rest of South East Asia.

Contrary to other countries in the region, the camps in Hong Kong were 'open' and the boat people were free to seek local employment while waiting for resettlement. For the Vietnamese, and in particular the Northerners who had come from the most impoverished part of Vietnam, it was a godsend. They now had a job at a decent salary, access to good medical care as well as food and housing, all of a far better standard than what they enjoyed in their home country.

None of these benefits proved effective in protecting Hong Kong from the wrath of the human rights activists. Camps in Thailand, Malaysia or Indonesia were all closed, run by the military in remote locations hours away from the capital. Government officials who ran the camps often spoke no English and had little patience with bothersome foreigners of little standing. In contrast, with its wide choice of hotels, tax free shopping, easily accessible camps, English-speaking authorities and independent courts, Hong Kong became the destination of choice of every refugee advocacy group on the planet, all trying to find fault with how Hong Kong was addressing the boat people influx and all vying with each other to demonstrate how much more active than the competition they were. This relentless fault-finding and the constant accompanying threat of complaining to London or to some US senator, not to say the media, put Hong Kong under considerable pressure and one that your honest, straightforward, Hong Kong British civil servant was not necessarily well equipped to handle. So in a certain sense my job consisted mostly of supporting Hong Kong by trying to deflect the constant denigration that it was submitted to by self-styled human rights advocates.

Except for clamoring for more resettlement slots there was not much Hong Kong could do about the continued influx of boat people as long as Vietnam did not seriously crack down on departures and Hanoi had no incentive to do so.

With things more or less under control in my area, the icing on the cake came when Dayal called me to his office. He would generally greet me with a smile but this time he was beaming. 'Hartling is invited to visit China,' he told me, adding, 'this time as High Commissioner.'

With Jacques in Beijing my contribution to organizing Hartling's mission was minimal and except for arriving in Beijing two days before he did, I had little to do but watch and follow.

Hartling arrived in Beijing in the late afternoon of August 31, 1981, with his wife and Dayal. From the airport he was driven this time not to a hotel but to a government guesthouse. It was a Soviet-style building with large rooms, heavy drapes, dark leather sofas and plush carpeting surrounded by a large, well-kept garden and staffed by any amount of servants who hovered silently in the background.

The Chinese had given us no indications as to whom we would meet and our expectations were not particularly high when, on the second day of the visit we were led to the Great Hall of the people and ushered into a vast, brightly lit room with high ceilings and brocade-covered walls in light yellow. There a small man was waiting and as we entered he walked up to Hartling with a big smile and outstretched hands. It was Deng Hsiao Ping.

Deng had been Hartling's host when he had come to China in 1974, and the two men were visibly at ease with each other. And while there was nothing for them to negotiate, the symbolic nature of Hartling being received at China's highest level could not be underestimated. Not that Hartling was one to lose his composure. As Deng went off on a long tirade, denouncing the Soviet Union and all the ills it was supposed to represent, Hartling interrupted him. 'But Mr Vice Chairman,' he said, 'I too am anti-Soviet.' There was a second of silence and then Deng laughed long and hard.

Over the previous year I had discussed at length with the Chinese the subject of them joining the Refugee Conventions and their constant reply was 'why,' to which I would answer 'why not'. My main argument was that they had nothing to lose. All the Western countries had adhered to them and as all the Soviet bloc countries were opposed to them on principle, adhesion by China would be a good cosmetic move that would further illustrate how far they were from the Soviet system.

I did not expect anything to come from these exchanges and was therefore totally caught by surprise when, that very afternoon, as if it was a matter of no great importance, one of the Chinese in our group turned to Hartling and mentioned off-hand that China had decided to adhere to the 1951 Refugee Conventions. I saw Hartling's face light up. As far as refugee law was concerned, he had made history.

In trying to convince the Chinese to adhere to the Refugee Conventions my main selling point had been that the obligations they entailed could be easily circumvented and all the signatories did so with gusto. Actually the Conventions simply provided only two main obligations for its signatories. The first was that any person claiming refugee status was entitled to a hearing so as to establish whether his claim was credible or not. The second was that a person recognized as a refugee, that is fleeing persecution for political, ethnic or religious reasons, would not be returned to a location where he would be in danger. The days when practically every illegal immigrant would claim refugee status either to stave off deportation or to prolong his stay for the duration of the procedure had not yet arrived and if and when they did there was little chance that China would either be subject to an influx or unable to handle it.

After two days in Beijing we set off by air for Nanning and then onwards by road to Beihai. We arrived in late afternoon and I did not recognize the city. There was now a proper port with a long jetty and wave breakers protecting the access. Apartment buildings had sprung up, three-storey affairs in concrete, painted white. Next to the port a large refrigeration plant was buzzing with activity. Apparently they had just signed a contract to supply deep frozen shrimp to Hong Kong and part of the profits was to be redistributed to the workers. I had brought some pictures of Beihai as Jacques and I had found it two years before and Hartling was appropriately impressed. The Chinese had done a splendid job and in the short span of two years Beihai had become a thriving community. It was on this happy note that Hartling returned to Geneva and I withdrew to the quietude my office.

A TOURIST IN HANOI

While China had now become the main focus of my professional activity the root-cause of the problem originated in Vietnam and though I had no official reason for visiting Hanoi plain curiosity urged me to do so. The Vietnamese no longer delivered tourist visas, an irrelevant restriction as there were no takers but foreign diplomats stationed in Hanoi had the possibility of inviting friends for private visits and the relevant visas would generally be granted. I had slowly built up a friendship mostly through correspondence with Mohamed Bouabid, the new UNHCR representative in Hanoi, and when I asked if he would invite me his response was an enthusiastic yes. So in early September 1982 I arrived in Hanoi with a tourist visa as the personal guest of Bouabid.

There were now direct flights from Bangkok to Hanoi, courtesy of Vietnam Airlines and a dilapidated Soviet-built Tupolev 104. The aircraft had been out of production for 22 years and the last models retired from service in the Soviet Union the year before but beggars can't be choosers and that was all the Vietnamese had available.

I found Hanoi not quite the city I had known five years previously but the differences were subtle. It was still an unhurried city moving at the speed of a leisurely driven bicycle but something had changed in its rhythm. It was less graceful, less fluid as if some sort of undefined disturbance had given it a ragged edge. The people looked haggard, rarely smiling, and shuffled about with a blank glazed stare. I had known Hanoi as a poor but clean and dignified city. It was still poor, possibly more so but the poise seemed to have worn out and for good reason too. Six years after the end of the war there was little the regime could be proud of.

While the average salary was still between 80 and 100 Dongs per month, the official state controlled food rationing distribution system had for all practical purposes collapsed and most Vietnamese had no alternative but to do their shopping on what stood for the free market. Officially it had been abolished in 1977 under the guise of 'building socialism'. However the state had proved unable to fill the gap left by the obliteration of the small household shop and while private retail trade had not officially been reinstated it was again tolerated, creating a grey area in which market forces rather than the state determined prices. The end result was the emergence of two parallel economies which the average Vietnamese had to navigate in order to make ends meet. How he did it was a tribute to his resourcefulness. On the free market rice stood at 15 Dongs the kilo, a chicken cost 60 Dongs and a bottle of beer 40 Dongs. As for the black market exchange rate of the dollar, it had gone from 9 Dongs to the dollar when I had left Hanoi in the fall of 1977 to 100 now.

That Vietnam's ills were self-inflicted and derived from a fundamental ideological and geo-political misperception was not something the ruling Politburo was willing to consider. So the regime soldiered on and though it was in no danger of being deposed some of the principles it stood for, or claimed to stand for, had started fraying at the edges. And one of the first symptoms of this slow decay proved to be prostitution.

Prostitution, so went the official wisdom in Hanoi, is a social disease and as there are no social diseases in socialist countries therefore there is no prostitution in Vietnam. This point of principle having been established, the chapter was closed and there was nothing left to be said. But this was Vietnam where nothing was what it appeared to be.

In 1974, Sweden had decided to donate to Vietnam what would be the world's most advanced automated paper mill. Located at Bai Bang, some 60 miles North-West of Hanoi and costing an estimated 170 million US $, it was supposed to represent a technological breakthrough which would set the pace for the country's development into an industrialized economy, combining a foreign technological input with locally produced wood pulp.

Even on paper it was not a good project. Vietnam had an excess of manpower and automation was the last thing the country needed but that was only the beginning. Once the project got under way everything that could posibly go wrong went wrong. The feasibility study had been somewhat optimistic and when test production started in 1980 it was belatedly discovered that locally produced wood pulp did not fit production norms. So to get the plant started wood pulp had to be imported from Sweden. Power proved the next hurdle and a massive generator had to be imported to make up for the erratic electricity supply. The end result over the years was a one billion dollar project, making it the most expensive mill in the world per ton of paper produced. Vietnam being what it is, production did finally take off but fifteen years behind schedule and never on a commercially viable basis.

In order to build the plant some 600 Swedish technicians had come to Vietnam and a prefabricated village was built for them at Bai Bang which included, in addition to housing, a cafeteria, a pool, a school and a clinic. Actually it was a small replica of a Swedish village to which its inhabitants attributed the name of Valhalla, the abode of the gods in Nordic mythology. While some of the Swedes had come with their families, most did not and slowly the inevitable came about. On one side there were lusty, affluent, blue-eyed Swedes and on the other, lissome country girls from the nearby villages. The two were fated to meet, and the world's most advanced paper mill became the bursary of the world's oldest profession.

The Vietnamese have a fierce ethnic identity with a strong racial connotation that, especially in the more conservative North, they never even bothered to disguise. Children of mixed origin, Western and Vietnamese, were in Southern Vietnam called the dust of life. In the North the description was more brutal: head of a chicken, ass of a duck. With this inbred racism compounded by the regime's total ban on any personal contact between a Vietnamese and a foreigner, what developed in Bai Bang, and not on a small scale either, should have been perceived by the authorities as having gone more than one step too far. But it was not. Maybe because they did not want to have to deal with a few hundred fidgety Swedes, perhaps also because Bai Bang was far away from Hanoi and so out of the limelight or maybe due to a combination of both, the authorities turned a blind eye to the goings-on, and the Swedes were free to live out their fantasies of an Asian nirvana. Not that it was a one way affair either. With the average per capita income in the countryside being about 5 US $ per month the funds that the hearty Swedes pumped into the local economy were, by local standards, massive and probably had a greater grass-root impact than the deficit-bound paper mill.

In early 1982, as the paper mill was being handed over step by step to the Vietnamese, the Swedes started leaving Bai Bang and a score of girls found themselves without an occupation. With no future prospects in the countryside they brought their skills to Hanoi where they came into competition with the locally available talent. While officially it had never existed and woe betide any foreigner who fell for their charms, there was one exception: the Russians. There were any amount of lusty Russian experts working in Hanoi and the Vietnamese were too worldly-wise to ignore their needs even if these did not correspond exactly to socialist norms. However, as long as the authorities could pretend that nothing was happening they were content to let things pass. This proved somewhat less easy when the Bai Bang contingent descended on Hanoi, hereby impacting the rule of supply and demand. And it was here that UNHCR came into its own.

In 1976, under the misguided impression that guest accommodation was lacking in Vietnam's countryside, Rizvi had procured for UNHCR a Volkswagen camping van with a large folding double bed in the rear compartment. The van never served its intended purpose but Bouabid and friends found a new use for it. The idea was for two prospective customers to cruise the dark alleys of Hanoi at night with the van's sliding door open. If luck was on their side, two damsels would hop into the van as it slowed down before resuming its normal cruising speed. The key was to keep on driving while each punter took his turn in the rear compartment. The van would then slow down again, the door open and the damsels disappear into the starry night. Occasionally the van would be loaned to so-called friendly embassies who supported the work of UNHCR and it became quite an institution in Hanoi with only the naive assuming that the Vietnamese police was unaware of these shenanigans.

Except for its van, there was little UNHCR had left to show for itself in Vietnam. The chicken breeding facility at Chem had never gotten off the ground. The buffalo breeding facility—we had imported from India 200 buffalos to improve the breed in Vietnam—initially fared better but then fell victim of 'building socialism'.

The Soviets had tractor stations where large numbers of machines were concentrated, serviced and then loaned to state farms and collective enterprises according to need. The Vietnamese, who dreamt of tractors but had few to show off, went for the next best thing and so they created buffalo stations. There the beasts which had been removed from their owners, were concentrated in large numbers and then temporarily allocated to whoever needed them. What the communist leadership had failed to realize was that buffalos were not machines. They were alive and while they were big nasty brutes they also had a heart. Deprived of their masters and loaned out to strangers who did not care about them the buffalos withered and then started dying by the thousands. With fewer buffaloes to till the land rice production plummeted and it was only at the brink of disaster that the ideologues in the regime belatedly realized that even buffaloes needed some affection and the few remaining ones were returned to their original owners.

But chicken and buffalos aside Hanoi's alignment with the Soviet Union and its occupation of Cambodia had taken their toll on the UNHCR programs. Donor countries, all of them industrialized democracies, had by now lost all incentive for providing UNHCR with funds to assist a Soviet client state and the only good reason for UNHCR's continued presence in Vietnam was the Orderly Departure Program.

The Vietnamese had seen ODP as a means of getting rid of people they did not want. Foreign governments hoped it would provide a credible alternative to illegal departure by boat. Both were disappointed. Foreign governments, by law, could only grant visas to Vietnamese who fitted their resettlement criteria and those who qualified under ODP were a minority. As for the Vietnamese authorities, having failed in their attempt to blackmail the Western countries and in particular the US into taking their outcasts through the ODP program they continued to encourage the boat people exodus while making it difficult for those who tried to leave legally to actually do so. Thus for those very few Vietnamese who wished to avail themselves of the Orderly Departure Program operated by UNHCR the challenge was equivalent to running an obstacle course blindfolded through a maze of constantly changing bureaucratic procedures that would have put Kafka to shame.

OF BOAT PEOPLE AND BUREAUCRATS

I I left Vietnam grateful that this was not a problem on my agenda only in time to find another one on my plate; Hong Kong

For a Vietnamese who made it to Hong Kong the going was good. He lived in an open camp where he did not need to pay rent, could work, enjoyed medical care and could send his children to school while waiting for resettlement. This, according to the Hong Kong government, had turned the colony into a destination of choice and with resettlement at an all time low something had to be done to slow down the influx. The concept of humane deterrence was born.

On July 1, 1982, the Hong Kong Government decreed that all camps in the Colony would from now onwards be closed, and the refugees would be confined to them until they were ready to leave for a resettlement country. Closed camps were the rule in all the other Asian countries. But coming after a six-year time span during which Hong Kong had been far more generous than any other government in the region, the backlash to the decision was massive. There was hardly any self-styled human rights group that did not go overboard, vociferously denouncing the closed camps as an Asian gulag at best irrespective of the fact that the inmates were getting better food, better housing, better medical care, schooling and clothing than at home in Vietnam. And while confinement might have had its discomforts, spending one's day chatting, playing ping-pong or watching films on TV was not exactly the Vietnamese definition of an inferno.

That this was not the image the closed camps projected was partly the fault of the Hong Kong government. The Hong Kong civil service was mainly made up of Brits of the old school. Solid, not excessively hard-working but basically efficient, they called a spade a spade, had little time for the required mendacity of their environment, and it never occurred to them to call the closed camps something more cosmetically agreeable such as Refugee Rehabilitation Centers. But cosmetics was not their forte and they paid the price for being out of step with a world ruled by form rather than by substance.

Whether the closed camps ever deterred any Vietnamese from proceeding to Hong Kong was never established, but their existence did serve the useful purpose of confirming to the local Chinese population that the Vietnamese who came to Hong Kong were not being given preferential treatment compared with Chinese coming in illegally from the mainland.

If 1983 was a good year for UNHCR in Asia, Africa was another matter. This of course was nothing new. Nothing ever worked in Africa but what in most parts of the Dark Continent was an everyday, run of the mill, below-the-horizon disaster had turned into a visible one in Sudan. Granted it was not visible to all, but to Hartling's chagrin, the few who did see it included one deceptively modest man who happened to carry a very big stick.

Arthur Gene Dewey had graduated from West Point in 1956 and then built up a career in the US Corps of Engineers and in the US army aviation. I had met him in Geneva in 1972 at the Graduate Institute that he attended for one year before becoming head of the Politico-Military department of the Pentagon before retiring from the Army in 1981 with the rank of colonel to assume the position of Deputy Assistant Secretary of State for refugees in the Reagan administration.

Dewey was a character straight out of a Norman Rockwell illustration. Clean-cut, with that particular gait of a retired officer, he was strictly a meat and potato man and a born-again Christian to boot. Idle talk, uncertain values or a tangential approach went against both his grain and his training as an engineer.

It would have been reasonable to expect a Christian soldier and a Lutheran headmaster to be on the same wavelength but they were not. Hartling the former Prime Minister was not impressed by a mere colonel and Dewey was even less impressed by what he viewed as UNHCR's operational shortcomings in the field, notably in Sudan.

The US-supported government in Khartum was at the cross-roads of an insurgency in the South, a civil war in Ethiopia and a lingering rebellion in Eritrea, resulting in a constant influx of refugees, and Dewey had been monitoring with increasing disbelief what he viewed as the poor performance of UNHCR in addressing the crisis.

Within UNHCR Sudan was the responsibility of a slightly pompous Australian, Nicholas Morris, who liked to put on the airs of an Englishman, spoke with conviction and oozed organized optimism. Dewey had repeatedly warned Morris to no avail regarding such things as a coming measles epidemic in the camps or the need to warehouse supplies for potential new arrivals and each time had been proven right. It took more however to jolt Morris into action and he shrugged off with disdain all the subsequent warnings by Dewey. In desperation Dewey went to complain to Hartling but got nowhere as Hartling defended Morris to the hilt.

Hartling had been elected High Commissioner for Refugees in 1977 for a five-year term that expired at the end of 1982 and he could normally expect to be re-elected for a second five-year term. But Dewey thought otherwise. He believed that Hartling was slipping and that a change of regime was necessary. Dewey might have been a mere colonel but he also represented the US government. The end result was that Hartling was re-elected for a second term of only three years instead of the usual five ending in December 1985. Hartling was not overjoyed but he was now past 70 and could look back on a well-filled life. Conversely his Directors whose administrative fate was more or less tied to him took it less well.

Of the four Directors, potentially the most important one was the Director for Assistance who was responsible for overseeing all the aid projects throughout the world. By engineering the choice of Maxime Zollner for the post the other directors had scored a bureaucratic victory of sorts. Though not intrinsically stupid, Zollner was incredibly lazy which ensured that he would never represent a threat to their authority. However, what might have passed off as a clever ploy in the rarefied atmosphere of the UN system soon badly backfired. Except for Asia where Rizvi kept a tight reign on operations and where I had the fortune of having good staff in the field, assistance activities in the rest of the world started to unravel. Africa, already in a pretty bad state, got even worse and as the grumbling of donor governments led by the United States increased perceptibly the Directors started to panic. Something had to be done, but what?

In May 1982 we were suddenly informed that in order to improve the efficiency of the organization a new bureaucratic layer had been created. Until then the assistance division had been divided into regional sections, three for Africa, two for Asia and so forth. From now onwards, between the section chiefs and the divisin Directors there would be a new layer; bureau directors would be created one each for Asia, Africa, Latin America, Europe and the Middle East and the section chiefs would now report to them rather than to the division directors. The rationale for this decision was never explained to us but we assumed that it was a cosmetic exercise to project a more operational image.

So overnight I had a new boss, an Asia Bureau Director in the person of an Iranian who went by the name of Jamshid Anvar. Anvar was a handsome man of elegant bearing with the full lips and generous nose of an Assyrian statue, emerging from a mass of abundant but carefully groomed hair and a flowering beard that he neither shaved nor cut but only trimmed. It was an incongruous sight that gave him the airs of a prophet offset by an engaging smile and a congenial personality. I had been introduced to him in the corridors and we would occasionally chat in the cafeteria where he seemed to know everybody, but that was the extent of our relationship. From what I had heard he had been trained as an accountant and after having briefly worked for an oil company in Algeria, had joined the financial section of UNHCR from where he had then moved into an administrative position in New York before returning to UNHCR. An Iranian citizen, he was also a Bahai but that he sought to disguise. What he did not was his hatred for the Shah. In New York, he and his French wife, whom he later divorced, had been among the more vociferous opponents of the Shah and loudly rejoiced in his overthrow.

At first sight I had no reservation about working for him but nonetheless sought to enquire why he had been chosen as Director for Asia. The explanation that filtered down to me was pure United Nations. The director for Africa was an African. The director for Europe was a European. The Director for the Middle East was an Arab so the director for Asia had to be an Asian. Iran was in Asia hence the choice of Anvar. That he had never set foot in the Far East, had never served anywhere as UNHCR representative and had never demonstrated any political acumen not to say interest in the region was irrelevant. An Asian is an Asian and Iran is in Asia.

The beginnings were auspicious enough. He told us that he trusted us, that our work was good and that as he was not a micromanager we should feel free to use our common sense and only report to him what we thought it was indispensable for him to know or needed his intervention. Then after two months on the job, by mid summer he disappeared. Why, no one seemed to know but the rumor was that he had been hospitalized with a nervous breakdown.

Life went on as before except that now I had a problem. Jacques Mouchet was due to leave Beijing at the end of his assignment and had to be replaced. I had identified a potential successor; a tall lanky American whom I felt had the right personality for the job. Chris Carpenter had spent part of his childhood in Beijing where his father had been the US Vice Consul before the communists came to power. After college he had served in the navy, very much the officer and the gentlemen, before drifting into UNHCR. Single, imperturbable, keen of mind and calm of demeanor, he was very much his own man who did his own thing, a condition somewhat facilitated by his having inherited a respectable trust fund. This, I decided was the man for the job and someone the Chinese would respect. The only problem was how to get him accepted by the Chinese. We had no formal agreement with them and therefore no procedure that provided for a change of representatives. Jacques had no idea of how to proceed but wanted out. I did not want to leave the UNHCR office in Beijing empty as it might have started a precedent so, short of a better solution, I had a travel authorization signed by Zollner's deputy and flew off to Beijing. Jacques was packing and had no idea what to do but he had hired a Chinese assistant who had good connections with the authorities and when I asked her for some advice she ventured that I should 'see Mr Wang from the Foreign Ministry'. Word was passed to the Foreign Ministry and two days later Mr Wang showed up at my hotel while I was having breakfast. The message I had for him was simple; Jacques was leaving and I had in mind a successor with whom I was convinced the Chinese would feel comfortable. So if we could continue with the current arrangement this was fine with us but we did not know how to proceed. Mr Wang thought for a moment and then suggested that Hartling write to the Foreign Minister informing him that Jacques was leaving and suggesting that he would like to send Chris Carpenter to replace him. There would be no reply to the letter but about two weeks later Chris would receive his visa. For me it was a tremendous relief and upon my return to Geneva I could inform Hartling that as far as China was concerned we were still on track.

One week after my return Anvar reappeared and I went to see him to brief him on my trip to China. I had barely started speaking when he suddenly went berserk.

'You have betrayed me,' he screamed at the top of his voice, 'you went to China behind my back, I can't trust you any more.' Invective followed invective as a small crowd gathered in the corridor outside his office attracted by the uproar. On and on he went, literally foaming at the mouth, before dismissing me with a loud, 'I don't want to ever see you any more.' Back in my office I could not make any sense of his behavior and what I subsequently found out about him was of little comfort. He was known in New York not only for losing his temper and erupting in uncontrolled fits of rage but also for developing violent aversions to some of those around him for no perceptible reason. It took some time to sink in but it slowly dawned upon me that I had a raving madman as a boss.

Overnight I became Anvar's 'bête noire' and there was nothing I could do with which he did not find fault. 'You don't deliver,' he would scream at me a the top of his voice without ever specifying what he meant. I put up with this tomfoolery for a couple of months and then went to see the head of personnel with a list of complaints. He was a good man who listened and, yes, he agreed that I had a pretty good case if I wished to make a recourse against Anvar for harassment at the UN staff tribunal. But he did not hide the fact that if I were to win such a recourse, which seemed likely, it would reflect badly on Hartling. Would I agree to put it on hold and if things got too bad he would try to intervene. Hartling, he told me, was very pleased with me and when Anvar had once tried to bad mouth me he had snapped back at him telling him that I had his full trust. The offer was reasonable and I certainly did not want to embarrass Hartling so I replied that for the good of the organization I would hold my guns. His relief was visible and short of getting rid of Anvar I had gained a massive amount of points. Fortunately, Anvar was often on mission and as he could not deny me the ones I had to go on, I saw as little as possible of him.

However much I tried to avoid Anvar, I failed on one count; for some undefined reason, he asked me to accompany him on his first mission to China. I wished he had not. Chris Carpenter was by then well ensconced in Beijing and after two days of meetings during which Chris did most of the talking we went off to Fujian province to visit some refugees.

The afternoon of our arrival we were brought to visit a temple and as we exited the main building we passed a group of children, wearing red scarves and impeccably clean white shirts. 'Oh,' said Anvar, turning to the two Foreign Ministry officials who were escorting us during our mission, 'are these children Chinese or Japanese?' I saw Chris freeze. 'Chinese,' answered the official dryly.

That evening, as I retired to my room after dinner there was a knock on the door. The two Foreign Ministry officials, stepped into my room: 'What did Mr Anvar mean when he asked if these children were Chinese or Japanese?' They knew the answer as well as I did. The children were clean and well behaved, not dirty and messy, so they must have been Japanese. It was not that Anvar had thought it all out. The man did not think, he just talked. I decided to play dumb. I don't know, perhaps you should ask him. 'Yes,' said the officials without a smile, 'perhaps.'

Three days later we were in Guangzhou where the authorities gave a farewell dinner for us. After the usual toast it was Anvar's turn to raise his glass. 'I would like to thank mainland China for what it has done for refugees,' were his words. The unflappable Chris almost dropped his chopsticks as the guests froze in silent disbelief. Mainland China. This was the expression used by Taiwan when referring to the People's Republic of China. What followed was predictable. I was barely back in my room when there was a knock on the door and the two Foreign Ministry officials stepped in. 'What did Mr Anvar mean by mainland China' was the expected question. By then I was pretty fed up with the whole visit. 'Listen,' I told them, 'the man is a fool and does not even know the meaning of what he is saying. So forget anything he says, it is not even worth listening to.' The officials nodded. But as they stepped out of my room it occurred to me that the days I had been proud of serving UNHCR were long gone.

It was my first mission with Anvar and also thankfully the last. In the spring of 1984 the UN created a new position of Assistant Secretary General for humanitarian assistance to Cambodia based in Bangkok. It was a purely cosmetic exercise with no operational need but in recognition of Japan's financial contributions to the UN, the position was given to a Japanese, Tatsuro Kunugi. Kunugi had specialized in international law and probably barely knew where Cambodia was on the map but that was irrelevant. His assignment was a candy to Japan. When Anvar heard about the post he started to pull strings at UN Headquarters in New York and building on his so-called expertise as director for Asia for UNHCR landed the position of deputy to Kunugi and the corresponding promotion to senior director. While this dynamic duo had all the characteristic of the blind leading the deaf it was a godsend for me and from one day to another Anvar disappeared into the nothingness from which he should never have emerged. As his replacement Hartling chose a Belgian who had been the UNHCR representative in Hong Kong. There were few more cultured, educated and well-mannered men than Jacques Terlin and having gone through purgatory I was now back where I could do my work without the interference of a madman.

PRELUDE TO LEBANON

I 'I want you, yes, you with your dubious origins, I need someone in Beirut, all the others are imbeciles, you are the only one who will understand something of the situation.' Ghassan Arnout had, as he was wont to do, entered my office without knocking on the door and was pointing his finger at me insistently. Clever, crafty, articulate, thriving on intrigue for intrigue's sake. For want of a more suitable candidate he had been assigned the post of Director for the Middle East. The position on paper also made him responsible for the running of the massive UNHCR assistance programs for Afghan refugees in Pakistan but that specific job he had wisely delegated to an American, Tom Barnes, who after having been heavily involved in counter-insurgency in Vietnam had joined UNHCR where he was now running the Afghan program as a closed shop.

This left Arnaout free to torment the handful of fellow Arabs who worked for him whom he would regularly browbeat and insult, connive with the Arab diplomatic corps in Geneva and roam the corridors in search of any gossip that came his way which he would then amplify, distort and disseminate to all comers. How he ever came across my 'suspicious origins', i.e. my Jewish-born mother, I never found out but it probably came from Rizvi to whom I had once described my family background. To his credit Arnaout was free of any prejudice and while he would regularly call the blacks the tragedy of Africa he did so to their face and they loved him for it were it only because no one took him seriously and they knew that, deep down, it was done without malice.

I would have taken Arnaout's invitation to go to Beirut as a joke had the rumor not spread that UNHCR had now a new personnel policy and its name was 'rotation'. On paper the concept made sense. UNHCR was supposed to be a field-oriented organization and the idea was that all officers would be required to rotate between field and Headquarter positions thus demonstrating that they were proficient at serving in both. This, hopefully, would have brought to an end the current system which saw one category of staff doing all the hard work in the field while others spent their time basking in the comfort of Headquarters or posted in developed countries where they could lobby at will for promotions. If the concept made sense, its implementation never did. Not only did the senior directors exempt themselves from rotation but it became increasingly obvious that a high percentage of the staff coming from privileged families in the third world were simply culturally unfit at any task that required more than writing memos and roaming the corridors. The result was a series of mismatches but the pressure was there; by the summer of 1984 I had been at my job in Geneva for five years and it was time for me to plan ahead without waiting to be encouraged to do so.

Several times a year UNHCR would advertise the posts that were due to become vacant. The staff would put down their name for the posts they were interested in and a board would then chose the apropriate candidates. These were then approved by the head of personnel except for the representatives who would be approved by Hartling. It was a common procedure for staff who did not want to leave Geneva to put down their name for posts for which they were so manifestly unsuited for that they would be rejected as a matter of certainty upon which they could claim that they had applied for field service but, through no fault of their own, had been turned down. However much I valued looking after my own interests this was one road I was not willing to embark on, and even more as it could backfire and I could end up in darkest Africa so a I went through the list of posts to be filled, put my name down for Beirut and Washington and waited.

One week later Hartling called me in. 'I saw,' he said 'that you put your name down for Washington and I want you to know that I think you would have been very good at it, but,' he slightly hesitated, 'there are other considerations and I can't give it to you.'

'Sir,' I answered 'I will try to do my best wherever you send me.'

'This I know,' he replied with a nod as I left his office. So I did not get Washington but his calling me in was a nice gesture. The one who did get Washington was our deputy head of personnel, Fiorella Cappelli, and it was the last thing she wanted. Fiorella was a genuinely good person, competent and trusted by all. She was also neither a politician nor a programmer and was perfect at her current job, but rotation was rotation and the fact that moving her was neither what she wanted nor good for the organization was irrelevant. Rotation was now the rule.

Two weeks later Arnaout stormed into my office waving a piece of paper. 'You have got it,' he screamed, 'Beirut, Regional Representative for the Middle East.' When I asked him how many other candidates there had been for the post he broke out laughing. 'You must be mad, don't you watch the news on TV?' Actually I did, and Beirut was a staple of the evening news; car bombings, kidnappings, street fighting were the daily fare. In comparison Saigon even at the height of the Vietnam war was a haven of tranquility. 'Other candidates,' he laughed, 'only you are mad enough to apply, you and your "doubtful origins" but don't worry you will make it through.' Why did I apply? I did not really know except that I was sure I would not get bored and then where else would I find such a unique chance to get to know the cradle of our civilization, the Middle East?

BEIRUT 1984

I landed at Beirut airport at 10 in the evening on Wednesday December 5, 1984, flying in from Geneva on Middle East Airlines, the only airline still flying to Lebanon and as I stepped off the aircraft two UNHCR staff members from the Beirut office were there to meet me. Both were Lebanese; Solh, whose uncle was one of the founding fathers of modern Lebanon and who had seen the UNHCR office in Beirut through thick and thin, and his program officer, Lina Sultani. As the other passengers trudged towards immigration they pointed me to a side door with a sign above it that said VIP. It was a large, poorly lit room with plastic covered armchairs. The windows were broken and the far wall was pockt-marked with bullet holes. As we waited for my passport to be stamped I could see that they were eyeing me with barely disguised suspicion. I was wearing jeans and a brown Chinese padded jacket under a lose raincoat, not exactly the attire that they expected in a UNHCR Regional Representative with the rank of ambassador. Arnaout had warned me. Solh and Lina had been in Beirut forever. For all practical purposes they had run the office and felt very proprietary about it. While they would put up the best of appearances I was not welcome and they would perceive me, at least initially, as nothing more than an intrusion, and an ignorant one at that.

Driving into Beirut from the airport was eerie. There were no streetlights and the road was a long sequence of potholes occasionally interspaced with the rusting hulk of a burned out car. The city was mostly in the dark and whatever lights there were came in concert with the buzz made by a swarm of small portable generators. As we reached one of the main avenues two men, waving powerful flashlights signaled us to slow down. As we did Solh rolled down one of the windows and one of the two men came up to the car. He was unshaven and as he handed him some sort of pamphlet he shouted, 'Allah el akhbar,' Allah is great. 'Allah el akhbar,' responded Solh in a slow controlled voice. 'Its the Hezbollah,' he said turning towards me as our driver slowly put the car into gear, 'they only distribute pamphlets,' he added, more I suspected as if to convince himself rather than addressing me.

After another twenty minutes of driving through a maze of small dark streets the car came to a stop. 'We have arrived,' said Solh, 'I have booked you a room in a hotel not far from the office.'

The hotel lobby was lit by a lonely light bulb connected to a small generator, but even in the dim light I could see that this was no luxury establishment. 'The car will pick you up at 8 tomorrow morning,' said Solh 'and in the meantime have a good night.'

Before closing my door the hotel attendant had handed me a flashlight and its pallid beam shed enough light on a room in which I would not have wanted to stay one night longer if possible.

Next morning, after a quick breakfast of French bread and black coffee in the deserted dining room, Solh showed up at precisely 8 am. Rather than the black turtleneck sweaters I was generally comfortable in I had put on a coat and tie and I could see Solh's approving look. Clearly, my scruffy appearance on arrival must have been puzzling to him and my present attire reassured him as to my propriety for the job of Regional Representative.

The UNHCR office located in the Ein Mreisse neighborhood on the sixth floor of a 12 storey building on the rue Kennedy overlooked the sea and the view from my office was breathtaking. To the right it extended all the way across the bay of Beirut. To the left one could see the elegant, palm tree lined avenue de Paris that paralleled the sea front with, at the near end, the burned out skeleton of what was left of the bombed American embassy.

All the staff was there to greet me; Mouna the secretary, a pleasant woman in her forties, and her assistant Maroun who was in charge of the accounts; the two drivers, both called Mohamed; Yussef, the legal officer who was Moroccan; Lina and her assistant Jumana who were in charge of programs and finally Solh who kept an eye on everything. They all looked friendly enough but I could feel that they were somewhat on their guard just as Arnaout had warned me: 'They all live in the fear that UNHCR will close the office in Beirut,' he had told me. 'You must reassure them,' he added, 'but if you do it too explicitly they will become even more suspicious so don't say anything but just act as if things are going on as usual.'

But for the moment all these considerations were premature and my priority was to find a place to live.

Luckily for me, Youssef lived in a small service apartment building two streets down the road from our office and a phone call ascertained that by pure chance the owner, Alex Fallalah, had a space available. The one bedroom apartment into which he ushered me was perfectly adequate, clean, bright and just off the office. 'There is only one small problem,' he said, 'very small but you know how things are in Beirut these days, most of the time there is no electricity.' When I asked him how he defined 'most of the time' he tried to evade the issue but finally conceded: there might occasionally be some electricity in the middle of the day but as far as the night was concerned it was off 90% of the time. 'No refrigerator,' he said, adding with a bright smile, 'but you can cook; bottled gas.' I looked at Solh who had accompanied me and he nodded his assent. 'Very safe,' he said and the deal was done; one month's rent to start with.

What I knew about Lebanon was that the country had been carved out of Syria by the French in 1920 after the fall of the Ottoman empire. The French had wanted to give their Christian Maronite allies a state of their own. So to the Maronite province of Mount Lebanon they added Tripoli to the North, the Bekaa valley to the East, Beirut to the West and Saida to the South and called it Lebanon. What emerged was a hodgepodge of some 12 communities including Moslems and Christians of all ilks that evolved into a complex power sharing political system based on religious affiliation. Loose government controls, a gift for trade and a society based on mutual tolerance conspired to make Lebanon the most prosperous society of the Levant and by the middle 1970's, Beirut, with its universities, hospitals, fashion houses, vibrant private sector and dynamic banking system could justifiably claim the title of the Paris of the Middle East. Foreign intervention, demographic shifts and sectarian divides brought down this elegant house of cards in 1975 when civil war erupted, tearing the country asunder.

The heart of Lebanon had been Beirut and it now became the main arena of the civil war. Initially, it had been a civilized war and while all the parties involved lobbied mortar shells and fired long bursts of machine gun fire at each other with gusto, there was an order to this exuberance. All sides held their fire between the first and the sixth of each month, which was pay week. Likewise firing was suspended between the 25 and 31 of each month when businesses closed their books. Shelling, when it occurred, started at 10 in the morning, after people had done their shopping and subsided at 11 am only to resume from 4 pm to 4.40 pm and, except for some occasional sniping, never on a Sunday.

This civilized routine did not survive the passing of time and when I arrived in Beirut the war had turned into a free for all in which a puzzle of militias, warlords, family clans and religious communities, all jealous of the local power they wielded and desperately holding on to it would let loose whenever their whim inclined them to do so with every gun, rocket propelled grenade, heavy machine gun or mortar they could muster.

Mount Lebanon and East Beirut were controlled by the so called Lebanese forces, a Maronite Christian movement which was divided into three groups, two minor ones, the Tigers and the Guardians of the Cedar, and a major one, the Phalangists, who, in turn had a radical wing, a centrist wing and a more moderate one. West Beirut, which included the southern suburbs and the airport, was controlled by four factions, theoretically allied but in practical terms each controlling its own part of town. These included Amal, a left wing Shiite group, the PSP (Popular Socialist Party) composed only of Druze, the upcoming Hezbollah with links to Iran, and finally the Mourabitun, a Sunni militia supported by Libya.

Each of these militias had its own stomping grounds and I only discovered much later in my stay that the rue Kennedy where we had our office was actually controlled by Amal while the nearby streets where my apartment was located was under Druze control.

The main distinction between East and West Beirut was the fact that the East was essentially under the responsibility of one group, the Phalangists, while power in the West was fragmented and in the hands of a variety of militias, local warlords and armed criminal groups. And while shelling and gunfire took its toll on both sides, it was anarchy on one side and some form of order on the other.

Dividing Beirut was the 'Green Line' a sinister swath of a few hundred yards wide made up of guttered building and barbed wire entanglements with the antagonists bunkered down on each side and occasionally taking shots at each other. The two main crossing points along the line were separated by a quarter of a mile wide no man's land through which a dirt track meandered around shell holes and skeletons of shelled buildings from one side of the line to the other. Most of the time the two sides would be in radio contact and agree when cars filled with civilians could cross either way but ultimately no rules applied; the line could be open for days and suddenly close. Snipers for no reason would take shots at the cautiously crossing cars anytime. Crossing the line was a gamble and those who did never knew if they would make it alive or get stuck on the other side and for how long. It was an ordeal that those who lived on one side and worked on the other—and this included part of our staff—had to go through daily, a nerve wrecking trial which, day after day, took its toll as people increasingly cracked under the stress.

Long periods of absolute calm, as there occurred when I arrived, if anything made things worse as they only heightened the expectation of inevitable trouble to come and it was no wonder that on an average per capita basis Beirut was the world's greatest consumer of Valium.

Solh suggested I do some shopping before going to my new quarters so, accompanied by Mohamed the driver, we set off on foot to what looked like a small store just behind the office on the rue Clemenceau. Actually, behind a modest facade it was a vast Ali Baba's cave and the shelves were piled high with every single possible delicacy available in the best delis of London or New York. In no time I piled a shopping cart full of spaghetti, canned tomato sauce, salt, sugar, coffee, tea, milk, two types of bread, eggs, various fruit and a small piece of butter—I remembered I had no fridge. As we proceeded to check out Solh pointed to a large flashlight and a camping lamp powered from a bottle of liquid gas. 'You will need them,' he said.

Night fell around 6 pm in Beirut and after having unpacked and prepared for myself a plate of spaghetti I set out to read by my gas lamp but soon discovered that it was not the best light to read by and turned it off.

The night was quiet and though it had turned chilly one could still do without heating. It had been a strange day, especially for a country at war but I recalled Arnaout's admonition that in Lebanon things were never what they appeared to be; wise words no doubt but I still had to decipher their full meaning, if any.

The next morning I was at the office at 8 am and had barely sat down behind a pile of papers on my desk when Solh came in and announced that he had just received a phone call from the Swedish embassy and that their Secretary of State for Immigration would be coming to see me within an hour. To say that I was ill prepared to receive him would have been an understatement but I had no option except to bluff my way through any question he would put to me, albeit with Solh and Youssef at my side.

Jonas Widgren was a tall emaciated Swede with a sallow complexion, high cheekbones below a large wide forehead and pale blue eyes of almost Mongol appearance. His English was unstructured and his rhythm staccato; eloquence was not his strong point but I had heard he had been a close collaborator of Olof Palme, the former Swedish Prime Minister, who was not one to suffer fools and this alone suggested that he was worth more attention than his first appearance commanded. Apparently, he explained to me, there were a handful of Lebanese in Sweden whom he felt did not qualify for refugee status and he wished to deport them back to Lebanon but was wary of the outcry by advocacy groups. 'How does UNHCR feel about repatriation to Lebanon,' he asked me, eying me with suspicion. Fortunately Solh had given me a short introductory briefing about the situation in Lebanon and while there were many blank spots it was all I had to go by so I decided to take the plunge. 'I can't answer you,' I replied, 'it all depends.' My answer must have taken him by surprise. 'Depends on what,' he said looking at me with a concerned frown. 'It is simple,' I said, 'it depends on who the people you are sending back are and where you will be sending them back to.' I could see that this was not the answer he was expecting and I had shot some of his bearings. 'Let me put it in another way,' I went on. 'You must look at Lebanon as it is. It is divided in areas controlled by various factions. This means that if you take a Maronite and sent him back to East Beirut he will be in no danger. The same applies if you deport a Shiite back to West Beirut, a Palestinian to South Lebanon, a Druze to the Chouf area or a Sunni to Tripoli. Granted on paper the country might be at war but overall there will always be a given area where someone from a given community will be safe from persecution. So, yes you can send people back but it all depends on who they are and to which part of Lebanon you return them to.' I could feel Solh next to me breathe a sigh of relief. He was deeply committed to his Lebanon and I had exactly reflected his feelings. As for Youssef, the legal officer and hence officially the keeper of the flame, he understood by now enough of Lebanon to concede that I was not in the wrong.

Widgren I could see was completely taken aback but quickly regained his composure. 'Do you mean,' he said, 'that I can actually send them back?'

'Of course,' I replied, 'but within the constraints I mentioned.'

'So is this the official position of UNHCR,' he asked as if he needed this last reassurance. 'It is,' I said as I turned to Solh and Yussef who nodded their assent.

I probably made Widgren's trip to Lebanon but a doubt must have lingered. 'Are you sure you work for UNHCR?' he said with a big laugh as he left my office.

Being UNHCR Representative in Beirut required that I introduce myself to the foreign embassies still in the city and I started doing the rounds with Solh. All had armed guards and took whatever precautions they fancied against whatever they felt might strike them. The British, whose office was located in a tall building facing the sea, had hung large nets from the roof which came all the way down to the ground floor, presumably in the hope of catching any rocket propelled grenade aimed at their windows. The Canadians had provided their ambassador with a massively armored limousine that was so heavy that it could barely negotiate the mountain roads that led inland from Beirut. The Swedes had been provided with special curtains that were supposed to catch shards of shattered glass and the Swiss had four guards in their lobby armed with automatic pistols with lead bullets that would not bounce off the walls if fired indoors.

The UN still had a presence in the city and its various agencies UNDP, UNICEF, UNRWA, WFP and others would meet every week mostly to discuss administrative issues such as salary scales for the local staff and which roads were safer than others. On my first meeting I was introduced to a UN security officer who advised me not to go out at night and gave me a portable radio to use in an emergency. 'To call, if you have a problem,' he said, 'just press this button and talk into the microphone let me show you.' He did and nothing happened. He shrugged his shoulders. 'It does not really matter,' he commented. 'If you get into trouble and have to call, even if you get through nobody will come.' After the meeting I showed my radio to Solh. 'Yes,' he said, 'I have the same one. There is no one at the other end. Actually,' he added, 'I don't think there ever was.'

The one organization Arnaout had recommended I absolutely steer clear from was UNRWA, the UN agency responsible for Palestinian refugees. UNRWA had been created in December 1949, and was responsible for providing assistance to Palestinian refugees. After the creation of UNHCR in 1951 the Arab league insisted that UNRWA carry on with its mandate and the organization thus became the only UN agency in history to be responsible for one single ethnic group to the exclusion of any other. The purpose of the exercise was never in doubt. On paper UNHCR tried to solve refugee problems, be it through return or local integration. Conversely, the task of UNRWA was to keep the problem alive. With the Arab states refusing to recognize Israel, their only card was the perpetuation of the Palestinian refugee issue as a useful tool to continue harassing the Jewish state. This required that the Palestinians be kept in camps rather than be integrated in the various Arab countries where they had fled to and UNRWA became the tool through which this was achieved. That the problem would backfire with the

Palestinian camps becoming the first incubators of terrorism was foreseen by none, but then the Middle East was not about thinking ahead. Perversely, the United States, which was the main supporter of Israel, was also the main contributor to UNRWA, thus adding to the sword of Damocles that dangled over the Jewish state. By 1984, the Palestinians had outlived their welcome throughout the Arab world in general and in Lebanon in particular. After having tried to overthrow the government of Jordan and then take over South Lebanon they now lived huddled in shanty towns in West Beirut detested by all. Fortunately, UNHCR had nothing to do with the Palestinians, but in a world where misunderstanding was the rule, steering a course far away from them was a wise thing to do.

The UNHCR Regional office for the Middle East had been set up in Beirut by Sadruddin in the early 1960's. Lebanon at the time was an island of peace, prosperity and tolerance in the Middle East and Beirut was a logical choice for an office that was supposed to cover the region from a supposedly neutral base. In addition, Sadruddin, through his wife whose first husband was from a great Lebanese family, had a romantic attachment to Beirut, hence his reluctance to close the office when the civil war started in 1975 and so the UNHCR office in Beirut had endured. By the time I arrived in Lebanon not only had Beirut, with its tenuous security situation, often closed airport, erratic telephone lines and unreliable tclex, lost all appeal as a UNHCR Regional Office but we also had practically no assistance activities in Lebanon. As a result of the civil war it was a barmy refugee indeed who would claim asylum in Lebanon and the few who did were provided with counseling by the Middle East Council of Churches to which we allocated 25,000 US $ a year for this service, a paltry sum by any standard and certainly not one that justified the presence of a regional office. Of course there were internally displaced Lebanese by the hundreds of thousands but these were mostly taken care of by their local communities or warlords. On paper we could have helped them but it would have been suicidal. Amal would have resented our helping the Maronites who would have resented our helping the Druze who would have resented our helping Hezbollah, making us a prime target for a massive hit from all sides. So lying low and doing nothing became the prime condition for our survival in Beirut.

The function of Regional Representative required that I be accredited to every government in the area—except Israel—and the first country on my list was Syria and for good reason. Not only did Syria play a major role—overt and covert—in Lebanon, but also as far as the numbers and needs of refugees were concerned there was a lot to be done. Getting on the good side of the Syrians was therefore a must and one week after I had arrived in Beirut I was in Damascus with Solh.

Damascus was said to be the oldest city known to man and whether this was true or not there was something in the air that suggested thousands of years of history. The main market, the souk Hamadie, had initially been the via Recta, the straight road of Roman times and the cobblestones that had seen legions of Roman soldiers march to battle showed barely a sign of wear twenty centuries later. Today Damascus was the seat of one of the hardest regime in the Arab world but the vicissitudes of politics had left untouched the sophistication of the city, the elegance of its art nouveau architecture and the urbanity of its inhabitants.

Solh knew everybody and was welcomed by everybody and for two days we did the rounds of ministries, embassies and restaurants where dignified maitre d's in white coats and black trousers, surrounded by swarms of attentive waiters, would proffer to our attention leather-bound menus of imposing proportions.

Much as I enjoyed playing the tourist in Damascus I still had to find a way of bringing some assistance to the Afghans refugees in Syria who, officially, did not exist but that problem was solved the next day; we were permitted to help the Afghans provided that in our books they would appear as Eritrean.

By December 14 I was back in Beirut and while by now I had my logistics more or less under control, as far as security was concerned I still could not make heads or tail of the situation. From Geneva, on TV Beirut looked like an inferno. Granted I had been in Lebanon for only two weeks but I had crossed the Green Line with no problem and heard no shooting by night. Conversely, the UN had just made a resume of the security situation in West Beirut during 1984 and a copy had landed on my desk. During the year there had been 214 major armed clashes, 185 major explosions, 7 foreign diplomats kidnapped, 37 foreign diplomats who had moved for security reasons to East Beirut, the crossing points of the Green Line had been closed 46 times, the airport had closed down for a cumulative total of three months, 100 major banks had been attacked and car bombings, which had peaked at a record number of 26 in one week had become so common that they were no longer reported. The same applied to kidnappings of Lebanese and political assassinations.

I made a note of these incidents and sent a copy of the report to Geneva on the assumption that my stay had coincided with a lucky break in the fighting and that I had not been assigned a holiday destination. As I gave a copy of my note to Solh he looked at me with visible dismay. 'Do you really want to send it,' he commented. It reflected a reality that he had gone a long way to overlook and had never reported to Geneva.

On December 18, after 13 days in Beirut I was back in Geneva for the Christmas holiday. Arnaout was rapturous when I explained to him how I had fiddled the program for Eritrean refugees in Syria to include the Afghans but while he professed to be glad that we had achieved something for the refugees it was the convoluted way it had been done that appealed to him the most. I also told Hartling and he agreed that given the circumstances I had done the right thing.

On Tuesday January 22, 1985, I was back in Beirut and while I had enough paperwork to keep me busy during the week my dread was what to do on the weekends. There was a well-stocked bookshop, chez Joseph, in the main shopping street, Hamra, ten minutes away on foot but just walking there and back while not exactly unsafe was not exactly safe either. With the total breakdown of order in West Beirut anybody could come up to anybody with a gun and while kidnappings of foreigners were generally targeted they were also becoming random. The Lebanese were born merchants and whenever they saw, or thought they saw an opportunity their penchant for trading would kick in. Thus, over time kidnapping had become an industry. There were now groups who would kidnap on order, groups which specialized in keeping custody of the kidnapped and groups who specialized in negotiating ransoms, all of course for a fee. It was also not unheard of for a person to be kidnapped by one group and then sold to another who hoped to get a better ransom. Likewise, anyone who looked like a foreigner stood the risk of being kidnapped on the odd chance that there might be someone willing to pay a ransom for his release.

This was not something that the people at my office would talk about but both the Canadians and the Swedes had been advised by their governments to keep a very low profile and possibly stay off the streets where they would be immediately recognized as foreigners. So the only safe option for me was to stay home on the weekends.

The main UN base in Lebanon was in Naquoura in the Israeli-controlled part of Southern Lebanon and as UNHCR representative it was difficult for me not to drop by at least once, were it only on a courtesy call.

Driving to Naquoura, some 60 miles South of Beirut, could take between 1 ½ hours and never, depending on traffic, shelling, the state of the road, the mood of the Israelis, the disposition of the local militias or all of the above.

With the UN flag flying from our car, I set out with Solh and after ten minutes on the road slowed down for our first checkpoint South of the airport, but we were waved through by a grubby, unshaven grim-looking man in worn green fatigues seated on the side of the road on an old chair with a gun under it. Over the next hour we went through six such checkpoints, all manned by the same sinister-looking characters and Solh would spell out for me to which group they belonged; Amal, Hezbollah, then again Amal, Mourabitun, again Amal but after we had passed the sixth he stay silent. 'And who was that?' I asked him. He looked at me somewhat surprised. 'It is the Israeli army,' he said. We had barely gone five more minutes when we reached another Israeli checkpoint and here things got difficult. 'Where you go?' asked one of the soldiers who seemed in charge in broken English. 'To Naquoura,' answered Solh. 'You can't go,' he replied. Solh stood silent and I felt I should take over. So I got out of the car and asked the soldier in an even tone 'why not?'

'Because I say so,' he snapped back.

'Listen,' I told him, 'we are from the UN and we have a meeting a Naquoura.'

'I don't like the UN,' he barked back.

'Neither do I,' I replied. He looked momentarily taken aback.

'Then why are you with them?'

'OK,' I said, 'do you like the army?'

'No,' he said.

'So, why then are you with them?'

'OK,' he answered, 'go, go.' I could see that Solh was puzzled but he said nothing.

The main focus of the meeting that day in Naquoura was the collapse of the Lebanese pound. In the first three weeks of 1985 it had lost 29 % of its value and the plunge showed no sign of abating. As the pound nosedived, merchants would adjust their prices daily with the result that all goods were now indexed to the dollar. With salaries not following, people were now hoarding whatever goods they possessed and many could no longer make ends meet.

For the UN staff still in Beirut, the consequences in terms of salary were not inconsequential. With our salaries paid in part in Lebanese pounds, our revenue on paper remained the same but its purchasing power took a nosedive. As for our monthly post adjustment which was paid in dollars it was also based on the exchange rate of the Lebanese pound and the result was that between January and April it dropped from 1,615 US $ to 49 US $. The UN had of course a mechanism to ensure that corrections were made to a post adjustment, but it proceeded at glacial speed while the Lebanese pound was in free fall. So for those staff members who could not put up with the drop in salary the only solution was to apply for a transfer.

The collapse of the Lebanese pound was only a symptom of what had developed into three wars in one.

The global context was the confrontation between the US and the USSR with each of the two superpowers supporting their respective allies namely Israel and Syria. On the regional level the conflict was more complex. Both Syria and Iraq were under the rule of the Baath Party but these were two rival wings of the Baath and they were at each other's throat. With Iraq at war with Iran, it was logical for the Iranians to allay themselves with Syria against their common enemy. That Iran was ruled by a Persian Shiia Moslem fundamentalist regime while Syria was a Sunni Arab nation controlled by an Alawite secular party was irrelevant to the issue. What was at stake was a geopolitical relation and not a love match. It was therefore in the order of things that, using Syria as an intermediate, Iran would arm and support in Lebanon an anti Israeli Shiia movement, namely Hezbollah. The same logic induced not only Israel but also Iraq to provide weapons to the anti Syrian Lebanese Phalangists who, as an added bonus, were both at war with the PLO and trading blows with the Shiia.

To add to the complexity of the conflict was the fact that it could not be summed up in one all inclusive formula. It was not a war between poor and rich because there were some of both on each side. It was not a war between Christians and Moslems because a majority in either group did not take part in the conflict. And while most of the Shiite were poor and all the Christians were not rich, it was the poorer of the Christian Maronites who tended to be Phalangists and the poorer of the Shiites who tended to be Hezbollah. Within this constantly shifting quagmire, alliances were temporary and betrayal the rule. Thus, when the mainstream Shiite movement Amal tried to maintain some order in West Beirut and had come to some agreement with the Phalangists it would be the Shiite Hezbollah who would create incidents to discredit it. Their main ruse was the truck mortar. It consisted of a 62 mm mortar bolted onto the bed of a pickup truck. The truck would emerge from an underground garage, fire a half dozen rounds in the general direction of East Beirut and then reverse into its lair. The Phalangist would then blindly fire back into West Beirut as the citizenry that thronged the streets would rush to find some refuge under the nearest doorway. Furious radio messages and phone calls would then be exchanged between Amal and the Phalangists before the shelling would subside. As the truck mortar constantly changed locations Amal could claim with some degree of credibility that it could not put it out of action and hence was not responsible for its shenanigans. Likewise, when a major car bomb would blow up, no one ever really knew who did it, why it was done, against whom and by whom pretending to be whom. Under these circumstances, and considering that there was no prospect of UNHCR having any role to play, humanitarian or other in Lebanon, the obvious question for me was what was I doing in Beirut? The implied answer in Geneva was that our presence had a symbolic value and were we to leave the Lebanese government would have felt let down. That explanation simply did not gel. First of all, for all practical purposes there was no longer a Lebanese government hence no one to feel let down. And as for our presence having a symbolic value this begged the question 'symbolic of what?' So ultimately the answer was simple. I was in Beirut because, due to bureaucratic inertia, no one at UNHCR wanted to take the initiative of closing down the office and moving it to another country in the region. Fortunatly, our Headquarters did not make any demands on us and left us to our own devices with one exception. There was a new Deputy Director at the Protection division, a pompous Bengladeshi named Shamshul Bari and he had set out to make a name for himself. So one day we recieved a communication informing us that he had heard about serious problems for refugees in the Bekaa Valley and demanding in no uncertain terms that we immediately go on the spot to investigate. Solh, who had read the message was nonplussed. As he explained to me the Bekaa Valley was under the control of various fundamentalist Shiia militias buttressed by elements of the Iraninan Revolutionnary Guards and no sanc person would ever contemplate even going close to the place. By now I knew enough about the UN never to say no. If an unreasonable request came my way the strategy was to say yes, deflect the thrust and turn it back to where it originated from. So I replied that this was an excellent idea but due to the highly sensitive security situation in the area this should be a high level mission ideally led by Deputy Director Bari. It was the last we heard about a mission to the Bekaa Valley.

I never considered being shot at, being maimed or being kidnapped as part of my UN job and I had no intention of making it such. Fortunately for me, the fact that UNHCR could not bring itself to move its regional office for the Middle East out of West

Beirut in no way demanded my constant presence in the city. I was after all regional representative and not just representative to Lebanon so I decided to play the part. It made sense professionally, it was wise in terms of my personal security and, last but not least, it enabled me to visit the Middle East in privileged conditions.

On all my tours I took Solh along and actually could not have done without him. He had an incredible number of contacts throughout the region, especially in government and all the officials we would go and meet seemed to hold him in high esteem. However from Amman to Kuwait to Qatar to Abu Dhabi, to Riyadh to Bahrain the one word governments did not want to hear was 'refugees'. And likewise, while they suffered from no shortage of funds, contributing to a UN organization as opposed to their own charities was simply not part of the picture. So our tours were actually a long sequence of courtesy calls with an occasional unexpected burst of activity. We had just arrived in Qatar on one of our tours when we received an urgent message from Amnesty International in London. According to their information an Iranian refugee who had sought asylum in Qatar had recently been arrested and was on the point of being deported to Iran where his life would be in danger. Amnesty International demanded that we immediately intervene to save this person's life.

The next morning Solh set off at full speed, contacting the government while simultaneous scouring all the police stations in case he was held in detention unreported. That afternoon we received another message from Amnesty International. This time they accused us of dereliction of duty, of being accomplices to murder and threatened to alert the press to our failure in upholding our mandate to protect refugees if the case remained unsolved. By now Solh was pretty unnerved as he set off for his second day of quest while I, being of no use to him, waited at the hotel. By noon he was back with a puzzled look on his face. He actually knew the refugee Amnesty International had referred to and while stopping by the most luxurious hotel in town to have coffee had run into him. The man had a suite in the hotel, had never been arrested and was actually by the pool reading his newspaper. Solh wanted to immediately revert to Amnesty International telling them, in a short message, that the case had been solved but I stopped him. Had Amnesty International simply alerted us to some information that had come their way and asked us to look into the matter that would have been fine and, in drafting my note to them, I told them as much. But they had taken the moral high ground as if they had a monopoly on it and in the process had accused us of dereliction of duty and that deserved an answer and they got it too. The message I sent Amnesty International was not the sort of thing I would copy to Geneva... Arrogant... pompous... publicity seeking... desk bound bureaucrats... moralizing from the comfort and safety of their London office... diverting our time and resources from more urgent tasks... we have kept this whole matter on file and if ever you have the arrogance of addressing us as you did we will release it to the media who will draw their own conclusions as to the credibility of your outfit... It was the last I ever heard from Amnesty International.

By now life for me when in Beirut consisted basically of making it to the office and back and staying holed up in my apartment the rest of the time. Kidnappings of foreigners, for whatever reason, were now increasing and a further turning point in the escalating violence was reached when three Soviets were abducted. It was a first; no Soviet citizen had ever been kidnapped until then and the whole of Beirut watched to see if and how the Soviets would react. They were not disappointed.

Following the abduction, the Soviets, acting through appropriate intermediaries, kidnapped the distant nephew of a major Lebanese religious figure—some said it was sheik Fadlallah but this was only hearsay—killed him, cut off his testicles and had them sent to his uncle with the following message: the Soviet Union has some 250 million inhabitants and a few more or less are of no concern to the Soviet authorities. However, the kidnapping was an insult to the Soviet state. This was unacceptable. So if within 72 hours our three hostages are not released, we will start killing every single member, man, woman and child of your extended family. When the religious figure protested that he had nothing to do with the kidnapping, the answer he received was unequivocal: we know you are not responsible. We know you did not do it. We are not accusing you of having done it. All we are telling you is what will happen to your family if our people are not released. Yes, we know it is unfair but then life is unfair and tough luck to you.

It was a masterly move and it worked. Two days later the three Soviets were released and no Soviet citizen was ever kidnapped again in Lebanon. The incident never hit the press and as news of it spread by word of mouth I marveled at the sophistication of the approach. Had the kidnapped been Americans, there would have been public statements followed by empty threats culminating into some sort of war dance leading to nowhere. The Soviets knew better. Their system might have been foul but intellectually they were far superior to the Americans. They did not threaten, they acted going straight for the jugular of the Arab world, the family.

I did not have behind me the protection of the Soviet Union, only of the UN, which did not even pretend to be concerned for our safety and the only precaution I could take was to concede to Maziad's, my driver, insistence that I not walk to the office though it was only a few minutes away but let him drive me there and back and accompany me on the way home to the supermarket to replenish my supplies. I never doubted Maziad's devotion to me but when I pointed out to him that I did not think the Colt 45 he carried in his glove compartment would serve much purpose he agreed. We need something better he said but it will cost 200 US dollars, a sum that I gave him with no hesitation. The following day he accompanied me to my apartment carrying something wrapped in a newspaper. 'Look,' he said with a big grin on his face as he unwrapped the paper. It was an AK47 with a folding stock, brand new, in perfect condition, one of the earlier models with a forged receiver rather than a stamped one, a thing of beauty. I kept it under my bed with two loaded magazines, and though, in an emergency it might have been only of marginal use, I liked to believe that from then onwards I slept better.

By early June 1985 I was holed up in my apartment on a Saturday afternoon with another lackluster weekend to look forward to when the phone rang. It was Georges Koulischer, the new UNHCR director for Administration, calling from Geneva. The line had been down for the past few days but it was obviously now up and working and as clear as could be. Koulischer was not one to beat around the bush and went straight to the point. He wanted to talk to me over the phone but preferred to do it from Cyprus so when could I get there? 'Is it urgent,' I asked. 'Yes,' was his reply. I remembered there was a daily Middle East Airlines morning flight from Beirut to Nicosia so I told him I could be there the next day. 'That would be fine,' he said, adding 'where are you spending the night?' 'In my apartment,' I replied. 'Well,' he hesitated, 'could you call Solh and ask him if you could spend the night at his place?' 'Sure,' I said, by now somewhat perplexed, 'could you give me some indication concerning what this is all about.' There was a moment of silence at the other end of the line... 'your mother,' he said. I got the point instantly. My poor Jewish mother. That was not exactly good news.

A WAR BY ANOTHER NAME

B By some miracle the telephone was still working after Koulischer had hung up and I managed to get through to Solh at his home in Saida. 'I had a call from Koulischer,' I told him, 'and he asked me to talk to you as soon as possible.' 'How soon?' he asked. 'Now, if possible.' There was no hesitation at his end of the phone. 'All right,' he said, 'I am coming.'

The drive from Saida to Beirut generally took half an hour if there was no firing on the way and this gave me just enough time to pack two suitcases before Solh rang the doorbell. He did not seem particularly surprised by my sudden call but then he rarely was and generally took things in stride with a touch of good humor. I briefly explained to him what Koulischer had told me adding in the missing pieces. 'Yes, my mother was born in a Jewish family. Yes, she had become a Christian when she had married my father. Yes, I had been baptized at birth, yes, I was a Christian although not a practicing one and Judaism was of no concern to me. Have you heard anything along those lines?,' I asked him. He hesitated. 'Yes,' he said, 'there were some rumors but I never heard anything bad said about you.'

Solh knew everybody in Lebanon and there was a good chance that if anybody had something against me he would have heard about it. A good chance, yes, but not a certainty and that was not good enough.

Solh's home in Saida was that of a wealthy Lebanese featuring heavy brocade curtains, gilded Louis XV style furniture and exquisite marble floors. His wife was what the French would qualify as a '*Grande dame*', gracious in manner and impressive in allure and the hospitality he extended to me included serving me dinner at 9 pm rather than at the customary 11 pm and letting me go off to sleep.

Solh had managed to get me a one-way ticket to Cyprus and drove me next morning to the airport. Check in was lax, no one bothered to weigh my luggage, there was no security control and soon, to my great relief, we were airborne. The flight was short and uneventful and by noon I had checked myself in a hotel in Nicosia and was on the phone with Koulischer.

According to his explanation, Hartling had gone to London to attend some sort of refugee conference and had taken him along in addition to Rizvi and his faithful personal assistant Marie-Thérèse Emery. They, and many of the delegates to the conference, were all staying at the same hotel and before dinner Marie-Thérèse and Rizvi went down to the bar for a drink. As Marie-Thérèse was to describe it, she was seated at a small table when Rizvi moved up to the bar to join a man whom she knew to be a representative of the Palestine Liberation Organization. The two starting chatting with at one point Rizvi putting on his mysterious air commenting 'I will never understand this organization.' What do you mean, said the PLO man. 'Yes,' said Rizvi, 'UNHCR, can you imagine, they sent a Jew as their regional representative in Beirut.' Marie-Thérèse was horrified, rushed up to Koulischer's room, told him what she had heard upon which he summoned Rizvi who claimed it was all a misunderstanding and Marie-Thérèse must have heard the wrong thing. Finally it all boiled down to Marie-Thérèse's word against Rizvi's and Koulischer told them to forget the matter. But Koulischer did not and he called me the following day.

For me, what had occurred was obvious. Marie-Thérèse had always looked on Rizvi with maternal concern and had no reason to invent such a story. Rizvi, as I knew him, could just not resist the temptation to make a show of himself by advertising the fact that he was privy to some information no one else had. Of course Rizvi knew perfectly well that I was not actually Jewish and that only my mother was of Jewish background but then saying that I was Jewish sounded better. Rizvi had also a love / hate relation with Arnaout and being able to claim that he, Arnaout, a Syrian had chosen a Jew as UNHCR representative in Beirut carried an aura of disbelief and ambiguity typical to the region. That I might get killed in the process as a result was purely incidental.

This left unanswered the question of what I should do. Kou-lischer had spoken to Arnaout who swore that he had only heard good things about me from his Arab friends, which was all well but did not answer the question. Koulischer also had mentioned that if I wanted to leave my post altogether and be reassigned to Geneva he could arrange it but I felt this was somewhat excessive. So I agreed with Koulischer that I would stay in the region for a few more weeks, avoiding Beirut, and then come to Geneva to review the situation.

After a couple of days in Cyprus I flew to Damascus where Solh and Maziad who had driven in from Beirut met me at the airport. Solh was most relieved to hear that I had decided to stay in the region but for what purpose? I had nothing on my agenda for the next ten days so I decided to take a tour of Jordan stopping first in Amman. As I was checking in at the front desk of the Marriott hotel someone called my name. There was Mike Molloy, the coun-selor at the Canadian embassy in Beirut together with the ambas-sador and an aide. They were also checking in but had only attaché cases as luggage. 'Traveling light,' I commented. 'Unlike you,' he replied pointing to my two large suitcases. Over coffee he let me in on why the luggage for the three of them consisted only of attaché cases. That morning they had received a coded cable from Ottawa: Leave Beirut immediately. Inform no one. Pretending to go for coffee they had left their office one by one, piled into the armored limousine of the ambassador and instructed the driver to head for Damascus and from there on to Amman. It was only once safely out of Lebanon that they had phoned Beirut informing their local Lebanese staff that they would not be back but that their salaries would continue to be paid while they would continue to look after the embassy offices. This took care of any doubts I might have had about leaving Beirut.

After one week in Jordan I was back in Damascus wondering what to do next when the decision was taken for me. On July 14, TWA 847 flying from Athens to Rome with 153 passengers on board was hijacked by two gunmen and made to land in Beirut. The cri-sis that followed and which was concluded when Israel set free 766 Shiite prisoners in exchange for the release of the passengers shattered whatever illusions were still harbored about security in Beirut. Overnight the whole UN system stampeded out of the city leaving behind a few token Lebanese staff members. For me, a possible return to Beirut was now even more out of question and I was pondering what to do next when the phone in my room rang. I picked up the receiver and was told that a Mr Dayal from New York was on the line and wished to talk to me.

After spending two years in Geneva as Hartling's assistant Dayal had gone back to New York where the current UN secretary general Pérez de Cuéllar had chosen him to be his chief of cabinet and had promoted him to the grade of Under Secretary General. The combination of his function and his grade made him one of the more influential senior UN officers and I could not help but wonder why he would wish to personally talk to a mere P5 like me. But I was soon to know.

Apparently, two years previously Pérez de Cuéllar had received 460,000 US $ to provide emergency assistance to Lebanon and the money had still not been spent. The donors were now asking how the funds had been used and de Cuéllar would find it extremely embarrassing to admit that nothing had been done with the money. So would I agree to assume the function of chairman of the UN Coordinating Committee for Emergency Assistance to Lebanon and ensure that the available funds would be disbursed at the earliest. This would enable de Cuéllar to inform the donors that the funds they had provided had been disbursed, the assistance distributed and the chapter could be closed to everybody's satisfaction. Dayal was not one to impose anything on anyone but I could hardly turn down his request.

I sat down with Solh and in one hour we drafted an assistance project for the 460,000 US $. With that sum we would request a number of local NGOs to procure blankets, mattresses, soap, stoves and cotton sheets, all on the Lebanese market. This assistance would be distribute in equal parts to East Beirut, West Beirut, Southern Lebanon and Northern Lebanon including the Bekaa Valley. Without mentioning it, in practice we would be covering all the areas controlled by the respective competing militias. The project, as we had drafted it, would be presented by Solh for approval to the

Lebanese government aid agency with one provision. If it was not approved within 30 days the funds available would be withdrawn and de Cuéllar would inform the donors that Lebanon no longer needed any assistance. 'Are you sure it will happen like this,' asked Solh. He had his own experience of the UN system and he knew that they never seemed to take any firm decisions on anything. I shared his doubts but this was not the time to waiver. 'Absolutely,' I told him. 'Either they accept our project as it is or they lose the money. The money has to be spent, now or never. I am sure you can explain this to them.'

While Solh would pass on the message to whomever he knew in the government I still had to deliver it personally to what stood for the coordination committee. So we left next morning at 5 am for Beirut where we arrived at 8 am. On the road Solh had managed to make a number of phone calls and half a dozen Lebanese were waiting for us at the UNHCR office. They were the leftovers of the UN agencies that had stampeded out of the city and, on paper, made up the coordination committee that I was supposed to chair. So chair it I did. Our meeting lasted barely half an hour but that was enough for me to impress on them the fact that our project was non negotiable and that they should try to impress on whoever was their interlocutor that if approval did not come within 30 days they could forget about the assistance. By mid afternoon, somewhat frazzled but none the worse for my six hours on the road and a dozen checkpoints to go through, I was back in Damascus. I had taken a gamble on the Lebanese but was pretty sure it would work and it did. To Solh's surprise, approval came within two weeks and shortly after I could tell a purring Dayal that that the project had been implemented and that all the supporting documents were on their way to New York.

The next day I took the Swissair flight from Damascus to Geneva and was back in my familiar flat. And yet something was missing and it took me a few days to get used to the deafening absence of distant firing echoing throughout the night.

Taking clear decisions was never the strong point of the UN and for once it played in my favor. Neither Arnaout nor Koulischer wished to close the UNHCR office in Beirut and move it somewhere else in the region but they also did not want to take the responsibility of putting me in harm's way. So the solution that was found was a compromise that suited everyone. Until now I had the authority to issue my own travel authorizations thought the Middle East. This authority was now extended to cover also Geneva, which meant that I could move about at my discretion. As for the Beirut office, it was left untouched with the clear understanding that I did not have to be physically there.

For me I could not have dreamt of a better solution. While both the telephone and the telex to Beirut were erratic they enabled me to stay in contact with Solh and had I been present there was nothing I could have done than he could not have done better. Actually the place had gone berserk; shelling was now almost constant and on most days our staff from East Beirut could not cross the green line and make it to the office.

So I found myself a desk in an office next to Arnaout's and, pending a new assignment, decided to take a back seat and lie low in Geneva. No one seemed to mind and even more so as by lying low I ensured that there be no need for anyone to take any decision regarding the future fate of the UNHCR office in Beirut.

September had now set in when one evening at home my phone rang. The call was from Washington and Gene Dewey was at the end of the line. As head of the US refugee bureau he would play a major role in the choice of Hartling's successor, but the last thing I expected was that that he would get in touch with me on the issue. Anyhow, as he explained to me, he had identified the perfect candidate in the person of Jean-Pierre Hocke, the current head of operations of the ICRC. I had worked for Hocke as a consultant for ICRC and could vouch for the fact that he was imaginative, decisive, had no patience with bureaucracy, knew how to cut corners and knew how to use good advice. Granted I had never been his direct employee but there was nothing I could object to as regards his suitability as High Commissioner. I also looked upon Dewey as a profoundly honest man with a lot of common sense and as he had worked many years with Hocke there was no reason for me not to trust his judgment. According to Dewey it was a done deal in the sense that Washington had persuaded the Swiss government to present Hocke for the post. That had taken some doing. Hocke was not part of the Swiss establishment and his somewhat imperious ways at ICRC had contrasted with a more traditional, not to say cautious approach that was the rule in Switzerland. But apparently Bern's initial reservations had been overcome and Switzerland was now firmly behind him.

The UN High Commissioner for Refugees was elected by consensus by the UN General Assembly upon the proposal of the UN Secretary General and the problem now was to convince de Cuéllar to propose Hocke for the post. Granted the US carried a lot of weight and being Swiss was a plus but it was not enough. Before presenting a candidate de Cuéllar had to make sure that he would be accepted by all government and therefore had to informally consult a wide number of states. The result was not a given and even more so as there was another candidate in the person of Boutros-Ghali from Egypt who was liable to benefit from African support. While Washington had pulled out all the stops and was lobbying worldwide for Hocke, some additional support was needed. Did I have any ideas, asked Dewey. My first thought was Arnaout. He might have been wacky but he had his contacts in the Arab world and they probably listened to him as one of their own. Then there was Antoine Noel, the UNHCR representative in New York. Noel was a megalomaniac Ethiopian, possibly even more demented than Arnaout, but he was thick as thieves with all the African ambassadors in New York. The two were close and were liable to embrace any scheme in which plotting and conniving was the daily fare and a possible promotion the distant reward.

I called on Hocke the next day. It was not yet publicly known that he was a candidate for the post of High Commissioner and he was somewhat taken aback when I told him I knew but relaxed when he learned that the information came from Dewey. As for using the services of Arnaout and Noel, he knew neither of them but not untypical said 'if you think it will work, go ahead.' Dewey, having known both had his reservations, but finally conceded that if one lived in a world of insanity one should know how to use lunatics. Not atypically Arnaout proved the hardest to convince.

'Are you sure it is not a trick,' was his first reaction but then he relented and promised to get Noel on board.

I did not follow closely the ins and outs of the campaign but Dewey kept me posted and apparently Noel and Arnaout had gone full blast among the Arabs and Africans in New York promoting Hocke.

December came, and with Hartling due to leave at the end of the month Arnaout got all his staff together and called me in his office. There he handed me an envelope. I opened it. It was a letter from Hartling promoting me to Director at the D1 level. It was the last thing I expected and it left me speechless but not Arnaout. 'I got it for him,' he announced triumphantly to those assembled. I suspected that my work in China had more to do with my promotion than my performance in the Middle East but kept this to myself. Granted Arnaout had probably also put in a good word for me, but being who he was he would have been quite capable of simultaneously supporting my promotion and knifing me in the back. Ten days later Hocke was confirmed as the new UN High Commissioner for Refugees and I retreated for the Christmas holidays officially still as UNHCR Regional Representative for the Middle East.

GUNFIGHT AT THE HOCKE CORRAL

Few if any High Commissioners raised such high expectations from the staff as Hocke when he assumed his office. He was young, in his mid forties and known as a man of action with little patience for burocracy and routine. The last years of the reign of Hartling had been disappointing with the organization run by a quartet of directors who spent most of their time quarrelling and it was time for a change.

Hocke's first appointments, made at the suggestion of Arnaout, were encouraging. As executive assistant he chose a Canadian with a razor-sharp mind, Carol Faubert, and as chief of Cabinet the rising star of UNHCR, Sergio Vieira de Mello, who, many years later as UN representative in Iraq, was to lose his life in the bombing of the UN building in Baghdad.

At the ICRC there were few constraints on Hocke for hiring, firing or moving staff as he pleased and he had surrounded himself with a retinue of loyal followers for whom protocol was non-existent, everyone was on a first-name basis and he was the undisputed top dog. From this inner circle Hocke chose three trusted cohorts which he brought with him to UNHCR. François Hohl was a loud mouthed, massively overweight, scruffy, untypical Swiss who made no secret of the fact that he was gay. Paul Adams, also somewhat rotund and unkempt, allegedly in charge of fundraising but rarely seen, and finally Bernadette. She was in her late twenties, five feet tall at most, with a slight build and the delicate features and diaphanous skin of an asexual Barbie doll. Meticulously put together, impeccably made up, not one hair of her 1930s-style hairdo ever strayed from its allotted place, as if it was frozen in time and space by a judicious spray of hair lacquer. Her official function was to be a '*lectrice*' which translated into a reader, a somewhat mysterious function until it was explained to us that her job was to read all the correspondance addressed to Hocke, divide it into sections and decide what should reach him. That such a function should be allotted to someone who had never operated within the UN system caused some eyebrows to be raised. But that reaction paled after Hohl made a tour of the office and proclaimed loudly to one and all that the good times were over and they all would be taught what real work was. In a few days Hohl almost succeeded in undoing Hocke's positive image and the early enthusiasm which greeted his coming was replaced by a general wait-and-see attitude.

The next to arrive on the scene was Gene Dewey. He had been the architect of Hocke's election as High Commissioner and he was now given his reward; the position of Deputy High Commissioner. Whether his function was to guide Hocke, assist him, support him, advise him, manipulate him or control him remained to be seen.

At the ICRC Hocke had been running a relatively small Swiss organization in which he reported to an all-Swiss committee made up of well-meaning worthies who seemed awed by his personality and practically gave him carte blanche.

Being head of a UN agency was an altogether different ball game. Now he had to contend with staff regulations, financial procurement rules, official salary scales and, above all, the likes of governments. These were not just the 40-odd members of his executive committee but also the full membership of the General Assembly with, in the background, the ever-watchful eye of the UN Secretariat and, lurking further behind, UNHCR's major donor and prime sponsor, the United States. The end result was that the bravado that had served him so well at the ICRC was now of little use and what the current situation called for was the deft use of a stiletto rather than the brutal wielding of a sledgehammer; but he chose the sledgehammer and on March 21, 1986, he struck. In one great sweep the four divisions, assistance, protection, external affairs and administration, were swept away and their directors sent packing to posts outside Geneva, albeit comfortable ones like London, Stockholm or Bruxelles. The five regional bureaus now became the focal points of all UNHCR activities, assisted by nine specialized support services and a new division for 'Refugee law and doctrine' to be headed by Arnaout who was promoted to senior director at the D2 level, the highest grade for a career UN civil servant.

Was structural reform needed? Many of us felt that what was wrong with UNHCR was not structural but the absence of policy guidance, leadership and inspiration. Experience had shown that even the worst structure, staffed with the right people would work and the best of structures, staffed with the wrong people would not. So was it change for the sake of change or was the purpose to get rid of the four directors but then why make the changes structural? What we also noted was that Hocke now had 15 units reporting directly to him and while on paper it meant that he had concentrated in his own hands an incredible degree of power there was no way he could keep up with such a workload

But the real issue was elsewhere. Dewey, who had worked closely with Hocke on the restructuring of UNHCR, was above all an engineer which made him essentially a systems man who went by set rules and well defined procedures. Cutting corners went against his grain were it only because the need to do so reflected a system breakdown. If Dewey was a chain of command freak, Hocke, as I had known him, was his opposite. At heart he was an anarchist, who acted on impulse or according to his gut feelings and was very much a law unto himself. Ultimately the two men were as compatible as fire and water and the big question mark was how the two would interface. By spring 1986, Hocke had the structure he wanted and, apart from Arnaout who no one took seriously, about as many good people working for him as were available at UNHCR. However, unlike his position in the ICRC, he was now operating within the constraints of the UN system and this, it appeared, he had not quite realized.

By early June, I was called in by Hocke. 'I have a job for you,' he said. At the ICRC he had commissioned what he called a 'special study' which provided for a complete reassessment of the organization, its purpose and its functioning. 'I need a special study on UNHCR he said, will you do it?'

It was not the job I had dreamt of. The current director for Asia had asked me to be his deputy and this was exactly what I aspired to: keeping out of the limelight, dealing with a region I knew and getting things done by working behind the scenes. But Hocke was insistent and I could not say no so I agreed. 'Good,' he said, 'this is what I want.' He rambled on for half an hour while I took notes. It all sounded rather confused and all that I got out of it was that I should brainstorm, get people together and send him papers.

So now I was no longer Regional Representative for the Middle East but the holder of the improbable title of 'Adviser for Special Studies', nominally a member of Hocke's cabinet and, on paper, reporting to him.

UNCHR had been created by sovereign states to manage their refugee policies and was being financed by them to that end. Questioning the foundations of the organization was therefore not within the terms of reference of its staff including the High Commissioner, but this said, room for improvement was considerable and especially regarding the choice and assignment of personnel. How should staff be hired? Should there be tests, interviews, a training period or an initial posting to an emergency field position? The issue was not so much that the staff, due to 'regional representation' came from the four corners of the world but that they inevitably carried their cultural background with them and the difficulty lay into weaving the resulting mosaic into one operational entity. While most staff from Western countries came essentially from a middle class background those from the third world came from privileged classed where domestic help was abundant and cheap, and most shared a clear aversion to physical discomfort not to say physical effort. Drafting memos, discoursing on world affairs and pacing the corridors they excelled at but not much more. Would sending all prospective staff members to South Sudan sleeping on camp beds next to a refugee camp eliminate most African or Indian candidates? The Japanese were another case in point. Coming from a society that functioned on consensus and respect for order, they made for hard working and efficient program officers but it was a rare Japanese indeed who could be sent to a crisis area to operate on his own with little or no instructions. And what about the lawyers swarming in the Protection division? Most of them had never seen real field service and operated in a abstract world with little relevance to reality. So, should there be parallel career paths with more circumscribed promotion potentials for those with more restricted areas of competence?

Soon I started sending papers to Hocke and the reaction was nil. So I started spacing my papers, again with no reaction on his side. At a loss about what to do I drifted into the equivalent of an internal exile with nothing to do and no one to report to.

Occasionally I would come across Arnaout in the corridors and he would tease me. 'Look at yourself,' he would say, 'you helped him and he gave you nothing. You did not get a promotion and you did not even get the job you wanted. The moment he did not need you anymore he sidetracked you. But I am smarter than you are. I stir up trouble for him and now he is convinced that he is surrounded by enemies and the more enemies he has the more he thinks he needs me. "El kalb, el khanzir", set the pigs against the dogs and the dogs against the pigs.'

By early 1987, two new characters appeared on the UNHCR scene. They were, we were told, consultants hired personally by Hocke with the purpose of reinvigorating the organization and they soon proceeded to organize a flurry of all-day meetings and weekend retreats. While an occasional truism might emerge during this exercise in micromanagement, the overall impression it made on the staff was one of bewilderment. These were people who had no clue how and under which constraints a UN organization operated.

Little by little a general climate of disbelief began to pervade the organization. I observed it from afar but could not fail to pick up the subtle but constant wave of rumors that came my way. Finances were in a mess, reserves were down, the consultants had been hired for an outrageous sum in flagrant violation of all UN procurement rules. Hocke had taken as a matter of routine to using Concorde when going to New York and would fly himself and his wife in first class by dipping into UNHCR funds and Dewey, who by now had been totally marginalized, had resorted to organizing prayer sessions in his office during the lunch hour.

For one year I savored the benefits of being ignored if not forgotten when out of the blue, on Thursday August 20, 1988, I was called in by Hocke The previous month, as he explained to me, accompanied by Arnaout he had gone to Moscow where he had met the Soviet Vice Foreign Minister Vorontsov.

According to Vorontsov some 50,000 Afghan refugees who had sought asylum in Pakistan had returned to Afghanistan and Hocke was invited to go to Kabul to meet the returnees. The ploy was not exactly subtle. With millions of Afghan refugees in Pakistan cared for by UNHCR and an active resistance to the Soviet presence in Afghanistan funded by the CIA, advertising the fact that there were 'returnees' to Soviet-controlled Afghanistan would carry a powerful political message that could seriously destabilize the resistance.

Did Hocke see the trap or was he carried away by his obsession for action? Two weeks after his meeting with Vorontsov he received an invitation to go to Kabul and his reaction was immediate: he accepted. Predictably, the US went ballistic and so much so that Hocke decided to go personally to Washington to discuss the matter. Now, he told me, he wanted me to accompany him and go a couple of days before his arrival to prepare his meetings. Why me? Perhaps he thought I had some privileged relationship with Washington but even if I had, this was a matter of policy, not personality. I would never know but the mission promised to be entertaining.

The morning of my departure, while on the way to the airport, I dropped by the office to see Hocke and found him in excellent mood. Here is a man who relishes a fight, I told myself. 'By the way' he added with a big grin as I was taking my leave, 'I will give you one guess as to who called me at home last night telling me I was crazy to send you to Washington and that you would betray me.' How a mere UN civil servant could betray a High Commissioner pertained to the world of the absurd but then so did Arnaout. 'El kalb, el khanzir', set the dogs to fight the pigs and the pigs to fight the dogs... sowing dissent, he could just not resist.

The evening of my arrival in Washington I had dinner with Jim Kelly from the Refugee Bureau of the State Department and the message he gave me was unambiguous. Hocke's mission to Kabul was an absolute no-go. It would give credibility to the Soviet-imposed Afghan government and destabilize the millions of refugees in the camps who would fear that they were being sold out. That much I knew already. The question, he said, was how to get the message through to Hocke. How would I know? After all, I told him, Hocke had been put in his current job by the US government and he was now theirs to enjoy.

Hocke joined me in Washington the next day and his visit was a two-day whirlwind. The National Security Council, the Deputy Secretary of State, the Refugee Bureau, various NGOs, they all had the same message: it is unacceptable to the US that you visit Kabul under Soviet occupation. In response, Hocke kept on repeating that he had only a humanitarian role and, on principle, could not ignore an invitation to visit refugees. Hocke was not one to understand the understated and it was finally up to John Whitehead, the Deputy Secretary of State, to spell out the US position at its most basic.

'We have,' he said, 'serious reservations on the wisdom of your visit in spite of its limited terms of reference. Your visit will give credence to a government that creates refugees and they will capitalize on it as proof of some sort of national reconciliation process that we know does not exist.' Whitehead could not have been more explicit and yet, after two days of hammering it looked as if Hocke still had not got the point...unless of course he had, but relished a confrontation not to say simply aggravating the US.

'I will refer the matter to the UN Secretary General,' he finally told his American counterparts 'and I will let him decide.' To me he confided that he was now certain that the Americans had no objection in principle to his visit to Kabul but were only opposed to the timing, and he would handle this later on. His conclusion seemed to me so insane that I felt obliged to call Sergio Vieira de Mello, his chief of cabinet in Geneva.

'He is mad,' said, Sergio, 'completely insane, you must call Dayal immediately.' Dayal was usually unflappable but when I told him that Hocke had told the Americans that he would refer the matter of his visit to Kabul to the Secretary General for his decision he almost went through the roof.

'It is outrageous,' he commented, 'if the Secretary General says yes he will have the Americans on his back and if he says no he will have the Soviets after him.'

Ultimately Hocke never went to Kabul and the issue drifted away but the damage had been done. Both Faubert, Hocke's wily Special Assistant, and Sergio, his chief of cabinet, could spot a sinking ship and both eased themselves out of Hocke's cabinet. Faubert assumed the title of Bureau co-coordinator, a meaningless function but one which moved him out of Hocke's orbit and Sergio was offered to become Director of the Asia Bureau. It was not the job he wanted and he came wailing to me: 'What should I do,' he moaned, 'I know nothing about Asia except that it is a mess.' But Sergio was a quick learner who knew how to put those around him to best use and I had no doubt that he would do well. So I advised him to take the post and we agreed to work together. By now we had established reasonably good relations and he looked upon me as a somewhat older person with no bureaucratic ambitions and therefore who could be trusted to provide advice he could follow without risking being knifed in the back.

Hocke, we now discovered, had a profound aversion for the UN system and one of his ambitions was to draw UNHCR away from it. Every year the UN in New York made a small financial contribution to the UNHCR administrative budget. It was only a token contribution but it underlined the link between the UN system and UNHCR. In 1987, as the UN in New York went through a belt-tightening exercise, Hocke told them that in order to help the Secretariat in reducing its expenses he could do without their contribution. They were not fools in New York and they realized that what Hocke was trying to do was to loosen the umbilical cord that made him part of the UN system. They insisted on continuing to contribute.

Hocke's attempt however damaged beyond repair the relation between him and the UN Secretariat. In-fighting within the UN system was something the bureaucrats in New York were used to and could put up with. But the head of a UN agency trying to steer away from the system was unheard of and not something they were ready to accept. And while the UN Secretariat was too timorous to move on its own, if an opportunity to get rid of Hocke came along, they would now be sure to take it. As for my 'Special Study', it slowly dawned on me that it was supposed to be a blueprint on how to detach UNHCR as much as possible from the fetters of the UN system. In itself, under different circumstances and under a different High Commissioner, it would not necessarily have been a bad idea, but it just could not be done unless supported by the main UN member states. When I explained this to Hocke after our return from Washington I saw a glint of resentment in his eyes: I had probably robbed him of his illusory quest for total power over the organization.

In December 1988, his term was coming to an end and the UN in New York was desperately looking for a suitable candidate to replace him. By then Hocke had alienated the staff, displeased the donor governments, irritated the recipient governments and had the UN system at his throat. All this was known and with the organization in such a mess, no alternative candidate applied for the post. Thus, for want of a better choice, Hocke was re-elected for a second term which the UN at least succeeded in reducing from the usual five years to three.

In mid-January 1989, I went to see him with the intention of discussing the possibility for me of working with Sergio in the Asia Bureau, but as soon as I started talking he cut me short. My continued presence at Headquarters, he told me, was out of the question and I was due to take a post in the field at the earliest. I explained to him that my standard allotted time in Geneva was not over and that as a senior officer I was entitled to ask for an extension; but of course I would not object to a post in the field, possibly somewhere my wife could work, and would therefore be interested in Bangkok or Washington.

'That,' replied Hocke, 'is out of the question. I don't want you in Asia and one cannot go from Geneva to Washington'—never mind that the past two UNHCR representatives including the one nominated by Hocke had. 'Either you come up with a suggestion for a field post or you suggest something else but the time has come for you to decide, the field or else...' he did not end his sentence.

After the meeting I wrote a note on my meeting with Hocke which I officially addressed to our Chief of personnel, Kamel Morjane, with copies to Hocke and Dewey. Hocke had effectively given me all the ammunition I needed for an appeal to a UN staff tribunal on grounds of harassment, intimidation and making false statements but it was necessary to put it on paper in the right terms.

After receiving my note Morjane called me in. He was from Tunisia, a good, decent man and he was chuckling. 'Listen,' he said, 'I don't claim to know everything but what on earth have you done to Hocke? He hates your guts and he is really after you.'

'I have no clue,' I replied, 'but you know Aranout, "el kalb el khanzir".'

'Ok,' he answered, 'dont tell me more, I got it.'

Apparently after receiving my note, Hocke had called Morjane in and had gone through the roof. It was a personal conversation, he told him, why in the hell did he write this? A personal conversation between the head of a UN agency and one of his staff who is told to find himself a field post or else... Morjane did not need an explanation, in UN lingo it was called staff harassment.

Hocke's re-election had been a miracle not to say a calamity. Dewey could probably have blocked it but this would have meant both admitting that his choice had been catastrophic and giving up his position as Deputy High Commissioner and he did not appear to have the moral courage to do either. So, having sold his soul to the devil he soldiered on.

I was still on paper 'Advisor for Special Studies' but, as far as Hocke was concerned, I was destined for the guillotine. However, my note must have destabilized him and he did not follow up on his threats which gave me time both to build up a working relation with Sergio and to reestablish myself within the organization.

By marking my note confidential I had ensured that it would be leaked and soon it was doing the rounds of the organization singling me out as another victim of Hocke. This in turn led Sergio to confide in me that a number of staff members had decided that, if only for the survival of UNHCR, Hocke had to go. They were all good people, the best UNHCR had, and they had all at one time tried to help him, but he was immune to any advice or opinion with which he did not agree.

'You don't understand,' was his standard reply.

'The man is beyond salvation,' commented Sergio, 'he has to go before he brings down the house. You must help us.' So overnight, having had practically nothing to do for three years, I now had two jobs. Helping Sergio on Asia and trying to ensure that the system would get Hocke before he got me.

To imagine that a handful of UN staff members could bring down a High Commissioner was ludicrous. Only governments could do so and Hocke's re-election, whatever the morale of the staff or his own shortcomings, proved that they were not willing to move. The only person who could remove Hocke was Hocke himself and he showed little inclinations to do so.

The range of complaints about Hocke was vast. The Swiss Foreign Ministry was embarrassed and the Federal Refugee office had never had such bad relations with UNHCR as under Hocke, but matters did not go further. Donor governments were unhappy but this did not translate into any form of action. Indeed what stood for governments were actually Foreign Ministries and these were staffed by genteel diplomats, not types naturally inclined towards confrontation. So except for moaning and groaning not much else was to be expected from them. And as for the recipient governments, while they were also disappointed in Hocke not having delivered the promised increase in aid, their opinion counted for little.

Last and least, while the UNHCR staff may indeed have become disheartened and demoralized, no one outside the UN cared. And the UN Secretariat in New York was far too timid to move against Hocke without some support from governments. The end result was that, while Hocke might have alienated every single one of his constituents, none was willing to do anything about it and unless he killed someone or set fire to the building there was not much that could be done to get rid of him.

The conclusion was that the only way to give him the chop was to panic him into resigning and this could not be done through the established system. The killing thrust had to come from outside the diplomatic establishment and this required not only a strong case but above all a smoking gun. 'Get us one' said Sergio.

As I sat in my office, ostensibly still working on the 'Special Study', a flow of information started coming my way. I had impressed on Sergio that what I needed was not rumors, insinuations or suspicions but hard facts, and I was getting them. Not only did it appear that there was hardly one single financial rule that Hocke had not taken liberties with but the very thrust of the organization's fund raising, programming and expenditure was off target. In terms of professional performance there was enough to hang him ten times over but that, in the never-never land of government bureaucracy, was not enough. I had the explosives but I needed a fuse to set them off with. Then, quite unexpectedly, the missing part came in from Hong Kong.

Rob Van Leeuwen was a graduate from Yale who had served as a lieutenant in Vietnam where he had been awarded a bronze star for valor and a purple heart for being wounded in combat. Apart from his height, everything about him was excessive. Incredibly articulate and equally argumentative, everything he undertook he did with a ferocious zeal compounded with a fearless perseverance, and once set on course he was as unstoppable as a bull dog on the rampage.

As staff representative he had taken Hocke head on and with his superior brain and razor sharp logic would regularly talk him into a corner. Likewise, he would take a perverse pleasure in unnerving Dewey by going to see him and pointing in the direction of Hocke's adjoining office saying, 'there is sin next door.' With UN staff rules rendering his dismissal impossible, Hocke in desperation had exiled him by making him Representative to Hong Kong from where he continued his jihad with undiminished zeal.

Sergio had mentioned to me several times that Hocke had taken to flying in first class, often taking his wife with him, and had made it a habit of flying Concorde whenever he went to New York. According to the recently revised UN rules only the UN Secretary General was authorized to travel in first class and all other staff members had to travel in business or economy depending on the length of the journey.

It was no secret that Hartling also traveled in first class and often took his wife along too, but it was understood that the Danish government had authorized him, in recognition for his services to the country, to deduct for his private use some funds from the overall Danish contribution to UNHCR and nobody saw anything wrong with it. Hartling was after all a respected figure of a certain age with an overall modest lifestyle and the financial situation of the organization was sound.

Hartling was also an astute politician and he had covered himself by informing UN Secretary General Waldheim that he was recieving some funds from his government for his personal use. Waldheim has reportedly told him that it was not quite legal—UN staff were not supposed to accept personal outside donations—but that it was done and it was allright so long as it was done discreetly.

Hocke on the other hand presided over an organization that was financially in the doldrums, had forfeited any respect that might have come his way and had no visible source of funding to cover his munificence, be it flights in Concorde or the lavish meals to which he treated his close associates complete with wines of the most prestigious vintages. Granted he could have paid for these indulgencies from his own pocket but he was not known to have any private income and his UN salary would have barely sufficed. Sergio and Carrol Faubert were almost sure that the funds for these extravaganzas came from the Danish account that had supported Hartling but they had no proof. If proof could be found, I felt the Danish Government would be obliged to claim that it was unaware that part of its contribution for refugees was used to pay for Hocke's carousing on Concorde and the resulting ruckus would ensure that he was toast.

Sergio, however, disagreed. 'Look at the programming figures,' he would tell me, 'that should be enough to kill him.'

'Not so,' I told him. 'This is substance but we are living in a world which caters to image and appearance. It is the cosmetics that count, not the substance. Look at Nixon. He fell on Watergate, a third rate burglary that killed no one, and not on the illegal bombing of Cambodia that killed thousands.'

I had no clue where to look for proof that Hocke was dipping into the Danish contribution to support his lavish travel style, so it was up to Sergio to do the rummaging. Initially he drew a blank. Then he remembered Rob Van Leeuwen. Although he was in Hong Kong, Rob, as staff representative, had his moles throughout the organization and in no time he struck gold. Apparently, in the dark recesses of the accounts department he had found a gnome who had access to Hocke's personal files. Yes, he confirmed, the evidence is there, bills, settled bills, bill after bill after bill, upgrades for Concorde for Mr Hocke, signed by himself with the comment to debit from Danish funds, first class tickets for *Madame* Hocke, it was all there.

But the gnome was a fearful creature. Like most staff he was despairing about what Hocke was doing to UNHCR but he wanted to make sure his name would never appear and he trusted no one except Van Leeuwen. Leave it to Rob, I told Sergio, but tell him if he does not come up with the proof he is the one who will have kept Hocke going. One week later Sergio called me to his office and drew out of his drawer a sheaf of faxes that had gone from Geneva to Hong Kong and back to Geneva. It was all there: the smoking gun. Now the only question that remained was how to proceed with it.

Hartling traveled first class and no one minded. But, unlike Hocke, he had not created a major budget deficit at UNHCR, disrupted the workings of the organization, aggravated every single government, got the UN in New York on his back and alienated his staff. And yet, just as these failings had not sufficed to prevent Hocke's reelection, 'Ticketgate' alone would not have been enough to have him pushed overboard. But both, combined into a critical mass, might do the trick.

How many UNHCR staff members were spending time digging for dirt on Hocke I never found out but I suspected that anybody who had anything on Hocke would come to Sergio the Maestro of this symphony of gloom and he in turn would pass the material on to me and to others. My job now was to process the material that came my way into one single document. In doing so I remembered Hartling's admonition that one should never give a government a paper that a 14 year old cannot understand. So I got down to work.

To be convincing my text had to be easy to understand, totally factual and appear devoid of any bias, partiality or prejudice. Drafting it proved no easy exercise and soon I had forgotten Hocke and his foibles and it became an end in itself like any piece of work which one wishes to do as well as one can because this is how one is. Many of the documents I received I did not use so as not to dilute the issue. Thus, the two consultants hired personally by Hocke in violation of all UN rules had been given an office in our building and allocated one of the UNHCR secretaries. One day she showed Sergio a printout of what she was doing. It had nothing to do with UNHCR; the consultants were using her, on UNHCR time, to prospect new clients. Interesting but distracting. On the other hand, some enterprising soul at UNHCR had gone to the city registry and found a record of the date on which the two consultants had registered their company. It was several weeks after Hocke had given them their contract. Now that was indeed relevant.

By and large the material I was receiving proved to be an education. I had no idea until then of the extent of the deficit the organization was burdened with nor that we had, by August only enough funds to operate for at best one month. I also had never gone into the intricacies of programming and fund raising. Now and finally I learned how the system actually worked, or in this case, did not work.

So, little by little, I coalesced the data that kept pouring my way into a draft of about a dozen pages aptly entitled: 'UNHCR's financial crisis; a man-made disaster'. The draft was then further fine tuned by Sergio and Faubert and the end result was a clean, professional document that read like an indictment from which there was no escape.

The substance was that Hocke, and Hocke alone, was responsible for the current financial crisis of UNHCR and that it could only be resolved through his removal.

Traditionally UNHCR budgeting followed a time-proven mechanism. Proposals for expenditures such as funding for a refugee camp were initiated in the field and then went through a series of checks at Headquarters before final approval by the Assistance division. While the proposals were being assessed, the External Affairs division would informally contact donor governments to try to determine how much funds they had available. Needs were unlimited but funds were not and a balance had to be struck between the two. The end result was that, when UNHCR would make a public appeal for funds, there would be no major disparity between what was asked and what was available. Finally, all projects were not of equal priority and some could actually not be implemented. By exercising restraint the organization was therefore able to save some 70 million US $ per year and this sum was used to cover the budgeting gap between one year and the next.

Hocke trashed this system. Not only did he request more funding than donor governments were willing to contribute but in an operational frenzy he spent all he budgeted for had thus reduced the carryover from one year to the next to zero. The outcome by 1989 was a 147 million US $ shortfall and no carryover.

This was the substance. I embroidered into it some reference to ongoing expenses as attachments that required no comment, namely:

1) A contract with a consultancy firm which, on the day it was signed, did not exist and which was not submitted to the UN contracts committee as required.

2) Other consultancy contracts also not submitted to the contracts committee included 750,000 US $ to Peat Marwick, 50,000 US $ to Battelle and 38,000 US $ to Price Waterhouse.

3) Thousands of dollars spent on first class air tickets for *Madame* Hocke and numerous upgrades for himself to first class or to Concorde, all taken from a special fund that the Danish government had set up for the personal use of his predecessor Hartling. The attachments include photocopies of the bills with Hocke's signature.

So we now had enough damning evidence to corner Hocke. The only question left was how to use it. I had made five copies of the 'man-made disaster' file, one of which I kept for myself and the remaining four I gave to Sergio complete with supporting documents and attachments and all that was needed was to identify the right time to unleash the dogs of war.

Hocke's relations with the Swiss authorities were appalling but he still had a following in the French-speaking Swiss media because of his past with ICRC and most journalists were unwilling to come to grips with what he had really been up to. Then fate intervened. I was in my office pondering about what to do next when the phone rang. On the line was Andreas Kohlschutter, one of the most prominent Swiss-German TV journalist whom I had me through some skiing friends. Andreas had heard that there were problems at UNHCR and I arranged for him to meet Sergio in Geneva.

Andreas was known to be something of a crusader and when he subsequently asked UNHCR for a TV interview with Hocke they should have smelled a rat. But the new chief at Information, an Algerian chosen by Hocke on Arnaout's recommendation, had no clue about who was who in the Swiss media. So the interview was granted and the subject agreed upon was UNHCR's financial crisis.

True to himself, Hocke started expounding at length on how wealthy governments were increasingly reluctant to contribute aid for refugees and how it was necessary for the organization to tighten its belt. At this point Andreas mentioned that there were rumors to the effect that Hocke was flying first class.

'That is not true,' he snapped back, 'I only fly first class when a friendly airline gives me a free upgrade.'

'Then what is this,' shot back Andreas, as he drew out two invoices signed by Hocke, and thrust them at him, 'here is a bill for Concorde and here is one for a first class ticket for your wife to Australia.'

'Cut, cut the camera,' screamed Hocke. It was the end of the interview and the result was devastating. The TV program started with images of a first class aircraft cabin. To the sound of soft music, beautiful hostesses were seen passing glasses of champagne to well-heeled passengers comfortably ensconced in their luxurious seating. Then, very slowly, the first class cabin faded away and was replaced by the sight of thousands of emaciated refugees in a camp in Africa; that in turn faded out as a picture of Hocke screaming 'cut, cut' slowly filled the screen. The show ended with Andreas standing outside the UNHCR building in Geneva and commenting that the reputation of Switzerland was certainly not enhanced by someone like Hocke as High Commissioner for refugees.

The TV program alone would not have precipitated the fall of Hocke but, in Mao's words, a spark can start a prairie fire. Henry

Kamm, the local *New York Times* correspondent, had been working on a story on Hocke and had done the rounds of the diplomatic missions in Geneva in addition to talking to the likes of Sergio and Faubert. As he was later to comment, he had not heard one good thing about Hocke. Spurred on by the Swiss TV program, he ran on October 5 a devastating piece quoting from a confidential US State Department memo that spoke of a 'crisis of confidence' within UNHCR. I knew Kamm casually and had not given him a copy of the file but others must have.

So now two of Hocke's bases had been shot to bits. His name was dirt in his own country, Switzerland, and Kamm's piece in the *New York Times* had shot whatever support Dewey might have tried to drum up for him in Washington. It was now time for the kill.

Anne Mette Skipper, the correspondent in Geneva of one of Denmark's largest dailies, the *Jyllands-Posten*, was a forceful woman who believed in right and wrong and when the Hocke file came her way she went all out. Hocke's use, for his own personal gratification, of Danish funds, collected from the Danish taxpayer and donated for needy refugees became front-page news in the Danish press. Suddenly the matter was no longer in the hands of timorous diplomats. It had became a domestic political issue. Questions were asked in Parliament and the Danish government was called to account. Twice, on October 13 and 19, the Danish Ambassador in Geneva, acting on instructions from his government called Hocke in for an explanation. While the Danes acknowledged that they had made a gesture to Hartling, albeit not a totally transparent one, they also claimed it had been a one-shot contribution to a Danish High Commissioner and former resistance hero and in no way was it intended to benefit his Swiss successor. With Hocke claiming that he been misled into believing that he could also benefit from the funds the Danes went on record by stating that the case called into question the High Commissioner's judgment, harsh words indeed in a diplomatic environment and on Monday October 23, they officially asked the UN Secretary General to carry out an official inquiry into the matter.

It was all that the UN secretariat needed to throttle Hocke. An inquiry would have been a major embarrassment to the UN and might also have shown that the Danish government had been lax in keeping track of its contributions to UNHCR. Clearly it was not the route to follow and the only alternative was to get rid of Hocke. On Wednesday October 25, 1989, Hocke, who had been summoned to New York by UN Secretary General Pérez de Cuéllar, was told that he could not remain in his post. That same day he handed the Secretary General his letter of resignation before boarding the late afternoon flight to Geneva. According to what had been agreed, Hocke, upon his return to Geneva, would first announce his resignation to the Chairman of the UNHCR Executive Committee and only subsequently make it public. But in New York they did not trust him and feared he might withdraw his resignation so as soon as his aircraft was airborne they made his letter of resignation public and when Hocke landed in Geneva next morning the news was already all over town.

I was away on leave in England during the fateful week and when I came back to Geneva Hocke was packed and gone, Dewey was about to follow suit and Arnaout was counting the days before he would be given the boot and sent into a comfortable bureaucratic exile.

The unsung hero of this sordid saga was the anonymous gnome in the finance section who had unearthed the smoking gun and had photocopied and given to Rob Van Leeuwen the vouchers for Hocke's travel extravaganzas which he had been careless enough to leave unguarded.

As for me, I derived no pleasure for having been a minor cog in this cabal nor did I flatter myself into believing that I had substantively contributed to Hocke's downfall; and if I had done my small part, it was essentially in self defense.

And yet, looking back at this whole sordid episode I could not help thinking what a waste. The man had boundless energy and knew when to take initiatives. He also had many good ideas and while most was not quite in conformity with UN rules, maybe slowly, step-by-step he could have created,in the interest of the organization, a special regime for UNHCR. And yet, was he so naive to believe that Dewey had put him where he was only on his merits and that he did not owe a debt to the US? Was he expecting a free lunch? Did he fail to understand that, beyond all the rhetoric, UNHCR was a political organization and that his planned visit to Kabul under Soviet occupation would be perceived primarily as a political gesture? Did he really think that by not following established fund-raising procedures he could force or shame sovereign states to contribute to UNHCR more than they had intended to?

Did he not realize that Denmark had stretched the rules in regards to Hartling and that if it became public knowledge that a Swiss was benefiting from the same munificence it would not sell politically?

Had he ever asked the advice of those close to him, not the half-whits he had brought in from the ICRC who knew nothing about the UN, but the likes of Sergio or Faubert who had their finger on the pulse of the international system? This was not the man I had known at the ICRC and I kept on wondering if some sort of demon had not taken possession of him so as to ensure that he would give no one the opportunity of helping him to save him from himself.

Ultimatly, the man remained a mystery to me. If Hocke went without a ripple, not so Dewey. Hocke had extended Dewey's contract for two more years until December 1991 and while he was willing to relinquish his post he expected the UN to give him another assignment at the equivalent level and pay; and when the UN refused he sued asking not only for two years of salary but also for compensation for 'moral injury'. A contract being a contract he won his case except for the claim of 'moral injuries' which was laughed off. None the worse for the calamity he had brought about, he reemerged as Assistant Secretary of State in the George W. Bush Administration. Ultimately Dewey, mild mannered, courteous, and possessed by the urge to do good proved the worst of the lot. His position in the US refugee bureau had given him tremendous power and in promoting Hocke as High Commissioner he had deceived both his government and himself. That he had done so with the best of intention carried no redeeming feature. If hell is paved with good intentions he was the master paver, and an unrepentant one at that. And when push came to shove, rather than acknowledging his guilt, he had sought to profit from it to the last drop.

Following Hocke's and Dewey's departure the UN in New York sent one of its senior officers to clean up UNHCR. His name was Kofi Annan and he was an instant success. In a matter of weeks the structure set up by Hocke was dismantled, Arnaout was packed off as 'Advisor for Arab affairs' and it was back to the business as usual.

But all this for me was immaterial. I now wanted out of Geneva, and fast. With Sergio Director for Asia I had engineered a posting in Bangkok for myself and after having been Adviser for Special Studies I was now Regional Adviser for Durable Solutions. On November 17, 1989, I landed in Bangkok with my wife, 150 pounds of excess luggage and a somewhat perplexed Siamese cat in a carrying case. 'Oh,' said the customs man at the airport as he surveyed the beast, 'Thai cat, coming home.'

VIETNAM REDUX

My assignment to Bangkok had not come as a last-minute upshot of the fall of Hocke but had been for one year in the making. Granted I was at the time, at least on paper, Advisor for Special Studies and Hocke, as my formal supervisor, was the only one entitled to authorize me to go on mission. But these bureaucratic niceties did not stop Sergio, as Director for Asia, from signing my mission authorizations and as no one in the administration of UNHCR sought to point out that the procedure was highly irregular I had set off on a series of missions for him mostly to Vietnam and Hong Kong. I never found out if Hocke was aware that I was now, in parallel to him, also working with Sergio but if he did he obviously did not care. So I was now back in my element albeit in violations of all rules.

By 1988, the arrangement reached in 1979 by which all Vietnamese boat people who reached the shores of countries of South East Asia would be permitted to land, automatically be recognized as refugees and all resettled in a Western countries, was coming apart.

While the arrangement was in keeping with the spirit of the time, it had also an in-built self-destruct mechanism. By guaranteeing automatic resettlement in a developed economy for any Vietnamese who left his country by boat it ensured an indefinite perpetuation of the exodus. This at the time suited everyone. Vietnam could proceed with its ethno-social cleansing and the US could continue to portray a Soviet-allied state as a brutal producer of refugees. It was an arrangement that the countries in the region had no objection to, considering they were not required to accept permanently any of the boat people, only to give them a transit right with UNHCR footing the bill for their temporary stay.

The system conceived in 1979 hinged on resettlement, and by the mid 1980s resettlements started to erode. Little by little a residual caseload of long stayers started to build up in the camps. These were mostly drug addicts, petty criminals or, in the case of Hong Kong, hardened North Vietnamese who no Western country wanted. At the same time Western governments were also cutting down on resettlement quotas for Vietnamese, claiming that the nature of the caseload had changed and that those leaving Vietnam now were now doing so mostly for economic reasons and not because they were being persecuted.

Thus in their view, what had started allegedly as a refugee flow in 1979 had now become 10 years later a migratory movement that included only a small percentage of genuine refugees, that is people fleeing persecution. The argument was spurious and had never been substantiated for the simple reason that until the mid-1980s no caseload analysis had ever been done. If it had it would have shown that a good number of boat people who had left Vietnam over the years in no way would have qualified for refugee status.

But in the wake of its defeat in Vietnam the US was unwilling to accept this reality. So the world's major superpower, to assuage its bruised ego, perpetuated the fiction that all Vietnamese boat people were refugees. The fiction endured for more than a decade, but fifteen years after the fall of Saigon reality finally started to catch up.

As the residual caseload started to build up and resettlement quotas started to shrink, the countries of South East Asia became concerned. The last thing they wanted was to get stuck with a local Vietnamese community so they took things into their own hands and embarked on the only policy that came naturally to them: push backs. The result was that more and more boats coming from Vietnam were pushed back to sea and those on board were left to drown.

This scenario did not develop overnight and in 1984 Jerry Tinker, an aide to Senator Ted Kennedy, had already concluded that only a minority of those who were leaving Vietnam could qualify as refugees. The situation, he believed, called for the setting up of a screening procedure to identify genuine refugees who would be resettled, while those who were not would be considered for repatriation. The time had come, he wrote in his report to Senator Kennedy, to negotiate a repatriation agreement with Vietnam.

Jerry Tinker had been ahead of his time but by mid-1988 a report from the Ford Foundation also concluded that the exodus had taken on a momentum of its own, irrespective of any need for asylum, and that with resettlement quotas shrinking the right of transit was collapsing, push backs were becoming the rule and a major new humanitarian crisis was around the corner.

By then Pierre Jambor, my former deputy in Hanoi, had been assigned as UNHCR representative in Bangkok where one of his responsibilities was to chair the monthly meeting of a small group of Thai officials and foreign diplomats including Americans, British, Malaysians, French, Canadians, and Australians whose task was to monitor the ongoing boat people exodus from Vietnam. By the end of 1988 the group had come to the conclusion that the system set up nine years previously was breaking down and a new approach was needed.

Setting up a new comprehensive system to deal with the outflow would however inevitably have required the involvement of Hanoi, but none of the governments represented in the group wished to take the initiative to invite the Vietnamese to their meetings, Pierre could not resist the temptation to stick his neck out whatever the circumstances and he took it upon himself to call the UNHCR representative in Hanoi, Charles-Henri Bazoche, and asked him to talk the Vietnamese into sending a delegation to attend the Bangkok meeting.

Charles-Henri Bazoche was reputed to be a defrocked priest and he certainly looked the part. He was tall, with a well-groomed beard, and I could visualize him in a white cassock and matching pith helmet somewhere in darkest Africa spreading the faith to the heathen.

Bazoche had moved out of the *Thong Nhut* hotel and lived in a small decrepit apartment of the type that the Vietnamese had belatedly allocated to foreign diplomats The standard of comfort was wanting but Bazoche more than made up for it by the standard of his fare, courtesy of *Monsieur* Binh. Trained by the French as a chef, he had put his talents into hibernation during the war years only to resuscitate them when Bazoche had come across him, through some mysterious contact. *Monsieur* Binh was a genius and his cheese souffle was the talk of the town. There was not a single ambassador who would turn down an invitation to Bazoche's dinner table and even high-ranking Vietnamese officials, though wary of all personal contact with the denizens of the capitalist West, would succumb to the lure of *Monsieur* Binh's art.

While the links Bazoche established could not transcend politics, they did create a semblance of trust and he was in as good a position as anyone could be to try to convince the Vietnamese to go to Bangkok.

A few years earlier it would have been a hopeless task but Vietnam was slowly changing. The failure of the policy of radical collectivization could not be disguised and while the regime's alliance with the Soviet Union was still unqualified, Hanoi was now trying to take the edge off its current confrontational relation with its Asian neighbors. So the time had come for some sort of gesture and in January 1989 Pierre's gamble succeeded. A small delegation from Hanoi arrived in Bangkok to attend the monthly informal get-together on the issue of the boat people.

While no concrete results emerged from this first meeting, the signal was clear. Hanoi was ready to talk, but about what? Everyone knew what the problem was but no one had yet put down on paper a blueprint for a solution. What followed was a drafting exercise which involved Pierre, Alan Jury from the US refugee bureau and Gervaise Appave from the Australian mission in Bangkok. Working in the shadows they drafted what became later known as the CPA, the Comprehensive Plan of Action for Refugees from Indochina, the first ever attempt to address the boat people issue with a mutually supporting set of solutions rather than blanket resettlement.

The substance of the CPA was common sense. All new arriving boat people would be screened for refugee status. Those qualifying would be resettled in Western countries and those who did not qualify would have to return to Vietnam on the understanding that they would not be prosecuted for illegal departure. In exchange, the right of transit for boat people in Asian countries was maintained and the resettlement countries committed themselves to ridding the countries of South East Asia of the residual caseload that had accumulated over the years.

In the context of the leftovers of the Vietnam war the CPA was a ground-breaking exercise. Not only did it introduce screening of the boat people and hence the perception that the simple fact of having left Vietnam by boat did not necessarily make a person into a refugee but it provided a new solution for those who did not qualify, namely return. Until then, return to Vietnam had been a taboo and just mentioning the possibility was anathema to Washington. Now the taboo had been broken.

The CPA had been conceived in a flash of brilliance but none of those who were part of the drafting team enjoyed stellar careers later on. They were too bright, too innovative or too irreverent to fit into a bureaucratic mold but the result of their collective effort, coming at the right time, opened the door for what was to be an honorable end to the boat people crisis.

Within UNHCR Pierre had done his part, laboring behind the scenes, and playing a major role in producing the goods. But he was altogether too abrasive, not to say mocking, to sell them properly. Sergio had initially been doubtful about the exercise but he now saw in which direction the wind was blowing and took over. His charm, looks, charisma, elegance, intellect, eloquence and hard work proved equal to the task as he went from capital to capital preaching the good word.

While these developments were unfolding I was nominally still assigned to working for Hocke in Geneva but I was spending more and more of my time in Asia sniffing around for whatever might come my way. But rummaging for what? I had not the least idea but Sergio had given me a blank check to travel in the region and this brought me to Hanoi. Bazoche had put me up at his apartment and the evening of my arrival gave a dinner at which I found myself seated next to a Vietnamese woman of distinguished demeanor who was introduced as *Madame* Lan. As we started chatting it emerged that she was the director of the press department of the Foreign Ministry and her husband, Vu Hoang, was Vice Foreign Minister. Together they made a formidable couple and one that would be plugged directly into the top levels of the leadership. She was fully informed of the ongoing negotiations regarding the nascent CPA but seemed to have some doubts as regards its effectiveness in slowing down the exodus. 'Perhaps,' commented Bazoche 'we could try and make sure people in Vietnam know about the CPA.' *Madame* Lan nodded. 'Yes,' she said, 'people must know.' But how could they be informed? Could some sort of information campaign inside Vietnam educate people about the CPA. 'Then, perhaps fewer people would leave by boat?' she added.

That she might even acknowledge that there might be such a need showed how far Vietnam had evolved over the years. After having encouraged, not to say provoked, the exodus the Vietnamese now saw it as an embarrassment though a difficult one to address. If they cracked down too hard on illegal departure they stood accused of violating human rights and if they did not crack down enough they would be seen as encouraging the export of a large slice of their population. The idea that through an information effort by UNHCR the exodus could be brought under control without repressive measure was a tantalizing one. 'I will arrange a meeting tomorrow for you with Pham Khac Lam, the director of Vietnam TV,' was her response.

Lam came from a prominent land-owning aristocratic family from central Vietnam that, in 1945, had thrown its lot in with the communists. The combination of impeccable revolutionary credentials with an upper-class French education and a somewhat irreverent disposition made for an entertaining personality and not one to beat about the bush.

'The government cannot tell people not to leave,' he said, 'they will not believe us. You must do it.'

My whole point, as I explained to him, was precisely not to tell people not to leave. 'That will not work,' I said. 'For the operation to work they must come to that conclusion by themselves. We can only provide the facts but they must be the ones to process them so as to come to the conclusion that it is no longer worth leaving by boat.'

The concept seemed to intrigue him. 'Where have you done it before?' he asked.

'Nowhere,' I replied, 'UNHCR does not speak to refugees, this would be a first.'

'Good,' he said, 'let's try. What do you suggest?'

'It is simple,' I replied. 'Let us send one of your TV teams to Hong Kong. They will film the camps, they will show that living conditions are not bad but they will also interview the authorities who will explain to potential boat people that the rules of the game have changed, there is now screening for refugee status, most of the boat people will not qualify and they will have to go back to Vietnam so is it worthwhile leaving?' As head of Vietnam TV Mr Lam enjoyed considerable authority, but his meeting with me had obviously been cleared by the authorities which meant that on principal he had been given the green light to collaborate with UNHCR. However, I suspected that Mr Lam had gone a bit out on a limb when he agreed there and then to my offer to send a TV crew to Hong Kong. Granted I would be covering all the costs but money, important as it may be, was not the main issue. The main issue was political; for the first time ever a TV crew from Hanoi would be coming to Hong Kong. I, of course, had also gone out on a limb. I had no guarantee that Hong Kong would grant the necessary visas or that UNHCR would endorse the project.

Back in Bangkok I linked up with Sergio and explained to him what I had in mind. Sergio was always open to new ideas and even more so if he could be convinced that they served his purpose. He did not ask me if the project would work because he knew that no one knew, but there was no downside to trying. Se we sat down and drafted an additional paragraph to the draft of the CPA. UNHCR will launch a Mass Information Campaign inside Vietnam to inform potential boat people of the provisions of the CPA so as to contribute to achieve a diminishing of the departure of people who would not qualify for refugee status. Or, in plain English, deterrence through information.

On June 14, 1989, the CPA was adopted in Geneva at a meeting of some 70 governments based on three principles. First, all boat people would be permitted to land in transit countries. Second, they would all be screened for refugee status with those qualifying for refugee status resettled and the others having to return to Vietnam. Third, returnees would not be punished for illegal departure and their reintegration would be monitored by UNHCR.

Included in the CPA was the provision for a Mass Information Campaign to, under the guise of providing information, try to deter potential boat people from leaving Vietnam illegally.

With this single paragraph I had designed a new job for myself. All that was left now was to ease myself into it. Money was not the problem. Just say refugees from Vietnam and funds would come pouring in but we had to go through procedures. 'You do it,' said Sergio, 'and I'll sign off.'

The first step was to create a post in Bangkok where I would be based. As director I was one grade above all the UNHCR representatives in the area and as most had exceedingly high opinions of themselves they would not have wanted someone looking over their shoulders. So in order not to unnerve them we called the post Regional Advisor for Durable Solutions, a meaningless title which achieved what it was intended to; no one is afraid of an advisor and no objections were raised. The next step was to nail down the qualifications of the candidates for the post. A degree, possibly a PhD in contemporary Asian studies, a minimum of 10 years of experience in East and South East Asia with special reference to both Northern and Southern Vietnam, at least ten years of professional communication experience including the production of TV and radio programs as well as familiarity with the written media and fluency in English and French.

The post was duly created and advertised and I kept my fingers crossed as staff members within UNHCR were invited to apply for it. Actually I should not have worried. Not only did no one have the qualifications to apply for it but no one was actually interested in it. It was too much off the beaten track and did not appear to lead anywhere in terms of promotion or career enhancement. So to no one's surprise I was the only candidate and while there were a few chuckles here and there form had been preserved. With the post came a car and driver, a secretary, an office within the UNHCR delegation in Bangkok, the authority to travel at will throughout East and South East Asia and an operational budget of 150,000 US $.

That the machination that resulted in the creation of my new posting had been undertaken while I was still 'Advisor for Special Studies' and thus nominally under the direct authority of Hocke was for Sergio a source of considerable hilarity. He too knew how to bend the rules but had never gone that far. So when Hocke fell I had already made my bed somewhere else, and luckily too. Apparently, one week before he was brought down he had, without telling me, abolished the post of Advisor for Special Studies.

By early December 1989 I was well ensconced in Bangkok and had my logistics under control. Every morning the driver would pick me up at home at nine and drive me to the office, some half an hour away. There I would read my newspaper, go through the mail and make whatever phone calls that had to be made. By then it was time for lunch with the choice being the UN cafeteria, a nearby Lao greasy spoon which specialized in grilled chicken and sticky rice or sitting down with one of the many foreign journalists or diplomats based in Bangkok. By two in the afternoon I would be back in the office, often with nothing to do and would then call the driver to bring me home.

If my daily scheduling was indulgent it did not release me from the obligation to figure out how to tell a Vietnamese who stands no chance of being recognized as a refugee not to leave Vietnam by boat. The more I thought about it, the more I came to realize that the answer to the question was deceptively simple. You don't.

Tell a Vietnamese something, anything, and his first reaction will be not to believe you. If what you tell him is not to his liking, he will believe you even less. And if you tell him that what you are saying is for his own good, then you can be certain that he will never believe you. So the approach had to be tangential. You don't tell him what to do, or in this case what not to do. You create an information input that will lead him to come to that conclusion all by himself.

This in turn required a strict adherence to four principles. First, the truth and only the truth. Stick to the facts and let them speak for themselves where possible. Second, ensure that the truth is credible. A Vietnamese government official telling people not to leave by boat is not credible. A US government official giving the same message is; and if, instead of telling them not to leave he just explains to them what the criteria for resettlement in the US are, he will be even more credible. So the truth had to be properly packaged if it was going to sell. Third, the visual image has to strike a cord on the Vietnamese psyche. And one of the most powerful messages is an image that speaks for itself. Last but not least never assume that anybody, and especially not a Vietnamese be it the simplest of peasants, is any less smart than you or I.

Having set up this theoretical groundwork in a totally empirical way with no guarantee that it corresponded to any reality, I then took one further step. Vietnam was now politically unified but it was still two countries in one. There were two mentalities and each had to be addressed in a specific fashion, if only because they corresponded to two distinct destinations. Northerners, and to a much smaller extent, people from Danang in Central Vietnam, had Hong Kong as their destination. Southerners aimed for Thailand, Malaysia and the Philippines. These two sets of destinations also corresponded to two very different sailing seasons, determined by weather patterns. The obvious conclusion was that, in order to have any chance of success, deterrence through information could only succeed if it was targeted at each specific group. In practice this meant a Northern strategy and a Southern one.

Three weeks after settling down in Bangkok I was back in Hanoi. Bazoche had been replaced by Jacques Mouchet who I had placed as the Representative in Beijing in 1979. Having him in Hanoi was great news. He had taken over Bazoche's apartment but also, more importantly, *Monsieur* Binh and I had a standing invitation to use his guest room and share his table. Jacques was on board from day one on the Mass Information Program and we both agreed that we would start with Northern Vietnam. This gave us about three months until the next sailing season to Hong Kong which started in April, peaking from May to August, until the fall monsoon made navigation too hazardous.

My next problem was to get visas for Hong Kong for the TV team which proved not too difficult but left unanswered the question of how to get them there as there was no direct air connection between Hanoi and the colony.

By now however, small numbers of boat people in Hong Kong, having been told that no Western country would accept them, had been volunteering for return to Vietnam and the responsibility for organizing flights had drifted my way. Normally UNHCR would have taken the lowest bidder which in this case would have meant finding a second rate transporter in the region but with repatriation already being a sticky operation I could not afford any hitches so, without looking for outside bids, I chose Cathay Pacific. I also felt that, in the long term, regular air links between Hong Kong and Hanoi would benefit both parties and if I could contribute to the process by bringing together Cathay Pacific and the civil aviation authorities in Vietnam it was worth the extra cost.

I therefore fiddled the schedules of the repatriation flight in such a way that the TV crew could go to Hong Kong with a returning flight and return to Vietnam with a flight bringing in returnees.

All went according to schedule and in mid-March 1990 the arrival in Hong Kong of the first ever communist Vietnamese TV crew made headlines in the colony. But to say that they were welcome would be overdoing it.

Robert Van Leeuwen, the UNHCR representative in Hong Kong, had been less than enthusiastic about the mission but he also had an ego of gargantuan proportions and that was the chink in his armor.

While the program in Hong Kong of the Vietnamese TV crew had been arranged by the authorities I had insisted that it start with an interview with Rob. He had been somewhat cool to the principle of repatriation to Vietnam and getting him on board for me was a must. The journalist on the TV team was a woman in her mid-30s of considerable beauty and Rob, who could be tremendously impulsive, developed an instant crush on her the moment she set foot in his office As the interview proceeded he became another person asserting with unfalteringly certitude that he, a decorated American Vietnam War veteran, was totally committed to promoting voluntary repatriation to Vietnam as one of the main solutions to the boat people exodus. Rob never did things by half and now with all his energy focused on repatriation I had gained a precious ally. But it was not my only stroke of luck.

On December 12, 1989, Hong Kong had implemented the first forced repatriation of 51 screened-out Vietnamese to Hanoi. The operation had been messy and the whole Hong Kong press corps was at the airport to witness the deportees being dragged to the aircraft, kicking and screaming. Once on board and with no audience to perform to, they had quieted down and the landing in Hanoi had gone without a hitch but in terms of cosmetics the damage had been done.

Protests came pouring in from all over the world to the point that Hong Kong decided to suspend forced repatriation for at least a year. From my perspective however the operation had been a success and enabled me to pass the message in both the camps and back in Vietnam that for boat people not recognized as refugees return to Vietnam was a given and that their only choice was between voluntary return and deportation.

To further emphasize the point Jacques had bought in Hanoi sets of Vietnamese schoolbooks which we sent to Hong Kong where they were distributed to the schools in the camps. The move was supposed to carry a message and it did. When the parents asked why Vietnamese school books, the answer was unambiguous; so that when you return to Vietnam your children will have no problems in going back to school.

I was fully aware that if I went on Hanoi TV and announced that for the average Vietnamese hopping on a boat no longer meant automatic resettlement in the US there was no guarantee that I would be believed. If however a US government official were to pass on the same message in Vietnamese this would be an altogether different proposition. I had identified exactly the right person for the job, Bill Fleming. He had spent years in South Vietnam, spoke the language fluently, was very much involved in ODP, was committed to the principles embodied in the CPA and had both his head and his heart in the right place. Unfortunately, as he explained to me, he would need authorization from Washington to appear on Hanoi TV and this would take months to get, if he got it at all. Of course, he added with a smile, nothing prevented him from giving an interview in Vietnamese to UNHCR. So I got my video camera and the message on the tape was clear and to the point.

Altogether the Hong Kong authorities did a pretty good job with the Vietnamese TV crew. In addition to letting them film the camps they also brought them to the stock exchange, the port and gave them a thorough tour of the colony. For the Vietnamese, this must have been an unsettling experience. They were all tried and tested communist party members and here they were, coming from a country that was rules by a superior socialist system confronted by a territory that was not only a colony but a capitalist one at that and yet in every way eons ahead of them.

There were some 80 returnees on the flight to Hanoi and the presence of a TV crew on board seemed, if anything, to thrill them; a sure sign that these were not people who feared to be mistreated upon return.

At the airport in Hanoi we were met by the three UNHCR monitoring officers, all fluent Vietnamese speakers who, by regular visits to returnees, were ensuring that Vietnam abided by its commitment not to penalize them for illegal departure. It was to become the largest monitoring effort anywhere in the world and the results were predictable. While the returnees included their lot of louts and petty criminals and some of them actually ended up in jail, none were harassed for the act of illegal departure and for good reason.

The main cause of departure from the North was the state of the economy and not an expression of political dissent. This was something that even the returnees did not hesitate to underline. Goran Rosen, a Swedish monitoring officer, told me how while going to visit a returnee he had problems identifying his address and had asked the help of a local policeman. When they both arrived at the man's home they were received with a shower of invectives. 'You want to know why I left,' he bellowed at the policeman, 'I will tell you, I fought during the resistance, I was at Dien Bien Phu, I have six decorations and I was wounded twice and now I can't make a living because there are no jobs, and you dare come to my home,' at which point the policeman beat a hasty and embarrassed retreat.

The editing of the film took one month and the end result was a clean, factual one hour long production which showed Hong Kong for what it was. Prosperous. And it showed also the camps for what they were. Not uncomfortable, the food adequate but the hope of being further resettled in the West at exactly zero. As for my direct contribution it consisted of a short interview at the end of the program. 'What is your advice?' I was asked.

'I have no advice to give anyone,' I replied. 'Those who have seen this program know the facts. They can judge by themselves so let everyone do what he thinks is best.'

Our film was aired on March 15, 1990, and rebroadcast by the TV on three successive evenings and it was with a slight touch of unease that I waited for its effect on the exodus, if any.

The peak of the sailing season in Northern Vietnam extended from April to August and the travel time from Vietnam to Hong Kong by boat was from six to eight days. In 1989, some 3,000 boat people had arrived in Hong Kong in April, going up to some 10,000 in both May and June for a total by September of some 30,000 arrivals. Six days after the first airing of the film, arrivals in Hong Kong were down by 70% as compared to the same period in the previous year and by August, when the sailing season was over, arrivals totaled some 3,500 that is to say a drop of some 87% compared to the previous year. In financial terms, considering that the cost for the upkeep of one boat person per year in Hong Kong amounted to some 1,800 US $, the total saving equaled to some 46 million US $. Granted I had kept irregular office hours and my way of doing things might have been somewhat unconventional but, were it only in monetary terms, I had more than paid my dues to UNHCR.

If the information program proved successful in stemming the outflow from Northern Vietnam, I was under no illusion that it would not have carried much weight had the regime not also started to evolve. Granted, it was still politically repressive, but it had become far less intrusive and the average Vietnamese was now free to set up a small business or to travel throughout the country without first having to require a police permit. Likewise, 'building socialism' had been consigned to the ideological graveyard where it belonged and the economy was slowly recovering from the ills it had brought about.

Ultimately, it was the cumulative effect of these developments plus the information program that brought about the ending of illegal departures from the North, a result that would never have been achieved by information alone. Conversely, change without information would have delayed by years the closure of this chapter of the boat people saga.

While the drop of arrivals of boat people gained me points with the Hong Kong government, considerable resentment against me was building up in other quarters. None of the UNHCR camp officers in Hong Kong would ever admit it, but they had developed a proprietary attitude towards the camp population and, with the drop in arrivals and increasing voluntary repatriation, I was depriving them of their cause and they could barely hide their hostility towards me.

The drop in arrivals and the pick-up in returns also did not go particularly well with the lunatic fringe of the Vietnamese community in the US as well as with a number of American Vietnam war nostalgics who were kept in business by the boat people exodus. In the name of freedom the Hong Kong government did not restrict mail to the boat people in the camps and a wave of letters and faxes originating in the US were now swamping the camps calling on the boat people to hold tight and resist any form of repatriation. Apparently the messages were now targeting me personally and the next thing I knew I had on the phone in Bangkok a euphoric Clinton Leeks, the Hong Kong refugee coordinator who, almost besides himself with laughter, informed me that in one of the camps I had been burned in effigy. 'They don't know what you look like,' he said, 'so they took some straw, made a big puppet put your name on it, which they misspelled, and set it on fire.' I could not have hoped for a better compliment.

While departures from the North had been dealt with, and would never pick up again, they continued unabated from the South. There the sailing season peaked in May and by now it was too late in the year to intervene and catch it in the upsurge which gave me a preparation time of about eight months to target the 1991 Southern sailing season.

The basis for my Southern strategy was of course the CPA and the provision that boat people not recognized as refugees would have to return to Vietnam. However, as opposed to Northern Vietnam I had two additional factors to consider. If departure from the North was rarely an act of political dissent it was much more so in the South, even if most of those leaving did not hide the fact that they were doing so essentially for economic reasons. The second was that the South had a safety valve that the North did not have: the Orderly Departure Program.

I was convinced that when the leaders in Hanoi had endorsed both the ODP in 1979 and the CPA in 1989 they had no intentions of fully abiding by its provisions. Granted they had slightly opened a door that might lead to a solution of the boat people crisis but initially at least the exercise had been essentially cosmetic so as to try and mitigate the appalling image that they had created for themselves throughout the world. This would have been consistent with their experimental approach; take a first step, see where it leads to, adjust your next move, seize an unexpected opportunity, backtrack if necessary, move sideways, rush ahead or take your time. But now procrastination was no longer an option. The Berlin wall had crumbled, the Soviet Union was following suit and overnight the regime in Hanoi which had imprudently put all its eggs in the Soviet basket had became a political orphan.

The collapse of the Soviet Union had a shattering effect on the communist power structure in Vietnam. For decades the Vietnamese communists had seen themselves as part of a great, worldwide revolution. Now there was no longer a revolution and in the process they had not only lost their ideological compass but also their only provider of weapons and economic aid. Overnight, taunting China, aggravating the United States and alienating all their Asian neighbors had lost its appeal. But the Vietnamese were not ones to linger in the past. A new situation had arisen; a new approach was required. Suddenly, the ODP which, for the Vietnamese began as a sideshow, had become one of the avenues through which Hanoi, by removing the thorn of the boat people issue, could start constructing a new non-confrontational relation both with the US and its

Asian neighbors. Thus ultimately, the success of the CPA hinged on the fall of the Berlin wall.

While Hanoi was becoming more co-operative in the overall implementation of the CPA an additional difficulty in stemming boat departures lay in the fact that far more Southerners than Northerners were liable to be granted refugee status and the example they provided was was still an encouragement for others to try their luck.

Regarding voluntary repatriation I also had to contend with the small hardcore of former Saigon military, all of whom had been recognized as refugees, who, while waiting in the camps for their resettlement to be processed, were also putting considerable pressure on the screened-out to refuse voluntary repatriation. This pressure in turn was keeping the camp population at unnecessarily high levels, which not only cost money but also tended to unnerve the countries of transit.

Addressing the former military was not a problem I could solve alone and I definitely needed reinforcements. Doing the rounds in Bangkok I had come across a retired US army colonel, Andre Sauvageot, who had been posted in Vietnam in 1964 and had spent the following ten years in the country neck deep in Saigon's political scene in cahoots with the CIA. A fluent Vietnamese speaker, Sauvageot believed that a page had to be turned and seemed totally committed to what the CPA stood for: asylum for refuges and repatriation for those who were not. This was the man I needed and I hired him on the spot as a consultant.

With his impeccable credentials Sauvageot was the only one who could convince the former military to back off but I could hardly expect him to advocate repatriation without having him first visit Vietnam. Getting the Vietnamese to give him a visa required some convincing but they finally relented and his visit to Hanoi proved an unqualified success. The Vietnamese loved him. Not only did he make no secret about his background but he came through as someone who genuinely liked Vietnam in addition to being highly entertaining. Sauvageot did wonders as he toured the camps and even more so as he could convince the ex Saigon military that they were not doing themselves any good by trying to talk others into refusing to return.

This was the good news. Now came the bad news. In January 1990, a new High Commissioner for refugees, Thorvald Stoltenberg, had been elected to replace Hocke and when he moved to Geneva he brought with him as his personal assistant a Dane, Jessen-Petersen, whom he had met at the UN in New York, where he had been detached for one year from UNHCR. Jessen-Petersen was a swaggering braggart whose crude manner and vulgar demeanor had earned him the nickname of the Danish peasant but he made up for it by an uncanny ability to suck up to his superiors or those who would be in the future. When Stoltenberg arrived at UNHCR Sergio was director for Asia but Stoltenberg had taken a liking to him and had promoted him to Senior Director and Head of External Relations, leaving the post of Director for Asia vacant. When the news spread Anvar, who had been twiddling his thumbs in Bangkok for six years, called Jessen-Petersen asking that he recommend him to Stoltenberg for the job. The two shared a long friendship and the end result was that Anvar was now back at his old post at UNHCR as Director for Asia. For him it was a godsend. From Bangkok he had repeatedly tried to get a posting in New York but the UN was now wise to him and nobody wanted him. With four years to go before his retirement, thanks to the patronage of Jessen-Petersen, he could now look forward to a cushy job in Geneva.

Sergio had called to give me the news and sounded slightly apologetic. He knew that Anvar was a bungling fool and that he should have put my name forward for the job but this would have meant confronting Jessen-Petersen, who still had the ear of Stoltenberg. Sergio could have lost the battle and he was not prepared to take the risk.

By now I knew Sergio in and out and did not hold it against him. He was a good friend but I also knew what not to expect from him. As for me, I was happy with my job and did not actually aspire to become Director for Asia All I would have wanted was a boss who was not loony but visibly this was too much to ask for.

After Sergio called I went to see Anvar who had his office three floors above mine in the UN building in Bangkok to congratulate him. He was all smiles and assured me that he was looking forward to working with me. Of course I did not believe a word of what he said. He was a sick, vindictive character who would knife me in the back at the first opportunity but it would take him some time to get his bearings and I probably had one more year left of working in peace. But in the back of my mind I did make a note to keep an eye open for another position.

Bad news rarely comes alone and the following morning I was told that a representative of Human Rights Watch was coming to see me. The woman who entered my office, accompanied by a dour looking young Vietnamese must have been in her late twenties and could be charitably called plain. She wore a white blouse in rough cotton one size too large, an ill fitting skirt cut out of what looked like curtain material and bare feet in thronged leather sandals. But what struck me the most were her thick, heavy calves covered with long black hair. This, I told myself, means trouble as she handed me a card. I glanced at it long enough to read Dinah Pokempner, legal counsel, Human Rights Watch, and I recalled my mother's words: a Jew looking for a cause.

Human Rights Watch had been created in 1978 as an upshot of the former Helsinki Watch and in 1985 had extended its reach to Asia where, like the new dog in town, it was peeing on every tree to stake its territory. They had already denounced the forced repatriation from Hong Kong of a plane load of boat people knowing perfectly well that none of them actually qualified for refugee status and that the Hong Kong government would never have taken the political risk of deporting a Vietnamese whose status was in doubt, but that was beyond the point. In the cut throat world of humanitarian advocacy where the name of the game was market share the loudest bird got the worm they were out to prove to the world that they were the best at denouncing human rights violations and if these were invented, who was there to know?

Now, she told me in no uncertain terms, UNHCR had to suspend repatriation to Vietnam because it was not safe and there was no guarantee the returnees would not be persecuted. I tried to explain to her that no Vietnamese who qualified for refugee status was ever made to return and those who did return were illegal migrants with no claim to persecution. Likewise, I told her, we had an extensive monitoring program in Vietnam and had never found any evidence that returnees were penalized for illegal departure and while Vietnam was still a dictatorship not every single Vietnamese could claim to have been personally persecuted for political reasons but I soon realized that I was wasting my time. Her mind was made up. Had she ever visited Vietnam I asked. She had not. Would she be interested in taking a repatriation flight and spending some time in Vietnam? 'No,' she answered, 'I don't want to be influenced by what I see.' Not influenced by what I see? Obviously she preferred to be influenced by what she was told by the young Vietnamese with her, who introduced himself as Thang, from SOS boat people. In fact he was just one demented kid with an inflated ego, but he had done a good job of misinforming her. Over the following years he became part of an attempt by a handful of American Vietnam-war nostalgics, wacky South Vietnamese émigrés and zany right-wing politicians to derail the CPA but to no avail. It was a pathetic effort, out of step with history and ultimately it came to nothing, but he certainly contributed to our workload.

My initial plan was to duplicate what we had done in the North and send a TV crew from Saigon to cover some of the boat people camps in the countries of South East Asia but this met with the absolute opposition from all the UNHCR representatives in the area. According to them the situation in the camps was so tense that the presence of a TV crew from Vietnam would lead to major rioting and this they did not want to put up with. The objections, I believed, made sense so I decided the TV crew would go instead to Hong Kong where it would cover the camp that housed the Southerners.

Basically the Southern TV crew brought back the same material as the Northern one had, which I expected, but the message we conveyed was somewhat different. The message in the North was basically: you can leave by boat if you wish but if you do not qualify for refugee status you will have to go back to Vietnam. The message to the South was the same but with an addendum. There is now a functioning Orderly Departure Program from Vietnam and if you qualify you can leave legally without risking your life on a boat. The example that we gave was that of a captain in the South Vietnamese marines. He had spent six years in a reeducation camp and had recently escaped to Thailand where he was told that, yes he qualified for resettlement in the US but the processing would take two years. However if he returned to Vietnam he could leave through ODP with six months. He gave it a try and it worked. I had sent a TV crew to cover his return and subsequent departure and the message he conveyed stood on its own.

The outcome of these efforts was a film that started by showing an elderly couple on a beach at sunset looking out to sea. In the background a voice was heard: their son had left by boat and has never been heard of again. Where is his body? Swallowed up by the sea, he has no grave. Will his soul wander aimlessly for all eternity like a ghost and who will pay homage to the grave of his parents once they have passed away? The program then went on to explain the refugee screening process as well as the return for the screened out and then, mostly through interviews with US officials, explained in detail the qualifications required and procedures of the ODP program. The overriding message was simple: things have changed. Now you know. Do what you think is best. In parallel with the TV program we prepared a briefing on ODP together with a form that prospective applicants could fill out, all to be published in a dozen South Vietnamese newspapers.

I had targeted the Southern information offensive to impact the annual May sailing peak of 1991 and the TV program was aired three months before the prospective exodus. May came and went and when the boat people arrival figures came in they were startling. While arrivals in South East Asia had stood at some 6,000 the previous year they were now down by some 93% to no more than 400.

By the fall of 1991, boat arrivals in South East Asia had come to an end but a small trickle of boat people from the North continued to land in Hong Kong. With voluntary repatriation in full swing the cause of this continuing dribble remained a mystery until the Hong Kong government, after minute interrogations of the new arrivals, finally put their finger on it. The cost of a boat ride from

Northern Vietnam to Hong Kong had dropped to 100 US $ but the repatriation allowance that UNHCR was providing to all returnees to assist them in their reintegration was still standing at 350 US $.

It did not take a genius to figure out that one rotation would net each returnee a profit of 250 US $ which was the equivalent of an average yearly salary in Vietnam. In a part of the world where no good deed went unpunished, it was the repatriation allowance that was now fuelling the exodus, and the record holder had made the journey six times.

The only solution was to abolish the repatriation allowance but this was a policy decision that normally should have been referred to Headquarters. However, with Anvar now Director for Asia a quick decision, not to say the right decision, was unlikely so Jacques contacted Rob Van Leeuwen in Hong Kong and they decided on the spot to suspend the repatriation allowance. On September 1, all the media in Northern Vietnam came out with the news that there would be no more repatriation allowance for anybody arriving in Hong Kong after September 28 and by early October the boat people exodus into Hong Kong was over for good.

As for me, having worked myself out of a job I now had to put up with a resurgent Anvar who slowly had started to turn the screws on me. My posting authorized me to travel freely throughout the region and that still stood, but he now requested that I inform him prior to any move. From a normal person the request would have been legitimate but coming from a psychopathic Persian it was easy to guess where it was leading to and I suspected that his next instruction would be that I ask for prior approval from him, which he would then proceed to delay, rendering my work impossible and then blaming me for any shortcoming that was inevitably liable to occur. Moreover, whenever he came to Bangkok he had gone back to his old habit of howling invectives at me, and I felt the time had come for me to jump ship. But where to? Fortunately fate intervened.

As the crisis in Indochina was coming to a close the Balkans were coming apart. Bosnia was in flames. Albania, which until then had been the world's most reclusive country, had collapsed into semi-anarchy and tens of thousands of Albanians were making their way illegally to Italy. With my attention still focused on Vietnam, the last thing I expected was a call from Sergio.

'I need you in Albania,' he said. 'What for?' I asked. 'Mass information,' he replied, 'we must try to stop the exodus.'

'But I know nothing about Albania,' I told him. 'Never mind,' he said, 'nobody knows anything about Albania but I am sure you will invent something.'

'When do you want me?'

'Next week.' But what about my house in Bangkok, my furniture and the rest? 'You can return later to pack.' So on April 20, 1992, I landed in Tirana. I had no idea of what stood in front of me but at least Anvar was now out of my way.

ALBANIA

While the first reference to an Albanian people dates from 400 BC it was only in 1912 with the collapse of the Ottoman empire that Albania became a sovereign nation. But even that did not last. In 1939, Mussolini invaded Albania, it's ruler King Zog fled to London where he settled at the Ritz and the country became an Italian protectorate.

The Albania which emerged from the Second World War was the only Eastern European country to be liberated by its own home-grown communist guerillas without the help of the Soviet Union and the only axis-occupied nation to emerge from the war with more Jews than it had started off with.

Once in power the Albanian communists, under the leadership of the French-educated Enver Hoxha, set up a regime unparalleled for its radicalism in the communist world. All private property, except for personal effects, was confiscated, religious practice was banned and the state became the only provider. In 1960, Hoxha broke first with Tito and then with Moscow, both of which he considered as having betrayed Marxist ideology and in 1979, he raised the ante and broke with China, which he also accused of ideological deviationism. By now Albania was in a self-imposed state of siege, a prison, hermetically sealed to any outside influence with weapons stockpiled in every village and concrete pillboxes, all facing Italy, dotting the landscape.

Hoxha died in April 1985 and while the regime initially survived without him, it collapsed in March 1992 bringing down with it the whole state apparatus. Freed from the fetters of absolute control the country descended into anarchy and literarily overnight every other Albanian became possessed by one obsession; to leave the country at all costs. While the full explanation of this sudden departure psychoses had never been fully document, television played a major role.

Albania was some 40 miles across the Adriatic from Italy and within reach of Italian television. During the Hoxha years watching it could land an Albanian in jail but most took the risk and they all focused on one program which became an object of fascination: the American series *Dallas* dubbed in Italian which they all understood. Watching Dallas became an Albanian addiction and the evenings when the program was broadcast the whole of the country came to a stop as the population stayed riveted to their TV sets. With time Dallas, in the eye of the average Albanian, became a mirror image of daily life in a Western Eldorado which was now within reach.

If the tens of thousands of Albanians who crossed over into Italy in every possible craft from fishing boats to commandeered ships did not exactly find upon landing a replica of Dallas, just the lure of the shop windows was enough of an incentive for them to leave in what had become a mass stampede out of the country.

The Italians were overwhelmed by the influx and were hesitant about sending them back least this violated the refugee convention which provided that no person claiming asylum should be repatriated before having been given a hearing and his case adjudicated as not valid. Then Sergio intervened. Speaking in the name of UNHCR he stated unequivocally that Albania was no longer a dictatorship, that no one could credibly claim that he had left the country to flee persecution and consequently the exodus was not a refugee movement and the refugee conventions did not apply. The lawyers in Geneva were furious but the point was indisputable. Sergio's pronouncement enabled the Italians to start deporting Albanians back to their country, but he wished to go one step further, or at lest appear to do so. Could the exodus be stopped or at least reduced to manageable proportions by an information campaign? There was no answer to the question, except: We will only know after we have tried. My job now was to try.

My first impression of Tirana was a vision from a nightmare. Except for a few government buildings built by Mussolini in the monumental style favored by the Italian fascists the city was one single expanse of ramshackle buildings all in an advanced state of disrepair. Garbage was no longer collected, electricity was erratic, the water supply polluted and the streets an unending stretch of potholes.

It was hard to imagine that just a few years earlier Albania had been one of the most regimented countries in the world, where there was even a rule on how women should carry their handbags and where whatever worked did so meticulously well and on time. While the leap from inflexible order to anarchy could be partly ascribed to the collapse of the regime this did not answer another question: where did the Albanians find the inner resources that enabled them to impose such a stringent order on themselves? The nearest I came to another answer was an Albanian joke that was making the rounds of Tirana. The government had imposed a curfew and had decreed that anyone on the street after seven in the evening would be shot on sight. It was six forty-five when a lonely cyclist arrived at a checkpoint. One of the two soldiers manning it waved him through but he had barely past it when the other raised his rifle, took aim and shot him down.

'Why did you do that,' asked the first soldier, 'it is only six forty-five.'

'Yes,' replied the other soldier, 'but I know where this man lives and he will never make it home by seven.'

If there was anything to be learned from this story it was that the Albanians could be emotional, systematic, irrational, forward thinking, cold blooded and erratic all in one. But this piece of wisdom did not provide an answer to my predicament. How do you get them not to leave?

With the fall of Hoxha the ruling elite had split in two. One side had created the Socialist Party and the other the Democratic Party. That the Socialists were not socialists and the Democrats were not democrats was besides the point. They had all been communists in the past, knew each other, had intermarried and all that divided them were personal affinities, not to say personal interest.

The local UNHCR representative, Olivier Guignabaudet, was an astute Frenchman with a sharp mind and an amenable personality but his ace card was his local assistant Tamara. A handsome woman of impeccable demeanor in her late 30s who was born within the power elite, she spoke five languages, knew everybody who was anybody and there was not a single door closed to her. As we did the rounds of ministers, journalists, academics and politicians it occurred to me that if Albania was Europe's poorest country, the small group at the apex of the pyramid was made up of some very educated people.

This did not exactly help me. Nor could President Berisha, who Tamara brought me to see, except for commenting that by definition anything the government said would not be believed and if there was a message to be passed on to the grassroots, I should pass it on myself. But what message, and, above all, how?

On my regular visits to the US I had, by accident, tuned in to some of the many Christian radio stations and while the quality of the message was not one I particularly cared for, I did like the congenial tone and the relationship of trust that had been established between the speaker and a rather simple audience. Could this, I wondered, be duplicated in Albania? And if the program was structured in such a way that we would be responding to listeners' letters, would this not be the best way to avoid giving the impression that one was trying to impose a message? But then, would the listeners have questions that they wished to be answered?

Radio Tirana happened to have the world's most powerful medium-wave transmitter which the Chinese had donated to the Albanians during their long honeymoon so they could disseminate their propaganda throughout Europe and while it was now underused and the equipment at least 25 years old it was still in working order.

The director of *Radio Tirana*, Bardul Pollo, and his technical coordinator, Yilli Pepo, did not need convincing. Yes, something had to be done to persuade people not to leave but what, he did not know. What he did know however was that no Albanian would ever believe anything said by anybody perceived as having any ties to the government. Actually, he added I don't think any Albanian will believe any other Albanian. 'You are Swiss,' he said, 'maybe they will believe you, you do it.'

So was born '*Voices from Home and Abroad*.' Miraculously, the postal system in Albania had survived the political turmoil and listeners were invited to write to me personally, care of *Radio Tirana*, with any question they might have regarding travel abroad. Tamara would then gather the letters, translate them into Italian and fax them to me in Geneva. I would then record an answer on a cassette in Italian and send back the tape with the corresponding letter on the Swissair flight. During the program the letter would be read out in Albanian, followed by my answer which would start in Italian and continue with an Albanian voiceover. The concept was to create a personal relationship between myself and the author of the letter and to provide information which other listeners could use, creating a multiplier effect. To be credible the program had to be oriented in such a way as to be perceived as a positive and friendly effort to explain to people how to leave legally. Deterrence for illegal departure had to be indirect as a collateral and not as the principal aim of the program.

News about the coming program was repeatedly advertised on the radio a month before it was to start and predictably, I did not receive a single letter. So, Tamara and I used a ploy commonly used in the media to jump-start a program: bogus letters which we wrote ourselves.

Six weeks later I had so many letters coming in that I was swamped. While almost all those who wrote wanted to know how to leave Albania, a considerable number of them qualified for a visa but did not know how to apply for one, not counting those who did not even know what a visa was. By now most of my answers went like this: Dear *Madame* so and so, Thank you for your letter and I hope you and your family are in good health. Regarding your question, you don't have to leave for Italy illegally. You actually qualify for a visa because your husband is legally in Italy. But if he were illegally in Italy then of course you would not qualify for a visa. So my advice to you is to go to the Italian embassy in Tirana and ask for a visa. Of course it will take some time because of the bureaucracy involved. If you decide to go illegally you will be there much quicker. However if you are ever discovered you will be arrested, the police will take your fingerprints and you will no longer be eligible to get a visa for Italy for the next five years. So the choice is yours. I would then indicate which documents she had to present to apply for a visa and also give her the opening hours of the Italian embassy in Tirana. Then I would conclude, I hope my answer has been useful to you and that you will soon see your husband. To both of you I wish good health and good luck.

The program, as I emphasized to the foreign embassies that I regularly briefed in Tirana, could not possibly have an immediate effect in regularizing departure from Albania. Rather it was a long-term educational effort targeted at a population who often did not know what a visa was, why visas existed, how one applied for them and why some people did not qualify.

As the program snowballed and hundreds of letters arrived, its scope diversified. People wrote asking about their pension rights and many did not understand why the benefits of the parents could not be inherited by the children. Women forced into prostitution in Italy would write for help, their letters alone being a far more effective warning than any I could give to Albanian women being offered undefined jobs abroad. Older people who had fought as guerillas against the Germans together with Italian deserters wrote indicating where Italians who had been killed had been buried. Other wrote with questions on medical problems with the under-lying assumption that to get proper medical care one had impera-tively to go abroad. By now I had enlisted the services of a Swiss doctor who, more often than not, would explain to a letter writer that, based on the information provided, he would reccomend the same treatment as the one currently prescribed by an Albanian doc-tor. With letters now also coming from Albanians all over Europe who were tuning into *Radio Tirana,* answering them required me to find a network of resources essentially in Italy, from the Ministry of Interior to the military as well as associations dealing in the traf-ficking of women. Soon I could no longer do it alone.

As luck would have it, I identified a young Italian who had just finished his assignment in Cambodia and was interested in the job. Giuseppe De Vincentiis was in his early 30s, came from Naples, was tall, good-looking, intelligent, astute, elegant, hard working and exactly the man I needed and by some miracle it only took me six weeks to get him posted as my deputy in Geneva. Together with a secretary we made a good team, albeit totally on the margins of mainstream UNHCR, where our work was looked upon as something odd to be tolerated but no more. Actually I did not ask for more and it was therefore very much from the sidelines that I witnessed High Commissioner Stoltenberg resign after six months in office and be replaced by a Japanese woman, Sadako Ogata. To me she was an unknown and all I knew was that Jessen-Petersen had succeeded in ingratiating himself with her, a task no doubt helped by his having a Japanese wife, and was now her closest confident.

With the crisis in former Yugoslavia, UNHCR had had to massively increase its staff and many offices, including mine, had been moved to a new building across the street from our main Headquarters. I occasionally would wander over to our main building and one afternoon as I was in the corridor where the Asia bureau was located I heard a massive commotion. It was nothing new. Anvar was known to scream and his bellows carried far but this time the pitch and volume was well beyond what we had become used to. When I cautiously inquired as to what was the cause of this outburst I was told by a secretary that *Madame* Ogata had just given him the sack.

Actually, Anvar's contract was with the UN Secretariat, not UNHCR, and when Jessen-Petersen had brought him in he had been given a two-year detachment to UNHCR. This had now expired and he was told it would not be renewed. Ironically, it had nothing to do with his performance, abysmal as it may have been. What proved to be his downfall were his mannerisms and the fact that *Madame* Ogata was Japanese. Coming from a society where form and demeanor were at a premium she had become increasingly irritated at his screaming and pointing his finger at her as well as his insensitivity to hierarchy. When flying back with her from Bangkok, he had pulled every possible string to be upgraded from business class to first, taking a seat next to her. That he had rattled on all night and kept her from sleeping was the least of her complaints. The peasant had had the impudence of seating himself next to the Empress. He had committed the unforgivable and had to go.

As a good Japanese, Ogata did not like to confront so she entrusted the task of giving Anvar the boot to Jessen-Petersen. So the man who had brought Anvar in—I suspect that he never confessed this to Ogata—was also given the task of showing him the door. It was the last we saw of Anvar. Apparently he was reabsorbed in the marshland of UN bureaucracy until his retirement.

We were all curious to see who she would chose as his successor and while her choice did raise some eyebrows, in particular with Sergio, for me it came as no surprise. She was a Japanese from the old school and most of those she had promoted or chosen as part of her inner circle were true to type; clean-cut and boyish looking of obsequious manners and respectful demeanor who only conveyed good news. In 1974 I had introduced Rizvi to a young Swiss, Werner Blatter, at the time the ICRC representative in Vientiane and he had hired him on the spot. Now some seventeen years later, Ogata had come across him as head of fundraising and he had all the qualities that appealed to her. There were no doubt worse choices and better ones too but she only felt comfortable with people she knew who would not stress her intelligence and he fitted the bill to perfection.

UNHCR at the time had not yet abolished its telephone switchboard operators, which meant that if someone from the outside called with a query, they would be steered in the right direction. One afternoon the phone in my office rang. It was one of the operators. Apparently she had on the line someone who wanted to talk about identifying lost children. She did not know who to address him to but had heard about our radio program in Albania and asked me if I would take the call. Children were not my line of business, but why not?

The man at the other end of the line identified himself as Ken Dodd and was calling from Texas. He worked for EDS, the data company created by Ross Perrot, but this call he stressed, was purely a personal one. A few days before he had been watching *CNN* and seen *Madame* Ogata the UN High Commissioner for Refugees, referring to the thousands of children in Bosnia who had been separated from their mothers by the fighting. Reuniting these children with their mothers was a major challenge and no one seemed up to it.

Ken and a colleague, Paula, wanted to help. New technologies were emerging that could be put to use to identify lost children and he could try and sell the idea to the board of EDS. It would all be for free, implemented by volunteers, and if the idea was accepted he felt it could be operational in 60 days. Was I interested?

The normal procedure would have been for me to write a memo and circulate it and it would be weeks, if not months before I would get an answer. So I decided to jump the gun and told Ken that yes, I was interested and would get back to him in one week.

Jacques Mouchet, who I had put as UNHCR representative in Beijing in 1979, was now head of the UNHCR office in Zagreb and when I phoned him he confirmed that he had heard of any number of children who had lost track of their parents, unaccompanied minors or UMs as they were called but nothing more. There was, he told me, a local NGO that went by the initials of UCE, which was involved with them. The best thing for me to do would be for me to go and see them. Three days later, under the somewhat dubious pretext that my Albanian radio program required me to go to Croatia, I was in Zagreb.

UCE was a small outfit, three women in all, financed by a grant from USAID. The head of UCE, Alenka, explained that they were trying to create a master file of all the children in Bosnia who had lost track of their parents. The idea was to leave the children in whatever care they were in and just to register them. Overall she felt there were 20,000 such children, half in Bosnia and the rest spread out in Serbia, Slovenia Croatia, Turkey, Hungary and Austria.

That was all the information I needed. There was a need, it was addressed peripherally and, last but not least, the victims were also the most vulnerable.

The next day I was back in Geneva and on the phone to Ken Dodd. Yes, I told him, there was a need and while I could not commit UNHCR, he could go ahead and prepare a proposal that I could submit to the organization. In the meantime he had got together with his technical people and a solution had been identified. For its time it was revolutionary.

The idea was to take a photograph of each child and then to digitalize it through a scanner. With the picture whatever information on the child that was available such as gender, name and surname, date of birth or approximate age, place of birth etc would be registered in a data base. That would be transferred to a new system which had just come on the market called CD-ROM coupled to a search engine. CD-ROM readers would be installed in every UNHCR office in all the countries that had received Bosnian refugees and parents could come to look for lost children The worst case scenario was a six-month-old baby of which one only had a picture and knew the gender. Other scenarios provided for the misspelling of names. The beauty of the system was that, through an off-the-shelf search feature, a mother looking for a lost child could go through the pictures of all the children of a certain age group and gender ensuring that even if the name was unknown or misspelled she could identify her child. Once a child was identified, it was up to UCE to ensure that the parents were who they claimed to be and only then would the location of the child be released.

To implement the project Ken Dodd proposed to work with one of EDS's parent companies, Bull, which was located in Paris and where a number of volunteers had already indicated that they were willing to spend time digitalizing the files. It all sounded pretty good but to sell the project within UNHCR I needed something more tangible. So with twelve files and photos provided by UCE, Ken had a sample CD-ROM made and sent it to me in Geneva together with a drive which he purchased from his own pocket. The installation was done on my computer by one of the IT technicians at UNHCR Headquarters and it worked. Now we had to sell it. Of the twelve children on the CD-ROM, one stood out. It was a baby less than one year old of whom we knew only the gender, male, and the name, Elvedin.

In order to get the project going, I needed to get it past *Madame* Ogata, and knowing that she always consulted her confidant, Jessen-Peterson, I first broached with him the possibility of showing her a demonstration of what I had termed Operation ReUNite. He was initially hesitant, made a few sarcastic remarks, but finally agreed and a computer in one of the offices next to hers was prepared.

Sadako Ogata carried with her an aura of authority. She was impeccably well dressed and, like many of her generation, slightly bow-legged, but unlike most of her kin her command of English was faultless and included a sense of humor that verged on the sarcastic. As the computer screen lit up, she looked at it with suspicion as I scrolled through the pictures of the children, unattractive pre-teen Balkans. Then I hit another key and Elvedin appeared. The change in her was instantaneous.

'Oh, a baby,' she cooed as her motherly instinct kicked in, 'how wonderful, what a good idea.' Jessen-Petersen was beaming as if the project had been his but I would have conceded anything to anybody in order to be left to do my work in peace.

So that was it. The empress had endorsed the project; operation ReUNite was on its way and anyone within UNHCR who demeaned it did so at his own peril.

While volunteers in Paris at Bull were busy digitalizing the first 5000 files we had received, UNHCR gave a press conference to announce the launch of the operation. The head of information, Sylvana Foa, was an eager, former American journalist with a sense of the theatrical and, when she presented the project she inflated initial the estimated 20,000 lost children to 30,000. We later found out that UCE had also been somewhat generous in its estimates and the total number of files did not exceed 10,000, which was in itself good news apart from the hype. The press conference made front page news, technology at the service of humanity, EDS was happy for the publicity and we were waiting for a first batch of 30 CD-ROM drives to be distributed throughout the region. Then all hell broke loose.

On May 18, 1992, the head of the ICRC delegation in Sarajevo, Frederic Maurice, had been deliberately gunned down. The killing stunned the organization, which had considered itself untouchable, into inaction and it took several weeks before it emerged from its stupor. Normally helping civilian victims in times of war was what the International Red Cross was all about. But it had freaked itself out of the picture and when it woke up it was too late. Ogata had stepped into the vacuum and the ICRC had lost its market share. With hundreds of UNHCR staff members now operating all over Bosnia the international community was now privy to the spectacle of a UN agency which was supposed to look after refugees, that is people outside their country of origin or internally displaced at best, spearheading a massive assistance program which brought relief to people who were not even on the move but cooped up in their own homes under siege. For all practical purposes ICRC was wiped off the map and all that was left for it to do was to distribute so-called Red Cross messages where the postal services had broken down.

The launch of Operation ReUNite added insult to injury. The tracing of adults or children was one of the core activities of ICRC and we had now usurped it. That the ICRC was not doing its job was not the issue. The issue was market share. If they did not do it, no one else should. The ICRC gripe came in the form of a letter from its President, Cornelio Sommaruga, to Ogata asking her to suspend Operation ReUNite. Sommaruga was a congenial, atypical Swiss from the Italian-speaking part of the country. Contrary to his tight-lipped predecessors he was boisterous and exuberant and would comment with abandon on anything that he came across. He got away with it as no one took him seriously and he could rave and rant about the state of the world to his heart's content.

Sommaruga's letter did not please *Madame* Ogata. She did not like confrontation and asked Jessen-Petersen to organize a meeting with Jean de Courten, Sommaruga's dour chief of operations, to try and come to a compromise. It was a waste of time. However much I explained the workings of the project de Courten was still adamant in his opposition. Finally, I asked him point blank why he was so opposed to it. The answer he gave was not one I was likely to forget. 'because it damages our institutional image.'

I had to restrain myself from answering that his institutional image had already gone up in smoke at Auschwitz when the committee who was aware of the Holocaust decided to stay mum so as not to provoke the Nazis. Our last resort was to offer to hand over the whole project lock stock and barrel to the ICRC including the hardware, the software and the files. They could continue working with EDS and run the project under their name but even this they refused so our meeting came to nothing. I was wondering where this would lead but it lead to nowhere. However upset the ICRC had been when Operation ReUNite was launched, they suddenly seemed to lose interest about the whole matter and their opposition just faded away.

But there was worse to come. While EDS was donating the technology of Operation ReUNite, we still needed an allocation to fund the implementation of the program. Money for Bosnia was plentiful but a specific budget source had to be identified and our finance department finally decided it should be the Soros fund. The financier George Soros was wary of the UN but, impressed by *Madame* Ogata's performance, he had made an exception for Bosnia and donated 50 million US $ to UNHCR. With the donation however he had put some of his people to supervise how it was being used. That was where my problem started.

For the professional humanitarians who dotted the American landscape the advent of Soros as a major donor to humanitarian causes was manna from heaven. Suddenly there was an abundance of jobs, positions, programs and they all scrambled for a slice of the pie. Among the various groups that Soros had engaged to monitor his Bosnian contribution was Lionel Rosenblatt, President of the advocacy organization, Refugees International.

Rosenblatt, a former US state department official, had spent some four years in Vietnam working, so he used to claim, on economic development. He had been in fact working for the Phoenix program, the CIA-sponsored assassination scheme that aimed at 'neutralizing' the Viet Cong infrastructure. Rosenblatt was a zealot for whom the Vietnam war had become a personal crusade. Years after the fall of Saigon, in cahoots with the lunatic fringe of the Vietnamese community in the US he had continued to fight his Vietnam war with fanatical zeal and Rob Van Leeuwen, the UNHCR representative in Hong Kong, told me once how he had seen him outside a refugee camp, bullhorn in hand, bellowing to the Vietnamese inside to hold fast and refuse repatriation. The end of the exodus, for which he held me and my information program partly responsible, had deprived him of a cause and I was told he had developed a personal grudge against me. When he found out that I was behind Operation ReUNite it was payback time and I was told that he tried to bloc Soros funding for the project.

Another source of opposition to Operation ReUNite came from the President of the Soros foundation, Aryeh Neier. Of German-Jewish origin Neier had been the founder of Human Rights Watch and had made a name for himself in the American advocacy community. Though an American citizen, Neier had remained very much a German, if not the caricature of one for whom everything had to be in the right place. Thus, tracing people was the job of the ICRC, and no one else and if they did not do it they should be made to, full stop. The issue here was order, 'Ordnung', not lost children and that was that.

Fortunately, saner minds in the person of Mark Malloch Brown, a lanky Englishman who was an advisor to Soros, prevailed. It was Mark who had kept me informed of Rosenblatt's and Neier's foibles and it was he who finally was able to put them to rest, although how he achieved this he never told me.

So Operation ReUNite proceeded but as we kept on registering children I was also thinking ahead. Double dipping, that is refugees using false names to obtain several times over their allotted rations or allowances, was an endemic problem for UNHCR costing us tens of millions of dollars per year. Here was a tool that could register hundreds of thousands of refugees including their picture and fingerprints thus bringing to an end double dipping and saving tens of millions of dollars. The possibilities were endless and I must not have been the only one to think so as out of the blue a letter arrived from the Smithsonian. Operation ReUNite had been chosen as one of the five finalists for their annual Technology in the Service of Humanity prize and I was invited to attend the closing ceremony.

It was a glittering evening and all of Washington was there in black tie for men and long dresses for the women. We did not get the first prize, it went to a system to locate policemen set up during the Winter Olympics at Lillehammer in Norway, but I received a beautiful crystal commemorative inscription that was duly delivered to *Madame* Ogata.

We now had CD-ROM readers in half a dozen locations in Bosnia with 6,000 children on record and while there was no rush to consult them the system had already enabled seven mothers to find their lost children. As for our Albanian radio program, it was going strong so basically we were on track when on a Friday afternoon I received a phone call from Sergio. Could I come and see him? He had now been promoted to the post of Head of Operations and I suspected that he had identified another area where an information program would be needed. I was wrong.

'Ogata has asked me to talk you,' he said. 'The CPA is in trouble. She wants to know if you would accept the position of Director for Asia to replace Werner Blatter starting on Monday but,' he hesitated, 'it would only be as Director *ad interim*.' Why ad interim? In rational terms it did not make sense and I could see Sergio thought likewise. Granted I was 59 and due to retire in ten months time but she had assigned other Directors in their positions for only two or three months before moving them so the fact that I had less than a year to go was not the key element in her decision. I also knew that, if the CPA was in trouble some tough decisions would have to be taken to get it going and this would require confronting governments. However, no government was going to take seriously a Director who was ad interim so by imposing this provision she was shooting herself in the foot. But she was also Japanese and therein lay the explanation for her wacky ruling. Nominating Blatter had been her choice and her's alone. It now had emerged that it had been a poor choice but she was the Empress and Empresses don't take poor decisions. Replacing Blatter would have implied that she had been wrong in nominating him in the first place but this she was not willing to admit. So in order to mitigate the affront that she had brought on herself, rather than chosing me as a replacement for Blatter, she put me in his job but only '*ad interim*'. The mental process was convoluted and ultimately did not make sense, but the fact remained that however well she spoke English, she still had the mind set of a Japanese and there was no getting away from it. 'Whatever you're thinking,' said Sergio, 'just take the job and never mention the "*ad interim*".'

The stern-looking woman who received me that evening at six did not move from her desk as I was ushered into her office and did not seem particularly pleased to see me either. 'So you accept,' she said coldly, 'fine,' she added, 'I want you to close the CPA.'

ENDING THE BOAT PEOPLE SAGA

T The following Monday I went to see Werner Blatter. We had not kept up over the years and I expected our meeting to be somewhat awkward but to his credit it was not.

'I know you have nothing to do with this,' were his first words, implying that someone else had. 'I will give you a short update and by tonight I will be out of this office.'

The update that Blatter gave me on the CPA was not good news. The UNHCR office in Hanoi had been without a Representative for over six months and while the exodus of boat people had not picked up again, voluntary repatriation had also come to a stop and some 35,000 boat people who did not qualify for refugee status were lingering in the camps. But even if they had volunteered to return, the system was also stuck at the other end. The repatriation procedure provided that each returnee had to be individually cleared by Hanoi before being authorized to return. And while 14,000 cases had been submitted to the Vietnamese and were waiting for clearance, none had come. With the CPA due to come to a close on July 1, 1996, and I due to retire from UNHCR on April 30 of that year I had no time to dither if I wanted to ensure that the end of the CPA stay on schedule. But as I embarked on what was to prove a deceptively easy task I could not help wondering by what strange set of circumstances the directorship of the Asia Bureau had come my way.

Nominating bureau directors was Ogata's prerogative and Blatter was someone she felt comfortable with. As such he was no worse than others she had graced with promotions to senior positions and under normal circumstances he would have done a reasonable job. Unfortunately for him circumstances were not normal and while he had been unlucky his being also unwise did not help.

Ogata did not like bad news and needed constant reassurance that everything was under control. Like many others, Blatter complied. Everything is working fine, he would tell her, the CPA is coming along and there is nothing to worry about. Then one day she took a trip to Washington and there the State Department came down on her like a ton of bricks.

The CPA is in a lock jam, she was told, the administration is under pressure from Congress over the boat people issue, repatriation has come to a stop and she had better get her act together and fast. It was not the sort of language she was used to hearing and she came back to Geneva considerably rattled.

To get a better perspective on the situation she decided to send Sergio together with her personal assistant, Irene Khan, and Werner Blatter to Hanoi. Irene, who had briefly worked for me many years ago, was a small dark brooding Bangladeshi with an Afro hairstyle, a law degree and a complete lack of a sense of humor. Except for one short year in Pakistan she had never served in the field and though credited with a sharp mind and an aggressive tongue I had never seen her use either for any practical purpose. Actually, she reminded me of a small dark hairy tarantula lurking in its lair. For some unknown reason Ogata had taken a liking to her and she skulked in her shadow. Having crept up the bureaucratic ladder on the merit of being a woman and an Asian, she now aspired to the post of UNHCR Representative in New Delhi. The position came within the precinct of the Asia Bureau and she needed Blatter's approval in order to get it. Blatter however, did not want her there and told her to her face that she would be given the post over his dead body. It was an assertion that the unwary Swiss would soon see come true.

Having alienated Irene, Blatter proceeded to do likewise with Sergio. In his new position as Assistant High Commissioner for Operations, Sergio expected to be looked up to by the Bureau Directors. It was mostly a matter of cosmetics, of coming to see him now and then in his office and they all complied. All, except for Blatter, who did not hide his disdain for him. It riled Sergio, especially as he had been personally involved in the CPA and had retained a special interest in Asia. So the team that arrived in Hanoi did not have Blatter's welfare high on their agenda and what they saw did nothing to alleviate their misgivings.

For six months Hanoi had been without a UNHCR representative and the acting representative, Carlos Zacagnini, an irascible Spaniard put in by Blatter, could hardly have been a worse choice. He was loud and offensive and screaming at the authorities was his way of trying to pass a message through.

As a result the Vietnamese had simply cut him out of the loop; his calls to ministries were no longer answered and it was as if UN-HCR Hanoi had ceased to exist.

The morning after their arrival Sergio and his team paid a courtesy call on the Foreign Ministry and before leaving were told that the Minister was giving a reception that very evening and that they were all invited to attend. After the meeting Sergio asked Blatter what he should wear for the reception. An open collar white shirt with no coat and tie, said Blatter. When they met that evening at the reception Blatter and Zacagnini as well as the minister and all the other guests present was wearing dark blue suits and ties. Only Sergio was in shirtsleeves. It was a slight that the dapper Brazilian would neither forget nor forgive.

If the visit to Hanoi was to prove a catastrophe that Blatter had only himself to blame for, he was also unlucky. In June 1995, a US congressman, Christopher Smith, introduced a bill to the House of Representatives which would provide 30 million US $ to resettle in the US 20,000 Vietnamese currently in camps. To justify his demand Smith claimed that the refugee screening procedure in the camps was flawed and that thousands of genuine refugees had seen their claim turned down. Smith was a fundamentalist Roman Catholic who had made his name in opposing any form of birth control, stem cell research and abortion—the abortion holocaust was a pet phrase of his—and he was happy to pick up any right-wing cause, real or imagined, that was steered his way. In this case the manipulator was Thang of Boat People SOS. The wily Vietnamese had become a master at disinforming naïve Americans and knew exactly which buttons to press on the American domestic political scene to draw attention to himself.

In practical terms Christopher Smith's agitation came to nothing but with Boat People SOS leading the way, it resulted in a flurry of leaflets, letters and faxes descending on the camps claiming that a new hope had arisen, people should not return and that those who did would all be sent to jail. These were outright lies but they had their effect. Overnight, voluntary return to Vietnam had ground to a halt.

While Blatter could hardly be held responsible for the turn events took he did not react either. That alone might not have carried any consequences for him had Ogata not been taken to task in Washington, had the UNHCR office in Hanoi been better staffed, and had both Khan and Sergio not had an ax to grind with him. But he had stacked the deck against himself and Ogata was put in a position where she had no choice but to remove him from his post. However, for her to accept that someone personally chosen by the Empress had underperformed was a step she would not take. So after she removed him from the Asia Bureau she sent him as Representative to Sarajevo and promoted him to senior director.

This left unanswered the question of who to replace him with. Sergio, for all his brilliance, was still a product of the UN system and while he was aware of its shortcomings he would suffer an occasional relapse into political correctness compounded by a complete misjudgment of people. The promotion of gender equality being a UN mantra and with the problems of the CPA originating in part in Washington, why not chose an American and a woman to boot for the post of Director for Asia? So the choice which he initially submitted to Ogata was Judith Kumin, currently UNHCR representative in Germany.

That the Asian experience of Kumin was limited to a short stint in a Bangkok back office processing resettlement cases was the least of her shortcomings. The flaw lay in her character. Give her a solution and she saw a problem. Give her a problem and she saw a worse one. This constant moaning walked hand in hand with a tendency to confront those around her, a trait that did not exactly make her popular with the German authorities.

Kumin was a single mother and by now her child was in his mid teens, well ensconced among his friends in his school in Germany and when she told him that she had been offered a posting in Geneva, he had a fit; he did not want to move. So Kumin turned down the job. Ultimately, I almost wished that she had not. Given her character, she would in no time have antagonized every single government in Asia, with dire consequences for UNHCR and the spectacle would have been hilarious to watch. But it was not to be and, by default, the job of Director for Asia landed on my lap.

I had barely settled down when an avalanche of letters, all originating from the US, arrived on Ogata's desk. The letters were all the same, and only the senders changed. Association of Vietnamese residents of San Jose, Association of Vietnamese professionals of Burbank, California, Association of Vietnamese communities in the US, Associations of Vietnamese accountants in Dallas Texas and on it went and they all carried the same message: Werner Blatter was an evil-doer but now even worse had come and they were protesting the nomination of the 'even more notorious Dr Casella' as Director for Asia. These were the same words used in a text put on the web by Boat People SOS so there was little doubt as to the origins of the message. Thang was back at his computer, spreading the word.

The letters unnerved *Madame* Ogata. She did not like confrontation or disagreement but would have been hard put to remove me from my post just because a handful of Vietnamese lunatics in the US were unhappy about it.

Werner Blatter seemed to have attracted an incredible amount of dead wood among the dozen people who staffed the Asia Bureau, but among them two pearls stuck out. Kapur was Indian, bright, personable, knew his job, was in charge of the sub-continent and needed no supervision. Colin Mitchell was a solid Australian with plenty of common sense and just the person I needed on the CPA. The rest of the staff I decided to just forget and left them to manage the day-to-day bureaucracy.

Blatter had gone out of his way to keep Sergio out of Asia. It was ridiculous. And counter-productive. Sergio was well known through the region, liked and respected and his charisma and energy could be put to good use. All the UNHCR representatives in the area respected him and if I wanted to pass a message, the most efficient way to do it was to do it through him. So my first foray out of Geneva consisted in organizing a meeting in Singapore for all the UNHCR representatives in Asia chaired by Sergio. For most of them it was a wake-up call. They had fallen into a routine and although they were fully aware that the CPA had come to a standstill, none of them knew what to do about it or had received any instruction to that effect, so jolting them into action became my first priority and Sergio the ideal instrument to do so.

In addressing the troops Sergio was at his best. Since 1979, he said, UNHCR had been in the lead as regards the boat people crisis. Now it had become passive as the CPA had become a football in an American domestic policy game. The time had come to regain the initiative and close down the CPA. If among the screened-out boat people there were some of special interest to the US, that was not the problem of UNHCR but something Washington and Hanoi should work out together. Today the boat people problem was anachronistic and if, 20 years after the end of the Vietnam War, there were still some people in Washington who were refusing to see reality, that was of no concern to UNHCR.

As for return to Vietnam this also had to be approached from a realistic point of view. Voluntary repatriation was all well and good, but it could not be viewed independently from deportation as one encouraged the other. Given that UNHCR had been asked, and had accepted, to monitor every Vietnamese who returned to Vietnam, either voluntarily or forcefully, the office ultimately was involved with deportation. Here we were walking a fine line. UNHCR could not refuse to fund deportation flights but could insist that excessive force not be used in getting the Vietnamese on the aircraft. What excessive force actually meant was not clear but the understanding was that it entailed refraining from actual maiming or bodily injury.

So the message was clear. UNHCR would facilitate any form of return with the understanding that it was pulling out from the Vietnamese boat people saga on June 30, 1996. And if there were any Vietnamese still left in the camps after that date they would no longer be of UNHCR concern.

It was the first time since 1979 that a clear policy line had emerged from Geneva and the drifting was over. Now the UNHCR representatives in the area knew what had to be done.

From Singapore I proceeded to Hanoi where my arrival was met with pleasurable expectations by the Vietnamese local UNHCR staff and with a snarl from Zacagnini who grumbled that the night of the long knives was just around the corner, and right he was.

The authorities were aware that I was coming and the following morning I met with Vice Foreign Minister Nien. He belonged to the new generation of Vietnamese officials and unlike my meetings in previous years, where we had spoken French, we now spoke English. There was also none of the posturing, the cliches or the ideological rhetoric I had come across in the past and he went straight to the point. Vietnam, he said, wanted to consolidate its relations with ASEAN, expedite the closing of the CPA and turn the page on the boat people exodus.

Finally, speaking slowly, Nien indicated that he would be grateful if UNHCR sent a proper representative to Vietnam because, in his words, without good co-operation it would be difficult to deal with the last stage of the CPA.

Coming from a Vietnamese official these were pretty strong words. I did not pass them on to Headquarters and even if I had, the wall of devoted Samurais that Ogata had built around herself to protect her from bad news would never have permitted them to come to her attention. But she had clearly made a bungle out of Vietnam.

If Nien operated at the policy-making level, implementation was in the hands of the Ministry of the Interior, that is the security apparatus and there something had jammed. The man to see, I was told was Senior Colonel Anh, but it proved to be a hard task. Initially, I was told by our local contact with the authorities Mr Son that Colonel Anh would not receive me but then he relented. Apparently he claimed he had met me in 1977 and for this and only this reason he was willing to see me but only outside office hours. Mr Son then arranged for us to meet that very evening for dinner at six in one of Hanoi's many small restaurants.

Colonel Anh looked vaguely familiar but while I would not have recognized him he seemed to recall me. Apparently, he was a junior Captain when we had met and he must have done well because he was now a senior Colonel which in a Western army would be the equivalent of a Brigadier.

Anh was a man of few words and our conversation started off haltingly. 'Are you still with UNHCR?' he asked, as if he did not know the answer. After I answered in the affirmative there was a long silence and then he interjected, 'I don't like them, they have insulted me.'

When I inquired who had been the author of this offense there was another long silence before he said in a low voice, 'the ape.' I could not make head or tail of this until Mr Son started whispering in my ear and slowly I got the message.

Several years earlier Clinton Leeks, the Hong Kong refugee coordinator, had told me how Anvar had bragged to him that he had made a tour of several villages near Hanoi telling the population not to leave by boat. Apparently hundreds if not thousands had come to listen to him and he seemed to derive great pride from this. Clinton seemed somewhat less impressed but had commented that at least Anvar had tried. Had he known the real explanation for Anvar's appeal to the populace he would have been even less impressed.

The Vietnamese, like all East Asians, considered facial hair except among the very aged and in small strands, repugnant, and more relevant to animals than to humans. Anvar had a full head of hair and a flowing beard, both of which he never cut and barely trimmed. Within this hirsute mass you could just about make out a long Assyrian crooked nose, full lips and two small porcine eyes. For a Westerner, the sight was awesome. For a Vietnamese peasant it must have been something akin to a nightmare. Soon the rumor spread like wildfire. A strange creature that talks but does not look quite human can be seen doing the rounds of some villages. Hundreds if not thousands flocked in to see this weird spectacle and speculation ensued; is it human? is it an ape? it does talk but what does it say? where does it come from? The matter was never settled to the farmers' content but one word stuck. He became known among the authorities in Hanoi as the 'ape'. But worse was to come.

There was a meeting in Hanoi with senior government officials and Anvar, as was his wont, lost his temper. 'He screamed at me and pointed his finger at me,' grumbled Colonel Anh. A senior Colonel in Vietnam's Ministry of the Interior was not someone to trifle with and if Anvar had not gotten away with screaming at the very Japanese *Madame* Ogata there was no reason why he would get away with doing it to Senior Colonel Anh. This time, however, he had not so much brought damnation upon himself as on UNHCR and from that day onwards Senior Colonel Anh did not miss one opportunity for making life difficult for the organization. That the Vietnamese system tolerated this idiosyncrasy said much for the way it operated. No one questioned that Colonel Anh had been insulted. He was therefore entitled to get even and as long as this did not compromise the overall functioning of the CPA there was no one to stop him.

'Where is he now?' he asked me.

'Oh,' I replied with feigned indifference, 'he is no longer with UNHCR, *Madame* Ogata spat him out like a cherry stone.' There was a short pause and then he asked, as if he did not know, 'and who replaces him?' 'I do,' I replied. 'Is that so.' He seemed to relax a bit, 'we will continue to accept returnees,' he said, 'but,' and he paused, 'we have some problems. We need to work with people who have some understanding, some good will and some brains. Recently we have had to deal with a person who had no understanding and no good will and there was no co-operation. This is the first time it happened and co-operation broke down. I hear a new UNHCR representative will be coming. I hope this time you will send someone with a brain.'

The message was clear. Zacagnini had to go, and fast. Appealing to Headquarters would serve no purpose. Dismissal was not in the picture and at best it would be months before a new posting could be found for him. My only option therefore was to keep him where he was, but neutralize him. Fortunately he was due to leave the next day for a two-week training seminar in Bangkok. He had barely left the office on the way to the airport when I called our local officer in Saigon, Imran Riza. Imran was Pakistani, educated in Canada and as good as they came. Would he accept the post of acting representative and share his time between Saigon and Hanoi? The request took him totally by surprise but fortunately he accepted. I then drafted a memo, copied to all the UNHCR representatives in the region informing them that Imran Riza was now acting representative in Hanoi. To everyone's great relief Zacagnini, while in Bangkok, found another position which had to be urgently filled and after a brief return to Hanoi to pack, proceeded to his new posting. I never saw him again but his performance in Vietnam proved no handicap to his career and over the following years he sailed unscathed from one promotion to another ending up with the grade of director.

Having stabilized our position in Hanoi I proceeded to Hong Kong where the situation was still very much in deadlock. With the camps open to a constant propaganda barrage from the US, voluntary repatriation had ground to a halt and the only returns were through occasional deportation flights. These however were increasingly difficult to implement, as extracting returnees from the camps required a major police operation and even by the most optimistic calculation, there was no way that the camps could be closed down by July 1, 1996, the official closing date of the CPA. This left me with only one solution; making an exception for Hong Kong and prolonging the CPA. In theory this might have ensured that the Vietnamese in the camps who were still refusing to return to Vietnam would linger in Hong Kong for years to come, I felt confident this would not occur and for good reason. Beijing had made it clear that they did not want a single boat person left in the territory by the date scheduled for the handover of the colony, namely July 1997.

News of this demand had never been actively disseminated in the camps so I suggested that a clear-cut message be passed on to the Vietnamese: you can chose between going back voluntarily to Vietnam now or staying in the camps but on July 1, 1997, the Chinese will take over and good luck to you. The Hong Kong authorities were worried that the message would displease the Chinese, but I convinced them that Beijing would be even more displeased if they found any Vietnamese in the territory on the day of the handover so they screwed up their courage and passed the message in the camps.

It hit home. The only people that the Vietnamese took seriously were the Chinese and as the handover date came closer, returns to Vietnam escalated.

From Hong Kong I proceeded to Beijing, more as a matter of courtesy than to discuss any matters of substance. The boat people crisis, which had cast the Soviet-aligned regime in Hanoi as the mad dog of Asia, had played into the hands of the Chinese. But with the collapse of the Soviet Union, Vietnam was no longer an issue for them and whatever happened to the CPA was now of no direct concern to them.

But there was one issue that they had not forgotten: the expulsion by Hanoi of its Chinese community in 1978. This was a subject which they were liable to reactivate any time they wished to put pressure on Vietnam so ultimately bringing it to a formal closing at an acceptable price would have been in Hanoi's interest.

The problem was not on my to do list and I did not expect the Chinese to raise it, but they did. Their suggestion was that UNHCR register all candidates for return with a cut-off date, that Hanoi approve some for return with a reintegration package from UNHCR and that China naturalize the rest, bringing the issue to a close.

There were two elements that made the offer credible in my view. First, it did not come from the Foreign Ministry but from the Ministry of Civil Affairs, which dealt directly with these people and had every interest in having the case closed. Second, the Chinese had not raised the contentious issue of the nationality of the Chinese from Vietnam, which meant that they were not looking for a confrontation but rather a solution.

Three days later I was back in Hanoi where I broached the proposal to Vice Foreign Minister Nien. His first reaction was surprise. Why would the Chinese raise this issue through UNHCR? he asked.

I told him that I did not know the answer to his question but my personal opinion was that if a token, face-saving return could be agreed upon, it was a worthwhile price to pay for China considering the issue closed.

Back in Geneva, to test the water, I sent an official letter to Nien, thanking him for having received me and adding that regarding the 'other matter'—I purposely refrained from being more specific—UNHCR is available to provide its services. The last thing I expected from him was a written reply but it came.

'The matter you mentioned,' he wrote, 'is rather delicate but under consideration.' He had not yet opened the door but at least he had not banged it shut either.

By now I had things more or less under control. Irene Khan had aspired to the post of UNHCR representative in New Delhi and as I did not care if she got it or not, I signed off on it. In retrospect Blatter had not been wrong in refusing her the job. After less than one year in New Delhi the Indian Ambassador in Geneva sent one of his diplomats to see the Deputy High Commissioner with an unequivocal message: either UNHCR withdraw Irene Khan from New Delhi or she would be formally expelled. Asked for the reason of this opprobrium he replied with one word: arrogant. India being the mother of arrogance he must have known what he was talking about. So she came back to Geneva her tail between her legs. But she was a clever operator and after Ogata's departure she jumped ship and suddenly emerged as Secretary General of Amnesty International, a position which enabled her to vent her aggressivity unrestrained. But even that did not seem to last. One year and two months short of the end of her second mandate she suddenly dissapeared from the Amnesty masthead to be replaced by an acting Secretary General. Why this sudden departure? No explanation was ever provided. Then, in February 2011, the *Daily Mail* let the cat out of the bag. One year short of the end of her second term the board of Amnesty International, dissatisfied with her performance, decided to get rid of her. To do so they had two choices. They could either sack her or pay her to leave. Fearing a scandal if they publicly sacked her they offered her a payoff of some 700,000 US $ if she agree to discreetly step down from her job. She took the money and ran and the matter would have remained confidential had not the *Daily Mail* spilled the beans and, in the process, seriously questioned the integrity and practices of Amnesty International not to say the greed of Irene Khan.

Six months after having taken over the Asia bureau, things has fallen unto place. In South East Asia all the UNHCR representatives in the region were on board and if they did not always follow my suggestions they did respond to what Sergio told them, so when required I used him to pass on the message. I had patched up our relations with Hanoi where Imran Riza could be counted on to do the right thing. Rob Van Leeuwen had left Hong Kong and I had been able to hand-pick his replacement, a deceptively cunning Swiss, able to outsmart any Vietnamese. So all I needed now was to empty the camps of some 35,000 boat people, none of whom qualified for refugee status, and all of whom were resisting repatriation. But not for long.

In January 1996, I arranged an informal ASEAN meeting in Bangkok about the CPA. Sergio was to be our star performer and we agreed that if there was need for a bad guy it would be me.

The real purpose of the meeting, which was presented as informal and piously defined as an exchange of views, was to force on a number of reluctant Asian governments the closure of the CPA. The issue here was not so much whether governments wanted to turn the page on the boat people crisis but how far would they be willing to go to do so. Clearly there were two approaches here, a Western approach and an Asian one. The Western approach, of which Hong Kong was a prime example, was to aim for a complete solution that demanded that all remaining screened out Vietnamese return to Vietnam followed by a closure of the camps.

The Thais, Indonesians, Filipinos and to a lesser extent the Malaysians were somewhat less clear-cut in their approach to the problem. For them life was by definition imperfect. Problems would always exist and keeping them under control to the point where one could disregard them was about as much as one could hope for. Granted they certainly did not want to see the arrival of any new Vietnamese boat people and were not contemplating accepting any for resettlement either but the continued presence on their soil of a few hundred Vietnamese in a small camp here and there for which they did not have to pay was something they could live with.

But not the US. Washington knew that as long as there were just a handful of Vietnamese boat people in even the smallest of camps in South East Asia these would provide the pretext for renewed assaults against the administration by radical right-wing congressmen and Vietnam War nostalgics. Washington therefore was aiming for a total end to the CPA and this was also the position of UNHCR. On the other hand Washington was still reluctant to endorse the principle of forced return and preferred to leave this responsibility to others.

So the undeclared purpose of the Bangkok meeting was to jolt Thailand, Malaysia and Indonesia into action, which in practice meant getting them to sit down with the Vietnamese and agree on a return scheme for the remaining caseload in the camps. That such a scheme could not rely only on voluntary repatriation but had to include a deportation component, now piously renamed Orderly Repatriation Program (ORP), was a given.

In substance, repatriation meant that a Vietnamese in a camp would be told, 'we have examined your request for refugee status; it was turned down because you don't qualify so no country will accept you for resettlement and, as you cannot stay in this camp for ever, you have to return to Vietnam. In doing so you will get a repatriation allowance (it had been cut only for the Vietnamese returning from Hong Kong) and once home we will monitor the commitment of your government not to prosecute you for your illegal departure. Now you have two choices. You can either volunteer for return and you will then board an aircraft and be flown back to Vietnam. Alternatively you can refuse to go back, upon which we will take you by the scruff of the neck, drag you onto a ship or an aircraft and with a policeman sitting on each side fly you to Vietnam with a reduced resettlement grant and a kick in the pants.'

The Bangkok meeting was the opportunity for me to agree with Sergio on what would be the UNHCR bottom line. We had enough funds to pay for the camps until June 30 and after that governments would be on their own. UNHCR was pulling out and if any government in the region wanted to keep any Vietnamese and pay the costs they were welcome to do so. In fact it was all a bluff. UNHCR still had more money than it could spend but if the governments in the region even suspected it, there would be no end to the CPA.

The task of convincing governments that we had reached the end of the road fell to me. Had they known that I was Director for Asia '*ad interim*' and was due to leave UNHCR within three months their most probable reaction would have been, let's wait and see what the next Director for Asia has to say. But they did not know and I was taken seriously.

Until now all returns had been by air, which was costly and limited the number of people that could be transported in one lot. Malaysia and Indonesia had, several months before the Bangkok meeting, raised the possibility of transport by sea but this had been rejected by the Vietnamese on the grounds that the numbers exceeded their capacity to process the arrivals on return. At Bangkok the option of return by sea was raised again but in a new environment. By now, normalizing relations with its neighbors was one of Hanoi's priorities. Likewise, the role of UNHCR as an intermediary was no longer necessary and could even have been counterproductive as that parties might have been tempted to evade their responsibilities by trying to shift them on to us. I therefore suggested that the issue of return by sea be discussed directly between Vietnam, Malaysia, Thailand and Indonesia in a closed meeting without my presence. The exchange only lasted one hour but when it ended the participants were beaming. The Vietnamese had agreed to returns by sea.

I had systematically been briefing journalists on the CPA and the announcement that it would be closed on June 30 made the front pages of the Asian media. The news then started slowly filtering into the camps that the end was near and that the likes of Lionel Rosenblatt, Boat People SOS and Christopher Smith had no chance of delaying the unavoidable. Little by little voluntary repatriation started to take off again.

With the dynamics of return now under way, Imran Riza's term in Saigon was coming to a close and I needed a replacement there.

While the post had been classified as a junior one by the UNHCR bureaucracy it was a key position because it included supervising the monitoring of the returnees in the South and receiving countless American delegations visiting Saigon, all looking for flaws in the monitoring process. Dealing with them required communication skills and a good knowledge of the region and there was no better choice for the post than Giuseppe De Vincentiis. His assignment in Geneva was coming to an end and while it took some doing I managed to get him assigned to Ho Chi Minh city.

Until then, following my assignments as ad interim Director for Asia, he had been running both our Radio program in Albania and Operation ReUNite single-handed and with his departure the two projects collapsed overnight to the complete indifference both of Ogata and the rest of the organization. Not only was the technology lost but also the investment made by UNHCR, namely half a million dollars from the Soros contribution, but I was not going to shed any tears over that. I had just found out that the year before both Rosenblatt and Thang from Boat People SOS had received a lifetime achievement award from the National Alliance of Vietnamese Service Agencies, an organization partly funded by no less than Soros's Open Society Institute. Soros could not possibly know where each of his dollars went but if this was the sort of people he was supporting, half a million of his dollars down the drain was not something I was too bothered about.

Yet I did regret the demise of ReUNite. While the technology was in its infancy it could have been developed and, in addition, there were still a sizable amount of mothers in Bosnia looking for their lost children but visibly this was not of great concern to Ogata. As for me, I had done my best but to no avail; pearls to pigs.

By March 1996, Giuseppe was well ensconced in Saigon and our new Representative, Catherine Bertrand, had arrived in Hanoi. She was French, had served in Hong Kong and although not a political mind, she more than made up for it by being solid, competent, friendly with a down to earth common sense. With Catherine having got the hang of things in Hanoi and Vietnam having accepted the principal of returns by sea only one thing was missing. Clearances for enough returnees to actually fill a ship. The only person who could do something about this was Colonel Anh and it was not without some apprehension that I went to see him taking Catherine along but I need not have worried.

Apparently he had agreed with the Malaysians to clear 2,200 returnees between mid-April and mid-May. Whether these would be forced or voluntary returns was now irrelevant. The boat people, with a police escort, would be put on four ships belonging to the Malaysian navy with the charter costs paid for by UNHCR, and brought back to South Vietnam.

'But,' said Colonel Anh, 'there remains a problem. Clearances.' Each candidate for return had to be individually cleared which meant checking his background and his last place of residence in Vietnam and this was not always easy. Many of the returnees had lived in remote hamlets, with no communications. This meant that the teams from the Ministry of the Interior, when operating from isolated hamlets then had to travel back to a larger village or small town where communications were available in order to notify the central authorities that clearance had been granted. This problem had not arisen in the North where most of the returnees were from the Hanoi and Haiphong area, but in the South the areas of departure were far more widespread and communications not so good. The end result was that clearances for the South were far more time consuming than in the North and he had problems keeping up with the agreed timetable for return. To expedite the matter Colonel Anh needed some communication equipment, specifically portable radio sets, so the clearance teams could report on their work even from remote hamlets.

That was fine with me I told him, but I needed specifics as well as his personal commitment that clearances would indeed be accelerated. 'Do you have a list of equipment and a costing?' I asked him.

'Yes,' he answered, drawing a sheet of paper from his desk, 'here it is.' I glanced at it. It was a list with, at the bottom of the page, the estimated cost of 60,000 US $. I passed it on to Catherine.

'It is fine,' I told him.

'Oh,' he hesitated, 'so you will send it to your Headquarters for approval?

'No,' I told him, 'I am approving it here, now,' I thought I detected a slight choking sound coming from Catherine, 'and when I go back to our office I will make a note for Catherine approving the disbursement and you can work out the details with her.'

Colonel Anh was momentarily stunned but he quickly regained his composure. 'This is good, he said, now the clearance teams can work well.'

Back in the UNHCR office I reassured Catherine. 'We have more money than we can use,' I told her and on the CPA Sergio had been more than clear. 'Do whatever has to be done but get the damn thing closed down and quickly.'

My next hurdle was Malaysia. The total boat people caseload stood at some 2,250 none of whom qualified for refugee status and all due to return to Vietnam. Egged on by a barrage of messages originating in the US suggesting that if they resisted repatriation there would be a last minute intervention to have them accepted by the US, they were becoming increasingly aggressive. Camp authorities were being regularly insulted and taunted, culminating in one group setting fire to their barrack in mid-January 1996. Police and firemen were brought in and what could have turned into a generalized riot was brought under control. However, rebuilding the barrack which the Vietnamese themselves had torched was not something the Malaysians, or even UNHCR, was even considering. So the boat people were given some plastic sheeting and told that this was what they would have to make do with. This was cause enough for Amnesty International to thrust themselves into the picture and they publicly denounced UNHCR for forcing boat people to live in the open without shelter. The fact that it was the boat people themselves who, by setting fire to their barrack, were the cause of their current predicament was of course carefully omitted.

The next person to join in the fray was Representative Christopher Smith. In a scathing letter to Ogata he bemoaned the fate of the refugees and demanded that their barrack be rebuilt at the earliest opportunity.

No one at UNHCR liked answering that type of letter and it ended up on my desk with a request that I reply under my name. I could not have asked for a better opportunity for some fun. The man, I remembered, was a radical right-wing Roman Catholic and the opportunity to address him with his own argument proved irresistible.

'Dear Representative Smith,' I wrote, 'I have been requested to extend to you our deepest appreciation for the letter you sent to High Commissioner Ogata expressing your concern for refugees. These, as you know, are people throughout the world who are often in very difficult situations. They deserve all the support they can get, and your concern for them is a great encouragement for us.

You will be very pleased to learn that that the Vietnamese you refer to are not refugees. After a very thorough screening, which has been systematically double-checked, it was determined that under current international procedure they do not qualify for refugee status. They are therefore due to return to Vietnam under an amnesty program that provides that they will not be held accountable for illegal departure. More than 70,000 have already retuned under this program and UNHCR, which has several monitoring teams operating throughout Vietnam, is satisfied that the Vietnamese authorities have abided by their commitment not to punish returnees for having illegally left the country.

Regarding the specific group to which you refer, it is correct that they are currently living under plastic sheeting in a situation which might be uncomfortable but is certainly not life-threatening. The reason for this situation is exclusively of their own doing. They used to live in a comfortable barrack until, in the course of a riot, they deliberately set it on fire, hence their current predicament. We noted your request that we should rebuild the barrack. This would not only entail considerable expense but there is no guarantee that they would not set it on fire again. But this is only one part of the problem. UNHCR is responsible for millions of refuges worldwide, many of whom survive in extremely precarious situations. In some situations we have major shortages of funds and refugees have to survive on less than one dollar per day. Under these circumstances we believe it would be profoundly immoral to deprive of assistance refugees in other parts of the world, who are on the edge of starvation, in order to divert funds to rebuild a comfortable and expensive barrack that non-refugees have taken on themselves to set on fire. We strongly believe that all individuals should be responsible for their own actions.

These Vietnamese are the guests of Malaysia and should behave accordingly. In your capacity as an elected member of the US Congress I ask you to call upon them and command them to abide by the laws of the land, respect their local police and refrain from committing arson and destroying public and private property. I am sure your voice will be listened to and that it will contribute to restoring law and order among this group.'

I obviously did not clear the letter with anyone within UNHCR, but I did show it to Sergio. He was the one who had forwarded it to me. 'I thought you would enjoy answering it,' he said laughing. My answer must have done the trick for it was the last we heard of Christopher Smith.

My other problem in Malaysia was in-house. Erika Feller, the UNHCR representative in Kuala Lumpur, was an Australian of German descent and a lawyer by training who had joined UNHCR in 1986. If there ever was a cliche of a Prussian schoolteacher it was her. Pig headed, unimaginative, dogmatic, never giving up she would get her point across through sheer perseverance and repetitive argument.

Her current job was to ensure the rapid conclusion of the forced repatriation of the remaining boat people caseload and the closure of their camp. This was a task that she was reluctant to undertake on principle, as UNHCR, in her narrow world, did not get involved in deportation. And the fact that sometimes in order to solve a refugee situation one had to also deal with non-refugees was beyond her grasp.

So she stonewalled but she also hated being away from Geneva and was only waiting for the day she could return and when I pointed out to her that this would not happen until she closed the camps, her personal interest got the better of her principles. With a clear goal now in sight she suddenly turned into a paradigm of Germanic zeal; in three quick ruthless sweeps by the Malaysian police, which she had enlisted for the job, the remaining boat people were hustled on to naval landing ships and dispatched to Vietnam with no more ado. Her forcefulness actually made her task easier. As more and more camp inmates realized that salvation from the US was not forthcoming and return inevitable, they chose to opt for voluntary repatriation as a far more comfortable way of return. Altogether three ships from Malaysia and one from Indonesia brought back the remaining boat people to ports in Southern Vietnam and on June 25, Sergio, at a ceremony held at the Sungai Besi camp in Malaysia, proclaimed the closing of the CPA and with it the ending of the Vietnamese boat people crisis. As for Erika Feller, she returned to Geneva where, over the years, she reached the rank of Assistant High Commissioner, an achievement made even more remarkable by the fact that except for 2 years in Kuala Lumpur all her time was spent at Headquarters. In an organization where promotion was allegedly subject to field service it was a record.

The last unsolved issue was the question of the Chinese from Vietnam who had been expelled to China. The Vietnamese claimed there was no problem and the matter was solved. The Chinese claimed there was a problem and the matter was not solved. Operating on the principle that if one of two parties in a disagreement claims there is a problem and the other claims there is none, there is a problem, I felt a last attempt to address the issue was warranted.

But with five days remaining between Sergio proclaiming the end of the CPA and my retirement from UNHCR, it was not to be.

ANOTHER WORLD

I left UNHCR on June 30, 1996, and some six weeks later Sergio called me. Apparently Ogata had just received a letter from the Chinese Minister of Civil Affairs suggesting that my expertise not be lost to UNHCR. The implication was clear. Not only did the Chinese want me to continue, in one form or another, to work on the issue of the ethnic Chinese expelled from Vietnam but the fact that the minister himself had chosen to write personally to Ogata showed that for China the issue was not unimportant. Faced with the request Ogata had two options. She could answer positively and retain me as a consultant, or she could answer positively and do nothing about it.

But she chose a third way. *Madame* Ogata belonged to that generation of Japanese for whom a difficultly in countenancing China was a given. It was not that she disliked the Chinese; they just went against her grain. During the Second World War her father had successively served as Japanese consul in Canton and Hong Kong and whenever the subject was raised she would speak unendingly about the good times she had in China as a young girl and all the pleasant memories she had come back with. That these were the darkest days of the Japanese occupation which brought about the death of millions of Chinese clearly did not occur to her. Once in Hong Kong during a press conference, it took all the persuasion her assistants could muster to discourage her from commenting about the fond memories she had of her stay in the territory in 1944.

It was probably unconscious on her part but telling a Chinese Minister to go fly a kite was a temptation she could not resist. So she wrote back telling him, as if he did not know, that I was no longer with UNHCR, that she had nominated a new Director for Asia and that was that.

It was the last I ever saw of *Madame* Ogata except for a brief encounter many years later, at Bloomingdales in New York. As we exchanged perfunctory greetings she enquired, 'How does it feel to have left UNHCR?' I did not pause to think. '*Madame,*' I replied, 'I don't know, I never joined.'

I came back from my twenty-year stint with UNHCR to a changed world. The end of the cold war combined with Asia's transition from an arena of confrontation to an arena of economic development had opened up a new era and while it was all for the better, with no wars to report on, no refugees to look after and no ideological confrontation to challenge the mind, the region was slowly becoming, as far as I was concerned, singularly boring. This, I realized, was a perception that did me no honor. Indeed the challenges of investment, development, trade and entrepreneurship were at least as exhilarating and certainly more constructive than the ones I had witnessed and they demanded participation while, over the years, I had essentially been an observer with an impact on reality that was more imagined than real.

The end result was that my terms of references, the French educated Vietnamese revolutionary with an uncanny sense of humor or the Chinese airline clerk who claimed that he did not work for money were now a thing of the past. So was the physical discomfort that was part and parcel of the thrill given by the illusion of having had a finger on the pulse of history. Spending two years in the *Thong Nhut* hotel in Hanoi between 1975 and 1977 had been an adventure. But when I went back to Hanoi in 1998 there was no more *Thong Nhut* hotel. The building was still there, carefully restored to its former glory but again directed by a French manager under its original name, hotel *Metropole*. During French colonial rule it had been the best hotel in Hanoi and some 45 years later in a unified and socialist Vietnam it was again the best hotel in Hanoi. As for room 324, my home for many months, it was still in the same location but the bathroom was in marble, the floor covered by a plush carpeting, the furniture fake Louis XVI and the purr of the central air-conditioning barely audible. What I had known as the last frontier had become mainstream.

Originally, I had drifted into UNHCR and now, although my contractual relation with the organization was terminated, I only slowly drifted away from the world of international bureaucracy in which I still kept a foot.

It is axiomatic of bureaucracies that it is not so much individuals as clans that rise and fall. Clans have leaders who drag behind them a retinue of aides, partisans, courtesans and hangers-on whose fate is directly tied to the one at the head of the herd. I was no exception to this rule and my bureaucratic fate, if there was to be one, was now tied to two individuals; Sergio Vieira de Mello and Jonas Widgren.

Sergio had left UNHCR and after a short stint with the UN in New York had been nominated as the UN top man in East Timor. We would call each other about once a month and I believed that he liked the idea that in case of need I would be available to him. He had many such relationships, both within and outside the UN system, and he made good use of them to further his career. But he also sometimes needed encouragement or the confirmation that what he was doing was the right thing and I obviously was someone he felt comfortable talking to. Last but not least, there was also a bit of the schoolboy in the inveterate Don Juan and he had to have someone to whom to crow about his feminine conquests.

It was an altogether different game with Jonas Widgren. I had met him in Beirut when he was the Swedish Secretary of State for Immigration and had kept up with him over the years. In 1993 he had set up his own shop, ICMPD, the International Center for Migration Policy Development. Based in Vienna it was essentially a think tank created by the Europeans to help them design their asylum, migration and border control policies. Jonas could be erratic, disorganized and impulsive but he was also incredibly intelligent, had vision and a touch of creativity and when he offered me to become ICMPD's representative in Geneva at a token salary I jumped at the occasion.

ICMPD was a purely European organization deeply involved in helping European governments address the population inflow that resulted from the Balkan crisis and representing it provided me with the unique opportunity of observing from the sidelines the slow, steady sinking of UNHCR.

In 1991, when *Madame* Ogata became High Commissioner, the organization had a budget of some 800 million US $ and a staff of some 2500. Then the Bosnian crisis erupted. It was to prove the acme of her stewardship of UNHCR. With uncanny political savvy and against the opinion of most of her senior staff she rushed in. On paper the war was a civil conflict outside the mandate of UNHCR, so normally, she should have stayed out. But there was a vacuum, ICRC had retreated into a stunned inaction, international NGOs were nowhere and governments expected that something be done, albeit not by them. Suddenly there was a window of opportunity and she stormed in. It was to be her apotheosis with one qualifier. Purely by chance, she had the right man at the right place at the right time. José María Mendiluce was a charismatic Spaniard with a gargantuan ego, a gift for leadership and a total disregard for red tape. Where others would have treaded fearfully he threw caution to the wind and charged ahead. When trucks were needed to deliver food he would rent them on the spot, have them painted white, the color of the UN and get them on the road in 24 hours, rather than, to the despair of the bean counters at Headquarters, go through UN procurement procedures and waste months in the process. The combination of Ogata in Geneva and the action man Mendiluce on the ground proved an overwhelming success. Suddenly UNHCR, and Ogata in particular, were day after day front page news. But it could not last. Peace came to Bosnia, Jose María Mendiluce had done his time and was shunted aside as UNHCR Representative in Bruxelles, possible the most bureaucratic assignment there was, before leaving the organization altogether and Ogata found herself again with a yearly budget of some 800 million US dollars but this time with 5,600 staff members. But worse was to come. Not only had she twice more staff than she had started off with but they were also increasingly the wrong people.

Madame Ogata, her sense of humor notwithstanding, came from a culture that was built on consensus and conformity and where there was no room for diversity of views. During her weekly directors meetings, more aptly described as her holding court, the participants would exert themselves to anticipate her wishes upon which she would address them with a satisfied nod and announce, 'so we have a consensus'. At heart she was a schoolteacher, vain, insecure, authoritarian, of imposing demeanor and yet only really at her ease when addressing the schoolchildren from the height of her pulpit, a cane close at hand. Little by little, over the years, every nail that stuck out was hammered in. Step by step she started shunting aside all those who stood out, who were maybe a bit too bright, too quick or too unconventional and with mediocrity feeding on itself the upper reaches of the organization slowly became a self-perpetuating haven for the second rate. It took some years of doing but by the end of her mandate the brilliant mavericks, the creative oddball or even the mildly unconventional had either been sidetracked, left the organization, sought early retirement or, like Sergio, had joined other organizations in the UN system. Granted they alone had not made what UNHCR had been at its best. But they, combined with the bean counters, the lawyers, the slogging field officers and the pedantic administrators, had contributed that extra spark of imagination and intelligence that had made UNHCR over the years the best of a bad lot. Now they were all gone. Ogata had leveled the field. Japan Inc had taken over.

On March 23, 1999, I attended with Widgren a meeting of European government representatives called by the Swiss authorities in Bern to discuss the potential crisis in Kosovo. While most of the participants adopted a wait-and-see attitude, Widgren was emphatic; any military operation in the region, he claimed, would be used by the Yugoslavs as a pretext to expel as many Kosovars as they could. Hundreds of thousands would converge on Albania and Macedonia creating a major humanitarian crisis.

The only dissenting voice came from UNHCR. Nicholas Morris some fifteen years previously had cost Hartling a truncated second term when he had failed to adequately plan ahead for a crisis that was looming in Sudan. Morris had all the qualities that appealed to Ogata—a well-mannered Australian with the airs of an Englishman who in public addressed her as High Commissioner, yes High Commissioner, of course High Commissioner, and was obsequious to perfection. She had promoted him to senior director and assigned him as her special envoy to former Yugoslavia in replacement of the flamboyant Mendiluce and history repeated itself. All is under control, explained Morris, we have planned for every emergency.

The following day, March 24, NATO unleashed its bombers to force Serbia out of Kosovo and what Widgren had predicted arrived. Hundreds upon thousands of Kosovars started pouring into Albania and Macedonia and within days UNHCR started blaring for help. Morris had repeated all the blunders that had cost Hartling so dearly. His advance planning had no bearing to reality and with some 850,000 Kosovar refugees pouring into Albania and Macedonia the whole UNHCR machinery in the region not so much ground to a stop but actually never took off. Conversely, the NGOs were ready and in a matter of weeks they occupied the ground leaving UNHCR on the side, a helpless spectator at best

On June 12, NATO forces entered Kosovo and the Kosovar refugees who had fled to Albania and Macedonia started to stampede back home. When the exodus from Kosovo had started Ogata had been unprepared to receive them. Now she proved equally unprepared for their return and as up to 40,000 Kosovars per day clogged the roads on their way home UNHCR had become irrelevant. By early July the game was over and they had practically all gone home. Japan Inc had missed the boat both ways.

Madame Ogata left UNHCR the following year, her reputation within the UN system in shambles but her international image intact. As for the UNHCR she left behind, it had become a self-perpetuating haven of mediocrity.

Sergio, after having spent two years in East Timor which he steered to independence, was now High Commissioner for Human Rights, a position which he did not particularly aspire to but which was the only one offered to him by UN Secretary General Kofi Annan. Sergio was particularly interested in a dialogue with China. We spent a lot of time brainstorming and finally concurred that few countries had made such progress in terms of human rights as had China over the last 50 years. Five thousand years of imperial power followed by 40 years of civil war and a Japanese invasion of incredible brutality had culminated in the coming to power in 1949, of a totalitarian regime in which the individual was perceived as nothing more than a tool of social engineering. Nonetheless, the regime had achieved the human right of national rule, political stability as opposed to anarchy, food, work, albeit badly paid, as well as basic education and some basic medical care. It had not been a linear progression and the aberrations that were the great leap forward and the Cultural Revolution cost the country dearly but by the time Mao died in 1976 China was again a nation and no longer the sick man of Asia. In the thirty years following his death the regime evolved from a totalitarian state which sought to create a new socialist man to a one-party dictatorship whose main concern was to retain political power rather than regulate the daily life of the average Chinese. But while in terms of human rights the regime was now not dissimilar from those the US had promoted in South Vietnam, Indonesia or Thailand during the cold war the international climate had changed. The end of the cold war, the revolution in communications, the emergence of a human rights industry promoted by the advocacy groups combined with evolving ethical principles which conveniently came about when the double standards of the cold war were no longer needed suddenly made human rights in China a front page issue. So paradoxically, as the respect for human rights in China slowly improved, the regime became increasingly susceptible to being attacked on that issue. By the same token however, it was not totally unreceptive to a dialogue on human rights.

Sergio, with whom I discussed the issue at length, was very sensitive to these developments and had decided to capitalize on them. However, what he sought were practical results not posturing.

In early 2003, Sergio was planning a visit to Beijing sometime in September, but he also felt his credibility would be hurt if he came out of China empty handed and by empty handed he meant with some pious statement and nothing else. What Sergio wanted was results but he also knew that obtaining them required time and careful planning. What he suggested therefore was that I go to Beijing prior to his visit in some sort of informal capacity as his adviser, discuss with the Chinese, see what they expected from him and, in the best case scenario, agree that upon his leaving China a couple of dissidents would be released and he could fly out with them.

I approached the Chinese mission in New York where I knew one of the ambassadors with whom I had worked 15 years prior on the Vietnamese refugee issue with this idea and the answer came back within days. The Foreign Ministry looked forward to receiving me and appreciated the form of the approach. Things looked on track and I made plans to go to Beijing sometime in August when suddenly SARS struck.

SARS as such did not worry me too much but getting stuck in Beijing in case the country proclaimed quarantine did. So together with Sergio we sent a message to Beijing saying that, considering how busy the Chinese authorities were dealing with SARS, it might be easier for them if I postponed my trip to September and Sergio's to October. Actually we need not have bothered. By September Sergio was dead and the whole exercise was off.

On March 30, 2003, the United States invaded Iraq. While the invasion had not been endorsed by the UN Security, the world body on May 22 adopted a resolution that provide for a significant UN role in the reconstruction of the country and the nomination of a special Representative of the Secretary General to be in charge of this new mission. Why UN Secretary General Kofi Annan asked Sergio, who already had a job, to take the position has never been fully clarified. President Bush had received Sergio, as High Commissioner for Human Rights, and the two had hit it off beautifully. So one rumor had it that it was Condoleezza Rice who had personally called Annan, asking that Sergio be nominated for the post. Others claimed however that it was Annan's idea to assign the post to Sergio. He knew the Sergio had made a strong impression on Bush and saw his nomination as some way of placating Washington with which he had had an increasingly tense relation. But whatever the explanation, the signature on the document assigning Sergio to Baghdad was Annan's and Annan's alone.

While the UN Secretary General is defined by the UN charter as the chief administrative officer of the organization, Annan and his minders had over the years inflated the position to that of some sort of a lay pope who embodied the principles of the UN charter. When the US invaded Iraq without UN Security Council's endorsement, Annan was caught at his own game. He had turned an administrative position into the likes of a moral entity. Now he was expected to pass judgment. That, however, went against his grain. He had built his whole career on not taking sides and while it was obvious from some of his ambivalent pronouncements that he was not in favor of the invasion, this was as far as he would go. In doing so he alienated everyone. The Bush administration resented his lack of support not to say his implied criticism of the invasion and those who opposed the invasion resented him for not taking a stand. Suddenly the man whom one of his close associates had described as the ultimate fence sitter found the fence too narrow to sit upon. So the choice of Sergio of all people, while there was no shortage of candidates for the post, whether on his own initiative or one suggested by Washington, could not have been anything else than an attempt by Annan to mollify the Bush administration. Whatever the ins and outs of his nomination what was sure was that Sergio did not want the job. Nor did any of his friends encourage him to take it either. Arnaout, whom Sergio consulted, was a buffoon but he was also far from stupid and, in addition to having a soft spot for Sergio had an uncanny feel for what the Middle East was all about. 'Don't go,' he pleaded with Sergio, 'don't go, they will kill you.'

But Sergio went and, being Sergio he set out to make a good job of the assignment with one provision however. It would be a temporary assignment. Annan had sent him to East Timor for three months and had kept him there for two years. This time Sergio did not trust him so he demanded that his assignment be for four months only and it be put on paper. Sergio's request was legitimate. He was after all High Commissioner for Human Rights. What was not, was Annan's acceptance. Baghdad was probably the single most important post for the UN and a four months long assignment flew in the face of common sense. But so it was.

On August 19, a suicide bomber leisurely drove a truck loaded with explosives up to the wing of the Canal hotel in Baghdad where Sergio had his office and blew himself up, killing Sergio and 22 other UN staff members. I heard of the bombing on the radio and immediately called him on his portable telephone. I got his answering machine and, believing him only to be wounded, I left him a message. 'Sergio, hold tight.' But then, having survived a couple of hours under the rubble and with no available equipment to rescue him, he was dead.

The attack sent the UN stampeding out of Baghdad and brought to a close any significant UN role in the future of Iraq.

Following the bombing, Martti Ahtisaari, a former president of Finland, was asked to make an investigation of the circumstances surrounding the attack. Ahtisaari's report was a damning indictment of the way Annan ran his shop and could be summarized in one word; dysfunctional. But was it? Granted, the attack could easily have been thwarted by setting up any sort of barrier that would have impeded the truck bomb from driving up to the building where Sergio had his office. Granted, the most elementary security precautions such as lining the windows with anti fragmentation film had not been taken, but then who was there to take them? The head of security for the UN was a genial Burmese and his deputy an American woman. Neither had any background in security but their choice did conform to UN standards. A unit, headed by a male from the third world with as his deputy a female from an industrialized country was the perfect combination of gender and regional balance. So, when all was said and done, what was dysfunctional? The way Annan was running his shop or the shop itself or both?

Visibly stung by Ahtisaari's report, Annan ordered a follow up study by a security panel to determine the level of personal responsibilities as regards the attack. A shudder of disbelief ran through the UN staff when it was announced whom Annan had selected to chair the panel: Gerald Walzer. Walzer was a high school graduate who had joined UNHCR as a finance clerk at the age of 19. Over the years the obsequious Austrian, laboring in the burrows of UNHCR's finances, had wormed his way up the bureaucratic ladder until he had caught the attention of *Madame* Ogata. She was, at the time, looking for a new Deputy High Commissioner and on a Friday had mentioned to Sergio that she was considering him for the post. Then over the week-end she changed her mind and on Monday announced that she had selected Walzer. From her warped perspective the choice made sense. In Walzer she found a reassuring figure who kept on guaranteeing that everything was under control without there ever being a risk that he would stress her intelligence. So Walzer became Deputy High Commissioner before retiring two years before she did, only to be resuscitated by Kofi Annan. Walzer's only qualification for the job was that he was an old friend of Annan. That his security experience was exactly zero was obviously irrelevant. On the plus side however he was not one to unearth what he was not expected to expose and the conclusions that he reached surprised no one. All those involved in Iraq bore some degree of responsibility for the security lapses that had led to the attack, all that is with one exception: Kofi Annan. He and he alone was innocent on all counts and white as snow.

President Harry Truman had a sign on his desk that read: the buck stops here. But that was the United States, not the United Nations. Had Annan acknowledged that having sent Sergio to Baghdad he was responsible to the best of his ability for ensuring his security and that of all the UN staff there, that he had been remiss in discharging his duty and wished to make public amends by recognizing his failings he might well have gotten away with it. But Annan was the quintessential representative of a bureaucracy where passing the buck was the rule and the word accountability not part of the vocabulary. So he chose Walzer, who duly produced the whitewash that was expected of him. But while the result of the exercise was predictable albeit craven, it was also surreal. Walzer was a non-entity and he could not, had he ever wished to, whitewash even his own backside not to say the one of a UN Secretary General. Ultimately of course Annan, if his ultimate aim was to hang on to the job of Secretary General and the perks that went with it, did get away with it. From this perspective the Walzer report served no practical purpose but it did earn Annan the dubious distinction of probably being the single UN Secretary General most despised by his staff.

As for me, the death of Sergio affected me more than I was at first willing to admit. His shortcomings notwithstanding, his looks, his demeanor, his eloquence, his intelligence, his charisma and his skill in dealing with people carried a message of hope, real or imagined but a message nonetheless. A few weeks after his death, as I proceed to erase his number from my portable phone I pressed the wrong button and the connection was made. There was his voice, clear, cheerful, thanking the caller for leaving a messages. It took many months before the UN finally cancelled his number.

The death of Sergio did more than bring to an end any professional relationship I might still have had with the UN. Its aftermath was so sordid and the efforts to dilute responsibility for the succession of lapses which had facilitated the attack so crass that I lost all empathy with the system.

But if I look back at my 20 year long detour in the world of international bureaucracy there is little I find to complain about. Granted, overall it was an imperfect system but not more so than the governments that had created it. And, ultimately, when push came to shove and the chips were down, UNHCR, be it in Sarajevo or in the closing days of the Vietnamese boat people saga, delivered the goods. As for me I could lay claim to a marked lack of bureaucratic ambition, to a not too overhelming ego and to a few good ideas none of which I could have implemented alone. All in all, it was an education and in exchange I had given it my best for whatever it was worth.

INDEX

TABLE OF CONTENTS

Hanoi, 1975, the author far right on a field trip with vietnamese officials.

Saigon 1965, Charles Regnault, left and friends.

ARRIVALS OF VIETNAMESE BOAT PEOPLE IN HONG KONG

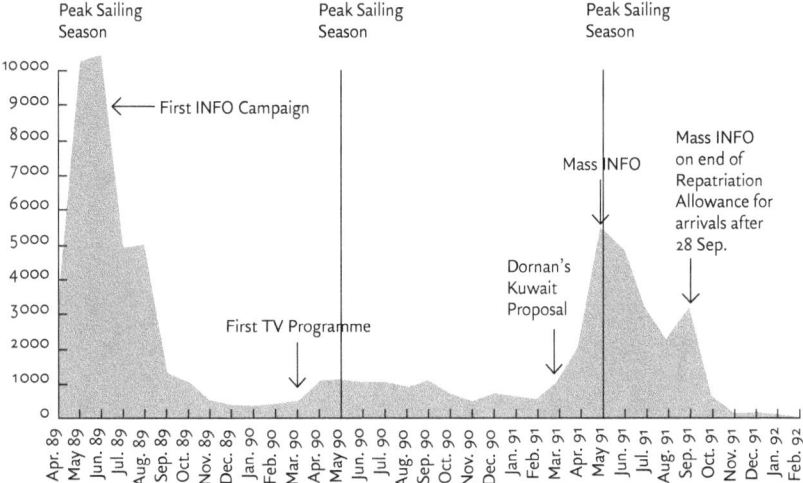

ARRIVALS OF VIETNAMESE BOAT PEOPLE IN SOUTHERN ASIA

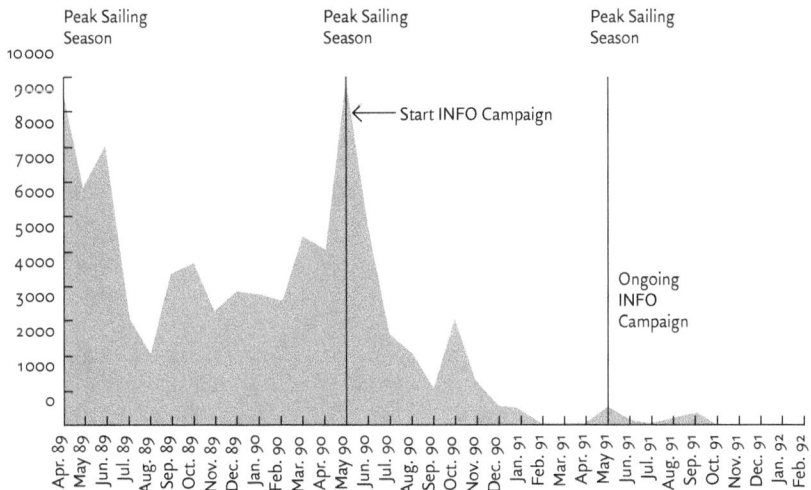

NATIONS UNIES
HAUT COMMISSARIAT
POUR LES REFUGIES

UNITED NATIONS
HIGH COMMISSIONER
FOR REFUGEES

Télégrammes : HICOMREF
Télex : 415740 UNHCR CH
Téléphone : 739 81 11
Téléfax : 731 95 46

Case Postale 2500
CH-1211 Genève 2 Dépôt

25 September 1995

Excellency

I would like to thank you for having received me and also for extending your welcome to our new Representative, Madame Catherine Bertrand. I am sure that she will preserve and further strengthen the close relation that UNHCR has established with your Government over the past twenty one years.

Regarding the CPA, we share your concerns. Problems have indeed recently been created which are beyond the making or control either of UNHCR or of Viet Nam. We will nevertheless continue our efforts and look forward to the successful closing of the CPA. UNHCR will, of course, continue its assistance and monitoring role in Viet Nam.

Regarding the other matter which UNHCR was requested to present you with, I am annexing some further details and clarification for consideration by your Government. UNHCR is available to provide its services to facilitate this humanitarian matter, subject of course to the concurrence of both Governments concerned.

I am taking this opportunity to again express the appreciation of UNHCR for the generosity with which your Government has treated returning Boat People.

Accept, Your Excellency, the assurance of my highest consideration.

Alexander Casella
Director
Regional Bureau for Asia and Oceania

His Excellency
Mr. Nguyen Dy Nien
Vice-Minister of Foreign Affairs
Hanoi

My letter to Vietnamese vice foreign minister Nien raising 'the other matter' that is the possible return to Vietnam of some of the Chinese that left in 1978.

MINISTRY OF FOREIGN AFFAIRS
SOCIALIST REPUBLIC OF VIET NAM
—

Hanoi, 25th October 1995

Dear Mr Director,

I have received with thanks your letter of 25 September 1995. The matter which you mentioned in the letter is under consideration. However, as you know, this issue is rather delicate. I shall keep you in touch when necessary.

With best wishes.

Yours sincerely,

NGUYỄN DY NIÊN
Vice Minister for Foreign Affairs

Mr. ALEXANDER CASELLA
Director Regional Bureau
for Asia and Oceania
GENEVA

...and the answer, guarded but an answer nonetheless.

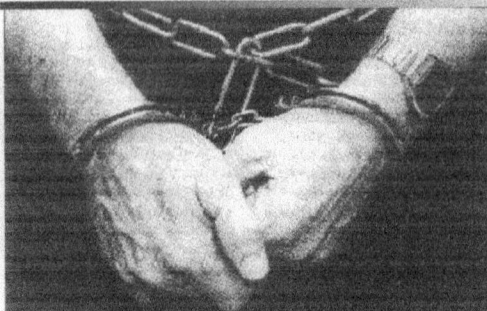

Prisons are the destinations of the refugees when they return to Vietnam

The repatriation policy adopted by the United Nation is wrong because the Vietnamese refugees will be treated as traitors once they are sent back to Vietnam. Many of these refugees are put in jails by the Vietnamese government and many other refugees are given hard labor so that they can be an exemple to other Vietnamese polple who also try to escape. These refugees are denied the right to join the army, the right to vote, and the opportunity to attend a University, where they can acquire a higher level of education.

Go to the previous page

The refugees's properties's are confiscated

Back to the first webpage

Return to my home page

Disinformation disseminated by the likes of Boat People SOS...

27 SEP 1995

Embassy of the United States of America
Hanoi

September 25, 1995

Ms. Supang
Officer in Charge
UNHCR - Hanoi

Dear Ms. Supang,

I am enclosing two items sent to me by the U.S. Department of State. The first is a letter from Boat People, SOS concerning allegations that families of asylum applicants are being harassed. I told the Department that without information on the names or addresses of the people allegedly harassed, neither we nor UNHCR would be able to investigate the claims. In any case, the letter sounds somewhat like an attempt to invent grounds for appeals of negative asylum claims. If you do have any information regarding these allegations, please let me know.

The second item is a letter from the Department to the Embassy regarding Vietnamese refugees in China. It suggests the possibility of a tripartite arrangement to bring them back, with UNHCR involvement. Perhaps we can meet or talk by phone this week, if you know anything about this matter.

...allegations from Boat People SOS but no names and dates.

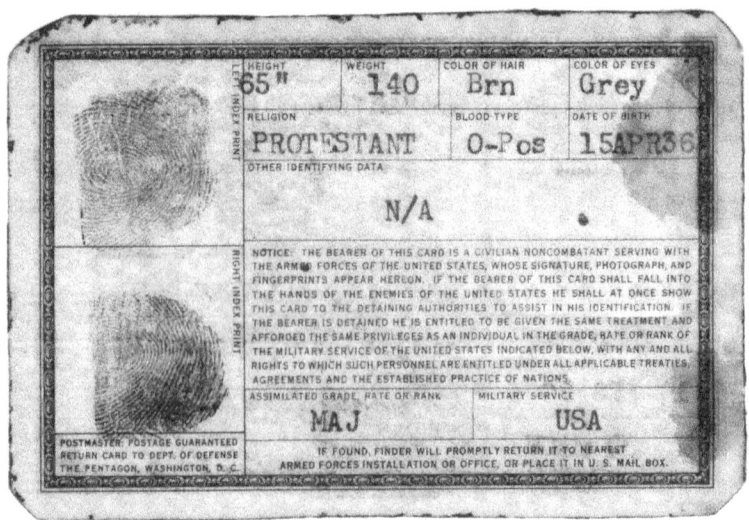

Not something you want to show the vietcong if captured.

Pierre Jambor.

THIS BOOK IS PUBLISHED BY THE ÉDITIONS DU TRICORNE, AND
PRINTED IN 2011. THE TYPEFACES ARE *Kaplun* FOR THE TEXTS AND
Hermil FOR THE TITLES, BOTH DESIGNED BY MATTHIEU CORTAT.

www.ingramcontent.com/pod-product-compliance
Lightning Source LLC
Chambersburg PA
CBHW060233290526
45789CB00001B/24